FLOWERS, BIRDS, WIND, AND MOON

JAPAN LIBRARY

FLOWERS, BIRDS, WIND, AND MOON

The Phenomenology of Nature in Japanese Culture

Matsuoka Seigow

Translated by David Noble

Japan Publishing Industry Foundation for Culture

Note on Romanization

This book follows the Hepburn system of romanization. Except for place names found on international maps and the author's given name, Seigow, long vowels are indicated by macrons. The tradition of placing the family name first has been followed for Japanese, Chinese, and Korean names. An exception has been made in the Notes section for authors whose works were published in the West.

Flowers, Birds, Wind, and Moon: The Phenomenology of Nature in Japanese Culture
by Matsuoka Seigow. Translated by David Noble.

Published by
Japan Publishing Industry Foundation for Culture (JPIC)
2-2-30 Kanda-Jinbocho, Chiyoda-ku, Tokyo 101-0051, Japan

First English edition: March 2020

This book is a translation of *Kachōfūgetsu no kagaku* (Chūōkōron Shinsha, 2004), which was originally published by Tankōsha in 1994.
English publishing rights arranged with the author.

Book design: Miki Kazuhiko, Ampersand Works

Printed in Japan
ISBN 978-4-86658-139-2
https://japanlibrary.jpic.or.jp/

Contents

Preface to the English Edition

Since ancient times, the Japanese have always cherished nature—the kaleidoscope of the seasons, and what I refer to as the phenomenology of nature, traditionally described as "flowers, birds, wind, and moon." Nature has inspired the essential motifs for the arts, from literature to design. Writers and artists developed these motifs by grasping the subtle changes presented by nature and expressing them through a diverse range of literary and design patterns. Their origins in nature explain why Japanese poetry, despite the brevity of the traditional thirty-one-syllable form, has been beloved for nearly two millennia.

In contrast, the Japanese have never put great stock in philosophical systems or rational thought. We celebrate the flowers as they bud, open, and scatter their petals; we are fascinated by the moon, and not just the full moon or the new moon—the phases of the moon that are celebrated around the world—but also the more nuanced intervals, such as the moon of the second, sixteenth, or twenty-second nights.

Japanese creative expression is grounded in the phenomena of nature. For decades I have been fascinated by the range of possibilities inherent in the capacity to sense the limitless gradations of subtle change. In this book, I also explore what new perspectives may emerge by examining this sensibility and its methods through the eyes of modern science.

I feel that, in particular, Japanese perspectives on time, *ma* (intervals), and *hoka* (otherness), though intuitive, have unique value—especially considering that science, since the development of quantum physics and the theory of relativity, has focused on issues of uncertainty, indeterminacy, probability, and ambiguity.

This book is a revised and expanded edition of a series of ten public lectures I gave in 1982, when I was thirty-eight years old. It would be gratifying to me if it now goes on to find a new audience in this English edition.

Matsuoka Seigow
Tokyo, January 2020

Introduction

Let's begin with a popular word in everyday use in Japan: *oshare* (stylish). Our current sense of the word derives from the Edo-period *share*, meaning fashionable, chic. It had associations with another word, *shadatsu*, suggesting something polished and refined. But at the same time, *share* could also mean jest, and even today we use expressions like *share o hasamu na yo* (stop kidding me, knock it off). *Share* also evolved into the expression *sharakusai*, meaning impertinent. In short, *share* had a variety of meanings and nuances depending on the situation. But today *oshare* has been reduced to a single meaning—stylish or fashionable—usually tossed off as a casual compliment.

The Japanese like to surround images with a certain multivalence and ambiguity, so that they may be adjusted to specific situations and circumstances. Take the word *aware*, as in *mono no aware*, meaning "sensitivity to the impermanence of things." Since the late eighteenth century, when the scholar Motoori Norinaga first drew attention to its importance, *aware* has been cited in almost every discussion of the defining characteristics of ancient Japanese imperial court culture. But then we have the word *appare*, meaning something like "splendid" or "admirable," which a warrior might have used to express approval of the exploits of another: *Appare na yatsu ja!* This word has a very masculine feel; in comparison, *aware* has a feminine sensibility.

But *aware* and *appare* are in fact the same word, modified by usage. *Aware* was employed by the court nobility to express the depth of emotion inspired by the changing seasons and the vicissitudes of all things, including human relationships. It is a word born of the refined sensibility of court culture. With the rise of the samurai class and the transfer of political power to the warrior houses, their leaders, beginning with Taira no Kiyomori (1118–81), began to aspire to the courtly beauty (*miyabi*) of the nobility and engage in a variety of elegant pursuits.

In the mouths of the warriors, *aware* became *appare*, acquiring a plosive pronunciation propelling it in a new direction that was quite different from the original *aware*. The pathos of a tragic hero like Minamoto no Yoshitsune (1159–89), which might have elicited a comment on *aware* from a courtier, was instead glorified when voiced as *appare*.

This book is an attempt to illuminate Japanese culture from a range of perspectives by taking up ten important themes from natural phenomena as embodied in the phrase *kachō fūgetsu* (flowers, birds, wind, and moon). It will investigate the origins and transformations of a number of images in Japanese culture, with the goal of following the complex processes by which these images gradually broke down into the building blocks for new permutations and variations. Meanwhile, I hope to also lend a voice in defense of the use of scientific imagery to elucidate the traditional phenomenology of nature associated with the phrase *kachō fūgetsu*.

Why do I want to do this? First of all, I believe we Japanese are losing our sense of the generative sources of the imagery created by our culture—as well as our sense of how to use this imagery. So I think it might help to retrace some of the paths we have traveled over the centuries.

Second, I think we need to foster the ability to discuss Japanese culture in suitable language. Particularly when addressing international audiences, we are sorely lacking in a clear and globally intelligible vocabulary capable of explaining the defining characteristics of our culture. Balancing global imagery and traditional Japanese references can be challenging, but it does not seem impossible, if we could simply find a consistent thread to follow. I have tried to find this thread or through-line in the phenomena of nature and the traditional Japanese phrase *kachō fūgetsu*.

In terms of the first objective, one issue we encounter is that the word "image" itself has become problematic. It is such a terribly convenient word that it tends to be a bit overworked. We often hear people say things like "I don't have a clear image in my mind of that project," or "That's perfect for our image"—in other words, it's used when people have difficulty conveying exactly what they mean. Many use it to mean little more than "impression." But images intrinsically have a history, a trajectory, an origin—or so I believe.

Call up for a moment the image of an apple (though almost anything would do). This "apple" already has a cloud of imagery attached to it. There's the apple representing Newton's theory of universal gravitation; there is William Tell's apple. There's Namiki Michiko's huge postwar hit,

"Ringo no uta" (Apple Song), which begins, "Bringing the red apple to my lips." And of course Apple Records, the label created by the Beatles; and the Apple of Steve Jobs and the Macintosh computer. They all use the image of the apple in different ways. New York is affectionately known as the Big Apple, and then there are the varieties of the actual fruit: Fuji, Mutsu, Granny Smith, and so on. One of my favorite musicians is Shiina Ringo (*ringo* is the Japanese word for apple). For each of us, the image of an apple calls to mind a host of people, places, and things.

Behind these symbolic uses of the apple lies a history of how the image has been used as an archetype. For Europeans, for example, underlying other images of the apple is the apple of the Garden of Eden, the fruit of the knowledge of good and evil, which, prompted by the serpent, Adam and Eve eat, disobeying God and committing original sin.

Western religion and folklore tell a wealth of stories centering on the image of a mythic Western Paradise where magical apples grow. The Celts called this paradise Avalon and believed it was presided over by Morgan, queen of the dead. In Greek mythology, Hera, the goddess of women and marriage, has an apple orchard guarded by a great serpent named Ladon. It seems that at some point these stories were absorbed into the Judeo-Christian narrative of the apple in the Garden of Eden, and thus the apple as the fruit of the knowledge of good and evil occupied center stage in Western culture.

Another major underlying foundation for images of the apple is that it is a fruit, a plant, and, fundamentally, *a living thing*. Every image has such links with the natural world and a background of universality transcending its individuality. In this book, I intend to focus attention on transformations of the Japanese imagery of nature—birds, flowers, wind, and moon—in the way in which we have just traced images of the apple and their origins and distribution.

In regard to my second objective for this book, the reason we have such difficulty trying to describe Japanese culture is that we lack access to an adequate set of imagery with which to explain its determinants. A definitive answer to this problem is beyond the scope of this book. Instead, what I wish to do here is to demonstrate that the images that enliven Japanese culture are the products of a thoroughgoing process of "data editing" involving the recombination of a relatively small number of concepts and keywords. The relationship between the words *aware* and *appare* touched upon earlier could be considered an example of such recombination.

The course I have charted for this book begins with an outline of developments in Japanese cultural history in the chapters "Mountains," "Paths," "Wind," "Birds," and "Flowers." The later chapters "Time" and "Dreams" form the nucleus of the book, with a presentation of some innovative concepts through which to think about Japanese culture. Along the way, chapters are inserted to explicate the themes—"Deities" and "Buddhas"—while the chapter "Paths" also includes some background explanation on the human processing of physical imagery. I will now provide a short preview of what is to come.

During the Jōmon period (c. 10,000 BCE–300 BCE) of Japanese prehistory, the matriarchal culture was gradually supplanted, principally by patriarchal social groups arriving from the continent whose growing strength was supported by the practice of settled agriculture. Here are the origins of one of the most basic distinctions in Japanese society, between native and imported—or, put another way, between mentalities of "here" and "there."

In 1954, in response to a question by the religious scholar Hori Ichirō, folklorist Yanagita Kunio summed up the impact of these external forces on Japan from the Yayoi period (300 BCE–300 CE) onward in a single phrase: *jidai shugi*, which might be translated as "subservience to power." This tendency has continuously dogged Japanese social and cultural history since ancient times and has been inherited by contemporary institutions, such as political parties, corporate interests, government bureaucracy, and the mass media.

Despite this radical shift in the earliest phases of its history, Japan somehow managed to engineer the institutions of state and a mythology to support it. However, because this system had not grown out of a clearly defined ideological core, but instead had been improvised to meet a mixed array of circumstances, it had to be given a central, anchoring pillar. Thus it was that Japan's earliest leaders created the concept of *makoto*, which signified sincerity in word and deed.

Yet even this *makoto* was, of course, a sensibility cobbled together from a variety of different sources. So the core of Japanese culture would remain vague and ambiguous, and its social and political institutions would be erected around this ambiguous center. This is the origin of what the Dutch journalist Karel van Wolferen described critically in his book *The Enigma of Japanese Power* (1989) as "The System."

By the period represented in the first major poetry collection, the

Man'yōshū (roughly the late seventh to late eighth century), this ethos of *makoto* had begun to possess great power. Alongside it was born a belief in *kotodama*, the spiritual power of language. But the pantheon of Japanese deities had been created from an assortment of narratives concerning deities borrowed from various parts of Asia, leaving it without an organized hierarchy. While the divinities of Japan were thus something of a hodgepodge (which is why, as I will explain later, rituals typically involve welcoming them into the community and then sending them away again), this did not diminish their status. Being an assemblage was part of their very nature, and as a result, the narratives concerning them and how they appeared in Japan became the sole form of information preserving their true character.

Another reason for the lack of a unified mythology was the impact of the arrival of Buddhism. The buddhas were initially seen as "alien gods" (*karakami*) no different from any other deity that had originated overseas, but the perception of the transitory nature of existence that was essential to Buddhism soon permeated Japanese society, while the advanced techniques of Buddhist art and architecture occupied the centers of Japanese intellectual life and craftsmanship and spread outward from there.

These circumstances resemble the way in which the sudden influx of American technology in the immediate postwar era spurred the majority of Japanese companies to adopt it and transform themselves.

As ancient Japanese society and culture took shape in this way, it chafed against the constraints created by the adoption of imported laws and institutions, and so the ways of thought imbued in the Japanese from time immemorial (what we will call in chapter 1 a "mountain" ethos, or the sensibility of mountain people) began to filter through.

This intermingled with the Daoist thought of the continent and overlapped with the already powerful Buddhist concept of the transience and ephemerality of all phenomena. The "mountain" ethos then descended once more upon the capital to influence the society of the nobility and powerful clans. Out of this arose the imagery of nature—flowers, birds, wind, and moon—and the sensibility of *aware* and *miyabi* that characterized classical Japanese culture.

With the powerful impetus of the Fujiwara clan, aristocratic society soon established a culture centered on the imperial court, and a self-consciousness of Yamato (Japan) began to emerge. The most readily apparent manifestations of this new awareness were the invention of the *kana* syllabaries and the compilation of poetry anthologies, the two greatest contributions to the development of *aware* and *miyabi*. We also should not overlook the ways in which a feminized courtly culture—the heir to the matriarchal culture of prehistoric times—propelled the evolution of this sensibility.

But as the newly rising warrior houses began to impinge upon this aristocratic aesthetic, *aware* and *miyabi* dissipated. On the one hand, *aware* slid over into the martial *appare* sensibility, as we saw in the beginning of this introduction, while on the other, attempts to somehow preserve its original sense resulted in new concepts such as *yosei* (overtones) and *ushin* (depth of feeling). In addition, there were those who chose neither the path of the nobility nor that of the warriors, but a third path known as "aesthetic reclusion" (*suki no tonze*) that took the form of hermitage or wayfaring travel. The twelfth-century poet-priest Saigyō and the poet and essayist Kamo no Chōmei personify this tendency. With these developments, a culture that embraced the phenomena of nature spread throughout the land—a culture whose keyword, "wind" (*fū*), is perhaps better translated as "air" or "atmosphere" in this sense, and is embodied in terms such as *fūai* and *fūzei,* describing a subtle aesthetic and stylistic sensibility.

There is another Japanese word, *susabi*, that possesses a dual meaning: the first a somewhat rough and ready, uninhibited energy reminiscent of Jōmon culture, and the other a quieter, more refined sense of play that recalls the Yayoi. These two streams of *susabi* intermingled, blended, and then separated from one another time and again in Japanese cultural history, and this book will pursue the traces of these interactions.

The phrase "birds, flowers, wind, and moon" (*kachō fūgetsu*), along with others such as "snow, moon, and flowers" (*setsugetsuka*), is often used in Japan to denote the phenomena of nature as they appear in our culture. Even so, there's no denying that phrases like these are all very fuzzy. They are rooted so deeply in the Japanese natural environment and sense of the seasons that it is difficult to grasp from the words alone what they are attempting to express.

In addition, it would give most of us pause if we were asked to identify precisely where our attachment to the poetics of *kachō fūgetsu* comes from. Did we learn it from our parents and older siblings? Was it cultivated through watching Noh plays, reading traditional poetry, and enjoying the tea ceremony? Or was it the result of seeing those things expressed in the works of poets such as Saigyō and the seventeenth-century haiku poet

Matsuo Bashō? Nor would we be able to say exactly what the appreciation of *kachō fūgetsu* involves. After all, it is not as if a love of flowers or an interest in birds is unique to the Japanese people.

The final question is whether there's actually any point to delighting in things like flowers, birds, wind, and the moon in this modern day and age. What is the use of such effete pursuits? Many would see them merely as a playground for aesthetes. You *could* possibly argue that this realm is what it is precisely because it doesn't try to be useful, but that won't likely persuade anyone. This is why the poetic engagement with nature is no longer as popular as it once was.

A number of possible phrases exist for summing up the essence of Japanese society. To name only a few, we have *wakō dōjin* ("softening the radiance and becoming one with the dust," a celebration of the virtues of humility and unobtrusiveness); *ichigo ichie* ("one opportunity, one encounter," the idea, central to the tea ceremony, that every encounter and experience should be appreciated as unique); *oyakata hinomaru* ("the patriarchal state," a Japanese manifestation of Big Brother); and the infamous dichotomy between *honne* (one's true feelings) and *tatemae* (outward show). Japan has also been termed a "village" (i.e., parochial) society (*mura shakai*) and a hierarchical society (*tate shakai*). These all appear to hit upon some unique aspect of Japan but at the same time are no help in trying to tackle any of the deeper questions about its essence.

What we need, then, is a new perspective, one that can connect the historical changes in the structure of Japanese society to the internal issues of sense and sensibility represented by *kachō fūgetsu* and the cultural construction of nature. For this purpose, we need to look at *kachō fūgetsu* as a system for producing new styles or patterns of thinking—what we might call *modes*—through a process of recombination of *codes*, that is to say, individual components such as "deities," "buddhas," "flowers," "birds," "grasses," "trees," "insects," "fish," "snow," "moon," "wind," "water," and so on. In other words, the Japanese phenomenology of nature is a system that maintains the realm of expression available to the people of that culture by offering modes concealing underlying codes; indeed, we might even be so bold as to call it a unique multimedia system developed since ancient times by the Japanese. This systems approach informs a number of the perspectives I have adopted in this book.

Here, I would also like to reveal some of my motives for introducing science-oriented discussions at various points in the following pages—a somewhat unusual choice in a book about Japanese culture.

First of all, I want to stress the dynamism of the nebulous-seeming phenomena and entities associated with the phrase *kachō fūgetsu*. Second, I want to demonstrate not only that the natural phenomena treated in Japanese culture possess many mysteries not yet explained by science, but also that the narrative-oriented perspective evident in such cultural interpretations is one that modern science itself would do well to adopt.

Third, I seek to argue that science needs to focus not only on the natural world, but also on the human perception and cognition of it. This is closely related to questions involving our physiological thresholds and the structure of our brains, which govern our perceptions. In the chapters "Paths" and "Dreams," I will provide limited but crucial discussions of these points.

Last, and most important for me, I am convinced that from now on all science must be information science, and that we must therefore greatly expand our understanding of what information is. It is precisely this "information" in the broader sense that has, through the medium of the *kachō fūgetsu* system, shaped developments in the realm of Japanese expression throughout history. This concludes my introductory remarks.

The first chapter, "Mountains," will start from a discussion of why we must have matrixes for our imagery, and why "mountains" were able to function as this common denominator. From the standpoint of the overall structure of the book, chapters 1 to 5 present the fundamentals of the argument.

CHAPTER 1 MOUNTAINS

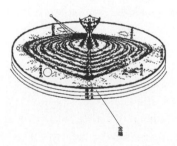

Land of mountains

Somewhere in our hearts we all harbor a profound awe of mountains. Even today, when every corner of the world is hedged in by asphalt and power lines and computer networks, we still experience both fear and wonder on entering the mountains at night. Thomas Mann in *The Magic Mountain* (1924) and Ernest Hemingway in "The Snows of Kilimanjaro" (1936) gave voice to this mixture of awe and dread, which was also captured by Kawabata Yasunari in *The Sound of the Mountain* (1949). In cities and towns where volcanoes are part of the landscape, the power of the mountains is all the more keenly felt. During a major eruption of Mount Aso in Kyushu, local elementary school children cried out, "The mountain is angry!"

Yet mountains also have a comforting presence that soothes the souls of those who look out at them every day. Mount Fuji is iconic in this regard, but every region in Japan has its own "incomparable peak" that vies with the others, from Mount Iwaki and Hayachine in northeastern Honshu to Hakusan and Hōki Daisen in the south and west.

Those who live in a city surrounded by mountains, such as Yamagata, Kyoto, Matsumoto, or Toyama, know that each morning's encounter with nature begins with the colors of the mountains—whether they are vivid and clear or clouded and sullen can shape the mood of the day. I was born and raised in the Muromachi and Nakagyō districts of Kyoto, and as a boy going to school I marveled at how different the hills of Higashiyama could look from day to day. The mountains enfold us in a comforting embrace.

Japan is a land of mountains. A mountainous land encircled by the sea—an island nation, and at the same time a nation of mountains. This is the essential topography of Japan. Many of the seafaring peoples who first came to Japan did not settle along the coast but headed inland, into the mountains. These peoples later developed what we now know as the Jōmon culture.

The Azumi, a seafaring people who presumably arrived in Japan by following the chain of islands extending into the southern seas, are one example. They first landed on the Atsumi (Azumi) peninsula on the Pacific coast in what is now Aichi prefecture, but then moved overland, heading northward to the Azumino, a plateau in the mountains of Nagano, and eventually ranging as far north as the area around Mount Hodaka. The deity enshrined at the summit of this peak, Hodaka no Mikoto, is the son of Toyotamahiko, a deity worshiped by seafarers, believed to be an ancestor of the Azumi clan. The *ho* of Mount Hodaka probably originally referred to the crest of a wave (*nami no ho*).

The mountains were populated by hunters known as *matagi*, charcoal makers who have given us folk tales such as "Sumiyaki Kogorō" (Kogorō the Charcoal-Maker), and craftsmen known as *kijishi* who worked with wood or bamboo. But there was a group who dwelt in the mountains even before them, remnants of the people who had created the Jōmon culture. Before the development of a culture based on paddy rice agriculture, the mountains were Japan's original home.

Looking at the mountains in this way, we soon discover that prominent peaks in every part of Japan are invested with their own particular mountain deity (*yama no kami*). Such mountains were regarded as sacred peaks (*reizan*), possessing power and authority as the transcendent custodians of the living things they watched over from on high. This concept is manifested in the word *okami* (literally, above, higher, and a colloquial term for rulers or superiors). The ethnologist Yanagita Kunio exhaustively researched the folk beliefs associated with these mountain deities and, in *Yama no kami to okoze* (Mountain Deities and Devilfish, 1936), argues that the Japanese have seen the mountains as the realm of their ancestral spirits. Later, Nelly Naumann of the University of Freiburg proposed that previous to this deification of ancestors, there had been a divine female ruler of the mountain hunting peoples, suggesting the possibility of the mountains themselves as a maternal archetype. I am one of those who finds Naumann's thesis persuasive.

It seems clear to me that, in brief, the earlier inhabitants of the mountains created an archetype of a maternal mountain deity, which was then gradually supplanted by the deification of the ancestors. Simultaneously, the custom spread of building *satomiya* (village shrines) in the foothills, distinct from the *yamamiya* (mountain shrines) deep in the mountains or at their summits. Fewer people inhabited the mountains, which became objects of fear and awe. But where did the former inhabitants of the mountains go? Over time they must have relocated to other, more remote mountainous areas. Mountain people likely appeared only rarely in the villages. Shy of contact, they probably retreated farther into the mountains after even a brief encounter with villagers. The mountains came to be regarded as the dwelling place of goblins (*tengu*), demons (*oni*), and other mysterious beings, and as a place of practice for the *yamabushi* (mountain ascetics) of the Shugendō sect. All of these developments lent complexity to the Japanese conception of mountains.

This complexity is expressed in Japanese as an equally rich vocabulary of images related to mountains. The brilliant colors of autumn leaves are known as *yama no nishiki* (mountain brocade); the silk tree is called *yamamame* (mountain bean); *yamaji* is the wind that blows down from the mountains as summer turns to autumn. Brigands and bandits were called *yamadachi*, and interestingly, in the argot of the pleasure quarters, Buddhist monks were known as *yama no kyaku* ("guests from the mountains"), since temples were often located in the mountains. Even today, in the bars, clubs, and geisha parties of Kyoto, one can frequently rub elbows with such mountain guests.

Magazines in Japan still commonly use the word *yamashi* to mean a speculator, con man, or swindler, but it originally meant a dealer in mountain properties or a mine operator and had no such pejorative connotations. The Edo-period physician and thinker Satō Nobuhiro was from a family of *yamashi* who were respected experts on mountains and mining. Even so, those who spent a lot of time in the mountains were viewed with suspicion by ordinary townspeople and villagers, and the term gradually came to reflect this.

Mountain imagery also pervades our everyday speech, even when it involves metaphors not directly connected with the mountains as real physical objects—such as when we refer to the "peak" (*yama, yamaba*) of an incident or occurrence.

On the other hand, in "Kiritsubo," the first chapter of *The Tale of Genji* (early eleventh century), we already find mention of the artificial mountains (*tsukiyama*) of the gardener's art. The Portuguese Jesuit missionary João Rodrigues, who arrived in Japan in 1577 during the Momoyama period, describes the huts built for the tea ceremony: "They called this in their language *shichū no sankyo*, meaning a lonely hermitage found in the middle of a public square."[1] The word translated by Rodrigues as hermitage is literally "mountain hut," conveying a simple shelter built in the recesses of the mountains. Constructing such huts in the midst of the city was an innovation of tea masters such as Murata Jukō (1423–1502) and Sen no Rikyū (1522–92).

In the Gion Festival celebrated every July in Kyoto, the floats that are the main feature of the ceremonial processions are divided into two main types, "mountain" (*yama*) and "halberd" (*hoko*), and the generic term for a festival float, *dashi*, is written with the characters for "mountain" and "cart."

The Naginata-boko float in the Gion Festival, Kyoto. Photo courtesy of Gion Matsuri Yamahoko Rengōkai.

So Japan is a land of mountains, and one that has always been deeply aware of their power. Naturally, a host of images have arisen involving mountains, so that metaphorical mountains abound even in places far removed from the actual ones. Yet I would like to think that there is an archetype that persists unbroken no matter how many images it produces. When we hear the word "mountains" and imagine goblins (*tengu*), it is because we sense the otherworldliness of the mountains. But I believe there is another, even older archetype that underlies our concept of mountains, one that we continue to draw on to create various ideas of what is "mountain-like."

So let's dig a bit deeper into where this shared archetype of mountains came from.

The archetype of Mount Sumeru

During the reign of Emperor Shirakawa in the early eleventh century, the imposing Hosshōji temple was built in the Okazaki district of Kyoto. This was followed by the construction nearby of other temples with the character *shō* (here meaning "superior" or "superlative") in their names—Sonshōji, Saishōji, Enshōji, and so on—for a total of six that came to be collectively known as the Rokushōji (Six Superior Temples). Among them, Hosshōji stood out for the octagonal nine-story pagoda that towered

82 meters above its precincts. Sadly, the entire structure was lost to fire. The medieval chronicle *Taiheiki* includes an account of the burning of Hoss-hōji, with this description: "The reverberations of the nine-story pagoda as it collapsed could be heard to the very depths of the earth [*konrinzai*]."

The word *konrinzai* has its origins in India, describing part of the structure of Mount Sumeru.

Mount Sumeru is a model of the universe in the cosmology of Indian Buddhism and other religious traditions in India. In the midst of the cosmic void floats a disk-like "wheel of air," surmounted by a wheel of water and a wheel of gold. The wheel of gold in turn is filled with a great ocean, in the middle of which towers Sumeru. And this is the derivation of the word *konrinzai*, for it literally means "to the margins of the golden wheel": an image of the farthest reaches of the universe inhabited by humans. Few people today know that *konrinzai* originally referred to this cosmological structure. In everyday speech, it is simply used as a negative intensifier: "I will never ever lie to you again" (*Mō, konrinzai uso tsukimasen*), for example.

In the ocean atop the golden wheel float four islands, one of which, Jambudvīpa, corresponds to our home, the earth—a relatively tiny place. The golden wheel is encircled by a ring of iron mountains. In the exact center, the cosmic mountain Sumeru looms over all. The scale of Sumeru surpasses almost anything in the history of the world's images—it's perhaps the most colossal product of the human imagination.

In ancient India, the *yojana* was a standard measure of distance, corresponding to about 7 kilometers. The wheel of air was said to be 1,600,000 *yojanas* in thickness; with the wheels of water and gold added, the total was about 20 million kilometers—certainly a fitting foundation for a cosmic mountain.

These mind-boggling figures were recorded in the *Abhidharmakośa* (Commentary on the Treasury of the Abhidharma) of the Buddhist scholar Vasubandhu in the fourth to fifth century. It is a famously thorny and difficult work: taking off from the old adage "Three years to fruit for peaches and chestnuts, eight years for persimmons," Japanese monks would say, "Three years for Yogacara studies and eight for the *Abhidharmakośa*." But it still makes for a pretty interesting read.

How well the Buddhist theology of the *Abhidharmakośa* was understood in medieval Japan is open to question, but it appears that everyone knew that Mount Sumeru was upheld by a wheel of gold. In the chapter "Pilgrimage to Chikubushima" of *The Tale of the Heike* (mid-thirteenth century) is the line "In Jambudvīpa there is a lake, in the midst of which a mountain of crystal rises from the farthest reaches of the wheel of gold [konrinzai], where heavenly maidens dwell."[2] (As noted earlier, Jambudvīpa is the human world in the Sumeru cosmology.)

Among the popular songs (imayō) recorded in Ryōjin hishō (Songs to Make the Dust Dance, 1169),[3] Mount Sumeru is mentioned as supreme among the highest mountains of the world. It is also referred to in a number of the Buddhist imayō in the same collection, including the following:

> Think of the white tuft between his brows / it is one of his bodily aspects / if you ask how vast is Sumeru, / it is 80,000 yojanas in length and breadth.
>
> When the Treasure Stupa emerged / Śakyamuni cast away Sumeru and the iron ring / transforming all into a vast realm of lapis lazuli / where the avatars of buddhas assembled.[4]

As the songs in Ryōjin hishō may be thought of as the popular songs of the day, the vocabulary found in them must have been widely understood. So to understand the Japanese concept of mountains, it is first necessary to understand Mount Sumeru.

But how did this image of an immense cosmic mountain first come into being?

The Mount Sumeru cosmology developed in India. From deep antiquity some believed that the Indian subcontinent had not always been there— that it had drifted there from elsewhere. This idea turns out to be true. In 1912 Alfred Wegener, a German polar researcher and geophysicist, proposed the theory of continental drift. According to Wegener, the Indian subcontinent was originally located near what is now the South Pole and moved northward at a snail's pace through the frozen seas, crossing what is now the Indian Ocean and eventually colliding with the continent of Asia. The shock of this encounter wrinkled the earth's crust to produce the Himalayas.

The name Himalaya derives from the Sanskrit himá (snow) and ālāya (storehouse; J. kura or zō). The word ālāya has great resonance in Buddhism, used metaphorically to speak of the entire Buddhist canon as a storehouse of the teachings; the "storehouse consciousness" (ālāya vijñāna) was seen as underlying all other forms of consciousness. It appears frequently throughout the "mind sciences" of India, but with regard to the Himalayas, *ālāya* is used to signify a storehouse of snow—and an experience somehow embedded in the deepest and most distant memories of the Indian people, something similar to Plato's vision of the sunken continent of Atlantis.

According to the continental drift theory and more recent advances in plate tectonics, the archipelago of Japan formed when land sheared off from the ancient continent Pacifica and collided with the landmass of Asia. Pacifica, which later sank to form an early part of the Pacific Ocean, was originally part of the Gondwana supercontinent. After the collision, the land that would become the Japanese archipelago adhered to the Asian continent, where it would encounter the last ice age before breaking away from the continent once again and acquiring something close to its present form. Until that time, it had been stuck fast to Asia.

As the Sea of Japan began to subside, the last remaining land bridges to the continent ran between what would later be the islands of Kyushu and Tsushima and the Korean peninsula. Eventually these too were severed and the Japanese islands were isolated from continental Asia. From a geological perspective, the Japanese archipelago has never stood still; this motion has resulted in it being an isolated chain of islands.

This sense of geological isolation underlies the famous "island mentality" (*shimaguni konjō*) of the Japanese people. I like to think of our archipelago as a handle attached to the doorway of the great continent of Asia, and it is from this vantage that we have striven to be recognized and accepted by the rest of the world.

As a side note, the standard way of writing Sumeru in Japanese is Shumisen, based on a transliteration of the Sanskrit. Since the Sanskrit *sumeru* originally meant a marvelously lofty mountain, it was often translated into Japanese texts as Myōkōsan.

Artificial mountains

Mount Sumeru is described as being formed of four treasures: gold, silver, lapis lazuli, and crystal. The portion of it rising above the ocean waves is essentially a cube, measuring 80,000 *yojanas* to a side. When the Buddhist song mentioned above refers to the white tuft of hair between the Buddha's eyebrows as being 80,000 *yojanas* wide, it means it is as big as one of the sides of Mount Sumeru—making the Buddha's face quite large indeed.

The lower half of this cube is four stepped verandas, the highest of which is occupied by the Four Guardian Kings (J. Shitennō), Jikokuten, Tamonten, Zōchōten, and Kōmokuten; the three levels beneath this are home to their subordinates and followers. Above the four verandas rises the Heaven of the Thirty-Three Devas, a magnificent walled city at whose center stands the palace of Taishakuten (Sk. Indra), the ruler of all, surrounded by marketplaces and the residences of the thirty-two other devas. It is a pretty lively place. These devas were also known as the "earth-dwelling devas," because their heaven is located at the summit of Mount Sumeru and thus still connected with the earth, while above them floats an immense pantheon of "sky-dwelling devas" who live in a series of heavens suspended in the void.

The first of these heavens, 80,000 *yojanas* above the peak of Mount Sumeru, is that of Yama, lord of the dead; the second, 160,000 *yojanas* above that, is the Tuśita heaven where future buddhas dwell; 320,000 *yojanas* higher still is Nirmanarati, "the abode of those born in bliss." Finally, 640,000 *yojanas* above is the highest of these heavenly realms, the Paranirmita-vaśa-vartin, the realm of Mara where the most exalted devas reside. It is a vertiginously majestic structure, these layered heavens, each double the height of the one below and inhabited by vast pantheons of deities.

This vision of Mount Sumeru was employed in almost every architectural structure in ancient East Asia. Not only temples and monasteries but also much humbler buildings borrowed from the structure of Mount Sumeru. In short, Sumeru served as a kind of master plan or archetype for the East Asian pavilion. A number of variations were built on the basis of this master plan, which also specified in detail the iconography for the deities and buddhas.

Buddhist images are enshrined in temples and subtemples throughout Japan. The vast majority of these images (with some variation among sects) are displayed on a dais or altar known as a *shumidan*, which is both named for and modeled upon Mount Sumeru. Buddhist images are placed on these altars in much the same orientations as those occupied by the Four Guardian Kings and other deities on the great world mountain. These temple altars underwent a further process of miniaturization, achieving a portability that resulted in the *butsudan*, the small Buddhist altars found in many Japanese homes.

The *butsudan* spread rapidly during the Edo period (1600–1868), but its prototypes existed much earlier in the form of *zushi* shrines designed as "miniature Sumerus" to be placed in one's room or even carried about. Indeed, the first major advance in portability came with the monks of Ippen Shōnin's Ji sect, who accompanied warrior bands into battle as chaplains and scribes. Because it was impossible to return the dead from the battlefield for a proper funeral, it became customary to conduct last rites on the spot, using a portable shrine, the precursor of the *butsudan*.

In Japan today computers have become a completely unremarkable part of everyday life—at work, at home, and in schools. But when first introduced, they were huge and unwieldy and attracted a lot of attention. Every organization and then, with the advent of the personal computer, every individual wanted one of their own. Buddhist statuary was a similar phenomenon. Using a single image as a model, Buddhist craftsmen replicated it, making numerous copies. The same happened for Mount Sumeru, the fundamental master plan for these images, which was reproduced and disseminated in the form of *shumidan* and *butsudan*.

When did this Indian imagery of Mount Sumeru first arrive in Japan?

The chapter of the *Nihon shoki* (Chronicles of Japan, 720) devoted to the reign of Empress Suiko (r. 593–628) relates that Roshikō, an immigrant from the continent, built a replica of Mount Sumeru and a Chinese-style bridge in the garden of the residence of the powerful leader of the Soga clan, Soga no Umako (551?–626). Thus it would appear that the image of Mount Sumeru had already reached Japan by the early seventh century, when the Soga were becoming seriously committed to Buddhism. Soga no Umako's recreation of Mount Sumeru was popularly called "the island" (*shima*) and became the prototype for later Japanese gardens. (Umako himself became known as "Lord of the Island.")

The Soga clan, during the era in which Prince Shōtoku (574–622) was serving as imperial regent and enthusiastically supporting Buddhism, were much admired as the aristocratic family that was the earliest to adopt the Mount Sumeru master plan and construct temple halls, pagodas, and gardens inspired by it. The *Nihon shoki* records that during the third year of the reign of Emperor Saimei (657), a model of Mount Sumeru was constructed to the west of Asukadera temple. An entry two years later, in 659, tells us that another Mount Sumeru was built along the riverbank to the east of a hill named Amakashi no Oka, and a banquet was held there for representatives of the Emishi from Koshi and Mutsu in northern Japan. A year later, a Mount Sumeru was built on the banks of Isonokami Pond, and entertainment held for forty-seven men of the Mishihase, an ethnic group from northern Japan. From this it would appear that construction of replicas of Mount Sumeru had suddenly become a fad.

We can surmise, on the basis of these accounts, that the Soga clan and other close retainers and advisors to the imperial house were in the process of mastering Buddhism and the "foreign deities" (*karakami*) imported from continental Asia, and wished to ostentatiously display this newfound power with the construction of gardens that emulated Mount Sumeru. In contemporary terms, this might be the equivalent of a country finally having the opportunity to host an international exposition, or to sponsor a national pavilion, or to build a state guesthouse for foreign dignitaries equipped with computers, large-screen televisions, and all the modern conveniences. In seventh-century Japan, the Buddhist thought and technology being imported from China and the Korean peninsula was bright and shiny and new and was displayed to impress, just as we use high-tech goods to impress others in today's world.

In this period, not only the gardens of the Soga clan but also gardens in general came to be referred to as "islands" (*shima*) and commonly featured a miniature Mount Sumeru in the form of rocks and plants arranged in the middle of a central water feature. The following poems from the *Man'yōshū* (c. 759), the oldest existing collection of Japanese poetry, reflect this type of garden design:

I see the garden
of my lord where mandarin ducks
do live on this day,
then there the [*ashibi*]
is at its best in flower.[5]

Here along the pond
its reflection blooms again
down in the water—
come pluck the shining *ashibi*,
strip its flowers unto your sleeves![6]

This garden which I, together with my darling,
laid out and planted,
has now grown waste and rife
with tall and wild-boughed trees![7]

Approaching the mountains

In Japan the image of the mountains was not shaped solely by that of Mount Sumeru. A variety of images grew out of the sense of awe inspired by the mountains and the religious devotion felt upon entering their fastnesses.

There are, fundamentally, two different ways of relating to mountains: one can gaze on them from afar, or one can enter them. In China, those who entered deep into the mountains were known as *xian* (J. *sen*), or immortals. In Japan they were called *yamabushi*—literally, "those who prostrate themselves in the mountains"—and their numbers were not limited to the common image of mountain monks engaging in ascetic practices and blowing on conch-shell trumpets (*horagai*). *Yamabushi* referred to all who entered the mountains to fully experience them, listening to their sounds, tracing their watercourses, mastering the lore of the trees, learning to forage for food. Yanagita Kunio called them *yamabito* (mountain people); more generally, ethnologists use the term *yama no tami* (people of the mountains).

The mountain people developed herbal medicine (*honzōgaku*) based on their experience; it was later expanded into a modern pharmacopeia incorporating this traditional knowledge. The mountains are filled with dangers, and techniques emerged for meeting and overcoming them. The mountain people were not ninja, but they engaged in a considerable amount of physical training to acquire survival skills that ordinary people lacked. All this gave birth to images of a realm of supernatural experience and to mysterious forms of thought.

There's a children's song with the lines "Spring has come / Spring has come / Where has it come? / Come to the mountains / Come to the villages / Come to the fields." In thinking about Japanese society and culture, it is common to distinguish between the realm of the mountains and the realm of the village. This is because the lifeways and mentality of the first people who settled in the mountains during the Jōmon period differed radically from those of the later settled agricultural villagers of the Yayoi period and onward.

The people Yanagita Kunio called *yamabito* were the earlier inhabitants of the mountains and regarded by the villagers of ancient and medieval Japan with a mixture of awe and fear. As a result, those living in the mountains came to be called *yamagatsu* (mountain outcasts), *yama no uba* (mountain crones), *oni* (demons or ogres), and the like. These were of course pejoratives; for example, *yamagatsu* was predicated on the notion that hunters, woodcutters, and other people were of low station. A line from the tenth-century narrative *Utsuho monogatari* suggests a view that these "mountain outcasts" were incapable of refined emotions or reason: "If heaven's laws prevail, she will become an empress or a lady. If they do not, she may become an outcast [*yamagatsu*] or a commoner." In medieval times it was believed that these people would occasionally descend from the mountains and appear in the villages.

Clearly, this is a distorted perspective, in which the "mountain realm" is seen (and judged) from the "village realm." But since the majority of cultural records would be produced from the perspective of the village (and later the cities and towns), it seems inevitable that it would become the dominant one.

This interchange between mountains and villages would provide the fundamental image of contact and exchange more generally in ancient and medieval Japan. In New Year's and Setsubun rituals throughout the country, one sees performances of demons and ogres and hags descending from the mountains into the villages, reproducing memories of contact long past between the two realms. And the history of this interchange between mountains and villages provided the background for the invention, mentioned earlier, of the tea house as a mountain hermitage in the midst of the city.

Why was it that villagers regarded those from the mountains with such fear? They also probably feared animals such as wolves and wild boar, but this was something different—fear of a unique spirit or energy descending from the mountains.

In the Shōnai region of Yamagata prefecture there are a number of mountains called *morinoyama* where the spirits of the ancestors are said to reside. These spirits are deities of the mountains (*yama no kami*), but in spring they descend to become deities of the fields (*ta no kami*) until the autumn harvest, when they return once more to their mountain homes. Near Mount Suganosen in Inaba in Tottori prefecture, on New Year's people smear red clay from the mountain onto pieces of paper that are then displayed as household decorations. In the village of Totsukawa in Nara prefecture, the custom is to go into the mountains on New Year's to hunt wild boar and deer, offering their hides and livers (the latter, known locally as *sanmai*, slit seven times with a woodsman's hachet) to the mountain deities. *Sanmai* has found its way into more general use as a word for guts or innards, as in the term for a way of filleting fish (*sanmai ni orosu*).

The *kadomatsu* New Year's decorations displayed at the gates of Japanese houses use the pine and bamboo that grow wild in the mountains as an invitation to the spirit of the mountains. Other seasonal decorations— *shimenawa* and *hōrai kazari*, for example—also make use of mountain symbolism, for the same purpose. The week following New Year's Day is often referred to as *matsu no uchi* ("within the pines"), signifying that during this period the spirit temporarily inhabits and recharges the village with its energy. The end of this period of recharging is marked by the Setsubun festival in early February, which customarily involves the scattering of beans to drive out demons; it is most easily understood as acknowledging the presence of the mountain people in the form of "demons" and thanking them by giving them beans—the symbol of settled village life—to take home with them. We may chant "Demons out!" (*oni wa soto*), but these demons represent a spirit and vitality required by the village to make it through each year. Setsubun is additionally rooted in an exorcism of plague deities and other evil spirits, which I will discuss in greater detail in the next chapter.

Mountain trees and vegetation such as pines and bamboo, when conceived as symbols inviting the habitation of spirits, are known as *yorishiro*. In contemporary terms we might describe the *yorishiro* as agents or representatives, and in principle a single pine branch could represent the entire tree and serve as the temporary lodging of the essence of the mountain spirit.

Many different things might serve as *yorishiro*. Flowering evergreen trees such as the *sakaki* or the camellia might provide a *yorishiro* for deities, inviting their presence. And they need not be growing in the ground; a branch might be broken off, but it would still preserve its power and function as a *yorishiro*. In this book I intend to use the concept of *yorishiro* to explain a number of Japanese ethnological phenomena. I will provide a much more detailed discussion of it in chapter 3, "Deities."

Ways of looking at the mountains

Customs initiated by mountain inhabitants have had an enormous influence on Japanese culture. But the mountains affect us even when we just gaze upon them from afar. Everyone has felt that sense of speechless wonder at the sight of mountains—often accompanied by a certain indefinable thrill of fear. This way of gazing intently at mountains eventually developed into an aesthetic appreciation of the landscape.

This appreciation is reflected in the ink-wash (*suiboku*) landscape paintings (*sansuiga*) that first developed in China and became popular in Japan during the era of the Northern and Southern Courts (1336–92) as one of the pastimes of Zen monks. The art of *sansuiga* was refined by the sensibilities of those who were drawn to the mountains. Its tradition was inherited by landscape painters in Japan such as Minchō (1352–1431), Josetsu (fl. 1405–96), and Sesshū Tōyō (1420–1506?), so we can safely say that the Japanese way of looking at landscapes began with mountains. The term *sansui* literally means "mountains and water" and was later used to refer to both landscape paintings and rock gardens in Japan.

Simply put, traditional landscape painting allowed the beholder to comfortably remain *here* while being provided a view of mountains in a distant *there*. As they worked, landscape painters sought to imagine themselves being in the mountains.

Looking closely at traditional landscape paintings, we find they fall into four main categories or stages: paintings that plant us squarely *here*, on this level relative to the mountains; paintings that place us on a level heading toward the mountains; paintings that imagine us as having entered the mountains; and paintings that produce in us a state of meditative relaxation as if we were living deep in the mountains, free of all worldly care. In other words, paintings for those who wish to gaze at the mountains, go to the mountains, live in the mountains, and die in the mountains.

Ink-wash landscapes employ a range of perspectives completely different from the single perspective used in European art. Known as *san'en* ("three distances"), the range includes a level distance, high distance, and deep distance. These are essentially views from three different vantage points: looking from nearby mountains straight across at distant mountains, looking up at the peaks from the base of mountains, and looking past mountains at what lies beyond. All three perspectives would be employed simultaneously in a single painting. This method was first analyzed by the Northern Song landscape artist Guo Xi (c. 1020–90) in his work *Linquan gaozhi* (The Lofty Method of Forest and Streams). In the twelfth century, the painter Han Zhuo proposed three additional perspectival distances: "broad distance," as when distant mountains are seen over a wide expanse; "hidden distance," when fogs and mist arise to conceal distant mountains rising above fields and streams; and "obscure distance," as when the entire scene is shrouded in twilight.

I suspect I am not alone in experiencing, with certain landscape paintings, the feeling that the mountains pictured in them were about to topple onto me. Fan Kuan (c. 960–c. 1030) was a wonderful landscape painter of the early Northern Song period, and whenever I look at mountains in his work I experience this sensation. Paintings of this sort invite us into a place of purity and beauty in the midst of nature; pastoral poetry does this as well. Tao Yuanming (365?–427) wrote many poems on such themes. Eventually, people began to seek out such spots for their "scenic energy" (*keiki*) and prize them as "famous places" (*meisho*).

Herein we see the birth of the landscape. A landscape is a place of just such outstanding natural power or energy. In modern Japanese, the word *keiki* has come to be associated with economic energy and prosperity, but it originally signified energy embodied in the landscape. The modern word *keiei* (meaning "enterprise" or "management") was once used in discussions of landscape painting.

The Six Laws of Landscape Painting, articulated by the Chinese painter Xie He in the late fifth century, are the following: (1) *qiyung shendong* (give vitality to the work through spiritual resonance), (2) *gufa yongbi* (use the brush to define the structure), (3) *yingwu xiangxing* (be faithful to objects in representing them), (4) *suilei fucai* (apply color according to the type of object), (5) *jingying weizhi* (attend to organization and placement), (6) *chuanyi moxie* (copy the classic models). Among these principles, the most important is the first, *qiyung shendong*, for the spirit and energy of a landscape painting depends on how well the artist is able to give active expression to its spiritual resonance.

But the other five principles are also significant, especially *jingying weizhi*, which addresses the crucial matter of composition in landscape painting. It is interesting that the present-day term for business management in Japanese, *keiei*, derives from this term *jingying*, originally applied to the spatial organization and composition of works of art.

I believe that what constitutes a landscape has been determined by the way in which people see it. And the way in which they see it is a judgment regarding whether or not it possesses *keiki*, the scenic energy or power mentioned above. In other words, what makes a "famous place" depends upon the alignment of aesthetics and expressive sensibility with a site-specific flow of scenic energy.

Being able to perceive this scenic energy first of all requires sensitivity to how well the site "invokes" the seasons (*kisetsu no yobiyose*). One must feel that the place is appropriately springlike in spring, autumnal in autumn. Then the quality of the view is important: are there panoramas, or does the place present itself best as a landscape to be strolled through? The view (*naga-me*) was the most important concept for the poets of the *Man'yōshū*, and the ideal, in their words, was a landscape at which one "never tired of gazing." Japanese aesthetic consciousness begins with this *nagame* of the Man'yō era.

Also of importance in determining a "famous place" is the scenic diversity it offers. The landscape surrounding the confluence of the Xiao and Xiang Rivers in Hunan province became a favorite theme of landscape painters in both China and Japan for the rich variety of scenic possibilities it afforded, which became codified into the Eight Views of the Xiao and Xiang: "Wild Geese Alighting on a Sandbar," "Sails off a Distant Shore," "Mountain Market in Clearing Mist," "Evening Snow Blending River and Sky," "Autumn Moon over Lake Dongting," "Night Rain over the Xiao and Xiang," "Evening Bell from a Mist-Shrouded Temple," and "Fishing Village in Evening Glow."

After the theme of the Eight Views of the Xiao and Xiang was imported to Japan, it inspired local variants, such as the Eight Views of Ōmi (Ōmi Hakkei), incorporating famous sites along the southern shores of Lake Biwa. In this way, this ideal Chinese landscape became a model and a prototype for Japanese landscapes.

My uncle, a Nihonga (Japanese-style) painter, made me memorize the Eight Views of Ōmi, which were selected by the poet and aristocrat Konoe Masaie in the fifteenth century: "Geese Alighting at Katata," "Returning Sails at Yabase," "Clear Breeze at Awazu," "Evening Snow at Hira," "Autumn Moon over Ishiyamadera," "Night Rain at Karasaki," "Evening Bell at Miidera," and "Evening Glow at Seta." In Ihara Saikaku's story collection *Nihon eitaigura* (The Eternal Storehouse of Japan, 1688), a character with too much time on his hands climbs to the viewing platform of a Kannon temple built on a mountainside overlooking the Eight Views of Ōmi but finds that even such spectacular scenery loses its charm when looked at all day long. The Eight Views of Ōmi are a kind of homage to the Eight Views of the Xiao and Xiang.

To become a famous place, a landscape must first of all embody a variety of the conditions by which scenic energy is judged. But it must also inspire a host of poets and painters to praise its beauty. Only places that meet both of these criteria become truly iconic famous places. Because of this, famous places are deeply entwined with a rhetorical device central to Japanese poetics: *utamakura*, or "poem pillows," place names that call up a rich store of traditional associations. The Uji River and Toba in Kyoto, Kasugano and Yoshinoyama in Yamato, Ōsakayama and Shiganoura in Ōmi, Suzukayama and Futamigaura in Ise, and Adachigahara and Miyagino in Mutsu—all of these famous places have been integrated as *utamakura* into hundreds, if not thousands of poems written over the centuries, so that the names themselves make these places famous.

In 1207, during the time of the third Kamakura shogun, Minamoto no Sanetomo, the imperial court poets who had been involved in the production of the *Shinkokinshū* (New Collection of Poems Ancient and Modern, 1205) produced another collection, *Saishō Shitennōin shōji waka*,[8] whose poems were themed on paintings decorating the sliding doors of the Saishō Shitennōin (Monastery of the Four Conquering Guardian Kings) in Kyoto, in turn representing forty-six famous places throughout Japan. Eight years after this, the anthology *Dairi meisho hyakushu* (A Palace Collection of One Hundred Poems on Famous Places, 1215) increased the number of places depicted by fifty-three. The additions—such as Tamukeyama, Ikomayama, Ōeyama, Tagonoura, Tsukubasan, Matsushima, and Sayo no Nakayama—suggest that a great deal of new information about the scenery of these places was being amassed at this time.

To summarize, I would like to stress that a famous place needs, above all, to be imbued with scenic energy. What scenic energy is, precisely, is difficult to explain. I believe, if you will continue reading, you will eventually come to understand it, because this book involves the fundamental nature of this idea.

Well, after having gazed at mountains, the next step is to visit them, for which we have an oft-used phrase: *monomi yusan* (sightseeing trips to the mountains). This is a valuable phrase in thinking about Japan. Let me say how I believe it evolved.

We'll start with the word *kunimi*, which means "land-viewing," gazing out over the land below from atop a mountain peak. A poem by Emperor Jomei (593–641) includes the lines "Ame no Kaguyama / noboritachi / kunimi o sureba" (Heavenly Mount Kagu: / When I climb it / And look out across the land);[9] in the *Harima fudoki*, an early provincial gazetteer, one entry reads, "The Homuta [Ōjin] emperor ascended this hill and viewed the land." It appears that for Japan's early rulers, such expeditions were a kind of duty, an assertion of their rule of all they could see. Of course, the act in itself involved nothing more than looking, as indicated by verses from the genre known as *kunimi uta* ("land-viewing poems"): "Gazing from this lofty peak / to the valley below / the cucumber and eggplant are in full flower." Here *kuni* signifies a unified community.

A "land-viewing" might be followed by *no-asobi*, an outing in mountain meadows. An excursion by Emperor Yūryaku in the late fifth century is famous as one of the first recorded examples of this pastime, but such pleasures were not reserved exclusively for the sovereign and court nobility; the common people also had a similar type of outing or festival, an *utagaki*, in which large numbers of men and women from neighboring villages freely associated with one another. Similar festivities are still being attended by large numbers of people in Yunnan province in China, even today. Another form of mountain pastime or recreation was hunting, and in chapter 5, "Birds," I will discuss falconry.

Eventually, as a number of specific locales became known for their scenic appeal—became established, in other words, as famous places—the common people began to frequent them as well, and *monomi yusan*, or sightseeing, became a popular pursuit. *Monomi* was originally a word in common use, meaning to experience a place that possessed scenic energy—one that was worthy of visual appreciation or that was bustling and lively.

A headnote to one of the poems in the *Kokinshū* (905), the first of the great imperial poetry anthologies, explains how the poem was sent to "a young woman who was out sightseeing [*monomi*] when [the poet] was at the Kasuga Shrine festival."[10] In the tenth-century *Tale of Lady Ochikubo* (*Ochikubo monogatari*), the main character, who is pregnant, says, "I am indisposed and know how unsightly I must be, and if I go out sightseeing [*monomi*] in the view of others I fear I will be a nuisance."[11]

I will speak of this more in later chapters, but the *mono* of *monomi* means "thing" in both the material and spiritual senses, referring to both physical objects and mental phenomena. Later, the idea of *monomi yusan* would connect with that of *yūraku*, meaning "leisure." *Yūraku* had its origins in the extraordinary popularity of parties for cherry-blossom viewing in spring, called *kaka yūraku* ("entertainment under the blossoms"), which then gradually expanded to include excursions to view the autumn leaves or sightseeing trips to places like the Eight Views of Ōmi. Entertainment beneath the cherry blossoms always included competitions in the composition of linked verse (*renga*) held beneath a *shidare-zakura* (weeping cherry). The impressive form of the weeping cherry tree had made it, since ancient times, a *yorishiro*—the temporary abode of spirits. But beneath all this, the sensibility of the *kunimi* and *utagaki* also lived on.

These forms of sightseeing and recreation are known as summoning or inviting the seasons (*kisetsu no yobiyose*). I mentioned earlier that Japanese gardens had their origins in the "island" of the Soga family in ancient times. Later, Mount Penglai (J. Hōraisan), the island of the immortals in Chinese myth, would supplant Mount Sumeru as the principal model for the central garden feature. In the Heian period (794–1185), there was a fad for *senzai awase*, a competition in which courtiers would collect wildflowers and grasses to plant in front of the artificial mountains in the garden. The garden manual *Sakuteiki* was compiled, promoting the use of stones in garden design to symbolize mountains.

Kingdoms in the mountains

The mountains have customs and ways of life proper to them. But the people of ancient and medieval Japan had no easy way to directly experience the separate, secret time and space of the mountain fastnesses. Naturally, this inspired speculation and stirred people's imaginations. Somewhere deep in the mountains, it was said, there is a magnificent palace, or a stupendous concealed treasure, or a place where reclining immortals dine on mountain mist, where ogres and evil spirits feed on human flesh—the settings of many a "true" story about imaginary kingdoms. If we trace all the variant versions of the folk tale concerning the demon king Shuten Dōji, for example, we find that there are mountains all over Japan analogous to Mount Ōe, his supposed lair.

Tucked away in the recesses of the Apostolic Palace in Rome are the Vatican Secret Archives, where the records and confidential correspondence of Catholic missionaries collected over the past 350 years are preserved. The Vatican is a strange and mysterious place, its strangeness brilliantly captured by André Gide in *Les caves du Vatican* (*The Vatican Cellars*, 1914), with its tale of con men attempting to dupe unsuspecting Catholics into believing that Freemasons have kidnapped and imprisoned the pope.

In the Vatican archives are detailed accounts, researched by Catholic missionaries, describing a number of expeditions sent by successive Chinese emperors to explore and survey the Kunlun Mountains and the mountains of Tibet. What was it the Chinese emperors were seeking in the depths of the Tibetan mountains? They believed that the Kunluns or the Tibetan Himalayas were the site of a legendary sacred realm.

China had its own version of Adam and Eve, named Fuxi and Nuwa. The two appear in the founding myths of China and are depicted as humans with the lower body of snakes with intertwined tails. They were believed to have been born on a remote mountain in Central Asia, called Kunlun, which was the realm of their mother, Xiwangmu (Queen Mother of the West), corresponding to Gaia in Greek mythology. In Chinese mythology, Xiwangmu lived in a magnificent nine-storied jade palace, resembling the Potala in Lhasa, and the emperors who sent the expeditions believed this palace truly existed.

In the palace of Xiwangmu stood a peach tree that blossomed only once in six thousand years, enveloping visitors in a fragrance that would almost dissolve them in bliss. The archetype of the apple in the Garden of Eden may have made its way across Eurasia, but in any case, somewhere in what are now known as the Kunlun Mountains or the Tibetan Himalayas there was believed to be a land protected from the icy winds, which, like the Peach Blossom Spring (a utopia depicted in a fifth-century Chinese fable), was always warm and pleasant. Outsiders bringing with them the cold breath of the surrounding mountains would be quickly turned away.

This was what, in modern scientific parlance, we might call a space-time singularity, a blissful peach-blossom paradise where the flow of time no longer had any meaning. Xiwangmu would appear to visitors to this realm in the guise of the bodhisattva of compassion, Guanyin (J. Kannon), and give them hints on how to rid themselves of earthly attachments and attain nirvana. It was also said that some of these travelers returned to China after their enlightenment, providing a source of the traditions surrounding Guanyin.

In records resting deep in the Vatican archives are reports that this land the Chinese spoke of as the realm of Xiwangmu was known in India as Katapa, and in Tibet as Shambhala. And it was through these reports, preserved by the Vatican for 350 years, that this illusory kingdom of Shambhala, hidden away in the mountains of Tibet, first began to receive attention from the outside world.

In my research, I have come across a seventeenth-century map, published in Antwerp, in which Shambhala appears as a place name. The Hungarian philologist Sándor Csoma de Kőrös (1784–1842), who around 1830 spent four years in a Tibetan monastery, wrote that Shambhala was situated north of the Syr Darya River, between 45 and 50 degrees north latitude.

On the seventeenth-century map, in the area marked as Shambhala there is also an explanatory legend reading "The place of origin of the Bon religion." Giuseppe Tucci (1894–1984), an authority on Tibetan religion whose work I deeply respect, hypothesized that Shambhala was located somewhere along the Tarim River. No trace of this land has yet been found.

A marvelous kingdom located deep in the mountains, or a mysterious hidden fortress—such ideas seem common to just about every era and people. Adventure stories, fantasy novels, and science fiction from Jules Verne onward are filled with such tales of fabulous palaces and secret sites. Steven Spielberg channeled this fantasy into the film *Close Encounters of the Third Kind* (1977). The storyline is simple: an ordinary guy working as an electrical lineman is so obsessed by a vision of a mountain that he neglects his family and begins building a huge model of it in his living room. The shape of the mountain is a kind of archetypal image for him; he becomes convinced that if he can somehow grasp it fully, something momentous will occur. This quest eventually leads him to a UFO landing site at the base of Devils Tower in Wyoming.

The outline of this story is essentially the same as that found in the documents held in the Vatican Secret Archives for more than three centuries: hidden deep within the mountains, there just might be another world.

The mountains as Pure Land

The concept of "another world deep in the mountains" (*sanchū takai*) has existed in Japan since ancient times. It was believed that after death, the spirits or souls of the deceased would travel to distant mountains to be reborn. In many parts of the country funeral ceremonies were conducted in the mountains or their foothills.

Even today, the belief that the souls of the dead return to the mountains remains widespread. Growing up in Kyoto, I was taught that Toribeno in the foothills of Higashiyama was a place where souls of the dead would congregate. Long ago, sky burials were probably conducted there. In some regions, similar funeral sites were called *akoya*; in the temple precincts of Rokuharamitsuji in Kyoto there is a small stone stele called Akoya that I suspect was once located at Toribeno. This in turn became associated with the story of Akoya, mistress of the warrior Taira no Kagekiyo, as told in the *sekkyō-bushi* (sermon-ballad) *Kagekiyo* and Chikamatsu Monzaemon's famous *jōruri* play *Shusse Kagekiyo* (Kagekiyo Victorious).

Eventually this idea of another world deep in the mountains mingled with Buddhist thought and helped nurture Pure Land beliefs—and the image that somewhere in the mountains, or beyond the mountains, lay a Buddhist paradise.

In Japan such beliefs focused primarily on the Pure Land of Bliss (Gokuraku Jōdo), the abode of Amida (Sk. Amitābha) Buddha believed to exist in the remote west. They originated in the doctrines of the Tendai sect, refined in the great monastery complex on Mount Hiei northeast of Kyoto. In the middle of the Heian period, these beliefs made their way down from the mountain and into the capital, where they began to spread among the general populace. Greatly assisting the popularization of these teachings was the treatise *Ōjōyōshū* (Essentials of Rebirth in the Pure Land) by the priest Genshin (942–1017; also known as Eshin Sōzu), which provided readers with vivid and easily understandable images of heaven and hell.

In the tenth century a group of aristocratic literati led by Yoshishige no Yasutane developed a deep interest in the Pure Land and the idea of rebirth. They created groups such as the Kangakue and Nijūgo Zanmaie that were devoted to practices that included the recitation of the *nembutsu* (Amida Buddha's name) and the composition of religious poetry. The millenarian ideas associated with the concept of *mappō*, the final period of the Dharma when salvation was tied to faith alone, spread with the Pure Land teachings. Many temples and halls dedicated to Amida Buddha or his attendant bodhisattva Kannon (Sk. Avalokiteśvara) were constructed, the most famous being the Byōdōin at Uji, south of Kyoto. These were attempts to create a "Pure Land in this world," modeled on descriptions in the Buddhist scriptures—an expression of longing to be reborn in the Pure Land and transported to the Other Shore (*higan*).

The Western Paradise, the Pure Land of Bliss presided over by Amida Buddha, was the most popular destination. But in the Buddhist teachings it was not the only Pure Land. In the east was the abode of Yakushi (Sk. Bhaiṣajyaguru) Nyorai, the Medicine Buddha, known as the Pure Land of Lapis Lazuli, or Rurikō Jōdo, and abbreviated as Jōruri. Later, *jōruri* became the name of the narrative musical accompaniment for the puppet theater that was the prototype for Kabuki, suggesting its similarity to the ethereal music playing in Yakushi's Pure Land of the East.

There was also a Pure Land in the north presided over by the bodhisattva Miroku (Sk. Maitreya) or the deva king Bishamonten (Sk. Vaiśravaṇa), and one in the south ruled by Shaka Nyorai (Sk. Śakyamuni, the historical buddha), but for some reason these were not as popular as Amida's Western Paradise. In any age, some images flourish while others fade.

Among the many images used to spread Pure Land doctrine in medieval times were the paintings known as *raigōzu*. Colorful and richly imaginative, we might almost think of them as a kind of Pop art, or Asian space opera.

Riding on the clouds, a gigantic Amida Buddha floats over a mountain range. In early paintings, he is usually depicted alone, but later, as people grew ever more eager for his coming, he was commonly shown descending accompanied by a retinue of twenty-five attendant bodhisattvas. For the impatient, there was even a genre of these paintings called *haya raigō* ("speedy advent") in which Amida is shown riding a particularly fast cloud to his earthly destination, accompanied by ethereal music provided by a host of bodhisattvas floating amid clouds and playing a variety of celestial instruments. These almost lead me to think that Kyoto should introduce a new festival themed on this epic cosmic opera.

Those impatiently longing for Amida's arrival began to act as if he had already descended into this world. The Amida and Kannon temples and the halls for walking meditation known as *jōgyō zanmaidō* are all tokens of this. During the era when the Fujiwara family controlled the imperial court (roughly from the late ninth to the late twelfth century), the nobility could not wait to be reborn in the Pure Land. They built temples near their residences where Amida Buddha and Kannon were enshrined. If they fell seriously ill, on their deathbed they would be connected to these images or paintings of Amida or Kannon by five-colored skeins of ribbons, the better to be guided to the Pure Land. Fujiwara no Michinaga (966–1028), arguably one of the most powerful statesmen of the Heian period, was filled with an almost desperate desire for rebirth in the Pure Land of the West and, when he was dying, used this method to connect with images of Amida.

From the middle of the Heian period onward, as predictions of the end times according to the doctrine of *mappō* were voiced ever more urgently, the construction of halls and temples to connect with the Other Shore reached a crescendo. And so it was that the "mountains" of the Pure Land came to be embodied within the cities and the villages, in miniaturized form.

Many of the world's mythologies posit an axis mundi, or world axis—a central pillar of some sort connecting our world to different levels of existence.

Frequently this axis mundi takes the form of a cosmic mountain such as Mount Sumeru, or a towering "world tree." The great religious studies scholar Mircea Eliade (1907–86) studied world trees throughout global mythology and argued that this "symbolism of the center" was the fount of all other imagery. According to Eliade's formula, the earliest sacred sites were all associated with legends involving fissures or ruptures, through which one might be transported to another world. This is a concept shared by many cultures. The site of such a rupture might be marked by a mountain, a tree, a river. Sometimes animals are used to emphasize the rupture, or the axis mundi is represented by a pillar or other manmade object.

Throughout Japan there are *bonten* and *onbashira* festivals whose centerpieces are colorfully decorated bamboo poles or enormous pillars made from tree trunks; in Europe, there is the tradition of raising a maypole. All of these are symbols of the world tree.

Once this idea of an axis mundi has taken root, and its symbol has been established, a succession of variant forms develop in different regions. Portable shrines (*mikoshi*) and floats (*dashi*) are standard features of almost any Japanese festival. They can be seen as miniature models of the cosmic mountain. This is why we often refer to festival floats colloquially as *yama*—mountains. The *mikoshi* are girded (usually twice) with massive ropes that suggest the world serpent. These *mikoshi* serve as palanquins for transporting deities.

A festival is a drama that announces, once a year, the presence of deities in our midst: a ritual for periodically reinforcing that awareness. Most traditional festivals convince us of our proximity to mountains and deities and allow us to enter a kind of trance state and enjoy that realm—they are devices for a sort of virtual-reality experience.

Almost all Japanese temples have "mountain names" (*sangō*) that precede the official temple name (*jigō*). Thus Naritasan Shinshōji, Zuiryūsan Nanzenji, and Kofukusan Kenchōji, where the suffix -san refers to mount and -ji to temple: Mount Narita Shinshō Temple, for example. This tells us that the temples and monasteries themselves were originally modeled on mountains.

So mountains are the archetype or matrix for a broad variety of images. They are the common denominator or, in other words, the basic stage setting for the drama of birds, flowers, wind, and moon—and a solid point of departure for the continuing story of the phenomenology of nature in Japanese culture.

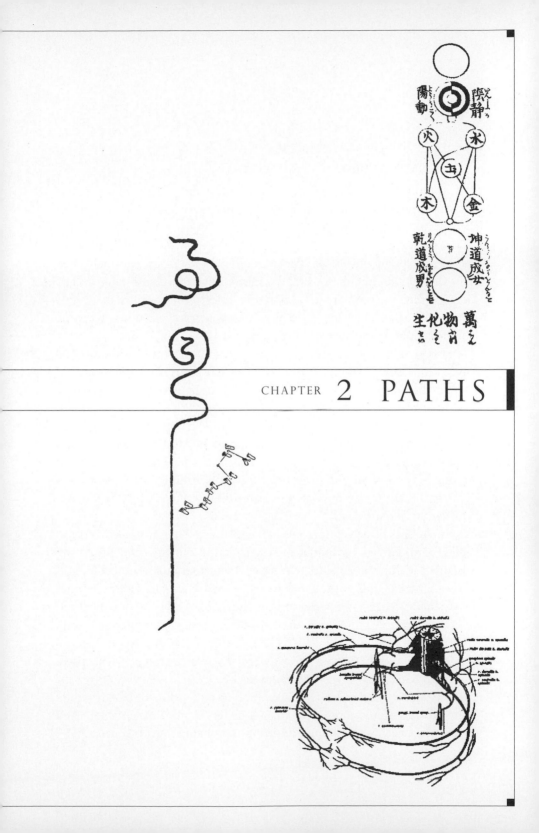

陰靜
陽動

火　水

土

木　金

坤道成女
乾道成男

萬物
化生

CHAPTER 2 PATHS

The uncanny valley

You've probably had this experience: you descend a flight of stairs, not really paying attention, and suddenly you run out of stairs before your feet are ready.

Mori Masahiro (b. 1927), a pioneering robotics engineer, once conducted an experiment a bit similar to an old *Candid Camera* episode. When we reach for a doorknob, we simply assume it will be a hard metal object. Mori replaced the standard doorknob with a soft rubber replica that had a shiny surface like metal and stood by to watch people's reactions. Everyone who took hold of the knob recoiled from it with a cry of alarm.

Our bodies are repositories of science—crammed with mysteries to be solved only through scientific investigation. The brain has a diverse molecular language of hormones and neurotransmitters, and our body as a whole is equipped with a variety of homeostatic settings that it strives to maintain: if we are cold, we get goosebumps; when we're hot, we sweat. Many of our daily activities are governed by an accumulation of habitual behavioral patterns. Consequently, the instant we grasp what we expect to be a metal doorknob and instead discover it to be squishy rubber, we experience a shock to our entire nervous system greater than that of simply having our expectations overturned.

Our patterns of perception and behavior have what are called "critical values." Ordinarily our activities and communication with other people are contained within these values. Grasping a soft doorknob and recoiling in surprise is an example of the shock we experience when one of these values is suddenly exceeded. But we are largely unaware of what sort of critical values are programmed into our bodies, nor do we understand them very well.

How do we experience a pathway, physically? Given a 10-meter-wide path, most people tested will walk right down the center. Therefore, ergonomically speaking, for foot traffic of one lane in either direction, a 10-meter width is unnecessary; a maximum of 3–4 meters is probably sufficient. At 5 meters wide, even a stumbling drunk could probably stay on course.

The science of ergonomics attempts to define and secure the minimum viable width. Yet a path adhering to this minimum width but with either side of it falling steeply away as sheer walls into deep valleys would cause most people to hesitate before walking along it. Why?

This is one manifestation of the phenomenon that Mori Masahiro has dubbed "the uncanny valley": a boundary beyond which we suddenly experience discomfort or aversion. Mori used this term to refer to the uneasy gap between humans and humanoid robots that are unsettling, even frightening, because they are uncannily close to "real" humans. But such uncanny cliffs and valleys lurk in many aspects of human perception. They are an excess dimension of space-time we carry about unwittingly within our psychology and consciousness, thought processes and images, perceptions and behavior. They form a physically unnecessary realm, a hollowed-out, negative space-time.

The human body is not merely what is wrapped in our external form, with its proportions beloved of artists since the ancient Greeks—there are many, many more things concealed within. We have only limited under-standing of what we actually contain.

In our senses and perceptions, there exist what are known as "transit points" indicating a certain level or volume past which a stimulus will produce a change in state or a shift in response. For example, if you scratch an itch too hard, the feeling of relief or pleasure can give way to discomfort or even pain. Even something that feels good can, through overstimulation, pro-duce an adverse effect. Mild teasing, if repeated enough times, will be met with anger rather than amusement. Physiologists call these transit points "thresholds," and they are similar to the critical values mentioned earlier. On a day-to-day basis, skillfully controlling these thresholds—and living things have a wide variety of them—plays a major role in our lives and work.

These issues of critical values, the uncanny valley, and thresholds all point to the hidden dimensions of our senses. And they prompt us to try to challenge the mechanisms underlying our senses, perceptions, and behavior. So we might drink ourselves nearly senseless, or act in outra-geous ways, or explore remote frontiers—all of which are impulses to defy the critical values of one's body and try to glimpse, even temporarily, the hidden dimensions beyond.

In the 1960s the American cultural anthropologist Edward T. Hall pro-posed the concept of proxemics as a way of looking at some of the hidden dimensions in our lives—specifically, the human use of space and the effects of population density. Proxemics was designed to better understand patterns of human behavior by collecting detailed observational data on a variety of thresholds: What is the range of the human sense of smell? How do we feel when someone else enters our "elbow room"? How do people seat themselves on benches in public places? These studies resulted in the discovery of a range of habitual behavior that normally goes unnoticed.

Now, as we begin to consider the significance of pathways, an examination of these hidden dimensions of the human body and mind will become quite important. Why? Because pathways are what people have constructed to explore unknown and hidden dimensions. Moreover, pathways are the basis for all cultural phenomena, from transportation and industry to civilization, language, and the arts. Without pathways, none of these are possible.

I think of pathways as the scars left after the adventure of challenging and exploring the dimensions hidden from us by the critical values of our bodies and minds. This is the definition of pathways that I am working with.

We see paths, roads, ways, streets, trails—all of which are expressed by the Japanese kanji 道 (pronounced *michi* or *dō*)—from two fundamental perspectives: the impulse to travel from *here* to *there*, and the somewhat anxious anticipation of what might be coming from *there* to *here*. It is the path that forms the connection between the two.

The last scene of many a film shows us the hero disappearing down a road. Roads and paths are always symbols of where we have been and where we are going, the past and the future. Charlie Chaplin's *City Lights*, Federico Fellini's *La Strada*, and Luis Buñuel's *The Milky Way* all devote considerable time and energy to depicting roads and paths and, by so doing, reveal our yearning for not only beginnings and ends but also continuity.

In Japan the *michiyuki* (literally, "road-going"; sequences usually depicting a man and woman traveling through a series of places on their way to a love suicide) made famous in the *jōruri* plays of Chikamatsu Monzaemon (1653–1725) are suffused with this longing for an eternal continuity.

Salt roads

The history of the world's trade routes is largely understood. In prehistoric Europe the Amber Road was widely known and traveled, bearing amber and furs from the shores of the North Sea and the Baltic to Hamburg and Kassel, and then down the Elbe and Rhine to the Adriatic Sea and Venice, or the Ligurian Sea and Marseilles. In ancient Persia the Royal Road, an extensive system of trade routes completed by order of Darius I, was traversed by inspectors and spies known as "the eyes and ears of the king." It ran from Ephesus in Asia Minor to Susa and Persepolis near the Persian Gulf.

The famous Silk Road traverses the entire Eurasian continent. Many other such roads existed in antiquity: salt roads, iron roads, rice roads, pilgrimage roads. Buñuel's *The Milky Way* depicts the ancient pilgrimage route from Paris to its terminus at Santiago de Compostela in Spain.

In Japan as well, roads were built from ancient times. In the eighth century the post-station system (*ekisei*) was introduced from Tang China, but there are numerous references to roads that predate this. These early roads were rather primitive: steep and often overgrown with vegetation. The section dealing with Japan in the *Wei zhi*, a Chinese chronicle compiled in the late third century, describes the roads on Tsushima, an island between Japan and Korea, as being "like the trails of animals," while the roads in the Japanese protostate of Matsura in Kyushu were "heavily overgrown with weeds, with no sign of previous travelers." Early Japanese construction used only earth and wood; roads were not paved with stone. If roads were not constantly maintained, it was no simple task to keep them from becoming completely overgrown.

Beginning in the Kofun period (c. 300–710), the power of horses imported from the continent was widely recognized, and roads were built specifically to accommodate them. In the chapter of the *Nihon shoki* devoted to the reign of Emperor Ōjin is a description of how the eastern Emishi who came to pay tribute were put to work on the Umayasaka (Horse Stable Hill) road. Particularly after the establishment of the Yamato court in the fourth century, we see frequent references in historical sources to *hayuma*, or "fast horses," written with a variety of compounds making use of the kanji for "post-station" (駅 *eki*), indicating how important these roads had become. No doubt the constant trampling of the vegetation by the horses' hooves helped maintain the roads.

Plans for developing major highways between the Yamato and Kawachi regions began in the seventh century during the reign of Empress Suiko. Three of these ancient roads ran north-south across the Nara Basin:

Kamitsumichi (Upper Way), Nakatsumichi (Middle Way), and Shimotsu-michi (Lower Way). Research by historians including Kishi Toshio has shown that Kamitsumichi intersected with Yoko-ōji, a major east-west road, thus serving as the point of departure for the eastern provinces; Nakatsumichi became the main route southward to Yoshino; and Shimo-tsumichi extended south from Suzaku-ōji, the main thoroughfare of the capital city of Heijōkyō, to connect to the Tajihimichi leading to Kawachi.

But we cannot see the real Japan by looking only at these major highways and thoroughfares. We have to enter a number of other paths and byways. The writer Shiba Ryōtarō's long-running essay series *Kaidō o yuku* (Along the Highways, 1971–96) takes us down those side roads. Among them, the "salt roads" were indisputably the most important to the lives of the common people of ancient times.

People cannot live without salt. The Kōshū Kaidō, originating in the Shinjuku district of what is now Tokyo, was one of these salt roads, as is suggested by the name of its terminus, Shiojiri, a city in Nagano prefecture near the border with Yamanashi prefecture. Similar place names like Shiotsu and Shioyama are relics of the ancient salt roads (the *shio* in these names meaning "salt").

Understanding the salt roads is key to understanding the foundations of Japanese culture. It can almost be said that Japan divides culturally along the ancient salt roads. For example, Suwa and Matsumoto in Nagano prefecture are quite close to one another, but the salt used in the Suwa region was transported upriver from the Pacific coast along the Tenryūgawa, while the salt used in Matsumoto was brought from the Sea of Japan along an entirely different river route, the Himekawa. The place name Shiojiri suggests precisely what it was—the terminus of the Himekawa route, just south of Matsumoto. Other regions of Nagano prefecture—Ina, Azumino, Saku, and so forth—were each served by a different route for transport of salt. Each of these regions had a distinctive culture, dialect, and folkways. The salt roads fed different sets of social relations.

In a famous anecdote, the warlord Uesugi Kenshin (1530–78) sent salt to his rival Takeda Shingen (1521–73), against whom he fought five major battles over twelve years. Shingen's supply had been cut off by another warlord family, the Hōjō, whom Kenshin criticized for unfair tactics, declaring, "I do not fight with salt, but with the sword!" There is reason to doubt the veracity of this tale, however, for Shingen was at that time based in Kōshū, a region that had no scarcity of salt; moreover, Shingen was the sort of commander who would have been quite conscious, tactically, of the need to secure logistics such as salt routes. The salt for Kōshū came up the Fuji-kawa from Suruga Bay, a route that Shingen made sure to control early on by seizing the territory of Ichikawa Daimon at the southern end of the Kōfu Basin. Not only that, Shingen developed a method of smoke-curing miso to increase its ability to store and preserve salt. "Shingen miso" still boasts the highest salt content in Japan. Miso made four centuries ago using this method has been found safe to eat even today. So why was Shingen said to have received salt from Kenshin? Probably because of a Chinese traditional anecdote about sending salt to an enemy that found its way into the *kōdan* storytelling tradition of Edo-period Japan.

The first researcher in Japan to explore the history of the salt roads and the salt industry was Shibusawa Keizō (1896–1963). Shibusawa was a finan-cier and statesman who served as governor of the Bank of Japan and minis-ter of finance. Politicians were considerably more cultured in his time than those today, and among other ethnological writings, Shibusawa left us *Enzoku mondōshū* (Dialogue on Salt-Related Customs), a survey of folkways and customs related to salt. After its publication, various scholars began to study this subject. Among them was Miyamoto Tsuneichi (1907–81), whose definitive work *Shio no michi* (The Salt Roads) is particularly well known.

How was salt produced in premodern times? For the most part, by sim-ply boiling down seawater. Transporting the salt inland from the coast, however, was very difficult. Because salt produced from seawater contains a deliquescent, magnesium chloride (known as *nigari* in Japanese), it tends to liquefy by absorbing ambient moisture—quite inconvenient for storing and transporting in the humid climate of Japan.

Consequently, in early times salt-cured fish and seaweed were used as a medium for the transport of salt. Even if salted fish lost its surface coating of salt, the body of the fish would hold its salt content for two or three years. This was the origin of *shiozake*, the salt-cured salmon popular in Japan, especially as a breakfast food.

The early salt-makers did not merely include the professionals living and working along the coast. Miyamoto Tsuneichi recorded the following example from Niigata prefecture. During the winter, people living in mountain villages would cut timber and drag the logs to a nearby river. Each household would mark its logs with an individual brand. When the spring thaw increased the river flow with snowmelt, they would float the logs downstream. The logs would be carried downriver all the way to the Sea of Japan, where nets would be set to catch them. They would then be used as fuel to boil water for salt, which the villagers would carry back into the mountains with them.

This suggests that the first salt roads were actually rivers. But eventually most people were buying salt from salt merchants, whose sales routes became the new salt roads. Oxen, better suited to traveling the narrow trails than horses, were the principal pack animals. The processing of salt was terribly hard labor, made worse by the exploitative behavior of the merchants and producers, as depicted in Mori Ōgai's famous story *Sanshō Dayū* (Sanshō the Bailiff, 1915) and the 1954 Mizoguchi film by the same name. Sanshō the bailiff was merciless in driving the workers who gathered and boiled the saltwater.

Deities of the roads

The salt roads were paths fundamental to supporting everyday life. But in ancient and medieval times, roads and trails were also believed to be occupied by a host of strange and motley creatures. Let's spend some time on this topic, as it is quite significant.

According to Shirakawa Shizuka, a noted authority on Chinese characters and their etymology, the kanji for road, path, or way (道) originally depicted a group of people walking toward an unknown destination with a human head (首) held before them in a ritual gesture of purification. In other words, this kanji signified advancing in pursuit of a hidden dimension. Kanji are constructed from a set of basic elements, called radicals, in different combinations; kanji with either the "walk" (辶) or "step" radical (彳)—such as 行, 途, 辿, 往, 復— all have something to do with roads or paths. For example, the kanji 術 (*jutsu*, technique or skill) was originally an image of performing some type of concentrated labor in the middle of a roadway. In the kanji 徐 (*jo*, slowly, gradually), the 余 originally meant "needle," which in ancient China was an extremely important scientific instrument and considered an antenna for communicating with the deities. The kanji 徐 is thus the image of a needle planted in a roadway, simultaneously pacifying the earth spirits and signaling the deities.

So for the people of ancient and medieval times, roads and trails were also important pathways traveled by the spirits. Crossroads (*tsuji* 辻 or *chimata* 巷) were believed to be where the spiritual power residing in words (*kotodama*) was especially powerful.

This poem by Kakinomoto no Hitomaro (active 689–700) references *kotodama* in a divination at a crossroads:

kotodama no	Through the *kotodama*
yaso no chimata ni	in an evening divination performed
yūke tō	at a multiple crossroads
ura masani noru	the prediction was clear:
imo wa aiyoramu	my love will return to me.[1]

Yaso no chimata (literally, "eighty crossings") is a poetic term for a bustling intersection; this divination technique consisted of listening to the voices of the crowd in order to hear what the *kotodama* had to say. That it is evening is important: twilight is known in Japanese as *tasogare* (derived from a phrase meaning "who is it?"), the hour when faces begin to be indistinguishable in the dusk—an hour in which people's spirits become elevated, purified. It was also known as *ōmagatoki* ("the hour of calamity"), when ghosts and evil spirits are abroad in the world. This method of listening for the *kotodama* at a crossroads in the evening darkness—a way of listening in on information from a hidden dimension—would continue through the Edo period, when it was known as *tsujiura* ("crossroads divination").

Thus, from ancient times, crossroads were imbued with a deep and complex significance. The place where two roads cross becomes the center of the four directions, where a variety of spirits and things congregate and collect, and where a variety of events may originate. As Buddhism permeated popular consciousness, so did the concept of *rokudō*, the six realms of existence (devas, warring titans, humans, animals, hungry ghosts, and creatures of hell), and of *rokudō no tsuji*, the crossroads of the six realms, as a kind of antechamber to rebirth into one of the six realms after death. From the Muromachi period (1336–1573) onward, it became common to enshrine images of the bodhisattva Jizō at crossroads throughout the country, since Jizō was revered as a protector of souls in the afterlife.

In the Greco-Roman world, a three-faced image of the goddess Hecate was placed at crossroads, to which it was customary to make offerings on the night of the full moon.

In addition to the *tsujiura* mentioned above, there was a similar divination practice called *hashiura* that took place on bridges. Like *tsujiura*, *hashiura* involved listening to the voices of passersby in a place of geomantic power—for bridges, like crossroads, were regarded as charged with significance and as powerful collectors of information. Bridges were also home to spirits such as Hashihime ("the maiden of the bridge"), the demonic spirit of a woman consumed by jealousy famously believed to haunt the Uji Bridge, as well as the demon disguised as a woman encountered by the legendary hero Watanabe no Tsuna (953–1025) at Ichijō Modoribashi bridge in Kyoto. Bridges are thus considered to be a node between this world (*here*) and the other (*there*).

The roads swarmed with spirits and sprites, ghosts and goblins—some benevolent, others evil. In Japan, this led to the positing of a deity known as *sae no kami* as the protector of roads. The use of *sae* is significant here. *Sae* means to block, to seal, to obstruct. In other words, the role of this deity was to protect *here* from the plague spirits and other evil spirits that might be coming down the road from *there*. *Sae no kami* was one form of the roadside guardians known as *dōsojin* (literally, "roadside ancestral deities"), who were also believed to know the fortunes of the villagers. They were represented by straw or wooden images and figurines beloved by local children.

To protect against plague gods and evil spirits entering the city, Kyoto had a special festival, the Michi no Ae no Matsuri (Festival of the Roadside Gods). Held on the last day of the sixth and twelfth months, it was conducted as a state ritual of protection against malevolent beings. Three guardian deities—Yachimatahiko, Yachimatahime, and Kunado—were celebrated, in the process breaking the "critical value" separating their hidden dimension from our own to appear momentarily here, in this world. The Shikaku Shikai no Matsuri (Four Corners and Four Borders Festival) were similar rites conducted to defend the capital from evil spirits from the four directions.

Representative of these malevolent forces attempting to enter the capital were "terribly polluted plague spirits" (*kegare ashiki ekiki*)—meaning infectious diseases—as they were called in the *Engi shiki*, an early tenth-century compilation of government regulations and ceremonial procedures. At the time, outbreaks of disease were believed to be the work of vengeful spirits (*mononoke*) or demons. The Four Corners and Four Borders Festival was aimed at repelling such forces at the points where major roads entered the city from the four directions. Since it would be constantly driving spirits away throughout the year, one large ceremony was conducted annually, at year's end. Also known as the Oniyarai (Demon-Expelling) or Tsuina (Calamity-Dispelling) ritual, this is one of the origins of the Setsubun festival still celebrated today.

The models for techniques of expelling demons and dispelling calamities were imported from ancient China, where, according to the *Zhou li* (The Rites of Zhou, second century BCE), a diviner or ritualist called a *fangxiangshi* (J. *hōsōshi*)—wearing a bearskin over his head ornamented with four golden eyes, clad in black with crimson skirting, and bearing a halberd and shield—led a retinue of retainers in a rite of exorcism. The Setsubun rituals at Yoshida Shrine in Kyoto, which feature a *hōsōshi* wearing a mask with four golden eyes, still preserve something of this archetypal ceremony.

Since the *hōsōshi* himself presented such a fearsome visage, in the popular mind the exorcist became confused with the demons he was exorcising. In the Setsubun ritual we are familiar with today, he scatters beans while chanting, "Oni wa soto, fuku wa uchi" (Demons out! Good fortune in!). But there were also instances like the Oni no Hōraku (Demons' Liturgy), held during Setsubun at Kyoto's Rozanji temple, in which demons are summoned. In any case, the Setsubun ritual was always one aimed at refreshing the spirit at the seasonal transition to spring.

The roads and byways teemed with a panoply of ghosts and spirits. When disease ran rampant, it was only natural that the common people wanted to dispatch the evil spirits down the roads and away from their villages. This urge took the form of another common folk ritual, *mushiokuri*, or "seeing off the insects." The villagers would gather to make straw dolls and form a procession to the outskirts of the village to send off harmful and crop-damaging insects. Of course this sent them on the road toward the next village, which would then have to conduct its own *mushiokuri*. I'm told that starting somewhere in Gifu prefecture, there is a chain of *mushiokuri* that sends the bugs all the way to villages along the Sea of Japan in Toyama prefecture. This custom is also sometimes called *sanemori*, in a somewhat far-fetched association with the legend of a Heike general, Saitō Bettō Sanemori, said to have died in battle after his horse stumbled in a rice field and threw him. Sanemori's spirit vowed to avenge this ignominious end by becoming an insect that would forever blight the harvests.

As we have seen, roads have many nodes—crossroads, bridges, and checkpoints—that have been accorded great importance. These various spots along the road serve as collection points for a mysterious voltage that, when it exceeds its critical value, can bring either unexpected good luck or misfortune. Or so it was believed. For readers who wish to explore it further, I recommend the ethnologist Akasaka Norio's *Kyōkai no hassei*

(The Origin of Boundaries, 1989) as a fascinating deep dive into this aspect of folklore.

The Daoist way

Let's shift focus for a moment to consider the forms of thought inspired in China by "path" or "way." The character for road, path, or way (道) is pronounced *dao* in Chinese. The philosophy that emphasized the Way in China is thus known as Daoism. There are many forms of Daoism, from folk traditions to more organized religious sects. In what follows, I will use Daoism as a generic term for all these variants.

Daoism has diverse origins, with at least five streams of thought intermingled. The first is the philosophy of Laozi and Zhuangzi, with its emphasis on non-action (*wuwei*) and harmony with nature. The second is a pursuit of immortality and a desire to emulate the lives of the immortals, known as *xianren* (J. *sennin*). The third is a cosmology founded in the *Yijing* (Book of Changes) and the concepts of yin and yang and the Five Elements. The fourth involves various forms of mysticism, from astrology and other forms of divination to traditional medicine. The fifth is the geomantic tradition known as fengshui. Add to this the festivals venerating various folk deities and magical beliefs employing a variety of charms and spells, and Daoism presents quite a complicated package of philosophy, sorcery, and religious belief.

The thought of Laozi and Zhuangzi revels in the concept of negation. More radically than the ancient Greek philosopher Heraclitus, it advocates relativism as the means for humanity to return to the original Way of nature. Laozi would later be deified as the original patriarch of Daoism. The Way of the Immortals, as described in *Shenxian zhuan* (Lives of the Deities and Immortals), a treatise attributed to the Daoist scholar Ge Hong (283–343), idealizes mountains as a sacred space and seeks to emulate the immortals believed to disport themselves there. The aesthetic appreciation of the mountain landscape, as described in chapter 1, "Mountains," largely originated in this way of thought. Yin-yang thought saw all the phenomena of the universe as produced and governed by interaction between *qi* 気 (J. *ki*)—a primal energy having two aspects, yin and yang—and the five elements of wood, fire, earth, metal, and water.

With this background, almost all variants of Daoism placed the Dao, the Way, at their core. The Dao was the core cosmological principle of ancient China. As it says in chapter 1, verse 42, of the *Daodejing*, "The Dao gives birth to one. One gives birth to two. Two gives birth to three. Three gives birth to the myriad things." The Way was seen as the genesis of all phenomena, preceding even the One.

In medieval China, the *taiji* (Great Unity) cosmology stated that in the beginning the Way manifested as a primal energy, or *yuanqi*, that separated into yin and yang, which then generated the myriad phenomena of the universe. Here, too, the Way was the ultimate source of all things—the origin of all origins.

The following table displays a "cosmogram"—an abbreviated diagram of the Daoist universe—provided by Ge Zhaoguang of the Chinese Studies Research Institute of Qinghua University in Beijing. Combinations of the various elements noted here have provided the principles for everything from the organization of rituals to the presentation of food—many of which have been adopted in Japan as well. One could almost say that the history of Japanese culture has consisted of selecting those principles that had the greatest appeal to the Japanese sensibility, and then refining them.

Great Unity
|
Duality
|
Yin-Yang

| Heaven | | | | Earth |
| Four Seasons | | | | Five Elements |

Four Seasons	Spring	Summer		Autumn	Winter
Five Elements	Wood	Fire	Earth	Metal	Water
Five Emperors	Taihao	Yandi	Huangdi	Shaohao	Zhuanxu
Five Deities	Gou Mang (spring/wood)	Zhu Rong (summer/fire)	Hou Tu (goddess of earth)	Ru Shou (autumn/metal)	Xuan Ming (winter/water)
Five Sacrifices (at protective loci of the household)	front door	hearth	central courtyard	entrance gate	roadway
Five Organs	Spleen	Lungs	Heart	Liver	Kidneys
Five Colors	Blue	Red	Yellow	White	Black
Five Tastes	Sour	Bitter	Sweet	Spicy	Salty
Five Aromas	Rancid	Scorched	Fragrant	Rotten	Putrid
Five Sounds	pentatonic scale pitches (jue, zhi, gong, shang, yu) corresponding to E, G, C, D, A on the Western scale				
Five Directions	East	South	Center	West	North

PATHS

These Daoist principles extended into all aspects of life, from the seasons and the cardinal directions to the perception of color and the human body. The landscape paintings discussed in the previous chapter also have a deep connection with Daoism. As well, veneration of the Kunlun Mountains and the Queen Mother of the West was an outgrowth of the Daoist tradition. In chapter 4, "Wind," we will see how Daoist concepts of fengshui and the ruling spirits of the four directions influenced the layout of the imperial capital of Heiankyō.

Even the "dry landscape" (*karesansui*) rock and sand gardens that are closely associated with Japanese Zen temples were originally modeled on Daoist gardens.

Knowledge of Daoism is essential to understanding Japanese intellectual and cultural history. Many aspects of Japan cannot be understood without some understanding of Daoism.

Japanese culture has many traditional practices that take the *dao* (J. *dō*) of Daoism as a key element in their name, usually translated into English as "way"—for example, the "way" of flower arrangement (*kadō*, also known as ikebana) and the way of tea (*sadō*, also known as tea ceremony, or *chanoyu*). *Bushidō*, "the way of the warrior," informed samurai life in the Edo period. The words for reason (*dōri*) and morality (*dōtoku* or *dōgi*) also include the kanji for the "way." In other words, the ultimate method for accomplishing something was conceived as a *dō*, or way. The scholar Okakura Tenshin (1862–1913) was the first to note this. And the phenomenology of nature in Japanese culture that we will gradually outline in this book is certainly connected with Daoism.

Serious study of the influence of Daoism on Japanese culture finally began in the 1960s with the work of Shimode Sekiyo (1919–98) on Japanese folkways and of Fukunaga Mitsuji (1918–2001) in intellectual history, but even today it remains generally unappreciated. I was fortunate to have studied in my twenties with Yoshioka Yoshitoyo (1916–79), a leading figure in Daoist studies in Japan, yet in the course of my longtime advocacy of the role of Daoism I have somehow been unable to persuade many people of how interesting and important a subject it is.

Traces of Daoism can be found throughout our traditions: the legends of Tanabata, Mount Hōrai (C. Penglai), and Kaguyahime, and the stories in many regions of the heavenly maiden and her feathered robe (*hagoromo*), to name just a few. Consider as well the custom, called *Kōshin-machi*, of staying up all night on specific days to keep the "three corpses and nine insects" (*sanshi kyūchū*) in one's body from causing harm. Another custom (*tsuki-machi*) involves staying up late on certain days of the lunar cycle to venerate the moonrise. The ritualized dance steps (*henbai*) that are performed in festivals all over the country have elements of Daoist origin.

With regard to dance steps, the *henbai* traditionally performed by a general before setting out for battle, as well as the familiar bobbing and weaving gait of participants carrying the portable shrine (*mikoshi*) in most Japanese festivals, resembles a well-known step used in Daoist ritual called *yubu* (J. *uho*, also known as King Yü's step), which follows a zigzag pattern based on treading the arrangement of the seven stars of the constellation known in the West as Ursa Major—and which, as my research has revealed, is also connected to the origins of the martial art of *taijiquan* (commonly known in the West as Tai Chi).

The *taiji* of *taijiquan* refers to Polaris, the North Star. As the single fixed star in the night sky, it was seen as emblematic of the ultimate Way of the cosmos (*taiji*, literally "great pole," was also sometimes referred to as *taiyi*, "great unity"). Practitioners of Daoist meditation would first cleanse their bodies and then dress in white, search for the North Star, and stand focusing their attention on the seven stars of Ursa Major glittering high in the northern sky. Then, controlling their breathing, they would slowly bring these seven stars down to earth, where, inhaling and exhaling deeply with each step, they would tread the pattern of those stars, one by one. With each step and breath, they would send energy into their arms and legs, and then slowly release it. This was the origin of what we know today as *taijiquan*. Similarly, *qigong*, the Chinese practice of meditative breath control, has also had a long and deep association with Daoism.

These "cosmic steps," as I call them, were imported to Japan and transformed into the martial *henbai* and the movements of those carrying the *mikoshi*. They were also quite possibly an archetype for the famous "leaping exit" (*tobi roppō*) performed by the character Benkei in the Kabuki play *Kanjinchō* (The Subscription List).

The rituals and thought of the Daoist masters were transmitted to Japan, where the Onmyōryō (Bureau of Yin and Yang) was created as an organ of the imperial government to oversee these esoteric practices. Abe no Seimei (921–1005) was a famous "master of yin and yang" (*onmyōji*), the Japanese version of the Chinese Daoist masters. It was Seimei who advised Watanabe no Tsuna (953–1025) to observe a period of ritual seclusion and abstinence (*monoimi*) as a precaution after his battle with the demon on the bridge at Ichijō Modoribashi.

The lore and techniques of Daoism and other mystical arts were also passed down as a secret transmission among the "mountain people" of Japan. The legendary En no Gyōja (634–706), said to be the original *yamabushi*, seems a thoroughly Daoist figure, and a wielder of Daoist magic.

Daoism also permeates traditional Japanese medicine, whose bible was the thirty-volume *Ishinpō* (The Heart of Medicine, 984), compiled in the mid-Heian period by Tanba no Yasuyori (912–995). This was in turn partially based on *Zhubing yuanhou lun* (Treatise on the Origin of Various Illnesses) by the Sui-dynasty writer Chao Yuanfang, which naturally included numerous aspects of Daoist medical practice.

Speaking very simply, the basics of Daoist medicine comprise six practices: *bigu*, abstinence from eating cereals and other cooked foods; *fuer*, the use of medicinal minerals and herbs to control the body; *liandan*, methods of formulating and preparing mineral and herbal prescriptions; *diaoxi* and *daoyin*, methods of breath control and massage centering on deep abdominal breathing; and *fangzhong*, certain sexual techniques aimed at restraining ejaculation during intercourse. Daoism was not puritanical about sex; it was quite tolerant.

All of these practices, in the final analysis, were techniques for achieving longevity or immortality. Imported into Japan, they became the foundation upon which were nurtured a variety of Japanese ideas about longevity and immortality. About a fifth of the texts in the Noh repertory are infused with a Daoist sensibility, and there is a distinctly Daoist coloring to such Japanese customs as moon-viewing. In a sense, Daoism is a hidden dimension of Japanese culture. As the folklorist Yoshino Hiroko has pointed out, it is striking that flags emblazoned with the characters 太一 (J. *taiitsu*, the *taiyi* mentioned earlier) are flown at Ise Grand Shrine, the most sacred site of the Shinto tradition.

Seen in this light, the idea of warding off plague spirits and other evil spirits at points where roads entered towns or villages was also probably influenced by Daoist notions of how to treat the spirit world.

In China, there were thought to be three types of immortals (*xianren*): heavenly immortals, earthly immortals, and "corpse-liberated immortals" revived from the dead. These last were greatly feared and probably inspired various aspects of the Japanese concept of demons.

To summarize what we have covered so far, we could say that roads and paths are the bearers of a diverse variety of information. Roads transport the materials of everyday life, such as salt; they allow the circulation of good and evil spirits, well-being and disease; and they serve as a pipeline for news and rumor—and thus they may be described as forming an "information highway."

The science of paths of light

In Daoism, the Way is the ultimate principle of the universe, but this was not envisioned as an actual road or path. The Way was a cosmic concept.

But there are real pathways that exist in the physical universe. Not the orbits of the planets or satellites sent to circle Earth but even more complex, fully geometric pathways. These are pathways of what is called space-time geometry, so-called paths of light. So let's explore the world of science for a time.

The science of geometry had its origins in geodesy, a field of study and technical skill aimed at measuring and surveying Earth. Greco-European geometry from Pythagoras and Euclid onward was basically premised upon geodesy.

For 1,500 years or so, Euclid's fifth postulate, which indicates that parallel lines will never cross, was believed to be absolute fact. And indeed, within the realm of real-world surveying and measurement, there was no reason to dispute it. However, if we think of these lines as *streams of light*, then in fact while running in parallel they can actually cross or diverge.

The paths followed by light can be described as following two major patterns. The first runs along the convex surface of a sphere; the second, along a concave surface like that of a horse's saddle. The concave space is called a Riemann space; the convex space is known as a Lobachevsky space, for the mathematician who discovered this form of geometry, Nikolai Lobachevsky. In 1826, at a presentation at Kazan University in Russia, he declared the birth of non-Euclidean geometry.

Euclidean geometry is applicable only to a flat world. And in that world, parallel lines will never meet. But in a different world, it is possible for them to cross one another. Lobachevsky thought the latter was the universal reality, and that the world in which parallel lines can never converge was merely a provisional one. This line of thought was further developed by Carl Friedrich Gauss. Gauss was a thoroughly courageous individual whose motto was *Pauca sed matura* (Few, but ripe).

Meanwhile, Georg Bernhard Riemann, in a lecture at Göttingen University in 1853 entitled "On the Hypotheses That Underlie Geometry," proposed the possibility of a world in which parallel lines converge. Thus, non-Euclidean geometry postulates that crossing and converging parallel lines are characteristic of space-time throughout the universe. With these developments, the concept of the absolute nature of space so firmly held from Newton onward suddenly collapsed. This prepared the way for Fermat's principle: that a ray of light will follow the path between two points that can be traversed in the least time. And this, in turn, would serve as a premise for Einstein's Theory of Relativity.

Imagine a bedsheet upon which a number of balls are randomly arrayed. The weight of each ball makes a depression in the sheet where it rests, wrinkling the material around it. If you roll the ball, the depression and wrinkles follow it. This was Einstein's explanatory image of the universe.

The balls are stars, the sheet is space (and the gravitational field). Light travels outward from the stars, not in a straight line, but following the curvature and wrinkles in the sheet produced by the force of gravity.

Now let's place a lead ball on the sheet. It will probably be so heavy that it will sink out of sight, swallowed into the sheet. This now becomes the center of a gravitational field. The wrinkles in the sheet are the deepest around this point, which can be described as a singularity in the sheet representing space.

In contemporary cosmology there is a concept called the Schwartzschild radius, derived from an exact solution to Einstein's equations for the gravitational field. It is the radius that defines a black hole: if the mass of a star collapses to within this radius, its gravitational field will become incredibly strong—strong enough to prevent the light emitted from it from escaping. So even the paths of light have critical values.

The paths of light are the tracks it follows to travel the shortest time between two points. Electricity, like light, is a form of electromagnetic radiation and thus behaves similarly. The easiest way to understand this is to look at the phenomenon of electrical discharge. Lightning is an electrical discharge seeking the paths of least resistance through the atmosphere, producing the zigzag pattern memorably depicted in the famous lightning strike scene from the illustrated handscroll *Kitano Tenjin engi emaki* (Illustrated Legends of the Kitano Tenjin Shrine, 1219).

The pattern formed by shards of broken glass also follows this principle of energy or force seeking to follow the fastest path. Terada Torahiko,

The lightning strike scene from the fifth scroll of *Kitano Tenjin engi emaki* (Illustrated Legends of the Kitano Tenjin Shrine), 1219. Photo courtesy of Kitano Tenmangū shrine.

an early twentieth-century physicist, hypothesized that the patterns on the coats of giraffes and cats follow a similar principle. In his book *Kirin no madara* (The Dapples of the Giraffe, 1975), his protégé Hirata Morizō argues that the zebra's stripes and the dapples of the giraffe are formed when the skin cracks along the paths of least resistance in response to pressure as the fetus develops inside the womb.

All around us run many pathways formed by natural phenomena. And we can say that all of them are attempting to follow the fastest route. The patterns of divergence followed by the branches and roots of trees, by rivers and streams, by electrical discharges, by the stripes of the zebra, by the nervous and circulatory systems of our bodies, and by the roadways and railways of our cities all follow similar network patterns.

The key point here is that all of these networks have formed and expanded as the most efficient paths for disseminating information. Energy cannot stand still. It always seeks to disperse, to leak, to discharge. And this takes the form of lightning, electrical discharges, the branches and roots of trees. To sum up, this means that all roads are networked.

Life and information

The human nervous system is also a divergent network.

The nervous system has created innumerable pathways along which it sends and receives signals from our sense organs. These pathways are of two main types: afferent and efferent. Afferent paths conduct information inward to the spinal cord, brain, and other elements of the central nervous system; efferent paths conduct information outward from the central nervous system to all of the body's constituent organs and peripheral systems.

The signals traveling along these pathways in our body take the form of an electrical pulse (0 or 1) that serves as a digital data carrier. But this pulse does not remain unchanged for long; when it reaches a nerve ending it is translated into chemical data. There is a minute gap between connected neurons, the synapse, where chemical compounds called neurotransmitters exchange and process information. So the nervous system constitutes a supremely capable electrochemical biocomputer; but the question is, how did it manage to get wired up? I think this is where things really start to get interesting.

To put it simply, it is remarkable that the wiring of this sensitive biocomputer is dangerously submerged in water—for our bodies are mostly water, as in most living things.

If you try to run wiring through a fluid, the first problem encountered is discharges or leaks. When there is a discharge, the electrical energy will disperse following a pattern of least resistance. And the network pattern of the nervous system takes the sort of fracture pattern that we would expect for electrical dispersion. In other words, our nervous system was created so as to follow the dispersion of electrical energy throughout our bodies.

This is an example of positive feedback, which entails the amplification of changes to a system. Positive feedback is rare in biology, as most internal biological functions are products of negative feedback—in other words, the inhibition or reduction of a response in order to maintain balance or homeostasis. But the information pathways of the nervous system are new circuits wired by positively feeding back responses to electrical dispersion, even at the expense of existing cells.

Why have I introduced this discussion into a chapter entitled "Paths"? First of all, because our nervous system is an excellent example of a type of pathway—but more important, because in order to properly address issues related to the sense and sensibility of nature, I believe we need to know more about the internal "thresholds" structuring the flow of information within our bodies.

The phenomenology of nature is another form of information. When we look at flowers, birds, or the moon, and when we express their images in poetry or pictures, we are interfacing with the flow of information conveyed by these natural phenomena. And if this is the case, then this information is being discharged to us and forming pathways through our culture.

I am somewhat disappointed that previous discourse on the phenomenology of nature in Japanese culture has not included this perspective regarding information. What exactly do I mean by information? Let's bring science into this once again, and I will explain.

Life on Earth began with a "seed" of information cast here from the depths of the cosmos when our planet was still a primordial soup. This seed was something like a program for the expression of information. I call it a metaprogram or archeprogram—in other words, a matrix for other programs. This matrix imprinted patterns of information into the malleable clay of our planet.

Eventually these patterns of information formed macromolecular states in order to maintain and preserve themselves. These were informational life forms—in other words, the prototypes of biological data. This was still essentially raw code. But at some point, through some process, these data macromolecules generated RNA and DNA, and the program discovered the mechanism of self-replication. This marked the appearance of what might be called the central tenet of genetic information. Next, these data molecules formed a biological membrane to enclose themselves: the cell membrane or plasma membrane, the original capsule for life itself. Primordial life was born.

These primitive life forms embedded with genetic information began their activities in the nutrient-rich waters of the oceans, where they began to produce oxygen. Surprisingly, prior to this time oxygen did not exist on our planet. Oxygen bubbled up out of the seas and began to collect in the atmosphere, and this oxygenated atmosphere provided the conditions for new forms of life to develop. These were really the first living organisms, some form of seaweed or aquatic plant.

With this began the process of biological evolution familiar to us from textbooks. Aquatic life forms developed, and eventually some of these sea creatures emerged from the waters to populate the land as well.

We should note here that the protagonist in this great story of evolution is information. Or, more specifically, the genes serving as the bearers of genetic information—which, in order to extend their own lives, replicated that information—making new versions of the biological capsule enclosing it, and thus contributing to the history of evolutionary biology. Richard Dawkins has described this process in his book *The Selfish Gene* (1976), which argues that genes use organisms to advance their own survival.

The next step in the evolutionary process was the creation of information pathways—routes for smooth and efficient data transfer—within the bodies of living organisms. In other words, the development of nervous systems. We find prototypes for our central nervous system beginning to develop in complexity from squids and cephalochordates onward.

Why were such information pathways necessary? Because genetic information alone was insufficient for adaptation to the environment. Genetic information is a blueprint for the creation of internal systems. But once an organism has been made according to this blueprint, it still faces the continuous violent changes of the natural environment. So there is a need for these internal systems to know what is coming at them from outside. For this purpose, sense organs—eyes, feelers, and so forth—are necessary. A mechanism is necessary to integrate the information coming from these various sensors, and a center that can decode these information inputs and issue new directives in response.

Thus, a complex network—a brain and central nervous system—gradually developed, not to process internal genetic information, but to deal with the information coming from the external environment.

When this process of animal evolution advanced to the point that the hominid apes were on the verge of becoming human, a major transformation occurred: one of them, for whatever reason, stood erect and began walking on two feet. This was an unprecedented development.

The birth of humankind

As we know, the early humans who began walking erect thereby freed their hands for making and wielding simple tools. Eyes, previously located on either side of the head, moved to the front, enabling parallax vision and, with it, depth perception and free focusing between closeup and distance vision.

These were epochal developments in evolutionary history, rivaling the appearance of the family Orchidaceae in the plant world (some of whose members broke the bilateral symmetry characteristic of plant life up to that time); the development of exoskeletons in the insect world (by externalizing their skeletons insects chose a path of miniaturization and diversity); and the arrival of the dinosaurs (for whom a design misfire resulted in prodigious oversizing). But there were some difficulties attendant upon this leap forward.

One was that the erect stance of early humans narrowed the opening of the uterus, making childbirth considerably more arduous. Despite longer gestation periods, at birth babies were still quite immature, necessitating a lengthy period of childrearing—the longest among all mammals. Humans also lost body fur, estrus, and the ability to run fast and leap great distances.

But humans also gained more than enough to compensate for these deficiencies. The narrowing of the uterine opening meant that human heads were small at birth but continued to grow through childhood such that on the whole they became larger—and the brain expanded considerably. The combination of this enlarged brain, freed hands, and parallax vision allowed humans to become human.

That the free use of hands enabled toolmaking probably requires no explanation, but what is less known is how it also led to the flexing and bending of the fingers and awareness of their articulation, and how, coupled with the differentiation of the central nervous system, this encouraged the discovery of the concept of numbers.

The parallax vision afforded by eyes placed at the front of the head enabled depth perception, which in turn nurtured a sense of focus on subtly shifting relationships of position, like the advent of autofocus on cameras: here, there, over there—where? right here! This instilled in human beings an innate visual curiosity. Many animals pay little or no attention to anything that does not involve their immediate survival. At zoos, people often try to get the attention of the animals, waving and calling to them, sometimes even clowning around in front of them, but the animals usually make little response. In comparison, human infants and children are extremely alert to what they see going on around them. Humans are eagerly visual animals.

As to the enlargement of the brain, there is as yet no full account of how exactly its effects unfolded. The brain is an organ of memory, of decoding, of command and control, but we don't really know in what manner these faculties contributed to the palette of human ability. What we do know is that the most significant development of all was the "discovery" of the capacity for language.

The reasons for the development of language remain unclear, but it seems that it may have arisen in response to a decline in capacity of other physical means of communication—and, perhaps, obstacles to sexual communication between males and females.

The erect stance characteristic of human beings was revolutionary in a number of ways, but one effect was to push the male sex organs to the front, while concealing those of the female. I suspect this may have been a recipe for trouble. In addition, all other mammals have specific periods when the female can conceive and will accept and mate with the male, but this clearly defined period of estrus is absent in humans. Males are more or less always ready to go; but how the female will respond is unpredictable. The sort of indiscriminate mounting behavior common to a number of other mammals is unacceptable; if the female is not ready, the male's advances might be sharply rebuffed.

So what's a fellow to do? Say something. "Hey there," or hopefully something more appealing. And this was probably one of the factors encouraging the development of speech.

Another factor in the development of language was the lengthy period of child-rearing necessary to bring a human being to maturity, which gave special importance to communication between parent and child. Just as the hiragana syllabary in Japanese first developed largely as a female form of communication, it seems likely that the archetype for spoken language among many human groups was created by women, and specifically mothers in the midst of raising their children.

One of the most significant aspects of the human brain is the fact that it developed comparatively slowly during the history of early humankind. In other words, our brains took more than ten thousand years to evolve into what they are today—in tandem with the gradual development of human civilization. This means that early humans went through a period in which they imagined and experimented with a variety of things using brains that were still not fully developed—an insight that has led to a number of interesting theories and hypotheses.

The American psychologist Julian Jaynes (1920–97), author of *The Origins of Consciousness in the Breakdown of the Bicameral Mind* (1976), argued that in ancient humans the two hemispheres of the brain were still not fully integrated. The brain of modern humans comprises two hemispheres, left and right, which are each responsible for a different set of functions (though there are identical or shared functions as well). If the connective bridges between the two are imperfect, problems arise. Patients with damage to one or the other hemisphere exhibit a variety of abnormal symptoms.

In ancient humans it appears that communication between the left and right hemispheres was not yet optimized, and they had to imagine a controller presiding over the two—and this, according to Jaynes, is how the concept of gods came into being.

This is the most powerful theory yet advanced for how the conditions and demands of our internal systems might have given rise to our sense of the divine. Never before had anyone proposed that god (or gods) was born out of an effort to connect the left and right sides of the human brain.

Another fascinating theory about the human brain—the idea that it is not a unity, but a trinity—has been articulated by the neuroscientist Paul D. MacLean in *The Triune Brain in Evolution* (1990). This perspective arose out of the developmental history of the brain. Examining the structure of the human brain, MacLean posited that it consisted of three distinct parts, which he called the reptilian brain, the paleomammalian brain, and the neomammalian brain, in order of evolutionary development. In other words, we made the jump from hominids to *Homo sapiens* while still preserving remnants of the brains of earlier animals in our heads.

The reptilian brain, also known as the R-complex, corresponds to that of crocodiles, lizards, and other reptiles. It is hierarchical and somewhat brutal. The paleomammalian brain, comprising the limbic system in humans, is similar to the brains of other mammals such as rats or horses. It is emotional, altruistic, and rather sly. And finally, the newest element, the neomammalian complex, essentially the cerebral neocortex, overlies these earlier structures. What this means is that our everyday activities are largely motivated by the reptilian and paleomammalian brains, which the "rational" neocortex tries to control and administer in some sort of reasonable manner.

One scientist described this triune brain in chronological developmental order as the ritual brain, the emotional brain, and the rational brain. While this classification may be a little too neat, there is something to it.

In any case, all three are active at the same time. When we are thinking, watching flowers and birds, or experiencing the wind and moon, all three of these brains are operating simultaneously. And when we encounter something the neural and semantic networks in these brains cannot interpret, we humans imagine gods and demons and evil spirits.

The pathways of the brain—this is what led our ancestors to conceive of the divine.

CHAPTER 3 DEITIES

Accompanied by sound

Deities are invisible. If they are seen, it is only in visions. They can be likened to light and shadow, signals and information. In this book, when speaking of the worlds of the deities and buddhas, I will generally treat them as manifestations of information.

In Japan the manifestation or advent of a deity is called *otozure*, a word rooted in the words for "sound" (*oto*) and "to accompany" (*tsureru*). It is not so much that they make noise as that their appearance is an ineffable event describable only as a kind of sound. There is evidence that in ancient times, this *otozure* was something for which people actively listened. A large bell known as a *sanagi* would be hung from a sacred tree, such as the *sakaki*, and people would stand calmly and quietly before it, patiently awaiting the sound of the wind to indicate the presence of a strong spirit.

In the beginning the *sanagi* had no clapper. So when the wind blew, the sound it would make was not like that of a wind chime; rather, it was the subtle sound of the breeze blowing into it. Listening intently, people concentrated their attention and experienced a heightened state of consciousness. This was called *tamafuri* ("a trembling of the spirit"). And it was not only the sound of the wind that was sensed; intermingled with it was information from the unknown.

Beginning in the Jōmon period, attempts were made to channel these visitations. The percussionist Tsuchitori Toshiyuki hypothesizes that some pieces of Jōmon earthenware were used as musical instruments in rituals to summon the deities. With the cooperation of the Jōmon archaeologist Kobayashi Tatsuo, he has actually played replicas of these pieces of earthenware to see what they sounded like; such efforts will likely shed more light on this subject.

From this point forward, I will refer to Japanese deities in general using the Japanese word for them, *kami*, and using the word "god" or "gods" for the more common or universal concept of divine beings.

I consider these Japanese *kami* as a kind of subtle movement of our senses, a tremor of intuition. In the canonical literature, the advent of a *kami* is frequently described with the word *yōgō* 影向, written with kanji that mean "image" or "reflection" and "to approach." "Approaching reflection"—truly an apt turn of phrase, one that conveys the image of a barely perceptible and unexpected visitation that we are uncertain of having actually sensed or not. The word *yōgō* was also used for *kami*, and for the manifestation of other supernatural beings such as buddhas and immortals. In all these cases, it refers to forms not clearly perceived—a momentary disturbance of light and shadow.

Various sources testify to the interest in how the *kami* manifest themselves. When *kami* appeared more substantively to the observer, they might be described with words like *gongen* (avatar). The expression *yōgō* came to be used for any sudden and extraordinary appearance—the very image of the advent (*otozure*) of the supernatural.

Such vocabulary enjoyed great popularity in the Kabuki dramas of the Edo period. For instance, a line in act 7 of *Reigen Soga no magaki* playfully compares the arrival of a courtesan to a *yōgō*. In Shinto art, depictions of the appearance of godlike beings are known as *yōgōzu* (*zu* meaning "picture").

To perceive the presence of these more subtle *kami* that appeared only as a tremor of intuition, some sort of special apparatus was necessary—a kind of "visitation device"—and the classic form this took was the *yorishiro* mentioned in chapter 1.

Yorishiro can take many forms. The *sakaki* (*Cleyera japonica*) is the prime example of a tree traditionally serving as such a temporary abode of *kami*. Various kanji have been used to write *sakaki*, including 榊 (*kami* with the tree radical), 境木 ("boundary tree"), and 栄木 ("flourishing tree"). It can be considered a world tree, as discussed in chapter 1. In Shinto it is known as the *tokiwagi* (evergreen tree) and regarded as a source of immutable information. It was believed that evergreens could serve as conduits for powerful energies emanating from the Other Shore.

The *sakaki* was not the only tree that served as a *yorishiro*. Depending on what grew in a particular region, many trees could play this role: *hinoki* (a variety of cypress), *kashi* (an evergreen oak), *tabu no ki* (*Machilus thunbergii*, a giant bay), *nagi* (*Nageia nagi*, Asian bayberry), *tsubaki* (camellia), *kuromoji* (*Lindera umbellata*, spice bush), *shikimi* (*Illicium anisatum*, Japanese star anise), *yanagi* (willow), *sugi* (cryptomeria), *matsu* (pine), and so on. For example, in the Dewa Sanzan, a group of three sacred mountains in northern Japan, the camellia is regarded as the most spiritually potent of all the *yorishiro*.

Later, some of these sacred trees (*shinboku*) were used as pillars in Shinto shrines. Called *mahashira* 真柱 ("true pillars") or *shinbashira* 心柱 ("heart pillars") they were regarded as deities in their own right, or representations of the divine. As the historian Hayashiya Tatsusaburō once remarked, Japanese antiquity was "an age of pillars."

Sacred trees needed to be marked in some way to indicate their special status. The ancient Japanese chose to do this with bundles of rice straw, redolent of the harvest, which eventually became the sacred straw or hemp ropes (*shimenawa*) we know today. The *shimenawa* might be supplemented with *gohei*—zigzag paper streamers—for additional power and efficacy. *Kami* were conceived of as powerful "information from the unknown" that required a variety of such devices to receive and contain them.

Gohei are an indispensable element of Shinto ritual, which anyone who has visited a shrine has seen, but their origins and function are quite complex. They also have a number of different names, all of which refer in some sense to the zigzag, fluttering paper. Generically, they are called *heihaku* (literally, "offering cloth"); other names are *nusa*, *mitegura*, *yufu*, and *shide*. Today, all of these are made with cut and folded paper, but originally a textile called *yufu*, woven from the bark fibers of the *kaji*, or paper mulberry, was used. The zigzag cut and folded paper of today's *gohei* was intended to mimic the way that *yufu* cloth draped. The name of the spa town of Yufuin in Kyushu refers to this cloth.

I also suspect that the zigzag cut of the paper is related to lightning (*kaminari*). Now written with the kanji 雷, *kaminari* used to be written 神鳴 り or 神なり (meaning the sound or voice of the *kami*); the element 申 on the right side of the kanji for *kami* expresses the shape of lightning.

The word *nusa* is known to many Japanese from a famous poem by Sugawara no Michizane (845–903) in the *Hyakunin isshu* (One Hundred Poets, One Poem Each) and the traditional card game based on this anthology:

kono tabi wa	On this journey
nusa mo toriaezu	I have no silk streamers to offer up.
Tamukeyama	Gods, if it pleases you,
momiji no nishiki	may you take instead this brocade
kami no mani-mani	of Mount Tamuke's autumn colours.[1]

The associations underlying this poem are richly layered. First of all, in that era travelers carried with them a small bag filled with *nusa*—finely cut strips of silk, linen, or paper—to scatter before the images of the roadside deities they encountered at entrances to villages and mountain passes in the course of their journey, a practice known as *tamuke* (the origin of the word *tōge* for a high mountain pass). Underlying it as well was the custom of "road-blocking" (*michikiri*), or placing straw ropes and other markers at important boundaries to thwart plague spirits. Such associations must be considered in understanding the contextual background of Michizane's poem, whose basic premise is that his quick departure on his travels means that he has not prepared *nusa* to take with him; instead, he imagines the brilliant fall leaves on the mountainsides as silk brocade, and wonders how the gods might respond to this offering. In the poem, *tabi* functions as a favorite device of Japanese poetry: a *kakekotoba*, or pivot word, that conveys two meanings simultaneously. Here, it means both "at this time" and "on this journey."

Gohei would also be attached to branches of the *sakaki* tree and offered to the gods; this is the *tamagushi* 玉串 used to this day in purification and other rituals at Shinto shrines. The *kushi* of *tamagushi* means "skewer" and can refer generically to any pointed object. It is related to *kushi* 櫛, meaning a hair comb (whose teeth are also pointed); such objects are antennas for channeling spiritual power (like the needles mentioned in the previous chapter). In ancient times, simply wearing a comb in the hair was regarded as sufficient to tune in to the power of the spirits. Gradually, however, the *tamagushi* that originally served as offerings to the gods evolved into the talismans, charms, and protective amulets (*ofuda*, *omamori*) available at shrines. The *ofuda* received during a New Year's shrine visit or other occasions are examples of this. *Gohei* have taken many forms over the course of their long history.

Yorishiro and *monozane*

Where no large trees presented themselves as natural abodes of the divine, people would plant four small trees and connect them with *shimenawa* to form a square enclosure called a *himorogi* to invite the visitation of the *kami*. The *himorogi* would be possessed by the *kami*, becoming the deity's temporary abode and a manifestation of its miraculous power. It was a device for summoning the presence of the divine.

Not only trees but crags or rock outcroppings, called *iwasaka*, might also serve as *yorishiro*. As at Mount Miwa in Nara, the summit and a number of large rock formations along the path to it would be demarcated as sacred space with *shimenawa*. The *iwasaka* may be regarded as evidence of an ancient Japanese veneration of large stones and boulders in their own right, at the same time suggesting the transmission to Japan of belief in Mount Sumeru, which we discussed in chapter 1, "Mountains." Models of the sacred mountain called *Shumisen-seki* were created for temple gardens and gardens for the aristocracy.

Other examples of stone *yorishiro* were the rocks representing protective deities such as the *sae no kami* and *dōsojin* mentioned in chapter 2; deities of good fortune, such as Ebisu; Daoist fertility deities; and "stone deities" with names such as Mishakuji, Saguji, and so on. The place name Shaku-jii 石神井 (literally, "well of the stone deity") in Tokyo derives from these beliefs.

Eventually, these places where there were *yorishiro*—temporary abodes of the *kami*—became more permanent shrines, or *yashiro*. This word was originally written *yashiro* 屋代, which suggests that their prototype was nothing more than a *himorogi* enclosure with a simple roof (*ya*). Gradually, the roof would become more elaborate; the enclosure would become pillars of *hinoki* (cypress) raising the structure above the ground; stairs and doors would be added; enclosing fences called *mizugaki* or *tamagaki* would grow more numerous; and the architecture of Shinto shrines as we now know it slowly took shape.

Shrine styles followed two different models. The model for the Ise Grand Shrine is a Yayoi-period granary; that of Izumo Shrine, the residence of a powerful clan of that region. This echoes how in Ise deities are worshipped in a space separated from that occupied by ordinary humans, while in Izumo the two coexist in a shared space.

In certain cases, a shrine might be built on a mountain and eventually the entire mountain would come to be regarded as a sacred space (*kannabi* or *mimuro*). The opposite was of course possible: the mountain itself might already be regarded as a *kannabi*, and a shrine would be built in acknowledgment of this. In chapter 1, "Mountains," I have already mentioned the practice of building *yamamiya* (mountain shrines) on the higher slopes and *satomiya* (village shrines) in the foothills; in Japan this sort of system for differentiating among deities is fairly common. The most famous example of this, Munakata Taisha in Kyushu, is made up of three separate shrines: Okitsugū, dedicated to Tagorihime, on the remote island of Okinoshima; Nakatsugū, dedicated to Tagitsuhime, on the island of Ōshima nearer the coast; and Hetsugū, dedicated to Ichikishimahime, in the city of Munakata on Kyushu. These shrines comprise a trinity: though separate, they are one.

As we have seen there are many different *yorishiro* that can serve as temporary abodes for *kami*. *Yorishiro* that are objects (as opposed to larger entities like trees or mountains) are often called *katashiro* or *monozane*.

Katashiro are substitutes for or representations of a deity: a prime example would be a figurine, doll, or statue. *Katashiro* sometimes function as stand-ins for ancestral spirits during memorial rites, and in that sense the earthenware figurines (*dogū* and *haniwa*) of prehistoric Japan may be considered a type of *katashiro*. In some Shinto purification rituals (*misogi*), a *katashiro* is rubbed over a person's body to transfer their energies onto it before it is set afloat on a river or other body of water. This is the origin of the *hina nagashi* ("doll floating") festivals in various parts of the country. The word *hina* for "doll" originally signified a *katashiro*.

Oddly enough (though this is quintessentially Japanese), a *katashiro* could also represent an absent lover. A poem in the "Azumaya" chapter of *The Tale of Genji* presents an instance of this meaning, an almost fetishistic image of the poet stroking the *katashiro* of a lover that he carries with him:

> If she is a paper doll
> of the one I knew,
> I shall keep her on me,
> Stroking her whenever
> I long for my lost lady.[2]

Monozane initially meant the origin or material substance of a thing but came to also refer specifically to something that *kami* were likely to bond with or inhabit. This bonding was known as *yorimashi* 寄座, which also became the word for the dolls or child mediums used by *miko* (shrine maidens, who functioned as shamanic priestesses) or practitioners of the Shugendō sect to serve as the temporary abode of *kami* they were attempting to summon in their rituals. Once this inhabitation had taken place, the possessed bodies were called *yorigara*. In practice, however, *monozane* and *yorigara* were most frequently used to summon and capture not so much deities as strange and malevolent spirits such as *mononoke*. In book 3 of *The Tale of the Heike*, for example, we find the following passage:

> Alert to her weakness, stubborn spirits [*mononoke*]
> seized upon this chance to invade her.
> Once Fudō's rope had bound the medium [*yorimashi*],
> these spirits then revealed themselves.[3]

In the *Kokon chomonjū* (Collection of Things Heard, Present and Past, 1254) there is a reference to Shugendō practitioners employing *yorimashi* in their rituals.

When written 憑人 instead of 寄座, *yorimashi* can signify women, girls, or young boys serving as shamanic mediums. Often selected for their beauty, and dressed in spotless white robes, they would be purified with a wave of the priest's streamer-tipped wand and would, in a trance state, deliver messages from the *kami* in mysterious speech and gestures. To this day, the young boy (*chigo*) who is selected each year to ride on the Naginata-hoko "halberd" float in Kyoto's Gion Festival undergoes a comparable ritual of spiritual possession prior to the procession.

In addition to being used in Shinto shrines, *yorishiro* and its variations such as *monozane*, *katashiro*, and *yorigara* are also active parts of everyday life in Japan. We see them in New Year's decorations and customs: sacred *shi-*

New Year's decorations: left, arrangements of pine and bamboo; right, a decorative rake (symbolic of raking in good fortune for the coming year) with lucky icons, from the double sea bream to the gold coins and the figurines. Photos © JAPACK/a.collectionRF/amanaimages and © imagewerksRF/amanaimages.

menawa ropes, arrangements of pine and bamboo at doorways, ceremonially displayed stacks of rice cakes, gift envelopes, bamboo rakes and treasure boats symbolizing good fortune—and also the various effigies and structures created for the *dondoyaki* ceremonies in which the decorations are burned.

And that is not all. The *mochibana* and *mayudama* New Year's arrangements of rice cakes and rice-flour dumplings beloved by children; the chopsticks, mirrors, hairpins, and combs treasured by generations of Japanese women; the knotted paper cords, decorations, and wooden platform trays used for gift-giving on special occasions; the rice bales, straw raincoats, scarecrows, bamboo ladles, and *tenugui* hand towels familiar to farmers—all of these things have functions as *yorishiro* or *monozane*. The circular lids on rice bales, called *sandarabōshi* or *sandarabotchi*, were used as offerings to the roadside gods (*dōsojin*); straw raincoats could become cloaks of invisibility (*kakuremino*) for the *kami*; scarecrows were originally images of Kuebiko (Yamada no Sohodo), a deity of knowledge and intelligence. The folklorist Yanagita Kunio, in the journal article "Tenugui enkaku" (History of the *Tenugui*, 1943), explains that the origins of this hand towel are in a strip of cloth called a *tana* used in Shinto rituals.

Many of the "mechanisms" upon which the phenomenology of nature in Japanese culture is premised are supported by these *yorishiro* and *monozane*. In fact, one of the hallmarks of Japanese culture is the omnipresence of *yorishiro*.

In Japan we often speak of "the myriad *kami*" (*yaoyorozu no kami*), but a multiplicity of deities is not in itself peculiar to Japan; Greek mythology also features a large pantheon. It is not so much that Japanese deities have numerous names and personalities as that everyday life in Japan is filled with objects in which the intimation of the divine might reside and be detected. I like to call such objects "mindgear": devices to which emotions may be entrusted.

Moreover, as I will explain in greater detail as we go along, the phenomenology of nature may be thought of as the gradual refinement of these *yorishiro* and *monozane* through the aesthetic consciousness.

As I will explain in the chapters "Flowers" and "Moon," the practices of flower arrangement had their origins in the appreciation of flowers as *yorishiro*, while the platform tray upon which dumplings are set out for the moon-viewing festivals in autumn, the dumplings themselves, and the sprigs of pampas grass accompanying them all developed out of earlier ritual objects and are infused with the concept of *yorishiro* and *monozane*. The pines in a Japanese garden and the pine tree painted on the Noh stage backdrop are also *yorishiro*.

The everlasting world of the Other Shore

The Japanese *kami* have no clearly defined physical form. As noted earlier, Shinto shrines were largely a development of *yashiro*, simple roofed enclosures, the majority of which did not originally contain a physical embodiment of the deity (*goshintai*).

The creation of physical forms for enshrined deities would come relatively late; a list of *goshintai* in the ninth-century *Kōtai Jingū gishiki chō* (Register of the Ceremonies of Kōtai Jingū) includes twenty-seven stones, five mirrors, water, and sixteen shrines that had no *goshintai* at all. We should note, however, that even in the absence of a physical embodiment, the people of ancient Japan were quite capable of sensing visitations by the *kami*.

This image of deities or spirits is not unique to Japan. In Southeast Asia visitations by similar ineffable beings, called *phi* in Thailand, are also welcomed. In Europe as well, there is a rich and varied vocabulary of spiritual visitation. Yet the Japanese *kami* possess special characteristics. In recent times the number of Japanese who can speak precisely and yet also subtly of the *kami* has radically decreased, but in earlier times the *kami* made frequent appearances in everyday speech.

The chapter of the *Nihon shoki* chronicling the reign of Empress Kōgyoku includes the following ancient song, which uses the verb *kikoeru*, translated here as "resounding" but literally meaning "audible, able to be heard"— and carrying the same sense of spiritual visitation as *otozure*, or a kind of "sound," as has been discussed.

utsumasa wa	"It's a god, a god!"
kami to mo kami to	so came its fame resounding,
kikoekuru	but Utsumasa
tokoyo no kami o	has struck down and punished it,
uchikitamasu mo	that god of Everworld!⁴

The word *kikoeru* originally carried the connotation of becoming clear, understanding, or being persuaded. A passage in *Tsurezuregusa* (Essays in

Idleness, c. 1330, by Yoshida Kenkō) describes a drunken elderly priest being supported by an acolyte, "staggering along, blathering incomprehensibly," using *kikoenu*, the negative of the verb *kikoeru*, to convey speech that cannot be "heard"—that is to say, understood. *Kikoeru* was also used in the sense of being informed of another's wishes, and when giving the name of a deity or distinguished personage, as in the well-known passage in the "Kiritsubo" chapter of *The Tale of Genji* that says, "all the world had heard of him as the Shining Prince." Kikoe no Ōkimi ("the great queen of whom we have heard") was the title given to the high priestess of Okinawa. Such is the significance of the word used to express the resounding fame of the deity in the poem from the *Nihon shoki*. But no less important is Tokoyo 常世 (the everlasting, timeless, eternal world or land), which also appears in this ancient poem.

The Eternal Land was given serious attention by the folklorists Yanagita Kunio and Orikuchi Shinobu as a reference to the original home of the Japanese people far beyond the sea. In *Kaijō no michi* (The Seaborne Road, 1961), Yanagita's meditations on this land beyond the sea are sparked by finding a coconut washed ashore on a beach in Aichi prefecture, while Orikuchi opens his *Kodai kenkyū* (The Study of Ancient Times, 3 vols., 1929–30) by remarking on this land as "the country of our foremothers." The ethnologist Tanigawa Ken'ichi devoted an entire monograph to this subject, *Tokoyo ron* (On the Eternal Land, 1983), arguing that "The Eternal Land is the foundation of the deepest layers of the Japanese consciousness." Tokoyo also appears in the *Man'yōshū*, in the following poem:

wagimoko wa	My own darling girl
tokoyo no kuni ni	must have been living somewhere
sumikerashi	in the Timeless Land:
mukashi mishi yori	she has grown even younger
ochimashinikeri	than when I saw her last.[5]

Here, the word appears to be emblematic of another world, remote from our own, like the deep-sea palace of the Dragon King visited by Urashima Tarō in the famous folk tale.

Mythic figures such as Sukunahikona, Mikenu no Mikoto, Tajimamori, and Inahi no Mikoto were said to have visited the Eternal Land. Tajimamori, whom we might call the Columbus of Japanese antiquity, was Japan's first ocean voyager. Dispatched by Emperor Suinin to seek the "fruit of timeless fragrance," he returned from the Eternal Land across the sea after a voyage of ten years with fruit-bearing branches, only to find that the emperor had died the year before and to follow him in death.

The "fruit of timeless fragrance" Tajimamori brought back with him was probably a variety of mandarin orange. According to one theory, the land he reached was actually Jeju Island in the Korea Strait. Tokoyo, the Eternal Land, is a vision of a utopia beyond the sea long cherished by the Japanese people. It was also called Ne no Kuni (Land of Roots).

As Buddhism spread in Japan, the image of Tokoyo blended with that of the Pure Land, with the flexibility characteristic of Japanese thought. Mount Potalaka (J. Fudaraku), the Pure Land of the bodhisattva Avalokiteśvara (J. Kannon), is regarded as one of the models for Tokoyo—a Pure Land said to be located in the sea south of India, as opposed to the Pure Land of Amida, associated with the mountains.

The Kumano region of the southern Kii Peninsula was a center of belief in the Pure Land of Fudaraku. Believers would row out from the shore at Nachi, seeking this utopia across the sea—a futile and desperate practice of faith that even the Shugendō specialist Gorai Shigeru speculates was a deliberate act of self-immolation. These "voyages to Fudaraku," as they were known, were possibly an evolution of the more general practice of seeking rebirth in the Pure Land through self-drowning (*jusui ōjō*).

At the same time, Nishida Nagao, a leading historian of Shinto, suggests that the "voyage to Fudaraku" concept was not unique to Japan, but can be found throughout maritime Eurasia. For example, Nishida calls attention to the considerable similarities between Kumano and Santiago de Compostela in Spain: Compostela is renowned as the terminus of one of Europe's greatest pilgrimage routes, while Kumano was one of the most sacred sites of pilgrimage in medieval Japan. According to Nishida, the two are linked by the ocean. Both were seen as sacred spaces, pure lands, places of last resort where people suffering from grave illnesses and severe disabilities might seek liberation from their ailments. If this was unsuccessful, then the seacoast at Compostela or Kumano-Nachi offered them the vision of a future beyond the waves, a point of embarkation for a final voyage to the Eternal Land. Some readers may recall Luis Buñuel's film *The Milky Way* (1969), a bold cinematic depiction of a modern pilgrimage from Paris to Santiago de Compostela.

Like Munakata Taisha in Kyushu, the Grand Shrines of Kumano are a trinity, comprising the Hongū (Main Shrine), Shingū (New Shrine), and the Nachi Shrine. Known as the Kumano Sanzan (Three Mountains of Kumano), they flourished from antiquity as sites for the worship of Amida and Kannon, and in medieval times were pilgrimage centers for people of every class in numbers so great that they were compared to swarms of ants making their way over the mountain trails (*ari no Kumano mōde*). This was probably the result of an overlap with the popular cult of Ise Shrine, as well as patronage on the part of the retired emperors who were the de facto rulers of Japan during much of the eleventh and twelfth centuries. While on a pilgrimage to Kumano, Ippen Shōnin (1234–89), founder of the Ji sect of Pure Land Buddhism in Japan, received a visitation from the *kami* there, which led to his belief in the recitation of Amida's name (*nembutsu*) to attain enlightenment.

Meanwhile, countless humbler folk who were truly desperate, especially those suffering from terminal illnesses or from leprosy, also undertook the pilgrimage as supplicants for the miraculous healing powers of Kumano. The story of Oguri Hangan and Princess Terute, later famous as a *sekkyō-bushi* (sermon ballad), revolves around the spiritual authority of the Kumano pilgrimage. In those days, leprosy was known as *gakiyami*. In his illness and distress, Oguri takes the name Gakiami (a portmanteau of "Hungry Ghost" and "Amida") to conceal his identity. In this guise he is aided by Terute and completes the Kumano pilgrimage, after which he is restored to robust health and vigor. This tearjerker of a tale is evidence of the storytelling and compositional acumen of the adherents of Ippen Shōnin's Ji sect.

Like Oguri Hangan, whose disease could be healed only at Kumano, people afflicted by illness and distress constantly sought salvation through the intercession of deities and buddhas. Such divine power may be considered a manifestation of information from the unknown.

And it is not only the people of the past who sought the aid of such power. Every age searches for information from the unknown. Intuition, gut feeling, spiritual possession, telepathy, synchronicity—all of these phenomena have intrigued people throughout history.

So let's set aside this talk of deities for a moment, and take a look at how science has dealt with the topic of information from the unknown.

The riddle of information

Modern science tells us that the universe began with the Big Bang, a colossal explosion that created a dense primal universe of plasma in less than three minutes. At first blush, a rather difficult story to swallow, and I myself have some doubts about it—even some scientists question the Big Bang theory. But as we look over the vast reaches of space-time comprising the history of the universe, we realize that there are a number of strange dramas taking place that might lead us to see in them the origins of our gods and of the information we sense coming to us from the unknown.

In the beginning, the entire universe was suffused with light, but as this light gradually diminished, matter—previously nonexistent—began to form. Soon there was more matter than light. This, in a nutshell, is the history of the cosmos. Looked at in the context of this history, the emergence of life and the birth of the human race occurred in a period in which matter, not light, was proliferating.

Yet in the physical universe there is something that is neither light nor matter, neither energy nor time. And that is information. I think that eventually this will come to be accepted as a scientific truth: information was involved in the birth of the cosmos from the very beginning. Along with light and matter, information should be regarded as one of the three essential forms of nature.

Religious traditions worldwide conceive of divinity as the source of light. It is a globally shared, archetypal image. Solar deities are to be found in every culture. Japan's Amaterasu is a sun goddess, and the story of her concealing herself in the cave of Ama no Iwato can be considered a variant of the solar eclipse myths found throughout Pacific and Polynesian cultures. This is all well and good, but people have sensed the presence of the divine and visitations of the gods at many different hours: not only in broad daylight but also at dusk or in the depths of the night. Often they have felt spiritual power to reside, as we have seen, in great trees, in crevices in rocks, in mountains and waterfalls.

In fact, pursuing this idea a bit further, we might say that when we recognize the presence of the divine we are responding not to day or night or any other visible phenomenon in itself, but rather to the reverence that we feel being excited in our hearts.

If this is true, then we may infer that god is not light, but rather the information that light has conveyed to us. Yahweh (Jehovah) would not reveal his physical form to Moses, speaking to him—conveying information—through a burning bush.

In every corner of the world there are stories involving divine pronouncements. One almost wonders whether any religion has begun without such revelations, or what we might call "meta-information." Since the true nature and source of this meta-information surpasses human understanding, however, I'll settle for referring to it simply as information.

But what is this "information from the unknown" that so many people have seen and heard throughout human history? Does it appear accompanied by a dramatic play of light and wind, as in Dante's *Paradiso*, Myōe Shōnin's *Yume no ki* (Dream Journal), or Hans Christian Andersen's "The Snow Queen"? Or does it appear in a vision like that of Kibi no Makibi or Hildegard von Bingen? Is it accompanied by voices such as those heard by Mohammed, Kūkai, Saint Francis, or Joan of Arc? Of course we cannot equate it solely with any one type of manifestation.

What are these things, these external visions or internal voices that psychiatry would probably dismiss as delusions or auditory and visual hallucinations? If they represent information, then of what sort? The search for divine information resembles the search for the locus of consciousness.

When people have an experience they cannot repeat or account for, they often attribute it to the intervention of some mysterious force. The truth, though, may be that we merely lack the vocabulary or scientific capacity to provide a sufficient explanation. If, then, we switch our perspective and work with that possibility in mind, we may be able to employ the concept of "information" to delve deeper into such mysteries.

Here, I should be offering some explanation of my image of information, but unfortunately that is a supremely difficult undertaking. So for the time being I will simply touch briefly on the concept of information as defined by contemporary information science, before proceeding with this discussion from a different perspective.

At present, the core definition of information comes from information theory, pioneered by Claude Shannon: information is the reciprocal of entropy. Entropy, a concept from thermodynamics, is a measure of the disorder of a system. If you leave a cup of hot tea it will cool. But it won't just keep getting colder; it will stop when it reaches the ambient temperature of the room. This what is known as thermodynamic equilibrium, and entropy is a measure of progress toward this state. In other words, entropy is the movement of the cup of tea and the room toward an undifferentiated thermodynamic state (temperature).

In Shannon's definition, information is by contrast the degree of order and differentiation among elements of a system. In short, information runs in the opposite direction of entropy: toward the creation of order.

Communications theorists identify the bit as the basic unit of information differentiation. For example, if we are given the block of information "North South East West," once North is determined, we know the other three directions, so this would be regarded as one bit. But to differentiate the elements in the block "Spring Summer Autumn Winter," we would have to split it first into "Spring Summer" and "Autumn Winter," and then split each pair again. Since it needs to be divided twice, this is a two-bit message. In other words, information is counted according to units of differentiation. Computers, which conduct calculations using the digital signals 0 and 1, work by constantly breaking information down into single-bit units.

But this definition of information is somewhat like saying that an origami crane is a piece of paper folded *x* number of times; it does not deal at all with the content of information, only with how it is divided, which is not really that interesting. The information I am interested in is semantic information, information with meaning.

In the previous chapter I discussed the information flowing within our bodies: genetic information, immunological information, information entering our brains. Words and images are information; gestures and facial expressions are information. Information flows to us through magazines, newspapers, television.

To reduce all of this to the number of folds in a piece of origami paper seems impossible. And such an approach is certainly useless if we want to consider information from the unknown. In thinking about questions such as how insects and flowers exchange information, what sort of data-processing systems animals have, how to teach robots, or even how our own brains edit information, we are always dealing with information as assemblages of signals or signs possessing *meaning*.

It is just that at this point we cannot fully explain these realities.

The "mindons" hypothesis

The popular expression *mushi no shirase* (literally, "insects' message") describes a sudden premonition, a feeling in one's bones. If, as I have suggested, the *kami* are a form of information from the unknown, then the type of intuition brought to us by these insect messages probably is too.

But the reality of insect messages, intuition, telepathy, or the sixth sense remains a mystery. If such things really exist in the world, then they must involve influxes of information, from time immemorial, along routes separate from those known to science.

Yet it is also true, as noted earlier, that we are altogether too inclined to dismiss experiences we cannot replicate or explain as puzzling oddities. It is time we brought the language of science to the sites of such experience—an effort that could shed light on the birth of consciousness.

Many theologians, religious figures, and philosophers have attempted to determine the origins of consciousness. In a previous book, *Yūgaku* (Intellectual Pursuits), I introduce the intellectual explorations of nearly 150 thinkers, about a fifth of whom addressed this theme, including Pythagoras, Plato, Mahāvira, Vasubandhu, Kūkai, Dōgen, Nicholas of Cusa, Paracelsus, Descartes, Leibnitz, George Berkeley, Swedenborg, Miura Baien, Jean-Baptiste Lamarck, Goethe, Hegel, Satō Nobuhiro, and Schopenhauer.

What is less known is that a number of established scientists also took up this challenge. Although their theories have been largely dismissed, the time has come for us to pay some attention to their adventures.

Such individuals began to emerge in the late nineteenth century, when the vocabulary of science had reached maturity. Évariste Galois, Claude Bernard, Carl Friedrich Gauss, Ernst Haeckel, Ernst Mach—they all make appearances in *Yūgaku*. William Crookes, inventor of the Crookes vacuum tube circa 1869–75, upon discovering a slight bending of the cathode rays in a Crookes tube, attributed the phenomenon to the "fourth state of matter," called "radiant matter," indulging in the rather far-fetched speculation that it might have something to do with the spiritual world.

Albert Einstein was another eminent scientist and inventor who early on developed an interest in spiritual matters, which seemed to deepen as he grew older. In his work on a unified field theory, he attempted to unify gravitation and electromagnetism as different aspects of a single field. If this could be accomplished, his theories of special and general relativity, published in 1905 and 1915 respectively, as well as the subatomic spacetime of quantum physics, might all be conceived as belonging to the same comprehensive informational space. Elsewhere, Einstein wrote that the transcendent space-time he was envisioning might be considered as something akin to mind, perhaps related to the emergence of consciousness.

After Einstein's death, the astronomer V.A. Firsoff hypothesized the existence of elementary particles he called mindons, which, as one might guess from the spelling, were material imbued with mind. Firsoff suggested that an equation equal in simplicity to Einstein's $E = mc^2$ might prove the basis for understanding this mental substance. Spurred on by this, other scientists commenced research into these hypothetical mindons.

H.A.C. (Adrian) Dobbs, a Cambridge mathematician, proposed the existence of particles he called psitrons (a name derived from the Greek word *psyche*, or spirit), as well as a fifth dimension of space-time to accommodate them. In addition to the standard four dimensions—three of space and one of time—Dobbs added a second dimension of time to arrive at his five-dimensional universe. He described the second dimension of time as being something like a wavefront of psitrons.

Dobbs suggested that psitrons continually stimulate the neurons of the brain, which by incorporating them bring them into time. In other words, time as we know it is no more than a field created by the neural network of our brains, what he terms the "time of psychology"; actual physical phenomena come to us from outside and are reflected back along various routes of response, existing in the "time of physics."[6]

Research on neurons by the Nobel Prize–winning Australian scientist Sir John Eccles had influenced Dobbs. As mentioned earlier, adjacent neurons are separated by a slight gap, called the synapse. When the pulse of a stimulus reaches the synapse, neurotransmitters are released from synaptic vesicles in the axon of the neuron, translating the information into chemical form.

Eccles's investigations led him to believe that a particular neuron was responsible for sending the initial pulse. Most neurons, when stimulated, would not convey information to the entire brain, but certain neurons, when properly stimulated, would transmit throughout the entire system. By positing the existence of such "critically poised" neurons, Eccles envisioned pathways by which psitrons did not necessarily act on all of the neurons of the brain but could stimulate only neurons in this particular state.

In this way, a variety of investigations commenced into the internal systems supporting our response to "insects' messages" coming from outside. Initially, these explorations were dominated by approaches like that of Eccles, focusing on the brain, but eventually approaches involving research into the ultimate forms of matter also emerged. Developed mainly by quantum physicists and electrical engineers, this was scientific research into the nature of consciousness, not the divine.

One of the leading contributors to this quest was the quantum physicist David Bohm (1917–92), who wrote that the human mind is conceivable only as a multidimensional fabric woven of waves or fields in which matter and spirit are intertwined. Bohm believed that our consciousness includes an "explicate order" accessible from outside and an "implicate order" that cannot be perceived by external observation. He argued that established scientific methods were inadequate to deal with this implicate order, and he experimented with the creation of a new scientific language, which he called rheomode, to address this issue. The implicate order he envisioned was complexly enfolded, a sort of "negative origami."

To date, there have been few results from the development of Bohm's ideas, but their boldness has been influential, a catalyst for new adventures by many sympathizers, including the cosmologist Freeman Dyson, the physicist Fritjof Capra, the neurophysiologist Karl Pribram, and the physicist Brian Josephson. Josephson won the Nobel Prize for his discoveries of what are now known as the Josephson effect and the Josephson device, but after encountering Bohm he devoted himself to studying the electromagnetics of meditative states.

Developments such as these have led an increasing number of scientists to conduct research into the phenomena underlying inexplicable experiences. But there is another group of scientists who have approached these phenomena from a completely different perspective—by studying them not as we experience them internally, but rather as they exist outside ourselves in order to understand their effects on us.

The Overmind

Arthur C. Clarke's novel *Childhood's End* (1953) regularly places among the top five in lists of the greatest science fiction of all time. The Overmind depicted in this novel is a cosmic intelligence whose representatives, the Overlords, arrive in spaceships that take up position orbiting our planet.

The Overmind is a superior intelligence that has come from the depths of space to help humanity achieve a transcendent state. The paintings of Raphael and Fra Angelico always show heavenly clouds occupied by angels sounding trumpets over the earth below. And as we saw in the "Mountains" chapter, in Japan we have the image of the descent of Amida to earth from the Pure Land. The Overmind is something like these messages of angels and buddhas.

In the novel, Clarke writes that it was in modern times (the twentieth century) that a longing for the Overmind gradually began to emerge. Wim

Wenders's film *Wings of Desire* (1987) is, in a sense, a lyrical cinematic tribute to something like the Overmind.

Pierre Teilhard de Chardin was a paleontologist, archaeologist, priest, and philosopher who argued in *The Phenomenon of Man* (1955) that something he called the noosphere was in the process of developing on our planet. De Chardin proposed that just like the ionosphere, the Van Allen belt, the stratosphere, and other layers in the upper reaches of the atmosphere, waves of human consciousness and spirit were gradually encircling the planet and forming a "planetary noosphere," or "thinking layer."

In the 1980s the English biologist James Lovelock proposed his Gaia hypothesis as an explanation of observed changes in the earth's atmosphere, stating that the interaction of nonliving and living elements of the earth works to form a complex, self-regulating system that can be considered a single organism—hinting at the existence of a new planetary consciousness.

In short, Clarke, Teilhard de Chardin, and Lovelock did not believe that mental substances (such as mindons or psitrons) existed in nature from the very beginning. Instead, they argued that the advent of human beings and human culture, and the history of human love and struggle and everything else that followed, gradually fostered a new and fragile umbrella of mind or cloud of consciousness on our planet. Unlike the earlier physical science approach seeking to understand mysteries from inside our bodies and minds, this was an attempt to get at the "veil of mystery" brought newly into being outside of us by the workings of consciousness. I will touch again on Lovelock's Gaia hypothesis in the next chapter, "Wind."

Here I would like to draw attention to the question of whether or not our consciousness or spirit is actually evolving. If in fact something like the noosphere is forming, then that probably means our minds or consciousness have been pumping out some substance like psitrons or psychons or mindons all this time—but is our consciousness really in the process of attaining a higher spiritual level as a result? If not, then all that mind stuff that we have been emitting, while it may not be quite the same thing as fluorocarbons, could be creating a noosphere that is no better for our well-being or our future. That is indeed a possibility.

Our attitude to this question of whether we are evolving beneficially, yes or no, could lead to completely different scientific implications.

If our answer is yes, then the story becomes one of a universe that started out as a purely physical structure, within which, on earth, remote from thermodynamic equilibrium, somewhat unusual structures of information formed that bestowed gradual effects on humans throughout biological history. If no, the story turns into one of a gradual progression within the cosmos from light, to matter, to information, to mind stuff, with life forms, including humans, having come by something that does not really harmonize with this flow. It's a thorny choice, certainly.

However, we can also switch perspective and think of these theories in terms of what we humans in the past were seeking to express by positing the existence of the divine—and what today, when the existence of the divine is denied, we are attempting to posit to replace it. Of course many people all over the world continue to believe in a god or gods; religion is deeply connected to their daily lives, and at times even reflected in politics. But in the advanced capitalist countries, the entrepreneurial class is attempting to substitute the economy for god; consumers arm themselves with a plethora of commodities. In this light, then, scientists such as the ones we have been discussing were trying to fill the void left by the absence of god with new science.

Have we really been able to create a system capable of replacing the one enabled by the gods and buddhas? Is that system no longer of any use, and is so many people's faith in it just a relic? Have our hearts and minds been taken over by something else? To me, it seems that questions like these have spurred the scientific interest in exploring the origins of consciousness.

But such questions and issues were present in antiquity as well. In the Japanese archipelago, earthenware figurines known as *dogū* were created in great numbers during the Jōmon period but disappeared in the following Yayoi period to be replaced by a different type of figurine called *haniwa*. This suggests a major transformation in cultural consciousness between the two eras.

The archaeological record shows that many *dogū* were deliberately demolished. They were made to be destroyed. The Jōmon people may have seen *dogū* as living deities, or as sentient beings with whom one might communicate. Another possibility is that the *dogū* of the Jōmon people somehow lost their power or efficacy and were destroyed by a new wave of Jōmon people or by the Yayoi.

It seems likely that human civilization and culture have frequently run into such problems and issues—and that history has rushed headlong from one era to the next without people really stopping to take stock of the whys behind these changes.

DEITIES

But there are other questions to consider in relation to the divine besides that of shifts in civilizations and cultural periods. Why, for example, is it possible for a little girl to have conversations with her favorite doll? Why can children be so convinced of the existence of imaginary creatures, as in the Miyazaki film *My Neighbor Totoro*?

Is it because for children, dolls and creatures like Totoro are like deities? That is the question. And not only for children; many adults continue to hold such faith. There is a story about the great philosopher René Descartes traveling with a large black suitcase containing a doll named Francine, named after his dead daughter, to keep him company. There are too many examples of things like this to deny.

To speak of the divine, it is insufficient merely to treat it in terms of faith or religion. Nor is it adequate to seek out the origins of consciousness of the divine (or of something approaching the divine) or to analyze the fetishistic tendencies we indulge in place of gods; the occult is the occult, nothing more. Of course, such things may be important to scholars, but as far as our imaginations are concerned, the most critical issue is how we express our experience of appearances of the divine, and how we receive others' such expressions of the experience.

Such phenomena are always linked to a "scene"—and it is this scene upon which we should focus our attention. Mircea Eliade, a twentieth-century historian of religion, referred to this sort of manifestation as an "epiphany," and took it quite seriously. It corresponds to the *otozure* or "visitation" discussed earlier. It is the moment, the scene, of this epiphany that is crucial—and crucial as well in the phenomenology of nature that is our theme.

Encounters with *marebito*

So far we have focused our discussion on manifestations of the divine as subtle presences, movements of invisible information, intimations in the human heart and mind. But this of course does not exhaust what can be said on the subject. There are also deities who present themselves boldly, forcefully, even roughly, and with distinctive qualities and features. We might refer generically to such deities as "strange gods" (*igyō no kami*).

In my mid-teens I moved from Kyoto to the Tokyo area, where I attended Kudan High School near Yasukuni Shrine, commuting from Sakuragi-chō in Yokohama on the Keihin Tōhoku Line to Iidabashi in Tokyo. For three years I saw the commute as the time when I could "edit" and organize my thoughts.

At the time I was fascinated by mnemonics, and I had by heart the names and order of the stations on my commute—Tsurumi, Kawasaki, Akihabara, Ochanomizu, and so forth—and many of the features in them. I would associate a variety of information I wanted to remember with these sites and features, making a mental data map. When one of the stations was renovated or reconstructed, it would wreak havoc with my scheme.

Training the memory is not that difficult. One way to do it is to run both forward and backward chronologically through your memory, developing the ability to do so rapidly and easily. Another is to create images in your mind of shelves, rooms, and even buildings in which information can be "stored" or "displayed." It's still a habit of mine to do this.

Back in high school, when I was using the Keihin Tōhoku Line as my data network, I felt that as long as the line existed, I would always be able to recall the information I had associated with it.

But at one point this conviction was shattered. One evening, as I was recalling the events of that day, I found that a chunk of memory had simply fallen away. It so happened that on that day, on the Keihin Tōhoku Line, I had encountered a very unusual individual. I hadn't even spoken with him, though our eyes had met. And as I sorted through my memories, it seemed that he was the one who had so easily smashed my mnemonic toolkit.

He had a strange appearance; his skin was perfectly and completely white, and he looked something like David Bowie in the film *The Man Who Fell to Earth* (1976). His skin was like nothing I had ever encountered before, emanating a kind of unearthly, indescribable beauty. He looked right at me. I couldn't turn my eyes away. The entire encounter was over in an instant, but later, no matter how hard I tried to recall it, my memories both preceding and following were very hazy. I know this sounds like something out of a science fiction or horror movie, but it was very real. And later, I came to think it might have been a meeting with a *marebito*.

The concept of *marebito*, which the folklorist Orikuchi Shinobu put such energy into elucidating, is a key for deciphering the workings of Japanese culture. It can be thought of as a term for spirits descending from the mountains or arriving here from the Eternal Land far across the sea.

Marebito can be written with the kanji 稀人 (rare person, unusual person) or 客人 (guest). Generally speaking, they were *kami* who appeared only occasionally in the villages and were seen by the ordinary residents (*jōmin*) as unusual visitors—strangers, in every sense.

Why did Orikuchi place such emphasis on the *marebito*? Because he had noted that Japanese *kami* were often "spirits from abroad" (*gairaikon* 外来魂) who come from far away and eventually return from whence they came. The Japanese *kami* are not given to taking up fixed abodes. They are usually to be found somewhere on the other side of the mountains or the sea (or else in constant motion), only occasionally appearing as strangers from strange lands—*marebito*.

Generally speaking, the *marebito* fall into two main categories, as the anthropologist Suzuki Mitsuo has pointed out. The first is of *kami* visiting from Tokoyo, the Eternal Land, while the second is of sacred performers who travel from village to village bearing the spirit of the *kami*. The first category includes deities like the Toshigami, who bring good fortune in the new year. The second type consists of itinerant artists who costume themselves and perform as *kami* but who are not divine in themselves.

In either case, *marebito* were treated as important guests. And for this reason, Orikuchi observed, many *marebito* wore broad straw hats and straw raincapes (*minokasa*) as an emblem of their status. Clad in this manner, the *marebito* presented a mysterious appearance. Clearly this was traveling garb. But where did these travelers come from? And where were they headed?

The anthropologist Komatsu Kazuhiko suggests that this is a costume for traveling from the other world to this one and back again. In other words, the straw hat and raincape are *yorishiro*. Donning them, people were transformed into *kami*—or at least something like a *kami*. To become a *kami* meant transcending day-to-day reality. And so, at certain times, people might choose to don such a costume and turn themselves into *marebito*.

Indeed, historical records from the mid-Edo period tell us that many participants in peasant protests dressed in hats and raincapes of straw. This was an expression of their desire to escape the reality of their existence. Similarly, participants asserted their solidarity with an oath that they sealed with "a sip of sacred water" (*ichimi shinsui*) to symbolize communion with one another and with the *kami*.

Other travelers wore not straw garb but deeper hats of bamboo bark or sedge and striped cloth raincoats. These were adventurers and vagabonds (*yūkyō* 遊侠), forerunners of the later gamblers and yakuza. I believe their costume, too, allowed them to adopt another identity. In their world, being installed as a "guest" (*kyakubun*) member of a group was a weighty and somewhat ceremonial matter; to me it seems similar to becoming a *marebito*.

Thinking about marebito leads immediately to insights on Japanese attitudes toward hospitality, or how one should treat a guest. For instance, it is common practice in Japan to give up your seat when an important guest arrives. When the giant of structural anthropology Claude Lévi-Strauss visited Japan in 1986, he remarked on someone vacating his cushion and turning it upside down to offer it to him as the honored guest.

During my childhood in Kyoto we lived in a typical townhouse (*machiya*) with a number of tatami rooms. During family meals my father would occupy the place of honor quite proudly, but when there was an important guest, his attitude immediately changed; he would turn his own cushion over and urge his guest to replace him at the head of the table.

I imagine similar scenes are being repeated tonight in any number of fancy restaurants all over Japan. If a department head is out with his section chiefs and one of the company directors shows up at the restaurant, he will immediately surrender his seat to the director. But if the company president should arrive, the scene will be played out again, with the director obsequiously urging the president to occupy the place he himself had taken not long before.

What is the meaning of all this? What I see is a changing of roles between host and guest. In Japanese culture, this kind of role reversal serves to maintain an exquisite interpersonal balance. I'll discuss this in greater detail later, but herein resides the essence of the Japanese concept of *utage*, or banqueting and social entertainment, as well as the consciousness of the roles of host and guest in activities related to the appreciation of flowers and birds, wind and moon. I encourage the interested reader to consult my book *Yugyō no hakubutsugaku* (A Natural History of Wandering, 1987), which treats this subject at length.

I think that the origins of this changing of roles between host and guest lie in the importance accorded to *marebito*.

One underlying factor may be the very nature of the subject in the grammar of the Japanese language. We Japanese have a truly unusual way of employing the subject in a sentence. In a restaurant, for instance, we respond to "What are you having?" with something like "Boku wa tendon" or "Ore, unagi"—literally, "I am tempura and rice," or "I, *unagi*"—placing self and the food on the same plane.

But there are even odder examples. The word *temae* 手前 is frequently used to refer humbly to oneself: *temae-domo no kaisha* (our company) or *temae-domo no kangae* (our opinion), and so forth. But then if our conversational partner starts getting annoying and we can't stand it anymore, we might bark out "Temē wa nā" (something like, "Listen, you!"). The *temē* here is the same word 手前 as the humble, polite term of self-reference *temae*, but pronounced in this rough way and used as a second-person pronoun, there is a remarkably dramatic shift in meaning. A humble way of speaking has been repurposed into an insult.

In the Kawachi region of Osaka prefecture, *ware* (a common first-person pronoun) can be used as a second-person pronoun even in situations where no insult is intended. This is similar to the way in which, historically, the *aware* of the courtier became the *appare* of the samurai, as described in the introduction.

This odd interchangeability of host and guest, subject and object is a stance fundamental to the aesthetic of flowers, birds, wind, and moon.

Wild gods

The most important deity in Japanese mythology from the perspective of social and cultural history is Susanoo. If I was asked to pick one deity from the Japanese pantheon, I would not hesitate to choose Susanoo—he's such a fascinating character. So let's take a look at him as a way of touching on some of the issues raised by the deities of the Japanese mythos.

Susanoo is the last of the three children born at the same time from Izanagi and Izanami, the primal couple. Amaterasu is his elder sister, Tsukuyomi his elder brother. Susanoo was a born ruffian, but he was also quite a crybaby. As he grew older, he continued to weep and moan so prodigiously that his father Izanagi expelled him from the Plain of High Heaven (this motif of weeping gods being expelled from Heaven is found in myths from all over the world). The banished Susanoo appealed to his sister, Amaterasu, for forgiveness and pledged contrition in a ceremonial contest known as *ukehi* (the vow), the nature of which remains a matter of much discussion. He managed to pass muster in the end, but his willful and arrogant behavior did not improve: he trampled the divisions between the rice fields and committed other violent acts. At first Amaterasu defended her younger brother, but when he flayed the piebald colt of heaven and flung its carcass into the room in which she kept her sacred loom, she lost all patience with him. Enraged, Amaterasu concealed herself in Ama no Iwato, the rock cave of heaven, plunging the world into darkness.

Incurring the wrath of the other heavenly deities, Susanoo fled to Izumo, which is equated with Ne no Kuni (Land of Roots; the underworld), landing at the headwaters of what is now the Hii River. His subsequent sovereignty over Izumo province then becomes a central part of the Susanoo story. However, the *Nihon shoki* records variants of this account that have Susanoo landing at the headwaters of Enokawa in neighboring Aki province, or descending with his son Itakeru to a place called Soshimori in the land of Silla (present-day Korea); the eighth-century gazetteer *Izumo no kuni fudoki* places the site of Susanoo's descent as Susanosato in the Iishi district (now part of the city of Izumo, Shimane prefecture). So this part of the tale is unclear.

After his descent, Susanoo slew Yamata no Orochi, a great serpent with eight heads and eight tails, and took Kushinadahime as his wife. Many children were born out of this union.

One of these progeny was Ōkuninushi no Mikoto, who was likely an actual historical figure, possibly the originator of the Izumo mythos. Yet the kingdom that he constructed seems to have been ceded rather quickly to the dynasty that founded the Yamato court—though it was probably much closer to a takeover. The deal may have been Japan's first example of collusion (*dangō*), and as is usual with most cases of collusion, we don't know the particulars. Therein lies the source of the contradictions in the Izumo mythos.

Ōkuninushi is also the protagonist in the cycle of myths associated with Mount Miwa in Nara, where he bears the name Ōmononushi or Ōnamuchi. In other words, the legend of Ōkuninushi ceding his land to Yamato could be describing either the Izumo or the Miwa dynasty.

Susanoo possesses the strongest character in the entire Japanese pantheon. The myths depict him as a wild and violent storm god, a rebel, a weeping and wailing deity, a god bringing death to living things. His realm is Sōkai 蒼海 (the Deep), Yomi 黄泉 (the Underworld), and Ne no Kuni. He is a multifaceted deity, a character as great and fascinating as Odin or Zeus in the European traditions, but his personality proves elusive.

If there was an actual human being who served as the model for Susanoo, then the identity of the clan from which he originated, identified variously as the Susa or the Ou, must hold all the secrets of the Izumo mythos, which was appropriated by the clan that founded the Yamato dynasty. Small wonder that so many researchers—notably Kadowaki Teiji and Furuta Takehiko—have been inspired to explore the historical background of Susanoo.

For example, there's an interesting hypothesis that Susanoo was the chieftain of the Susa clan, which had the backing of a guild of ironworkers from the Korean peninsula. There's no real evidence to support this, but also none to deny the possibility that Susanoo had connections to a guild of ironworkers. This would suggest that Susanoo's strength derived in part from his being an early adopter of the most advanced metallurgical technology from China and Korea.

Susanoo's rough and violent energy has something of the image of the forge about it, and the Yamata no Orochi myth might be interpreted as the conquest of a forge in the mountains. (According to the myth, Susanoo broke his sword killing the eight-headed serpent Yamata no Orochi, only to find another sword inside the serpent's body—the sword Kusanagi, which he presented to his sister, Amaterasu. This sword is one of the three Imperial Regalia.)

The *Izumo no kuni fudoki* provides a clue, telling us that Susanoo is a god of mountains and waters (both strongly associated with ironworking). If so, then perhaps the stories about Susanoo damaging Amaterasu's fields and loom reflect the threat posed to Amaterasu's group, which presided over the arts of agriculture and textile production, by the competing new technology acquired by Susanoo and his people.

Susanoo is a versatile and flexible deity, capable of transforming into a number of other deities and rulers. For example, Yasaka Shrine in the Gion district of Kyoto enshrines a rather strange deity imported from India known as Gozu Tennō (Ox-Headed Heavenly King), believed to be the *honjibutsu* (original Buddhist form) of which Susanoo is the local avatar (*suijaku*). Arahabaki, a powerful deity said to have dominated the Tohoku region in ancient times, was thought to be an avatar of Susanoo. There is even a bold suggestion that Susanoo and his brother, Tsukuyomi, are actually a single deity. This hypothesis claims that Tsukuyomi makes surprisingly few appearances in the *Kojiki* and *Nihon shoki*, the key chronicles of the age of the gods, because his activities were absorbed into those of Susanoo.

I first became interested in Susanoo when I began to wonder what the

Susa in his name signified. There are a number of theories. Kadowaki Teiji argued for a connection to the place-name of Susa in the San'in region. A little research will show that Susa comes from the verb *susabu*, which has the nominal form *susabi*. This *susabi* evolved over time to eventually become a key for unlocking some of the puzzles associated with the phenomenology of nature in Japanese culture.

Susabu was originally written 荒ぶ, meaning to behave in a rough or violent manner. *Kaze ga susabu* may be translated as "The wind blows harshly and wildly." Eventually *susabu* and *susabi* broadened semantically to include usages such as *kuchizusamu* (to hum, croon, sing to oneself) and *tesusabi* (diversion, something one toys or fiddles with to pass the time). *Kuchizusami*—written with the kanji 口遊 (mouth + play)—was the title of an eleventh-century primer for young court aristocrats, who were expected to chant or sing the lessons in order to memorize them. In short, at some point the original connotation of wildness and roughness (荒ぶ) for *susabu* somehow morphed into a sense of amusement or play (遊ぶ, also read *asobu*; nominal form *asobi*).

This semantic shift has considerable importance for cultural history. Initially, there was a time when things considered wild and rough—*susabi* in the earliest sense—were deemed evocative or elegant. A decaying roof, a garden overgrown with grasses—such scenes were positively appreciated as examples of *susabi*.

This sensibility gradually became an object of *asobi*: play, amusement, entertainment. It is not entirely clear whether the settings and activities associated with *susabi* invited or inspired a sense of play, or if these settings and activities served as catalysts for perceiving *susabi* as *asobi*, but in any case, there was an overlapping of the two concepts, culminating in an interesting shift from *susabi* as wildness to *susabi* as play. In other words, within Japanese cultural history the notion of play or entertainment has always been underpinned by the sensibility of wildness or roughness embodied in *susabi*. I believe that the name Susanoo is probably connected to this. This is a crucial point, one that I will return to in later chapters.

Susanoo is the original wild god: a type of deity whose tradition is reproduced again and again in the performing arts in Japan. For instance, in the Kabuki theater there are two styles of acting, known as *wagoto* ("gentle style") and *aragoto* ("rough style"), the latter corresponding to the image of Susanoo. *Aragoto* protagonists in Kabuki—Soga no Gorō, Sukeroku, Kamakura Gongorō, Benkei, and others—resemble Susanoo in their rough, wild, unrestrained behavior. Their wildness provides a grand vehicle for popular entertainment.

In this chapter we've looked at how the desire for information from the unknown inspired people to imagine the divine; how the invisibility of the *kami* led to the creation of a variety of receiving devices and arrangements; how in the twentieth century the same concerns led scientists to become interested once again in the search for psitrons and other evidence of the interaction of mind and matter; and finally, how the urge to commune with the divine served as the seed of the phenomenology of nature in Japanese culture.

The phenomenology of nature in Japanese culture is a multimedia experience, and indeed, information from the unknown was brought to us through a diversity of media, including the wind and birds. Our next topic will be wind, one of the delivery vehicles for these intimations of the divine.

Winds with names

The Japanese children's song "Kaze" (The Wind) is based on Christina Rossetti's poem "Who Has Seen the Wind?" And indeed, the wind is a strange thing, its true form invisible to us, yet we can see how it comes and goes and the results of its passage.

In *Kaze no Matasaburō* (Matasaburō of the Wind, 1934), Miyazawa Kenji (1896–1933) takes up this mystery. His protagonist is Takada Saburō, the young son of a mining engineer who transfers from Hokkaido to a small rural school in northern Japan on September 1 (in the old Japanese farming calendar, the day marking the height of the typhoon season). Only two weeks later, on the day of a storm, he is gone with the wind—transferred to another school, leaving with no farewells. His classmates remember him as Matasaburō of the Wind.

I imagine that Miyazawa conceived the idea for this story one day while listening to a gale whistling through the power lines. The lines serve as a resonator, like a tuning fork or the cavernous spaces between tall buildings in the city.

Kaze no Matasaburō did not originate with Miyazawa. In northern Japan—the Tohoku region and Echigo province (present-day Niigata prefecture)—this is the name for a wind deity who is also called Kaze no Saburō-sama in Niigata. There was a time when children believed the wind to be a ghost or spirit. *Jikkunshō*, a thirteenth-century collection of moral anecdotes, records examples from Shinano province (Nagano prefecture) and elsewhere of priests called *kaze no hafuri* who conducted rites to pacify the deity or spirit of the wind.

When I was in my early twenties I wrote a song called "Hie-oroshi" about the wind blowing down from Mount Hiei, northeast of Kyoto. Komuro Hitoshi, who at the time was a member of the group Rokumonsen, liked it and recorded it with a synthesizer arrangement—still rare at the time—by Tomita Isao. After that, it was covered by singers like Kobayashi Keiko, Yuki Saori, and Miyako Harumi.

In the Kansai region, the *oroshi* of "Hie-oroshi" refers to a strong wind that blows down out of the mountains in the vicinity of Lake Biwa and Osaka Bay in winter and early spring. People of Kyoto, Osaka, and Shiga prefectures use this term for a number of winds: there is the Ibuki-oroshi of Mount Ibuki and the Hira-oroshi (also called Hira-hakkō) from the Hira mountains in Shiga, as well as the Rokkō-oroshi in Kobe immortalized in the fight song of the Hanshin Tigers baseball team. I remember running through the howling Hie-oroshi to buy cigarettes for my father at the corner store.

The Hie-oroshi blows down off the slopes of Mount Hiei into the streets of Kyoto, but the wind heading down the same mountain on the other side, toward Ōmi Hachiman and Azuchi in Shiga prefecture, is known as *dake* or *dakekaze*. The winds blowing from Kyoto into the surrounding rural areas are known there as *kamikaze*, though few but locals use that term. So the winds are given different names in different areas, depending on the direction from which they are blowing. Along the coast of the Sea of Japan, what is called *oroshi* in Kansai is known as *dashi*. In Niigata, *nanoka-dashi*, the "seven-day wind," refers to a strong, dry wind that lasts for a little over a week, known as a foehn by meteorologists.

There are many intriguing names for wind in Japanese. Yanagita Kunio, in *Fūikō* (A Study of the Winds, 1935), and subsequently Sekiguchi Takeshi, originally of the Central Meteorological Observatory (now Japan Meteorological Agency), have provided us with an exhaustive survey that inclines me to believe that virtually all Japanese folk culture could be interpreted based on analyzing the vernacular names of the winds.

The most common of these names are probably *kochi* 東風 (east wind), *hae* 南風 (south wind), and *yamase* 山背 (northeast wind). *Kochi* is especially well known from the poem by Sugawara no Michizane:

kochi fukaba	When the east wind blows,
nioi okoseyo	send me your fragrance,
ume no hana	plum blossoms:
aruji nashi tote	although your master is gone,
haru o wasuruna	do not forget the spring.[1]

One can easily imagine Michizane in exile in Dazaifu in Kyushu, thinking of the wind blowing from the east and longing for the plum tree in his Kyoto garden. We should note, however, that *ayu no kaze* is actually more common nationwide than *kochi* as a term for the east wind.

In particular, *ayu no kaze* or *ai no kaze*, not *kochi,* is used along the coast of the Sea of Japan to indicate the slightly northeasterly cool winds of spring and summer. This poem by Ōtomo no Yakamochi opens with a reference to *ayu no kaze*:

ayu no kaze	Fiercely the east wind blows
itaku fukurashi	the Nago fishing dinghies
Nago no ama no	row into hiding.[2]
tsuri suru obune	
kogi kakuru miyu	

Nago refers to the waters of Toyama Bay east of Fushiki harbor in what is now the city of Takaoka, Toyama prefecture—visible from where Yakamochi was stationed when he served as governor of Etchū province in the eighth century.

Hae is an expression for the south wind used primarily in western Japan. It is probably related to the use of *hae* for "south" in Okinawa even now. *Yamase* is a cold northeasterly wind of early summer, known for the crop damage it causes in the Tohoku region. When it blows, the temperatures can fall below 20°C (68°F), damaging various crops, especially rice.

However, according to Sekiguchi, the association of *yamase* chiefly with the destructive winds experienced in the Tohoku and Sanriku regions is a product of media hype; in reality the word is used throughout the country to simply mean a wind coming out of the mountains. There's a folk song from Sado Island with these lines:

aiya yamase ni	Oh, now with the east wind
haya noborasete	sent off toward the capital
tono ga kudaru o	all we have to do
matsu bakari	is wait for my lord to arrive.

One word for wind that is somewhat tricky is *arashi*. Today, the word connotes a storm, with high winds and rain. But this does not accord with the use of the word in classical literature. For example, in the following poem by Fun'ya no Yasuhide, which can be found in the *Hyakunin isshu* collection compiled in the early thirteenth century, the image is not of a violent storm, because the verse is clearly equating a simple mountain wind (*yamakaze*) with *arashi*.

fuku kara ni	As soon as it blows
aki no kusaki no	the autumn trees and grasses
shiorureba	droop, and this must be why,
mube yamakaze o	quite rightly, the mountain wind
arashi to iuramu	is called "the ravager."[3]

In *The Pillow Book* (1002), Sei Shōnagon writes of *arashi* first as "the soft wind of the third month that carries in gentle gusts of rain at evening." In the same section she continues, "The wind mixed with rain that blows in the eighth and ninth months is a very moving thing. . . . And I love it when you open the lattice shutters or double doors at daybreak, and a sudden gust of stormy wind stings your face."[4] Neither of these suggests a fierce storm, but rather a cool wet breeze coming down out of the mountains.

The word *arashi* also appears in the *Man'yōshū*, in a poem written on the occasion of a visit to Yoshino by Emperor Monmu:

miyoshino no	Evening in the cold
yama no arashi no	of fair Yoshino's mountains,
samukeku ni	swept by the harsh wind
hata ya koyoi mo	will this be another night
a ga hitori nemu	when I must sleep alone?[5]

Here as well, if *arashi* meant a violent windstorm, Emperor Monmu would have felt more than a chill. It seems that in classical times, *arashi* signified a cold mountain wind and nothing more.

In Japan there are more than two thousand names for different types of wind. This is a prodigious number, even by global standards, but what is odd is that we have so few deities associated with the wind. In the *Kojiki* there is only one, Shinatsuhiko; the *Nihon shoki* has the same deity under a different name, Shinatobe. The tenth-century *Engi shiki* also lists Shinatsuhiko, called here by the name Ama no Mihashira no Kami, and a spouse, Shinatsuhime (Kuni no Mihashira no Kami).

The deity Fūjin (literally, "wind god"), immortalized in the famous screen painting by Tawaraya Sōtatsu (c. 1570–c. 1640), was not widely known before that. In Greek mythology we have Boreas, the north wind, blowing his conch shell; Notus, the south wind, dumping rain out of an upturned water jar; Zephyrus, the handsome god of the west wind, with

Tawaraya Sōtatsu, *Fūjin raijin-zu byōbu* (Wind God and Thunder God screens), seventeenth century. Kenninji temple, Kyoto.

his lover Flora, goddess of flowers; and various others, amounting to at least a dozen wind deities. So why so few in Japan?

Musing on Miyazawa's *Kaze no Matasaburō* brings to mind another work of fiction, J.G. Ballard's *The Wind from Nowhere* (1961). From the opening pages, the wind is blowing—blowing at gale and then hurricane force around the entire globe, bringing destruction to all the world's cities, one after another. Amid the chaos, one man begins constructing an enormous, wall-like pyramid. This was Ballard's first full-length novel, an epochal first step for science fiction's New Wave of the 1960s.

Somewhat later, I became the first Japanese to interview Ballard in his home on the outskirts of London, and it suddenly occurred to me to ask him, "Why the wind?" He replied that, up to that point, science fiction had focused solely on worlds people had no possibility of experiencing. He said he wanted to write about an event that anyone, anywhere in the world, might be caught up in. He thought that the wind represented a power we are all familiar with, and yet at the same time it issues from a mysterious place deep within us.

The true nature of the wind

The wind is indeed mysterious. It is hard to pin down precisely where it comes from.

It *is* possible to identify where a typhoon originates, but that is an exception to the rule. Winds are currents of air in the Earth's atmosphere. Viewed more broadly, the flow of electromagnetic particles from the sun constitutes the solar wind; the atmospheres of other planets also produce winds.

The Earth is wrapped in a voluminous atmosphere. How voluminous? Approximately 5 quadrillion 600 trillion tons, or about a million tons per capita for the entire population of the planet. The average human being takes about 10 million breaths a year, consuming about 5 million liters of air. This means that there is enough air in our atmosphere to supply each person presently on Earth for about 160,000 years.

The lower atmosphere grows progressively colder as altitude increases. With every 150 meters in altitude, the temperature drops 1°C. In the lowest layer of the atmosphere, called the troposphere, air currents are constantly in motion. What we know as "weather" (*tenki* 天気 in modern Japanese) is solely a phenomenon of the troposphere.

In the classical era in Japan, *tenki* meant heavenly or divine energy, as *ninki* meant the energy of the human body. As far as I know, the first use of *tenki* in the sense of "weather" is in the *Wakan rōeishū*, a poetry anthology compiled in 1013. And its current usage in phrases like "Otenki ga ii!" (Nice weather today!) didn't become common until the Edo period, encouraged by appearances in the works of Saikaku and other popular writers of the time.

Above the troposphere is the stratosphere, a shallow layer of relatively thin air divided into a number of even thinner layers, quite beautiful when seen from a jet aircraft. In the stratosphere, around 15 to 30 kilometers above the Earth's surface, is the ozone layer. It is extremely thin, and easily damaged by chemicals such as chlorofluorocarbons (CFCs) from aerosol sprays and coolants, but it protects us from ultraviolet radiation.

Above the stratosphere is the mesosphere, a cold layer about 80 to 100 kilometers above the Earth, where the temperature can be as low as –140°C. Noctilucent clouds, though very rarely observed, are a phenomenon of this layer; when meteorites fall, they leave behind dust that sometimes forms these shining clouds. Above the mesosphere is the ionosphere, which produces the aurora borealis. Out this far, the particles making up the atmosphere are extremely thinly distributed.

So we can see that our planet is wrapped in dozens of layers of atmosphere, each with its own winds, though what we normally experience as wind is limited to the portion of the troposphere closest to the Earth's surface.

Winds come in a variety of magnitudes. Among the most powerful are the trade winds, born in the subtropics and blowing toward the equator; the westerlies, blowing in middle latitudes from 30 to 60 degrees; the jet stream, which can affect air travel; and the polar easterlies, in both polar regions. All of these winds have shaped the history and cultures of the world's seafaring peoples. The monsoon is a mid-range wind familiar to us in daily life; in meteorological parlance it is known as a seasonal prevailing wind. What this means is that in different seasons it changes direction, sometimes blowing from the land to the sea, sometimes from sea to land. These monsoon winds underlie the sense of the seasons so fundamental to the phenomenology of nature in Japanese culture.

When a wind rises, the particles comprising it move in unison. Why do they move in this way, as a group? Because of the Earth's rotation. It would seem, therefore, that winds would always go in the same direction, like a merry-go-round, responding to the rotation of the planet. But this is not the case, for several reasons: the planet is not a perfect sphere; the linear velocities of the Earth's surface differ between the two poles and the equator; and the Coriolis effect influences the air's movement.

Explaining the Coriolis effect is a bit complicated, but bear with me. Gaspard Gustave de Coriolis was a nineteenth-century French physicist who described the principle that the path of objects (in this case, the air) moving across a rotating body is deflected by inertia. Since this may be rather difficult to understand, let's try a simple visualization.

Hold an orange in one hand with the navel up, and with your other hand position a felt-tip pen against this "north pole." While slowly turning the orange in a counterclockwise direction to simulate the Earth's rotation, guide the tip of the pen downward, pressing lightly against the skin of the orange and aiming as much as possible to draw a straight vertical line. What you will find is that as you progress toward the "equator" of the orange, your vertical line will gradually deflect to the right. If the same operation were to be performed drawing a line from the "south pole" up toward the equator, the line would be deflected to the left. This deflection is the Coriolis effect.

When air is warmed by the heat of the sun at or near the equator, it begins to rise, giving birth to typhoons, for example. The Coriolis effect then immediately comes into play. Under its influence, winds blowing toward either the north or south pole will have radically altered direction by the time they reach 30 degrees latitude, changing direction even more as they cool and descend. This type of activity is constantly occurring. As the winds cool and descend, they are affected by mountain ranges, the temperature of ocean currents, and other factors. And so the caprices of the wind take shape.

Thus, the wind is the product of a complex interaction of many factors, including the Coriolis effect. Yet even as we say "product," we must acknowledge that the only producer is the Earth's atmosphere itself and the particles that comprise it, and we go back to where we began: explaining the winds as atmospheric currents and flows.

As far as this atmosphere is concerned, I mentioned in the previous chapter the astonishing Gaia hypothesis advanced by James Lovelock, which argues that the activities of the life forms inhabiting Earth have partially formed our atmosphere and also affected the ratio of its constituent elements. According to Lovelock, this is the conclusion that follows when we consider how the level of gases such as oxygen and ammonia in the atmosphere has been maintained at an optimal level to sustain life—a delicate balance that, if deviated from even slightly, would pose a major threat to life as we know it.

This idea that the Earth's atmosphere is a biological product—or even a biological construct—was so radical at the time it was first proposed in 1969 that, aside from the microbiologist Lynn Margulis, who would collaborate with Lovelock to develop the hypothesis, it was greeted largely with incomprehension or indifference.

The Gaia hypothesis had touched on a fundamental truth. When the planet was first formed, oxygen was not one of the main components of the atmosphere. In fact, as noted in chapter 2, oxygen was nonexistent. But a "seed of information" dropped into the ancient seas, which eventually spawned the earliest aquatic life forms. These life forms produced oxygen that bubbled to the surface and was gradually absorbed into the atmosphere. Today's plants are engaged in the same type of respiration.

Thus, conceiving of the atmosphere as an extension of the biosphere was not in itself so startling; however, many scientists still balked at the idea of the atmosphere as a living thing. It was Lovelock who made this great leap.

I have no doubt that the atmosphere is alive. And of course the winds are alive. They bear pollen; they carry viruses. Not only that, but the winds teem with a diversity of information. There are several Japanese words that seem to suggest this: *fūbun* 風聞 ("wind news") and *fūhyō* 風評 ("wind opinion"), for example, both of which mean "hearsay."

The astronomers Fred Hoyle and Chandra Wickramasinghe pursued research along the same line of thinking. Hoyle is known for his steady state theory of the universe (an explicit rejection of the Big Bang) and as the author of science-fiction novels such as *The Black Cloud* (1957). Wickramasinghe, born in Sri Lanka in 1939, was a student of Hoyle's at Cambridge and collaborated with him for more than forty years.

Hoyle and Wickramasinghe deployed the panspermia hypothesis, originally proposed in the nineteenth century, to argue that the seeds of life on Earth originated in interstellar dust clouds and were borne here by comets. Not only that, they also hypothesized that seeds of alien life continue to fall to Earth from time to time. They assembled a variety of data in support of this hypothesis, including that on wind-borne influenza viruses.

Japanese newspapers once gave names like the Russian flu or the Spanish flu to each year's influenza outbreak. But if you went to Spain, they would be talking about the Asian flu. If you went to Russia, it was the Spanish flu; in France, they were worried about the Turkish flu. Pretty strange. In the course of their research, Hoyle and Wickramasinghe found that wherever a major flu outbreak was supposed to have originated, the people there always claimed it had come from someplace else.

With things like plant pollen, it is usually possible to determine the origin and vector of transmission, but this is a much more difficult proposition with viruses. Hoyle and Wickramasinghe, trained as astrophysicists, applied their hypothesis and came to the unusual conclusion that viruses had not originated on Earth, but had come here from outer space.

The Hoyle-Wickramasinghe hypothesis has yet to be proven. Yet no matter where they have come from, viruses are unquestionably transported by the wind. And not only viruses, but a diversity of other information is mingled with the breeze. This is why once upon a time people listened carefully for windborne news and rumor.

So the wind is a strange thing, always carrying something to somewhere else. It's only natural that the Japanese people have given it keen attention—keener, perhaps, than that given by people of many other cultures.

Wind and the Japanese

Many Japanese words incorporate "wind" 風 (read *fū* or *kaze*), with meanings concerning everything from natural phenomena to human manners and customs. *Fūkei* 風景, *fūkō* 風光, and *fūdo* 風土 all relate to scenery or landscape.

Fūbutsu 風物, *fūshū* 風習, and *fūzoku* 風俗 refer to scenes, objects, customs, or manners distinctive to a particular locale—a combination of the cultural and the geographical. *Fūzoku* in particular has been in use for a very long time; at one time the characters were read *fuzoku* and occasionally even *kuniburi* ("local customs"). The character *fū* 風 is also used in compounds suggesting the passage of time or turns of events. *Fūka suru* 風化する means to weather or fade; *fūsetsu ni taeru* 風雪に耐える is literally to endure wind and snow, and metaphorically to bear hardships; *fūun kyū o tsugeru* 風雲急を告げる implies that a crisis in human affairs is "being announced by the wind and clouds."

Social trends and the currents of speech, rumor, and opinion are described with other "wind" compounds: *fūchō* 風潮 (trend), *fūki* 風紀 (morals, discipline), *fūsetsu* 風説, and *fūbun* 風聞. *Issei fūbi* 一世風靡—used in the name of a 1980s rock group, Issei Fūbi Sepia—means something like "taking the world by storm," suggesting how rumors and fads, popularity and fame seem to spread instantly, as though carried by the wind.

"Wind" words are also frequently used to describe human characteristics and temperament: *fūkaku* 風格 (character, personality, style), *fūsai* 風采 (presence, air, manner), *fūgi* 風儀 (manners, demeanor), *fūbō* 風貌 (countenance), *fūshō* 風尚 (nobility, taste), *fūtei* 風体 (appearance, dress), *fūshi* 風姿 (appearance, looks, figure). Someone of slightly eccentric character or unique sensibility might be immediately labeled *fūryū na hito* 風流な人 (a person of taste and refinement; an artistic sort). *Fūryū* connotes a friend of the wind and moon (and pronounced *furyū*, with a short initial vowel, also refers to festival floats and other elaborate decorations, as I will explain later in this chapter). This artistic eccentricity, taken to an extreme, may lead to instability (*fūkyō* 風狂, literally "wind madness") and vagrancy (*fūten* 風癲). Tora-san, the lovable ne'er-do-well of the long-running movie series, went by the epithet *Fūten no Tora*, and other tramps and vagabonds similarly drawn to an eccentric and unmoored lifestyle are called *fūraibō* 風来坊 or *fūrabō* 風羅坊, connoting someone blown hither and yon by the wind.

And then there are many words—such as *fūmi* 風味, *fūai* 風合, *fuzei* 風情, and *fūshu* 風趣—full of vague and indefinable nuance and used to describe an atmosphere, flavor, sense, feeling. Yet if you say, "Fūmi ga aru ne" (That's tasteful) or "Ii fuzei da" (Nice atmosphere), most Japanese will somehow know quite well what you are saying. These "wind" words are interesting for being rather vague and yet managing to convey something quite subtle and precise at the same time.

A rich variety of expressions in Japanese refer to the wind: *kaze kaoru* 風薫る ("the wind smells sweet"), describing the blowing of a soft spring breeze through young leaves; *kaze no tayori* 風の便り ("message of the wind"), rumor, news brought on the wind; *kaze no suji* 風の筋, the wind's passage; *kaze no shirabe* 風のしらべ, the melody of the wind; *kaze o kiru* 風を切る, to cut the wind, meaning to move at great speed; *kaze ni tsuku* 風につく, to be carried by the wind; *kaze no iki* 風の息, the breath of the wind, used when the wind is variable, like human breathing. *Kaze no te* 風の手, hands of the wind, refers to a situation in which many things are being thrown about by the wind as though it had many hands, while *kaze no sugata* 風の姿, the shape of the wind, alludes to the way willows and other trees bend and sway in the breeze.

Kaze no ka ("fragrance of the wind"), itself a most fragrant expression, appears in this well-known haiku by Matsuo Bashō:

kaze no ka mo	The wind's fragrance
minami ni chikashi	nearby to the south
Mogamigawa	Mogami River

Kaze tatsu is another distinctive turn of phrase, one made famous by the title of Hori Tatsuo's novel *Kaze tachinu* (The Wind Has Risen, 1936–37). The protagonist, Setsuko, is a young woman quietly facing death in a tuberculosis sanatorium. As the story opens, the narrator, her fiancé, recalls sitting outside with her one late summer afternoon: "At that moment, a wind suddenly rose out of nowhere," moving him to recite to her, "The wind has risen; we must do our best to live."

This is a translation of a line from a 1920 poem by Paul Valéry ("Le vent se lève! . . . il faut tenter de vivre!"), elegantly rendered into Japanese by Ueda Bin and Horiguchi Daigaku. In the end, Setsuko passes away on a snowy day, with her father and fiancé at her side, her last words a faintly uttered "Love, there is snow in your hair."

Why is it that Japanese has so many "wind" words? The passage of time, the currents of social life, people's temperament and character, expressions, rumors, gossip—all are conveyed in the Japanese language through the image of the wind. But what, then, is this imagery that Japanese have invested in the wind? Already in the *Kojiki* and the *saibara* songs of the imperial court, we find examples such as these:

Saigawa yo	From Sai River
kumo tachiwatari	clouds rise and spread across the sky
Unebiyama	Unebi Mountain
konoha sayaginu	rustles with the leaves of trees:
kaze fukamu to su	a wind is about to blow.
Unebiyama	Unebi Mountain
hiru wa kumo toi	in the daytime streams with clouds
yū sareba	and when evening falls,
kaze fukamu to zo	because of the wind about to blow,
konoha sayageru	rustles with the leaves of trees.[6]

In both of these poems from the *Kojiki*, we see the first stirrings of the leaves sensed as a sign of the wind's "visitation" (*otozure*). The following lines from a *saibara*—a response to the first half of the poem, in which someone asks a seagull to fetch a pearl from the depths of the sea—describe the play of wind over the water's surface:

kaze shimo fukeba	The wind blows
nagori shimo tatereba	raising ripples on the water
minazoko kirite	it clouds what lies beneath:
hare	Oh!
sono tama miezu	I cannot see that pearl!

This famous poem by Ōtomo no Yakamochi appears in the *Man'yōshū*:

wa ga yado no	In the small clusters
isasa muratake	of bamboo around my house
fuku kaze no	a wind is stirring:
oto no kasokeki	tonight the faintest rustling comes
kono yūhe kamo	across the dusky air.[7]

In ancient Japan, attention to the many nuances of the wind was already well developed.

The Japanese are said to have a keen sense of the changing seasons, and indeed most of the classical arts use an invocation of the season (*kisetsu no yobiyose*) as a prominent technique. Put another way, this might be considered a reflection of how the actual seasons in Japan undergo a finely graded series of changes, known as *utsuroi*. *Utsuroi* is a key concept that I will take up in greater detail in chapter 8, "Time."

These subtle changes are sensed, first of all, visually. The mountains shift in color; spring greenery appears, flowers bloom. Then we hear the voices of the cicadas or the cuckoo, or the whispering of a mountain stream. But there is also a sense of the seasons that cannot be perceived by the eyes or ears alone, one that is brought to us in large part by the movements of the wind. This is the sense that Fujiwara no Toshiyuki captures in this poem from the *Kokinshū*: "Though it is not clear to the eye that autumn has arrived, I find myself surprised by the sound of the wind" (*Aki kinu to me ni wa sayaka ni mienedomo kaze no oto ni zo odorokarenuru*).[8] The wind heralds the seasons.

As a haiku poet, Bashō first came into his own with the travel diary *Nozarashi kikō* (Journal of Bleached Bones in a Field, 1684). There he writes of his departure, "It was the first year of Jōkyō, autumn, the eighth moon. As I left my ramshackle hut by the river, the voice of the wind was somehow quite chilling," followed by this haiku:

nozarashi o	Bleached bones
kokoro ni kaze no	on my mind, the wind pierces
shimu mi kana	my body to the heart.[9]

Here, the cold autumnal wind is described as piercing to the heart. Bashō was not the first to use the expression *shimu* (pierce) in relation to the wind; many others did before him. One of my favorite poems is an impromptu *imayō* composed by Major Captain Tokudaiji Sanesada when he returned to Kyoto to visit his sister, Senior Grand Empress Tashi, after Taira no Kiyomori had moved the capital to Fukuhara in 1180. The *imayō* were popular songs of the era, a style given even greater currency by the retired emperor Go-Shirakawa after years of study with a master of the form, a former courtesan named Otomae from Aohaka in Gifu. These songs were sung in four lines, each composed of twelve (seven plus five) syllables. Here is Sanesada's song:

furuki miyako o	Coming again to visit
kite mireba	the old capital,
asajigahara to zo	I see it sunk in ruin,
arenikeru	a reed covered moor.

WIND

tsuki no hikari wa	The brilliant moonlight shines
kuma nakute	in every cranny;
akikaze nomi zo	The chilly wind of autumn
mi ni wa shimu	pierces to the bone.[10]

Thus, in the context of flowers, birds, wind, and moon—the phenomenology of nature in Japanese culture—the wind occupies a special position.

This is because the wind is invisible. Flowers, birds, and the moon can be seen, but not the wind. The wind must be sensed by the movement and flow of *other* things. For example, connoisseurs practice the tea ceremony precisely to be able to say things like, "Did you hear the breeze passing through the bamboo just now?" A tea master serves tea in a setting where the wind will do just that. He offers you the bowl right as the wind begins to rise. You sip the tea, and someone says, "It's the wind," and then someone responds, "Yes, it is." That's it. An exquisite moment.

The wind, like the sense of a divine visitation, is a form of information. In China, the compass of the wind was divided into twenty or thirty cardinal and intercardinal directions, which were then associated with the movements of natural phenomena and of human affairs and thought. The wind's directions were further combined with the sixty-four hexagrams of the *Yijing* divination system. This is the origin of "wind" words signifying human customs and manners such as *fūshū* and *fūzoku*.

The Japanese took this sensibility a bit further, finding notions of elegance, taste, and aesthetic refinement in a subtle interaction with the wind. Everything came to be felt in relation to the wind. This form of communication, using the wind as medium, was not limited to that between human beings; one could enjoy an elegant moment in solitude, with only "the wind and moon as companions."

Taking such pleasures to the limit leads to what is known as *suki* 数奇, which we might translate as artistic passion or devotion to aesthetics. This could take two different forms.

The first was to invoke the four seasons with one's surroundings, leaving worldly affairs behind to commune with flowers, birds, wind, and moon— and then to express this in poetry, prose, or music. This was a type of aesthetic hermitage known as *tonze*, also referred to as *wabi-zumai* ("living in genteel poverty"): the same word that appears in the stock haiku expression "living in poverty [*wabi-zumai*] in the hamlet of Negishi," describing the area of Tokyo that was home to the poet Masaoka Shiki (1867–1902), among others.

The other method was to travel in search of aesthetic experience in what was known as *hyōhaku*, drifting or wandering. This word appears in the opening prose passage of Bashō's most celebrated travel diary, *Oku no hoso-michi* (The Narrow Road to the Deep North, 1689): "For some time since I know not when, tempted by the torn clouds adrift on the wind, I have been unable to suppress my desire for wandering [*hyōhaku*]."

There were pleasures to be had in running even closer to the edge—in savoring being driven "mad" by the wind. Let's talk about that, for we are now closing in on the subject of the phenomenology of nature in Japanese culture.

From aestheticism to eccentricity

The word *fūryū* 風流 (literally, "currents of the wind"), as touched on earlier, means elegant, artistic, tasteful. People say of individuals who have turned their backs on worldly affairs and concerns, "Aitsu wa fūryū na yatsu da na" (That guy is such a dreamer). This might imply that he does only what he pleases, or he lacks any concern for worldly realities.

The protagonist of Nagai Kafū's novel *Sumidagawa* (The Sumida River, 1911) is a haiku master named Shōfūan Ragetsu who has led a life devoted to *fūryū*: disowned by his wealthy family for his dissipated ways as a young man, he falls in love with a prostitute, marries her, and rejects mainstream society. What an enviable man, to be able to live completely immersed in aesthetic pursuits! This is the type of life Japanese describe as *fūryū*.

A line in the Kabuki play *Hiragana seisuiki* (1739) describes the character Kajiwara Genta Kagesue "the most elegant [*fūryū*] man in Kamakura." Originally, *fūryū* meant inheriting and maintaining the style of one's predecessors. It carried implicit praise for the more leisurely way of life in former times, and for this reason the word eventually came to connote the pursuit of aesthetic pleasures, or *suki*. But such a lifestyle was difficult to maintain. Many failed at it, and it caused problems for others. Even so, to say of someone "he led a life of *fūryū*" is a uniquely Japanese compliment of the highest order.

Read *furyū* (with an initial short vowel), the word has different meanings: it refers to the gorgeous costumes, floats, and decorations used in festivals, as well as to a broad category of folk dances often involving such ornamentation.

In medieval and early modern genre paintings of popular amusements, we frequently find gaudily dressed crowds dancing wildly amid colorful *hanagasa* (hats or umbrellas decorated with flowers)—many of them worn by the revelers, others large enough to shelter five or six adults. Such gaily decorated festival costumes and decorations were known as *furyū*, and the festivals themselves were called *furyū matsuri* (*furyū* festivals) or *furyū odori* (*furyū* dances). *Furyū* still figure today in Kyoto's Gion Matsuri with its elaborate floats; the Tanabata Matsuri of Sendai and Hiratsuka with their giant decorations; and Aomori's Nebuta Matsuri with its illuminated floats. In short, *furyū* signified gaudy and colorful decoration, as well as the excitement and high spirits that accompanied it.

In 1096, the first year of the Eichō era, the city of Kyoto and its environs were caught up in a strange popular enthusiasm for a form of folk dance called *dengaku* ("field music"). As Ōe no Masafusa (1041–1111) wrote in his account of this phenomenon, *Rakuyō dengakuki* (A Record of Field Music in the Capital), "It was as though all the people of the city had gone mad. They must have been possessed by foxes or spirits." Masafusa was one of the great literati of his day and the author of many works including *Honchō shinsenden* (Lives of Immortals of Our Realm), *Kugutsuki* (A Record of the Puppeteers), and *Gōdanshō* (Selected Conversations of Ōe). I regard him as one of Japan's foremost encyclopedists, yet the *dengaku* craze seems to have startled even him.

The diary of Nakamikado Munetada (1062–1141), *Chūyūki*, attributes the same craze to the "strange rumors of the times." Here, as well, we see how surprised the aristocracy was by this popular outburst—both by the gaudy display and the wild revelry it inspired. But then the aristocrats themselves were swept up in the mania of the Great Dengaku of Eichō, as it came to be called. About this time, the Kamo Festival in Kyoto inspired similar enthusiasm. "The decorated floats [*kasaguruma no furyū*] and costumes for the child attendants waste the fortunes of ten households," groused one contemporary account of the spectacle's lavishness.

From the Nara period (710–94) onward, the imperial government issued a variety of edicts forbidding extravagant display by the general populace—specifically, gaudy colors and unusual dress and appearance. But nothing previous had reached the wild intensity of the Great Dengaku. The aristocrats complained that this enthusiasm was "excessive" (*kasa*) but then became carried away by it as well. Today we would probably describe it as "radical."

No matter what era, it is impossible to repress people's enthusiasm for novel styles. In the years since my youth, a steady parade of fads and fashions has captured popular attention: rockabilly; the *taiyōzoku* ("sun" tribe); *bōsōzoku* ("speed tribes," motorcycle and car gangs); the dandyish *miyukizoku* (named for a street in the Ginza district in Tokyo); "happenings"; avant-garde Butoh dance; underground theater; the pop music of "group sounds"; street performances; glam rock; heavy metal; *takenokozoku* ("bamboo-shoot tribe," a dance and fashion fad named after a Harajuku boutique); punk; and so on—there's no end to it. The bizarre makeup of rabid J-League soccer supporters and girls inhabiting discos like Juliana's Tokyo or the Maharaja Gion in Kyoto are other examples.

In Japan the eleventh and twelfth centuries were a decisive era in which such outpourings of popular energy could no longer be suppressed by those in authority. One can see in this the complete collapse of the *ritsuryō* system, the centralized imperial government modeled on that of Tang China. After that, popular fads like the *dengaku* took on a religious cast, as in the *nembutsu odori* dances performed while chanting the name of Amida Buddha. They never waned—or, perhaps more accurately, never retreated into the background—but instead maintained a remarkable continuity over the centuries.

In the twelfth century, in addition to the Great Dengaku craze, countless examples of *kasa* took over Japan. A fad sprang up for the popular song genre *imayō* that had so captivated the retired emperor Go-Shirakawa; people went wild for *shirabyōshi*, a form of song and dance performance by women in male costume; and the swift rise of the Nihon Daruma-shū, a homegrown sect of Zen Buddhism founded by the cleric Dainichibō Nōnin, held people in its sway. The aristocracy was not immune to such excess. These haughty souls gathered quietly behind the closed gates of their mansions for poetry competitions to which they brought a similar passion. The aesthetic hermitage of figures such as the poet Saigyō (1118–90) originated in an attempt to escape an overheated social and cultural atmosphere.

This sense of "overdoing it," of "excess," found expression in the terms *kabuku* 傾く and *kabuki* 傾奇, literally meaning to tilt, to be out of alignment, and, by extension, to deviate. The use of *kabuki* already occurs in a 1032 entry in the *Shōyūki* diary by Fujiwara no Sanesuke describing the Kamo Festival. On that day, the imperial regent Fujiwara no Yorimichi dressed his pages in gorgeous costumes as attendants to the procession of the Saiō, an imperial princess serving as a priestess of the Shimogamo shrine, prompting Sanesuke to comment, "Today the regent evinced a deep feeling of *kabuki*." This word would become the origin of the name for the later Kabuki 歌舞伎 drama.

When *furyū*, *kasa*, and *kabuki* took even more gaudy and extreme forms, it was called *basara*. Basara (Sk. Vajra) was the name of one of the Buddhist protector deities known as the Twelve Heavenly Generals, and also of a ritual weapon symbolizing the power of divine wisdom, the diamond-hard brilliance of which can shatter all material things. By extension *basara* was used to describe wild music and dance as well as unrestrained and uninhibited behavior.

Basara became a fad during the fourteenth century. At the beginning of the *Kenmu shikimoku* of 1336, a collection of edicts issued by Ashikaga Takauji that laid the legal foundation of the Muromachi shogunate, a passage reads, "In recent days, under the name of *basara*, a love of excess has prevailed. Rich embroidered silks, finely wrought silver swords, and elegant [*furyū*] attire all cannot but astonish the eyes. One might almost call it madness."

Two years prior, the *Nijō Kawara rakusho*, a famous lampoon of the times posted anonymously at the Nijō Kawara riverbank in Kyoto, also mentions the *basara* craze. The text begins "These are the things currently popular in the capital," followed by a list; about midway down it makes fun of those wearing "oversized swords made of lead, hung so they sag in front with their hilts in the wrong direction" or carrying "*basara* fans with only five ribs."

So by this time, *basara* had already become a rampant trend. Sasaki Dōyo has been popularized as the foremost among the "*basara* daimyo," but other individuals of the Muromachi period, from Ashikaga Yoshimitsu to Oda Nobunaga and Izumo no Okuni, were also classic *basara* figures. In short, *basara* connoted both liberty and license, freedom and disorder.

If *basara* represented the extreme of radical eccentricity in external appearance, *fūkyō* 風狂, "wind madness," suggests the corresponding extreme within hearts and minds, though this term was not used in medieval Japan.

The word *fūkyō* began to be used in early modern times to describe an aesthetic sensibility that had gone too far—tipping over into eccentricity and even madness. *Kinsei kijin den* (Biographies of Eccentrics of Recent Times, 1790) by Ban Kōkei includes as its subjects those who "squandered their fortunes in the uncompromising pursuit of elegance [*fūkyō*] or abandoned their families for a life of dissipation." The extremes of a decadent lifestyle were what was described as *fūkyō*. In his book *Edo no fūryūjin* (Aesthetes of Edo, 1980), the poet and critic Katō Ikuya surveys such notable eccentrics of the era as Enomoto Kikaku, Hanabusa Itchō, Ōta

Nanpo, Awashima Chingaku, Ryūtei Tanehiko, and Santō Kyōden. While these men may not have abandoned their families, their sensibilities and proclivities went beyond the mere pursuit of aesthetic refinement (*fūryū*) toward something more extreme and eccentric (*fūkyō*).

These currents of eccentricity had first emerged much earlier, in the turbulent times preceding and continuing into the Sengoku (Warring States) period (1467–1568). The representative figure of that trend was the great (and notoriously unorthodox) Zen master Ikkyū.

Fūkyō originally signified a wildly blowing wind. *Fūryū*, too, meant the flow of the wind, as well as the abandonment of oneself to that flow. Something akin to these sensibilities of *fūkyō* and *fūryū* were already to be found in the ideals of *aware* (the capacity for deep emotion, often tinged with a gentle melancholy) and *okashi* (a more carefree or lighthearted response to the world) central to the aesthetics of the Heian imperial court. Responding spontaneously to the invitations of the wind with a sense of delight and pleasure has always been an aspect of the Japanese sensibility.

Ikkyū the eccentric

I'd like to say a bit more about the noted eccentric Ikkyū Sōjun. Ikkyū was born in 1394, just before the *basara* shogun Ashikaga Yoshimitsu built Kinkakuji (Temple of the Golden Pavilion) in the Kitayama district of Kyoto. He died in 1481, when Ashikaga Yoshihisa was shogun. The Ōnin War (1467–77) had drawn to a close, but the Kaga Ikkō Ikki, a century-long series of revolts in Kaga province by adherents of a popular Buddhist sect, was growing more violent. Earlier, Ashikaga Yoshinori had implemented a reign of terror, only for his weakness to be revealed when he was assassinated by one of his vassals in 1441. Ikkyū was an unorthodox Zen master, well equipped for living through such turbulent times.

Ikkyū is rumored to have been the illegitimate son of Emperor Go-Komatsu and a daughter of a high official of the former Southern Court. Although the veracity of that claim remains a mystery, we do know that when his mother became pregnant, she was expelled from court and gave birth to Ikkyū in a commoner's dwelling. Ikkyū was thus a fatherless—and unwanted—child, though his entry into Buddhist monastic practice at the age of six was not unusual in those times.

After being entrusted as an acolyte to Ankokuji, a temple in Kyoto, the young Ikkyū (whose childhood name was Sengikumaru) moved to

Kenninji to study Chinese poetry, and at the age of seventeen began Zen practice under the tutelage of Ken'ō Sōi at Saikonji. Ken'ō was a Zen cleric in the line of Kanzan Egen.

At the time, Zen Buddhism in Japan was dominated by one lineage rooted in Musō Soseki, founder of the Gozan (Five Mountain) system of major temples, and another lineage headquartered at the great Daitokuji temple complex in Kyoto that traced its origins to Shūhō Myōchō (better known as Daitō Kokushi). Kanzan Egen was a high disciple of Daitō Kokushi and was also the founding abbot of Myōshinji.

The master-student relationship in Zen is absolute. For the student, the teacher is everything; even when he is wrong he is always the master. There's a famous story about a roshi who was having a meal with his students. He had a bad cold, and the snot was dripping copiously into his udon noodles, which he was obliviously slurping up. But it would have been impossible for any of his students to point this out, and instead they all felt compelled to imitate him, letting their noses run as they ate. This is a true story from the life of Ōmori Sōgen Roshi, with whom I once studied.

Despite his lineage, Ken'ō died in extreme poverty, leaving Ikkyū despondent and without a master. He set out for Ishiyamadera, a temple on the shores of Lake Biwa. Ishiyamadera is one of the stops on the famous Kannon pilgrimage, and sites like it were believed to be manifestations in this world of Potalaka (J. Fudaraku), the Pure Land in the south inhabited by the bodhisattva of compassion. By retreating to Ishiyamadera, Ikkyū hoped to heal his grief over his teacher's death and achieve salvation. But he did not find the relief he sought, and, completely distraught, he decided to drown himself in the lake.

When Ikkyū's mother heard that her son had shut himself up in Ishiyamadera in despair, she dispatched a servant to him. It sounds like one of the tall tales that collect around great men, but it has been said that just as Ikkyū was about to throw himself into the lake, this servant stopped him. Ikkyū's mother was a formidable personality who in Ikkyū's younger days had supposedly exhorted him to become an extraordinary monk, remarking that if he turned into a regular run-of-the-mill monk he would be no child of hers. Although Ikkyū was saved, he now faced the shame of having survived. There's an expression in Japanese, "the great death" (*daishi ichiban*), which originally comes from Zen and means to strive at something as though one is ready to die for it; similarly, once a resolve is formed, there is no turning back. Ikkyū had no choice but to die or else to live on in shame with no more left to lose—and so he roused himself to find an even greater teacher than Ken'ō with whom to study.

At this time word of a Zen master named Kasō Sōdon reached Ikkyū. Despite having been ordained in the Daitokuji line, Kasō was something of a maverick, declining residence at Daitokuji to live instead in a modest hermitage called Zenkōan in Katata, a small town on the western shores of Lake Biwa. Accepted by Kasō as a student after much difficulty, Ikkyū devoted himself to a rigorous regimen of Zen practice, bearing up under the fierceness of Kasō's instruction.

The rigors of training gradually left Ikkyū exhausted, debilitated, and weak. One day while doing zazen, he entered a trance state. His body was a wreck, but the teacher he had chosen continued to make stern demands. Meditating in this state, he heard the fluttering and flapping of a bird's wings. When Ikkyū opened his eyes, a large crow cawed at him. It is said that at that moment, Ikkyū achieved enlightenment.

Enlightenment stories of famous monks often don't make a lot of sense, and in Ikkyū's case as well, this story about a crow cawing is about all that has come down to us. The painter Hirafuku Hyakusui has left us a marvelous visualization of this scene in his work *Katata no Ikkyū* (Ikkyū at Katata, c. 1929).

Having experienced enlightenment though, Ikkyū abandoned traditional Zen. The early thirteenth-century Chinese koan collection *Wumenguan* (J. *Mumonkan*; The Gateless Barrier) contains the famous line, "If you meet the Buddha, kill him." The warlord Oda Nobunaga is said to have been quite fond of this phrase, which distills the fierceness of Zen thought: as is stated in a similar passage in another text, the *Linji yulu* (J. *Rinzai roku*; Record of Linji), if you meet the Buddha, kill him; if you meet a saint, kill him; if you meet your parents, kill them. Ikkyū delighted in this thinking as well. He believed that Zen practitioners must kill all ideas. You can't speak of ideas if you don't have the power to kill them head-on; so first off, you must be willing to kill the Buddha.

This was the point of departure for Ikkyū's eccentricity (*fūkyō*), and he would push ahead with it consistently throughout his long life. Asked to chant sutras at a funeral, he blithely agreed, only to arrive at the gravesite in ragged robes, which he then raised before shitting in front of the grave and departing. When asked what is the Buddha, or what is Zen, he would spit on the questioner and hurl all manner of abuse at him. He seemed to revel in playing the bad guy, in being a contrarian.

Ikkyū saw all good intent as hypocrisy. He believed that do-gooders are always trying to hide something bad; that was his starting point in an attempt to eradicate the evil lying within. Ikkyū had practiced deeply enough to be able to accomplish this, and so he abused hypocrites as a way of exposing their inner evil. In effect he was throwing dynamite to blow up latent evil, concealed and repressed evil. Anyone who made a gesture of wanting to understand him would be subject to a withering assault. It is recorded that even the shogun sighed and said, "There's nothing to be done about Ikkyū."

> I, Kyōun, am truly the heir of Daitō,
> in the demon's nest of the dark mountain,
> what could be worthy of respect.
> I remember once, the melody of the flute,
> the clouds and the rain in the evening,
> and refined youths who brought down barrels of wine.[11]

This poem of Ikkyū's is unprecedented in its content. By this time Ikkyū was styling himself Kyōunshi, or "Crazy Cloud," and his collected poetry in Chinese would be entitled *Kyōunshū* (The Crazy Cloud Anthology); it was a fitting sobriquet for a man living an aesthetic (*fūryū*) and eccentric (*fūkyō*) life. The poem, in short, declares his embrace of "madness," which certainly is nothing if not outrageous. Ikkyū even opens another poem, entitled "On Myself," with the lines "Eccentric madman / Stirring up a crazy wind" (*Fūkyō no kyōkaku / Kyōfū o okosu*).

The Daitō mentioned in the first poem is Daitō Kokushi, founder of Daitokuji; the "demon's nest of the dark mountain," a reference to towering and forbidding peaks where demons might dwell. Ikkyū asks, What use is it to practice Zen in such a place? Recalling the past, he states that he did no such thing; instead, he sported with women and drank wine from golden barrels—and precisely because of this, he can lay claim to being Daitō's true heir.

An ideology of otherness

At the time, Japan was embroiled in the turbulence and chaos of the Ōnin War. Stories of Ikkyū reached the ears of the rulers of the day, who concluded that he was just the man to lead the world of Japanese religion and appointed him abbot of Daitokuji.

Ikkyū's response was typically unprecedented: he simultaneously submitted a letter of acceptance and a letter of resignation. He remained in Katata, refusing to attend the ceremony of his installation as abbot at Daitokuji. Instead, he announced that he would use the title to raise money among the rich merchants of the port of Sakai to reconstruct the temple after the damage it had suffered during the Ōnin War. Normally, an abbot too enthusiastic about fundraising might cause people to question his character. And indeed, Ikkyū was subjected to considerable criticism in this regard, but he was willing to trade his reputation for donations from far and wide. Not a penny of it found its way into his pocket; it all went directly to the temple.

Ikkyū was critical of his fellow monastics. Despite its title, *Jikaishū* (Self-Admonitions), a collection of more than one hundred poems, is filled with diatribes and invective against another of Kasō Sōdo's disciples, Yōsō Sōi, and Yōsō's dharma-heir, Shunpo Sōki. He was likewise scathing of Hino Tomiko, a powerful figure of the day as she was wife of one shogun and mother of another. Ikkyū—who styled himself as a madman, eccentric, "crazy cloud," and hooligan—feared nothing and no one.

When I consider the wildness of Ikkyū's attitude and lifestyle, I realize anew that Japanese history has always been one of status, forms, and etiquette being challenged by the exceptional, the eccentric, and the outrageous—and moreover, that it is precisely when these challenges arise that history reaches a major turning point.

Status and rank are always the symbols of authority. Violators of their conventions are unfailingly criticized and ostracized. Yet at some point the times always advance toward the destruction of convention. For the imperial court, the samurai were the destroyers; the Tokugawa shogunate was in turn challenged by the samurai of the Satsuma and Chōshū domains. In the history of calligraphy, we see similar rebellions and deviations from the established order. The most significant was the emergence of the phonetic kana 仮名 as a "provisional script" in opposition to kanji, which were regarded as *mana* 真名, the "true" or orthodox script. The "scattered writing" (*chirashigaki*) and insertion of spaces between words (*wakachigaki*) that became a part of kana orthography would have been unthinkable in the orthodox line of Chinese calligraphy beginning with Wang Xizhi.

Formal conventions are the creations of authority. For example, the early tenth-century *Engi shiki* (Procedures of the Engi Era) determined the conventions of Japanese society for a long time, and the Hōjō regents established the *Jōei shikimoku* (Regulations of the Jōei Era) as the formal legal code of the Kamakura shogunate in 1232.

The aesthetic consciousness of every age, too, has its formal conventions. From the perspective of classical Gagaku and Bugaku, such popular forms of music as *dengaku* and *shirabyōshi* appeared strange and crude. *Sarugaku* also seemed odd when it first appeared, and it was not until its refinement by Zeami and his aesthetics of *yūgen* that it attained the formal beauty that transformed it into Noh drama. But then, from the perspective of Noh, the early forms of Edo Kabuki (*wakashu* and *yarō* Kabuki) were similarly regarded as strange and unorthodox. And eventually, when Kabuki had established its status as a traditional aesthetic form, the Shingeki (New Drama) of the early twentieth century and the postwar experimental Kabuki of Takechi Tetsuji (1912–88) seemed unorthodox, and the Butoh dance of Tatsumi Hijikata (1928–86) represented an even more extreme challenge to artistic convention.

The same holds for Japanese ceramics. In the beginning, the Six Ancient Kilns (Rokkoyō) of Bizen, Echizen, Seto, Shigaraki, Tanba, and Tokoname produced simple functional ware, but gradually there developed a range of kilns creating pottery with considerable aesthetic richness. Chōjirō's Raku tea bowls, adopted by Sen no Rikyū as essential utensils of the tea ceremony, possess a depth that draws and captivates the eye. Placed beside such pieces, wares with distorted and warped forms might certainly seem odd; nonetheless, the *hyōgemono* (oddities) favored by the great tea master Furuta Oribe (1543–1615) changed the art of their era by introducing a "beauty of insufficiency" that posed a direct challenge to the aesthetics of fulfillment and satisfaction.

In many eras, violations of etiquette and propriety have expressed the spirit of opposition and resistance.

An extreme example was the Bureikō (Rude Society), a group of court nobles, clerics, and provincial warriors who gathered around Emperor Go-Daigo in support of his efforts to eliminate the Kamakura shogunate and restore direct imperial rule. Although unsuccessful, it ushered in the era of the Northern and Southern Courts, shattering convention within the emperor system itself and creating a major turning point in Japanese history. Also a failure, but indicative of the direction in which the winds of history were blowing, was the February Twenty-Sixth Incident of 1936, a violation of the established order that took the form of an attempted coup d'état by young army officers mentored by the right-wing radical Kita Ikki. And it seems likely that the 1591 suicide of the tea master Sen no Rikyū under pressure from the warlord Toyotomi Hideyoshi involved some form of resolute defiance as well.

Of course there are also examples in which the flouting or shattering of convention led to triumph. One of the most obvious is that of Oda Nobunaga (1534–82), who began as a minor warlord of the Sengoku period. No warlord was more enthusiastic in violating propriety and convention than Nobunaga. The earliest example of flouting convention recorded in Japan's history is perhaps Prince Naka no Ōe's successful assassination plot against Soga no Iruka in 645. Such examples are not limited to Japan, but what fascinates me is that in Japan they are understood in terms of the wind—in other words, as a history of new winds, or *ifū* 異風 ("unusual/different winds"), supplanting the old.

Past the age of seventy, Ikkyū fell in love with a blind singer, a woman he referred to as Shinnyo (Lady Mori). This relationship once again provided Ikkyū with experience of a realm of life outside the reach of the ordinary Zen monastic.

Zen monastic precepts discouraged sexual intercourse with women, but Ikkyū vociferously proclaimed his taste for both women and men. He was a man of intense convictions, openly consorting with women while pursuing a heroic Zen practice and rebelling against all the social authorities of his day. It seems likely that his sexual experiences opened up a world for Ikkyū beyond anything he had hitherto experienced in Zen.

This image of Ikkyū overlaps with that of Ryōkan (1758–1831), a Zen monk of the late Edo period who also led a life devoted to aesthetic pursuits and had a late-life romance, in his case with a nun named Teishin some thirty years younger. I've written of this in greater detail in the book *Soto wa, Ryōkan* (Ryōkan on the Outside, 1993).

Both Ikkyū and Ryōkan approached old age with erotic involvements. But this was no longer merely *fūkyō*—eccentricity or unconventionality. Instead we should see it as a case of unconventionality transcending itself to become a powerful means of arriving at something pure. Here is poem from Ikkyū's *Kyōunshū*:

The mad wind conceals nothing in this universe.
The crazy clouds it stirs up pile madness upon madness.

Who can know the place where the clouds are quieted and the wind
    settled?
From the eastern sea, the sun rises first in Japan.

"The clouds are being blown madly about by the wind—who or what on
earth can possibly tame them? I will," Ikkyū seems to be saying in this
poem, with pride. He's declaring that when day breaks over the eastern
seas, he—Ikkyū Sōjun—will be there to control the mad wind.

Wind and breath

The essence of the wind is that it blows. In ancient Greece this was called
pneuma and in India, *prana*; both words signify both wind and breath.
They are translated in Chinese and Japanese as *qixi/kisoku* 気息 (breath) or
fengqi/fūki 風気 (wind).

What this means is that from very early times in India and Greece, and
China and Japan, the idea of wind had two overlapping images: the wind
that blows in the natural environment and the breath that animates the
human body.

Wind and breath both flow in and out. This input and output is central
to the image of the wind, but not something science has especially concerned itself with. It has received real attention only from adepts of various
physical disciplines, from yoga and Daoism to the martial arts.

The out breath eventually became connected to language. Wind is
breath, and through breath it becomes language. People do not speak on
an inhalation, except when making a very few sounds; one must exhale
to talk. That words are almost always carried on the out breath should be
significant to all users of language, but it is not often acknowledged.

In India, the concept of prana gave rise to a spiritual practice. The initiation
of breath was conceived as opening the mouth wide to form the sound *a*;
its end, as closing the mouth with the sound *um*. In between, all the possible
intermediate vibrations were imagined. And this continuum of sound was
sustained as long as possible on a continuous exhalation. The result was
the sacred syllable *aum*, or *om*, used in virtually all classical Indian and
Tibetan mantras and chants (dharani), such as *om mani padme hum.*

Before exhaling and producing sound, one breathes in with the entire
body, inhaling the entire universe, incorporating all the nonverbal energies

of the cosmos. In the martial arts, deep abdominal breathing is a common practice—the lower abdomen is expanded to draw air slowly into the lungs. Breathing techniques in the martial arts developed around a set of postures and stances that would facilitate this type of breathing.

Having inhaled deeply, one next exhales slowly. One then gives voice to the exhalation, beginning with *a* and gradually closing the mouth to end with *um*. Imbedded in this practice is the belief that you are moving from the sound that originated the universe to the one that will terminate it, and that all possible sounds are encompassed between them. This is similar to the process by which black seeds send forth soft shoots from which green leaves emerge and a riot of colorful flowers bloom, which eventually turn brown and return to the black earth from which they arose—thus passing through all the possible colors of the natural world.

In China, *a* was rendered with the character 阿 and *um* with the character 吽. This was transmitted to Japan, where it appears today in colloquial expressions like *a-un no kokyū*, or "om breathing," meaning two people or things in perfect coordination with one another. In the paired statues of lion-dogs (*koma-inu*) at the entrances to shrines or of Niō guardian deities flanking the main temple gates, one member of the pair always has its mouth open wide to form the syllable *a* and the other has its mouth firmly shut, forming the syllable *un*. Invited into this great circulation between *a* and *un*, we are encouraged to engage in spiritual experience.

Kūkai (774–835), founder of the Shingon sect and the great monastic complex at Mount Kōya, brought great clarity of thought to the relationships between wind and breath, language and orthography. Near the beginning of the main text of his treatise *Shōji jissōgi* (Voice, Letter, Reality) we find this statement: "No sooner does the inner breath of living beings vibrate the air of the external world than there arises voice (*shō*)."[12]

Kūkai conceived of the wind as being composed of particulate matter, seeing in it the microcosmic movements of the "six sense-fields" (*rokujin*). Moreover, as is indicated by his statement that "all in the six sense-fields are letters," he embraced an image of the winds of the cosmos as filled with the dance and play of the written word. The line comes from the following verse in the *Shōji jissōgi*:

> Vibrating in each other's echoes are the five great elements
> that give rise to languages unique to each of the ten realms

all in the six sense-fields are letters, the letters
of the Dharmakaya, which is reality.[13]

This gives us an image of a colossal recirculation of energy: sound echoes through the universe, reverberating through the mountains and rivers, grasses and trees, to become human voice, which, while passing through the human body to become language, returns once again to the vastness of time and space. The spacious vistas afforded him from his monastic retreat atop Mount Kōya, his ascetic meditations in the waterfalls of the Ishizuchiyama range in Shikoku, and his practice of an esoteric mnemonic technique involving the mantra of the bodhisattva Kokuzō—these factors brought Kūkai to the point where all particles of light, all the flecks of dust in the wind, could be seen as letters and heard as sounds and voices. This is what this famous verse of his tells us.

Among Kūkai's treatises is one entitled *Unjigi* 吽字義 (Concerning the Character *Un*), a unique work in which he sets out an entire philosophy of wind based on an analysis of the character *un*. He distinguishes four separate aspects of this character, emphasizing that even in a single syllable different phases of cosmic harmony are expressed. Everything that exists is contained in a single breath of wind, and when we breathe it in, we breathe in tandem with the universe. "One is not one, and yet it is one; the innumerable form a unity. Suchness is not suchness, yet is ever present; giving rise to identity and relation."

The wind is breath. Breath is the wind. By virtue of the wind and breath, our words go out and in. And so our words are also the wind. Words are, as the original Japanese etymology has it, "leaves of language" (*koto no ha*), dancing in the wind.

The link between wind and breath is an essential perspective to consider when thinking about the wind. We've investigated a number of interesting perspectives on the wind in this chapter. In conclusion, I would like to offer this encapsulation of the fundamental nature of the wind: for me, the wind is a medium, a bearer of information. It is an invisible medium that is the first to bring us information from over *there* to where we are, *here*.

CHAPTER 5 BIRDS

The adventure of the salmon

As salmon enter their spawning season, they seek out the rivers in which they were born. Returning from the ocean in late autumn, they spawn and then die within a few weeks. When the waters warm again, the young salmon mature and make their long journey back to the ocean. This migratory life cycle of the salmon in Hokkaido, Siberia, Alaska, and other areas has been known since ancient times.

I once watched a documentary film on the Alaskan salmon, whose journey to their ancestral home is truly heroic. They are seeking not their birthplace but the part of the river where they grew to adolescence or maturity. Their intense struggle to return is thought to be prompted by some form of memory of place; the theory is that they are responding to the scent or other chemical or environmental cues recalling the stretch of river in which they spent their youth. As they head upstream to spawn, they stop eating altogether; swimming resolutely against the current, they move at an average speed of 14 kilometers a day.

Farm-raised salmon cannot make this return journey unless special fishways or ladders are built for them. Construction projects along rivers and nets present additional barriers to the salmon's progress upstream. Salmon attempt to leap, repeatedly, over barriers along their path. They never give up. Watching their determination in overcoming the myriad obstacles is a deeply moving experience.

What is the basis for this homing or migratory instinct of the salmon, which is familiar to most of us but whose mechanisms are still not completely understood? Many animals, including humans, emit chemicals called pheromones. Research into insect pheromones has made significant progress, whereas the operation of human pheromones is less well understood. Perfumes and colognes have been marketed claiming to incorporate pheromones for attracting the opposite sex, but I have no idea if such claims have any validity. These olfactory compounds might be described as scent signals that elicit certain behaviors on the part of the recipient. It was once proposed that salmon produced some sort of pheromone related to the mating cycle, but that hypothesis has been rejected, at least for now.

As river water warms in the spring and the environment begins its seasonal changes, the bodies of the young salmon become extremely sensitive, gradually taking on a shiny silvery coloration. This phenomenon is known as smolting. Their skin is transformed into a light-sensitive substance analogous to the silver halide used in traditional photographic film and paper. It has been argued that this smolting process is what initially sets the adolescent salmon on their course toward the ocean.

A compound in the skin called guanine has been identified as the cause of this silvering. Even if guanine is released into the river water, it seems unlikely that it could linger in detectable quantities during the rapid swelling of the waters in spring following the snowmelt. And even if some pheromone or other scent trail were released marking the journey to the sea, it is inconceivable that sufficient traces of it would remain, perhaps years later, to guide the return trip. So how is it that salmon are able to traverse such enormous distances to return unerringly to the streams where they were born?

And it is not just salmon that do this. Japanese freshwater eels known as *unagi* go to the ocean to spawn, and their offspring somehow know the way back to their parents' riverine home, enacting a similar (though reverse) drama of homecoming.

Although I've observed the migratory life cycle of salmon, read monographs on it, seen films, and talked to a number of zoologists, I have still not arrived at a solid explanation. But I've become convinced that the phenomenon known to zoologists as "imprinting" holds some valuable clues.

Imprinting is also very important to us as human beings. It poses the question of how much of our behavior is determined by our genes and how much by factors such as education, by what we've learned unconsciously from our parents' behavior or by what we have picked up from interactions with our environment or with others. The patterns encoded in DNA alone seem incapable of providing an explanation for the homing or migration instincts. Yet at the same time, it is also highly unlikely that they are entirely the product of learned behavior.

So how should we think about this? It seems likely that there is a command embedded in the genetic code awaiting release, along with some kind of mechanism ensuring that learned elements will activate the command and shape behavior. In this way, organisms undergo effective imprinting keyed to environment and locale—or so we can surmise.

Humans also imprint. The first researcher to emphasize this was Desmond Morris, a leading British expert on animal behavior. Employed by the Zoological Society of London, he studied the behavior of a variety of animals and wrote the global bestseller *The Naked Ape: A Zoologist's Study of the Human Animal* (1967), as well as *The Biology of Art* (1963) and *The Human Zoo* (1969), which helped to create a new science of human zoology. Lyall Watson, author of *Supernature: A Natural History of the Supernatural* (1973), *Lifetide: A Biology of the Unconscious* (1979), and *Earthworks: Ideas on the Edge of Natural History* (1986), was a doctoral student of Morris's at the University of London.

Morris stresses how important the phenomenon of imprinting is for human behavior in areas ranging from sex to food preferences, illustrating this with fascinating examples. For instance, some people quickly respond to certain events with defensive or aggressive behavior; careful observation reveals that these responses are closely related to that individual's attitudes toward sex and food as well as their personal manner and habits—and indeed, by extension, to their entire view of life. It is difficult to see this as anything other than the result of "information" imprinted at a particular point in their development. Why? Because in many cases this "personality" or "manner" resembles that of their parents or close friends to an astonishing degree.

Morris does not view all human behavior in a positive way, instead alerting us to the existence of behavioral imprinting that is hidden and difficult for the individual to resist. Especially in today's world, aspects of society, education, and the family environment may appear harmless enough but are actually producing lasting physiological imprinting that Morris warns could have an adverse effect on society as a whole.

Konrad Lorenz delivered a similar warning but used a much sharper tone. The winner of the Nobel Prize in 1973, Lorenz is the author of numerous books, including my particular favorites: *Behind the Mirror: A Search for a Natural History of Human Knowledge* (1973), *The Waning of Humaneness* (1987), and *Das Wirkungsgefüge der Natur und das Schicksal des Menschen* (The Causal Structure of Nature and the Fate of Humankind, 1983). Lorenz was the founder of the field of ethology, but in his later years he focused on the growing failure of the human system.

Two internal clocks

As scientists have delved into what sort of imprint could be guiding salmon to return to their natal rivers, they have hit upon another clue. And that is the concept of the internal clock—something present in all living things.

The two internal clocks—one governing circannual rhythms (having a period of roughly one year) and the other governing circadian rhythms (having a period of roughly one day)—interact in complex ways that affect animal behavior. Although invisible, the clocks reveal their presence in a range of subtle and sometimes puzzling animal behavior and habits. The Japanese biologist Uo Junko, for example, has been studying the internal clocks of cockroaches.

Examples of circannual and circadian rhythms are plentiful. To cite one well-known example, oysters dramatically open their shells at high tide. This was long believed to be a response to the tide itself, or to the waves, until one scientist conducted an experiment in which oysters were placed in beakers of seawater and taken to a lab far from the ocean. Sure enough, the oysters opened their shells at exactly the time of the high tide at the seashore where they had been collected. Somehow they knew what time it was at that seashore. They had an invisible clock keyed to the cycle of the tides.

The fiddler crab is known as *shiomaneki* ("tide summoner") in Japanese because the male looks as though it is waving in the tide with one of its claws, which is much larger than the other. When the tide comes in, the crabs all disappear into holes in the sand; when it goes out, they all pop out of their holes and head toward the water. It's an impressive sight, as though they, like the waves, are being pulled to and fro by the moon. The crabs emerge from their hideaways in the beach sand to play amid the waves and foam of the shoreline; near sundown, they head back up the beach. Watching them perform this operation again and again, it seems these crabs are themselves a wave, or perhaps moon sprites taking on the guise of a wave.

The tides are of course influenced by the gravitational pull of the moon. But this pull is felt not only by the oceans; the land as well is subject to it. Data show that during the course of each day this gravitational force pulls Earth out of shape by about 3 centimeters on the side facing the moon.

This phenomenon has been occurring for three or four billion years, long before life emerged on our planet. The history of life on Earth is only a tiny, recent sliver of our planet's history. Thought about this way, then perhaps it is the great vibrations of the moon and Earth that have been attuning themselves to the circannual and circadian rhythms of life, rather than the other way around. It seems conceivable to me. I've written elsewhere—in the book *Runatikkusu* (*Lunatics*, 1993)—about such mysteries of the moon.

As we have seen, animals benefit from various sorts of internal clocks creating rhythms, gauging timing, and interacting with one another to regulate the organism's relationship to its environment. But we still don't understand what serves as the "master clock." In mammals, the supraoptic nucleus of the hypothalamus was once a candidate for this role, but this theory has since been questioned. The hormone melatonin, secreted by the pineal gland, has been proposed as a chemical bearer of information related to the circannual and circadian cycles and as a regulator of responses to light, but details of this process have yet to be fully understood. Even so, it has become obvious that a wide range of organisms appear to be equipped with quite precise and complex regulatory mechanisms that rely on internal clocks.

Earlier I mentioned the discovery of powerful pheromones in insects; ants are guided by such chemicals, for example. In a classic experiment, a petri dish of sugar water was placed some distance from an ant colony. Eventually one of the ants stumbled across it and returned to the nest to alert the others, retracing the meandering path it had originally taken to get to the dish. When the other ants went to get the sugar water, they followed the same zigzag path. For some time this was considered evidence that the ants' behavior was controlled by a pheromone secreted from the abdomen of the first ant.

In 1947 a scientist conducted another experiment that would overturn this thinking. He conducted the experiment outdoors, in natural light, while trying to eliminate all traces of the pheromone pathway. The ants still followed the exact path of the first ant and found their way to the sugar water. This experiment revealed that ants have some form of solar compass that functions as an internal clock.

That was a landmark year in zoology, with many new discoveries and research reports. It was the year in which Karl von Frisch published his research on the dances of honeybees. He discovered that they perform two main types of dance to convey information regarding food sources to the other hive members. When they perform a "round" dance, it indicates that the flowers they have found are within 50 meters of the hive; a "waggle" dance signals that the flowers are at a distance of 100 meters or more. Moreover, based on repeated observation, Frisch was able to theorize that bees have an internal solar compass. He advanced the bold hypothesis that bees are able to detect and use the polarization patterns of sunlight to determine the direction of the flowers and then integrate this information into their dances to convey it to the others.

There was more. During the time it takes for the bee that discovers the nectar to return to the hive, the sun's position in the sky will have shifted ever so slightly—and this information, too, is integrated into the bee's dance, relaying the message that if you fly at this particular time at this compass point you will find some tasty nectar. In other words, bees are equipped with a kind of high-performance clock as well.

The scientist investigating the communication of ants also revealed that it was not only pheromones but also a solar compass that allows them to convey information to their fellows. Before long, it was discovered that such solar compasses and internal clocks are also deeply involved in the behavior of birds.

What I hope to emphasize with all this discussion of various organisms is that many animals—from salmon and crabs to ants and bees and birds and humans—possess quite precise and complex internal clocks that are probably driven by similar embedded "oscillators."

Secrets of the birds

Birds grasp the geometries of the heavens. Their migratory journeys are evidence of this capacity. The mechanics of bird migration were long a mystery, but since the 1970s a significant body of research has accumulated to clarify this process.

Initially birds were believed to navigate using the sun by day and the stars at night. Then it was thought that they sense the earth's magnetic field. In recent years we have come to understand that birds also use subtle changes in the patterns of polarized light between themselves and the sun in order to determine their position. To understand why birds possess this capacity, we must take a look at their evolutionary development. Birds evolved from reptiles; they are basically lizards that grew wings. In a poultry shop the evidence is there in plain sight. Plucked chickens look almost exactly like skinned lizards.

Life began in the oceans—birds, mammals, human beings were all born of water. First there were various forms of marine life, then fish. Eventually a few adventurous outsiders resembling mudskippers and climbing gouramis emerged, perhaps fleeing stronger predators in the water, and began the battle to occupy the land. At first they did little more than cling to the base of trees at the water's edge, but eventually they developed defenses against the light and heat of the sun. Scales were replaced by the warty skin characteristic of amphibians, and eventually salamanders and frogs appeared. Next these animals developed thicker, tougher skin to resist predators, and they gained the ability to survive away from streams and ponds, thus evolving into reptiles.

As reptiles developed robust systems adapted to life on dry land, one group headed toward gigantism. This was the failed evolutionary experiment that led from crocodile-like creatures to the dinosaurs: an experiment that did not calculate for the efficacy of size. The dinosaurs proliferated during the course of the Jurassic period, and then suddenly vanished—a mass extinction that may have been triggered by an asteroid, volcanic activity, or both.

Some creatures evolved along a different line. The secret of their success was viviparity—live birth following the development of the embryo within the body of the parent. The first step in this direction was monotremes, mammals like the platypus that incubated eggs internally for a significant period before laying them. The success of this experiment encouraged the development of nocturnal mammals, four-legged beasts of various sorts, and, eventually, human beings.

Other creatures continued egg-laying while avoiding the evolutionary missteps of the dinosaurs. These were the birds. They began as reptiles but extended their lives into a realm that other animals had not yet explored: the air. Developing a brilliant physiological solution to flight, birds advanced along an evolutionary path that humans could not follow. We have a special relationship with these other proud two-legged members of the animal kingdom.

In addition to flight, birds have developed a number of other capabilities. Their vision, for example, is superb. We often hear the derogatory term "birdbrain" for someone lacking in intelligence, but this is absurd: for their overall size and weight, the brains of birds are quite large, and the largest portion is taken up by the optic lobes. Hawks and other raptors are well equipped for sighting prey such as rabbits from great heights.

In the eyes of hawks there is a comb-like structure called the pecten oculi that contributes to their visual acuity, which is far sharper than that of humans. Moreover, with the exception of owls, whose eyes face forward like our own (yet are close to ten times more powerful than ours), birds' eyes are located on either side of their head. This gives them a field of vision approaching 360 degrees. When birds bob their heads while walking, they are scanning this 360-degree visual field in minute increments, which they can do because their eyes can operate independently of each other.

Birds' tongues are also marvelous devices, though sometimes they appear rather gruesome. Most people would probably be quite surprised at how long they are. The tongues of woodpeckers wrap all the way around their skulls. The tongues of hummingbirds have grooves that make it easier to sip the nectar of flowers, while parrots have thick tongues covered with minute papillae that help them taste and select their food. This sensitive tongue is thought to be one of the reasons that parrots are adept at mimicking speech. The legendary Tang-dynasty beauty Yang Guifei is said to have taught a parrot called Xueyinu ("snow-clad maiden") to recite the *Heart Sutra*.

The legs of birds are also unique. When a bird's leg is extended, the four toes of the foot open out; when the leg is bent, the toes contract. This is because the knee and ankle joints are directly connected to the tendons of the feet.

The reason that birds do not fall out of trees even when they are asleep is because this configuration of their legs and feet automatically tightens their claws around a branch when they settle in to rest. In flight they also tuck in their legs, toes retracted. As they come in for a landing, the legs extend and the toes open. It is rather amusing how many traditional Japanese paintings depict cranes and hawks but show a lack of understanding of this basic anatomy.

As an aside, the motifs of cranes alongside pines and cranes flying with pine branches in their bills are common in traditional Japanese painting and decorative arts. Both motifs were altered in transmission from their original source: originating in ancient Persia as a bird with foliage in its mouth, in China it became a bird carrying flowers, and in the Japanese art of the Tenpyō period (mid-eighth century) the motif transformed into the pairing of cranes with pines.

Hummingbirds have unusual—one might say artistic—abilities in terms of flight. They can hover in midair in front of trees, flowers, and their nests, wings beating so fast as to be unseen, and yet they are able to maintain an absolutely fixed position. Viewed in slow motion on film or video, the wings move like a Moebius strip, inverting midway through their circuit.

So we see that birds possess a number of characteristics that we might find attractive and enviable. Many inventors wanted to become birdmen and engrossed themselves in attempts to create devices that would enable them to fly through the air like birds. The myth of Icarus, the Montgolfier balloon, and the early flights of the Wright brothers were all born of this desire to fly like a bird. Our dream eventually resulted in airplanes, the space shuttle, and efforts to travel in outer space.

But human fascination with birds did not limit itself to the dream of flight. Another dream was to speak the language of birds or to commune with their spirits.

Bird deities

Birds twitter, chatter, and chirp, as though they are speaking a special language. And so, from ancient times to the present, beliefs and customs have evolved that are associated with the attempt to understand the language of birds.

The Japanese word for twittering, *saezuru,* derives from an ancient phrase (*sahe izuru*) meaning "to create difficulty"—in other words, to speak in a way that is difficult to understand. People speaking an unintelligible language were called *sahegi*. The ancient Greeks referred to people speaking unfamiliar languages as *barbaroi* (barbarians), and the Chinese had a similar term, *jueshe* (literally, "shrike's tongue"). To imply that other people spoke like birds was of course derogatory, and the linguist Matsuoka Shizuo, younger brother of folklorist Yanagita Kunio, speculated that *sahegi* meant to block or to forcefully resist, and *kotosahegu* meant the impediment or incomprehension of speech, so that by extension, *sahegi* became a term for barbarians who refused to accept civilization. At one time, the Korean language was derogatorily referred to as *kara saezuri* ("continental chatter").

I've been interested in the history of the word *sahegi* for quite a while. It is the root of the ancient clan name Saeki. In my book on Kūkai (774–835), founder of the Shingon sect of Buddhism, *Kūkai no yume* (Dreams of Kūkai, 2005), I point out that Saeki was Kūkai's family name and suggest that the Saeki clan was known for being adept in matters having to do with language and storytelling.

Traditions around the world hear the voice of the divine in the language of the birds. In some cultures this developed into full-fledged systems of divination; in others, birds themselves were deified, as in ancient Egypt, where the moon god Thoth was depicted with the head of an ibis, and Horus, the god of light, was identified with the falcon.

In addition, auspicious or mythological birds arose in various cultures: the stork and nightingale in Europe, the Garuda or Garutmān in India, the *fenghuang* (phoenix) in China, and the *suzaku* ("vermilion bird"; C. *zhuque*) in Japan.

Throughout Eurasia birds have been thought of as spirit-bearers, and as sacred or spiritual beings. In Japan the crow (*karasu*) has been widely venerated, particularly in the form of the *misaki-garasu*, divine messenger crows that are believed to guide us toward the future (*misaki* refers to a guide or envoy from the heavens). In Japanese mythology, a giant crow called Yatanokarasu (also known as Yatagarasu) guided Emperor Jinmu on his campaign to unify the realm; this idea of the crow as guide probably stemmed from the image of crows returning to the forested mountains at dusk, which overlapped with the mystery of what happens to the human spirit after death—inspiring the belief that the future course of our lives might be divined by observing the movements of crows.

The Yatanokarasu is often depicted as a three-legged crow, a rather unusual image that has its roots in China. The messenger of Xiwangmu, Queen Mother of the West, the three-legged crow (C. Sanzuwu, Jinwu) was regarded as an avatar of the sun. In Japan the three-legged crow became the symbol of the Kumano and Sannō Hie shrines. In modern times the Japan Football Association adopted the three-legged crow for its logo. The original design was created in 1931 by the sculptor Hinago Jitsuzō, and contemporary sources suggest that he based the image on the description of the three-legged crow in the *Huainanzi*, an early Daoist text, along with other inspirations, including the myth of Yatanokarasu.

Related to these topics is the pictographic *karasu moji* ("crow script") employed on talismans distributed by the Kumano shrines. In it, lively flocks of stylized crows congregate, jostle, and overlap to form the kanji of the text.

Crows are associated with the founding stories of many Shinto shrines, including Itsukushima Shrine in Hiroshima, Ise Grand Shrine, and Tamatsushima Shrine in Wakayama prefecture. Perhaps even more famous are the doves associated with the more than ten thousand Hachiman shrines nationwide, some of which use a "dove script" (*hato moji*) on sacred talismans, similar to the "crow script" of Kumano.

Several shrines venerate birds other than the crow or dove as messengers of the deities. Suwa Shrine in Nagano prefecture venerates the night heron and the grey heron native to the region; Mishima Shrine in Ehime is linked to the white heron that led Kōno Michiari to victory in repelling the Mongol invasion of 1281; Kashima Shrine in Ibaraki is associated with the golden eagle that was the mount for the deity Amatsukoyane; and the Keta Shrine on the Noto peninsula is associated with the cormorant. Certainly, many Japanese shrines are linked to birds.

The idea of birds as spirit-bearers gave birth to the image of a birdlike spirit boat, known in Japan as Ama no Torifune ("heavenly bird-boat"), which was perhaps inspired by the journeys of migratory birds.

Two shrines, Tamasaki Jinja and Tamayori Jinja, stand at opposite ends of Chiba prefecture's Kujūkurihama (literally, "the beach of 99 *ri*," or about 60 kilometers). During the course of researching the Kujūkuri area some years ago (the Kujūku Project), I discovered that the archives of these two shrines hold writings that give a detailed version of the Ama no Torifune myth. They relate that a boat appeared out of the heavens, made of rock and camphor wood (*iwakusu*). In it rode a company of gods who scattered beautiful jewels. These jewels fell into the ocean, and where they washed up on shore, at opposite ends of Kujūkurihama, the Tamasaki and Tamayori shrines were constructed. The boat in which the gods rode was called Ama no Torifune.

Ama no Torifune is also associated with the motif of the *utsurobune* ("hollow boat"), to be discussed in more detail in chapter 8, "Time," and references to it can be found in a variety of legends, folk tales, and stories, including the fantasy novel *Utsurobune* (1986) by Shibusawa Tatsuhiko.

Another Japanese myth centers on a bird, presumably a rooster, called Tokoyo no Naganakidori ("bird of the long cry from the eternal world").

It is said to have lured the sun goddess Amaterasu out of the Rock Cave of Heaven with its song. Amaterasu had hidden herself in the cave, plunging the world into darkness.

In ancient times roosters were kept by the Haji clan, caretakers of the imperial tombs and artisans who fashioned earthenware *haniwa* figurines. Roosters are kept as sacred birds at the Ise Grand Shrine to this day. They have always been valued as birds of liminality, crying out at the threshold between night and day.

Japanese are fond of symbols demarcating the boundaries between light and darkness, this world and the next, life and death. The dawn cry of the rooster was described using the word *tōtenkō* ("the eastern sky is crimson"). A scene in the Kabuki play *Sugawara denju tenarai kagami* pivots upon the untimely crowing of a rooster. When we were young, my sister and I delighted in reciting it because *tōtenkō* sounded to us like the cry of the rooster. The villain in this scene, Haji no Hyōe, holds a rooster over a corpse to make it crow in order to send a false signal that daybreak is near; that he bears the surname Haji, like the caretakers of the imperial tombs and rooster-guardians of antiquity, is surely not coincidental.

Ancient birdkeepers were called *torikaibe* (鳥飼部 or 鳥養部) or *torikaibito* 養鳥人, the origins of the present-day surname Torikai. And indeed, the name of Tottori 鳥取 prefecture derives from bird-hunting, but I will discuss this a bit later.

At this point we do not really know how birds were used in divination and fortune-telling in ancient times. But we do know that the direction of bird flight was used to predict the future or determine omens in rituals, and that all over the world ancient royal courts and palaces customarily caught or raised birds for the purpose of such divination.

Tales of catching or chasing after birds are common around the globe, including the European legends surrounding the bluebird and Chinese tales of bluebirds and red sparrows. *Soushen houji* (Continued Records of the Search for the Supernatural), a collection of stories attributed to the Chinese poet Tao Yuanming (365–427), includes the tale of two men who become lost in the mountains, where they are seduced by beautiful maidens. On leaving the mountains to return home, the men are each handed a pouch that they are warned not to open; when one pouch *is* opened, out flies a bluebird, and the man's soul along with it. The birth of Emperor Wu of the Han dynasty in 156 BCE was supposedly heralded by the appearance of a flock of blue sparrows. Nakano Miyoko, a specialist in Chinese literature at Hokkaido University, has studied a great number of such stories.

Many stories of this kind can be found in Japan as well. They frequently have an unusual plot centered on a person who is unable to speak until an encounter with a bird. The legend of the prince Homuchiwake is one such tale. Mute since childhood, Homuchiwake dramatically utters his first word upon seeing a white swan flying overhead. This legend as related in the *Kojiki* closely resembles similar legends of Ajisuki Takahikone, son of the deity Ōkuninushi, and of Homutsuwake in the *Nihon shoki*. These legends have interested me for some time, so let me elaborate on them a bit.

The language of birds

The Homuchiwake legend is a child-rearing tale that takes up almost a third of the section devoted to the reign of Emperor Suinin in the *Kojiki*. It gives Homuchiwake, son of Emperor Suinin and his consort Sahajihime, the epithet *ōmiko* 大御子 ("great august child"), leading scholars to suspect that it relates events of great symbolic significance. The story relates that Homuchiwake was born in a burning fortress (to which his mother had retreated to be with her brother, who had rebelled against the emperor) and that even after he grew to be a robustly bearded man, he still could not utter a word, continuing merely to cry like an infant. One day a white swan flew overhead, and hearing its cry, Homuchiwake uttered his first word. The emperor, delighted, sent a man to pursue the bird and capture it, but though he brought it to the palace and showed it to the prince, Homuchiwake would speak no more. The emperor, dejected, had a dream in which he was told that if he built a shrine, the prince would speak again. To discover who had spoken to him in the dream, the emperor ordered a divination, and it was determined that the deity who needed to be appeased was the Great Deity of Izumo. By praying to this deity, the prince gained the ability to speak, and later he married, and a magnificent shrine was built in Izumo.

The story would appear to be related to the origins of Izumo Shrine, but here I would like to draw particular attention to the fact that it was upon hearing the cry of a bird that Homuchiwake was enabled to speak. The more one ponders this, the more puzzles surface.

The first is the close resemblance between the Homuchiwake legend and the legend recorded in *Izumo no kuni fudoki* concerning Ajisuki Taka-hikone. Son of the deity Ōkuninushi, Ajisuki Takahikone could not speak, even after growing up to be a bearded man. He cried and wailed like an infant. His father put him in a boat and took him on a grand tour of many islands, but still he would not stop crying. One night Ōkuninushi had a dream in which he asked a god why his son wept and wailed, and was told that his son would begin to speak that very night. Delighted, he went to his son and encouraged him to speak, whereupon Ajisuki Takahikone uttered a single word: "Misawa." His father asked, "What place do you call by that name?" The son immediately set off, crossed a pebbled riverbank, climbed a hill, and at its summit said, "Here." As soon as he spoke, water sprang from the rocks, and Ajisuki Takahikone performed a purification ritual, cleansing himself with the spring water.

The tale of Ajisuki Takahikone closely resembles that of Homuchiwake, though there are also significant differences. In both there is a boat and the father receives a message in the form of a dream, but only the Homuchi-wake legend explains why the son was unable to speak—namely, because of a curse placed upon him by the chief deity of Izumo.

In another legend, Ajisuki Takahikone so closely resembles the deity Ame no Wakahiko that at Ame no Wakahiko's funeral he is mistaken by the mourners for the dead god restored to life, much to his anger. Ame no Wakahiko's death had been brought about by Ame no Sagume (a precursor of the Amanojaku, a trickster and troublemaker in Japanese folklore), who had convinced Ame no Wakahiko to kill a female pheasant sent to him as a divine messenger, saying its cries portended ill. When Ame no Wakahiko drew his bow and shot the bird, the arrow passed straight through it and continued up to heaven, where the god Takamimusubi caught it and threw it back, killing Ame no Wakahiko. Ajisuki Takahikone is thus also connected with birds in this rather roundabout way.

The *Nihon shoki* contains another variant of the Homuchiwake story. In it, Homutsuwake (Homuchiwake) is thirty years old, yet still cannot speak and instead cries all the time. On the eighth day of the tenth month, Emperor Suinin and Homutsuwake are standing together in front of the palace when a white swan flies overhead. Upon seeing it, Homutsuwake suddenly says, "What is that?" Delighted, the emperor dispatches Ame no Yukawatana to catch the bird that has inspired the prince to speak. Yukawatana pursues the swan as far as Izumo (some accounts say Tajima) and on the second day of the eleventh month presents it to the emperor.

From this time onward, Homutsuwake begins to speak. Yukawatana is richly rewarded and given the title Tottori no Miyatsuko ("imperial bird-catcher"). This is the origin of the name of the province (and modern prefecture) of Tottori, where Izumo is located.

If we may conclude anything from these three stories, it is the centrality of the motif in which speech or language is encouraged by birds—in which, small differences in details aside, the flight paths of birds inspire the *kotodama*, or spirit of language. Into this main theme are then introduced other elements such as the transformation of the speechless weeping deity, the origins of Izumo Shrine, and so forth.

As noted earlier, the archetype of the weeping and wailing god is Susanoo. That being the case, we may assume that the image of the rough god stands behind Homuchiwake and Ajisuki Takehikone as well. The rough gods, like the actors playing *aragoto* parts in Kabuki drama, speak little aside from a few highly charged lines.

The mythological association between the movement of birds and the secrets of language is common to many cultures. In Balinese mythology, the god of language—a parrot or parakeet—figures prominently. Our ancestors linked the twittering and chirping and cries of birds to their coming and going, high in the sky, to strange and unknown places, and imagined that somewhere lands existed where the language of birds was spoken.

Imagery of birds

As we have seen, the manner in which images of birds have been handled gives us insight into Japanese thought and cultural traditions. Not only that, but an understanding of the imagery of birds is essential to understanding certain aspects of the Japanese classics and the traditional Japanese aesthetic.

For example, episode 50 of *The Tales of Ise* (*Ise monogatari*, ninth century) begins with the following poem:

tori no ko o	How can I love someone
tō zutsu tō wa	who would care nothing for me
kasanu tomo	even were I able
omowanu hito o	to pile up hens' eggs
omou mono ka wa	ten wide and ten deep.[1]

If *tori no ko* ("birds' children") were understood to be baby chicks, this poem would make little sense. But the word means the eggs, not the chicks. From it came *torinoko*, the name, derived from the creamy color of an eggshell, for a type of handmade Japanese paper used for folding screens, sliding doors, and card stock for calligraphy and small paintings. *Torinoko* paper was an indispensable element of traditional Japanese furnishings and decoration. Today it has become much less common, but at one time, *torinoko* from Goka in Fukushima prefecture, and from Nashio in the present-day city of Nishinomiya in Hyōgo prefecture, were prized as being of the highest grade. When I do calligraphy for seasonal greetings or to amuse myself, I always use this type of paper.

In "Kochō" (Butterflies), chapter 24 of *The Tale of Genji*, a passage begins, "'The Birds' resounded bravely amid warblers' sweet carolings."[2] What does this signify? "The Birds" is the title of a well-known piece in the Gagaku repertoire, the music of the ancient Japanese court, and by extension refers to any piece of traditional music with a similar style in which the tempo rapidly increases. Gagaku compositions are usually structured in three movements (*jo*, *ha*, and *kyū*), from slow to fast, with the middle movement serving as a transition. "The Birds," which consists of a *ha* and *kyū* written in Sōjō (a somewhat unusual mode corresponding to a G Mixolydian in Western modal terminology), was so titled to distinguish it from "Kalavinka," the earlier work from which it was transposed, consisting of a *ha* and *kyū* written in the more common Ichikotsu-chō (D Mixolydian). The motif of birds did not end with the music; it was also featured in the Bugaku dance performed to it, in which the dancers wore bird wings and leggings called *chōsoku*, or "birdsfoot." The dance was traditionally paired with another called "The Butterflies," presenting performers in costumes with butterfly wings; Murasaki Shikibu's fondness for these dances gave her the seed for this chapter of her epic novel, as well as its title.

Birds are the source of several key images in folk culture and performing arts. One of these is *torioi* (bird-chasing). Originally this referred to the efforts of farmers to scare off birds that might damage their crops, and there is a Noh play titled *Torioi* (The Bird-Chasers) in which the characters do exactly that. *Torioi* was also a seasonal ritual practiced in many parts of Japan at "Little New Year," the first full moon of the year, in which the youth and children of the villages would go from house to house making a racket— as they might when frightening away birds—using household implements such as bamboo whisks, ladles, and mallets. This was similar in some ways to the *mushiokuri* (insect-chasing) rituals mentioned earlier in chapter 2.

Later, *torioi* came to refer to beggars who would appear at the front gates of houses at New Year's, singing celebratory songs while beating time with paper fans. And in the Edo period, it came to refer specifically to itinerant female entertainers who wore deeply folded straw hats (called *torioigasa*), playing the shamisen as they strolled from house to house on various occasions, including New Year's.

These forms of street entertainment are said to have originated with an individual named Yojirō who lived in the village of Hiden'in in Kyoto, so that the early *torioi* beggars were also known as *tataki no Yojirō* ("clapping Yojirōs"). The word *torioi* immediately brings to mind the celebratory New Year performances associated with Yojirō and itinerant female singers.

So we can see that *torioi* is part of the framework of popular performing arts that developed around New Year's festivities and wishes for health and long life. Even the stand-up comedy of *manzai* performances can probably be traced back to the *torioi* tradition.

The shrine gates called *torii* (literally, "bird perch") are one of the unique forms of Japanese design. I am quite fond of torii gates, and my heart leaps when one suddenly reveals itself amid the dense greenery of the mountain foothills, or I see the weathered wood of a torii standing beneath a coastal cliff or at the entrance to a lonely stretch of seacoast. It never pleases me to see these replaced with shiny concrete replicas.

Torii are quite mysterious. I have devoted much research to them, and still don't fully understand them. Some claim that they derive from Indian *torana* stone gates like those at the great stupa at Sanchi, or from the wooden gates in south China and northern Thailand decorated with bird figures along the top. I have given up trying to discover the origins of customs such as painting torii a bright vermilion, or setting large numbers of them in long colonnades as at Fushimi Inari

Lusheng pillar with bird totem, Miao people, southern China. From Hagiwara Hidesaburō, *Ine to tori to taiyō no michi* (The Way of Rice, Birds, and the Sun; Taishūkan Shoten, 1996).

Shrine. It is also unclear why so many shrines have a series of torii that must be passed through on the path to the main building.

Painting torii vermilion probably has something to do with warding off evil, but it is impossible to tell whether the custom originated in the use of vermilion during the Kofun period, as in the sixth-century Hinooka burial mound in northern Kyushu, or whether it derives from the vermilion associated with the Niu cult that drew Kūkai's interest after his introduction of esoteric Buddhism from China to Japan in the early ninth century. While I suspect that the Niu cult and the significance it placed on vermilion can be traced deep into Japanese antiquity, and that vermilion was used from ancient times in funerary applications and to protect against evil, the connections with torii are still unsubstantiated.

One reason is that the archetypal style of Japanese shrines, which is modeled on ancient raised-floor residences and granaries, featured unpainted wood, meaning there should have been little need for introducing vermilion paint. But vermilion was considered to have magical powers by the Daoist alchemists of China, who believed that minute amounts of what they called *dansha* or *zhusha* (literally, "cinnabar sand" and "vermilion sand"; powdered mercuric sulfides), skillfully formulated, could be turned into an elixir of longevity or immortality. In Japan sources of cinnabar were called *niu* and written with the kanji 丹生, "cinnabar-producing." The Chinese word for alchemy, *liandan* 錬丹, likewise contains the character 丹 for cinnabar, indicating its importance to the art. The painting of torii and other shrine structures with cinnabar-based vermilion pigments probably arose out of a belief, similar to that of the Daoists, that this precious mineral had properties related to longevity.

Yet as we know from the Minamata disease of the 1950s and 1960s, which was caused by mercury poisoning from industrial pollution, mercury ingested in even relatively small quantities can result in serious neurological damage, abnormalities in children, and even paralysis and death. Ancient records tell us that the gilding of the Great Buddha of Nara required huge volumes of mercury, and that many involved with the work fell sick or died from mercury poisoning. Even so, mercury was a precious commodity, and it is believed that fierce struggles erupted over control of the principal mercury deposits distributed through the island of Shikoku and the provinces of Kii and Ise.

Kūkai also had a deep connection with *niu*. The temple complex that he founded on Mount Kōya on the Kii peninsula lay in an area known to have some of the richest mercury deposits in Japan. Ancient documents state that Mount Kōya was ruled by a female deity called Nibutsuhime 丹生都比売, in what is probably a reference to the Niu clan of mercury miners who controlled the region and who worshipped Nibutsuhime as their tutelary deity. While doing research for an NHK documentary, I learned about a series of mercury deposits along the Japan Median Tectonic Line linking Shikoku with the Kii peninsula, with evidence of a number of ancient mining operations distributed along the pilgrimage routes linking Mount Kōya with Yoshino and Ise. Not only that, more than a third of the eighty-eight temples on the pilgrimage route associated with Kūkai encircling the island of Shikoku are located on sites rich in mercury. So I would conjecture that Kūkai negotiated with the Niu clan to obtain this precious resource, leading him to establish the monastic complex at Mount Kōya as his base of operations.

Such is the background behind the mercury sulfide used to make the vermilion pigment painted on torii. The painting, then, seems to have been done to make the torii serve as some sort of sign or marker, though of what no one knows for certain. Yet whatever else it might signify, the torii has undoubtedly always stood as a demarcation between this world (*here*) and the other world (*there*). And it follows that the removal of a torii would invite bad luck.

Songs of Birds and Insects by Mountain Folk

To better understand how the Japanese saw birds in relation to their daily lives, let us turn to popular culture. Here, I would like to introduce a selection of lyrics from *Sanka chōchū ka* (Songs of Birds and Insects by Mountain Folk), an Edo-period compilation of songs for Bon festival dances that popular writers of the period such as Ryūtei Tanehiko used as source material. The songs illustrate some of the conventional ideas about birds within mainstream Japanese culture.

washi wa yamagara	I am a *yamagara*
e ni otosarete	lured by feed
akari shōji no uchi ni sumu	into living behind *shoji* screens.
	(Yamato region)

The *yamagara* (*Parus varius*) are wild birds that were caged and kept as pets in the Edo period. They appear in poetry and songs as a metaphor for the women of the pleasure quarters, whose entrapment behind the shoji screens of teahouses and brothels is compared here to that of birds in a cage. As we saw in chapter 1, "Mountains," the women of the pleasure quarters spoke a language full of coded words, such as the term "mountain guests" referring to visiting Buddhist clergy.

hitori yamamichi   Traveling alone on this mountain path
monosugo gozaru   is awfully lonesome
hayaku koe dase   so hurry up and sing to me,
hototogisu   cuckoo!

(Yamato region)

This is the classic treatment of the cuckoo in Japanese verse; its lively voice encouraged travelers on their way.

kiji no mendori   The female pheasant
susuki no moto de   weeps plaintively
tsuma o tazunete   amid the pampas grass
hororo utsu   searching for its mate.

(Yamato region)

The pairing of pheasants with pampas grass is typical. The cry of the pheasant sounds to Japanese ears like weeping, and is frequently likened to it, as in this poem from the *Kokinshū*:

haru no no no   My tears overflow
shigeki kusaba no   like the sad call
tsumagoi ni   of the lone pheasant
tobitatsu kiji no   flying up to seek a wife
hororo to zo naku   sweet as the young grass in the spring fields.[3]

omoinaoshi wa   Will you not have a change of heart,
nai ka yo sama yo   my husband?
tori wa furusu e   don't the birds also return
kaeranu ka   to their old nests?

(Yamato region)

This song is based on a famous poem by Emperor Sutoku:

hana wa ne ni	Flowers have returned
tori wa furusu ni	to their roots and birds have gone
kaeru nari	back to their old nests
haru no tomari o	but no one knows where the spring
shiru hito zo naki	will find its final haven.[4]

The song transforms this into the plea of a woman addressing a wayward lover. The Noh plays *Tōboku* (Northeast) and *Ebira* (The Quiver) also make use of this image of flowers returning to their roots and birds to their former nests.

hiyohiyo to naku wa	The one crying *hiyohiyo*
hiyodori	is the bulbul
nakanu wa	those who do not cry
ike no tomo ni	are the mandarin ducks
oshidori tsurete yuku	traveling the pond with their companions.

(Izumi region)

This is the original of a number of variant versions distributed through western Japan. It plays the typical Japanese image of mandarin ducks as symbols of conjugal love fairly straight, while also adding a pun on the name of the birds (*oshidori*) and the word for "mute" (*oshi*). The bulbul is a solitary bird.

tori mo kayowanu	Though this place
miyama no oku ni	is so deep in the mountains that
sumeba miyako ja no yo	even the birds don't frequent it—
tono yo	"Home is where you make it," isn't it,
	my husband?

(Settsu region)

"Even the birds don't frequent it" is a stock phrase that suggests how much the Japanese associate birds with coming and going between distant places.

tsubakuro mo	The swallows, too,
noki no sumika ni kaeru	return to their homes beneath the eaves

| kimi wa nani yue | so why is it that you |
| kaeranu zo | will not come home to me? |

(Iga region)

The image of swallows returning to their nests was initially borrowed from Chinese poetry, but by the Edo period, virtually every home in Japan had swallows' nests under the eaves.

kimi wa kogarasu	You are like a young crow
ware wa mata	making me burn for love
owa o karasu no	while I too flap my wings like a crow
hane bataki	with tail feathers in miserable disarray.

(Tōtōmi region)

This verse hinges on two sets of puns: *kogarasu* means "young crow" as well as "to cause to burn (for love)," and *karasu* "crow" as well as "to make wither, to make shabby." "To have one's tail feathers in disarray" is a stock expression still used in Japan to describe falling on hard times. The song describes the plight of a man who has been ruined by a courtesan.

tsuma wa kitaguni	My husband is in the north country
mada kaeranu ka	and still cannot come home
fumi o yaritashi	perhaps I can send word
kaeru kari	with the returning geese.

(Kazusa region)

"Message of the geese" is a poetic expression for letters and other missives. Here the feelings of a wife waiting for the return of her spouse are expressed through the image of migrating geese. In the phenomenology of nature in Japanese culture, geese are a symbol of winter frequently depicted in traditional paintings.

aita mita sa wa	Though my longing for you
tobitatsu gotoku	leaves me all aflutter
kago no tori ka ya	I am, alas
urameshiya	but a bird in a cage.

(Shinano region)

| kago no tori de wa | It is not that |
| washa gozaranedo | I am a caged bird |

```
oya ga dasaneba          yet until my parents free me
kago no tori             a caged bird I am.
```
(Shinano region)

Fans of the popular music of the Shōwa era (1926–89) will recognize these two songs as sources for the well-known ballad "Kago no tori" (Caged Bird), in itself an indication of how deeply the image of the caged bird—as a metaphor for the life of a woman trapped in the pleasure quarters—resonated with the sentiments of the people.

```
washi wa kono chō no     I am a sparrow living
nokiba no suzume         under the eaves of this town
koe de kikishire         know me by my voice
na o yobu na             but do not call me by name.
```
(Kōzuke region)

From long ago, the sparrow has been one of Japan's most popular birds, and a synonym for chatterbox. It was also a slang term for streetwalkers.

```
shirasagi ya             The white egret
fune no hesaki ni        makes its nest
su o kakete              in the prow of the boat
nami ni yurarete         where, rocked by the waves,
shan to tatsu            it stands so straight and tall.
```
(Shimotsuke region)

The egret is a bird familiar throughout Japan that is often seen standing amid the fields and paddies, head cocked and alert. This image was also used in a well-known Shōwa-era popular song by Takada Kōkichi. Egret-themed dances are a part of many Japanese festivals, most famously the Gion Festival in Kyoto.

```
kigisu no ni sumu        Pheasants in the fields
hibari wa yama ni        skylarks in the mountains
uzura awabo ni           quail amid the ripening millet
tsuma omoi               all long for their mates.
```
(Noto region)

For some reason, in Japan the pheasant and the crane were considered to possess deep parental and filial sentiments. Quails feed on millet; when it was ripening in the autumn, the birds were thought to feel especially strongly for their mates.

tsukiyo karasu wa
mayōtemo naku ga
washi ga shinjitsu
omou demo nashi

On moonlit nights
the crows cry out when led astray
and though you cry after me too
you don't think me true.

(Echigo region)

This song picks up on a theme found in the *kyōgen* play *Hanago* ("Here in this forest in the mountain's shadow, the crows always caw on moonlit nights") and in an earlier type of popular song known as *ryūtatsu-bushi* ("On moonlit nights the crows cry longingly; perhaps I am a crow, to weep so longingly for you"). It was based on the notion that crows cry because they mistake the brightness of a moonlit night for the dawn; by extension, "crow on a moonlit night" could also mean a fickle lover. The *ryūtatsu-bushi* was a song form that became popular in the Momoyama period (1568–1600) and was a precursor of the songs collected in *Sanka chōchū ka*.

tani no koyabu ni
suzume wa tomaru
tomete tomaranu
iro no michi

The sparrow stops
in a valley thicket
there's no stopping
the way of love.

(Tanba region)

"Sparrows and bamboo" is a motif originally borrowed from China, where it was a popular theme for ink paintings. But here this inky solemnity is mocked in the popular imagination by giving it an erotic twist.

tori mo harahara
yoru mo honobono to
kane mo narimasu
teradera ni

The birds flutter aloft
in the brightening dawn
as the bells resound
from temple to temple.

(Awa region)

Harahara represents the sound of the wings of a flock of birds taking flight; *honobono* expresses the gathering light of dawn. Mimetic words such as these have been an integral part of the Japanese language from earliest times.

Hawks and bells

In 1972 Andrei Tarkovsky made a brilliant film adaptation of Stanislav Lem's celebrated science fiction novel *Solaris* (1961). In it, footage of Tokyo's expressways was used to represent a city of the future.

A crucial element in the film is the appearance of a mysterious woman—Hari, the dead wife of the main character—in a space station orbiting the planet Solaris, whose sentient ocean has given embodiment to this apparition of his guilty conscience. Hari's appearance is heralded by the tinkling of small bells that adorn her dress.

The instant I saw this scene it brought to mind the bells of Siberian shamans. The shamans of the Gilyak (Nivkh) and Ural-Altaic peoples in Siberia wear tubular iron bells suspended from their hips that sound as they walk, leading them to a higher state of consciousness. In the early twentieth century, research by the Finnish ethnologist Uno Harva on shamanism and by archaeologist Fujimori Eiichi on Japanese prehistoric bronze bells (*dōtaku*) provided a wealth of information on this subject of the spiritual uses of bells.

At the beginning of chapter 3, "Deities," I mentioned similar customs in Japan when I discussed divine visitations (*otozure*) and the bronze bells called *sanagi* that our ancestors used to elevate their consciousness. The staging by Tarkovsky of Hari's appearances in *Solaris* resonate with this.

Bells are instruments for channeling the spirit and altering consciousness. This is why the female attendants (*miko*) at Shinto shrines shake clusters of bells during ceremonies and rituals. Bells were also tied to the feet of birds in traditional falconry.

Falconry has its basis in the veneration of birds and appears to have been practiced widely throughout the world. It was part of the Egyptian, Assyrian, and Persian cultures. In Carolingian Europe, large-scale hunts involved large numbers of falconers. In East Asia, the gyrfalcons of the Liaodong peninsula were especially famous, and there are records of falconry being enthusiastically practiced in Korean states such as Goguryeo and Joseon, and by the Jurchen tribes of Manchuria.

Historical dramas on film and television tend to give the impression that falconry in Japan was limited to the Tokugawa shoguns, but that is not the case. This style of hunting was practiced since ancient times—from the establishment of the Yamato court in the third century, or perhaps even earlier—accompanied by a special ritual called *hōyō* ("release of hawks"). The thirteenth-century chronicle *Azuma kagami* (Mirror of the East) cites the claim that falconry was first practiced in Japan in the ninth month of the forty-third year of the reign of Emperor Nintoku (traditionally identified as 357 CE).

Falconry was originally a method of hunting food. But in Japan it developed into something more akin to an outdoor sport, in addition to gaining great symbolic significance, as we can see in the custom of attaching small gold- or silver-plated bells to the birds' feet or tails before releasing them.

When hawks and falcons wearing such bells were set free to hunt, the sound of the bells would float through the air, demarcating the entire region within earshot as a special place, a *kuni* (domain or realm). Seeing these majestic birds circling high overhead did something to elevate and calm the human spirit. Since references to falconry abound in Shakespeare as well, it appears that people in both the East and the West attached special significance to hawks and their bells.

As an aside, I would point out that what Tarkovsky was able to achieve with the bells in *Solaris* is something too often missing from Japanese cinema. Japanese tend to be overly concerned with psychology, and to focus too much on dealing with human relationships while not giving sufficient attention to depicting as background the kind of scene that Tarkovsky inserts to such great effect in *Solaris*.

Futagami no	Hither and yon
otemo konomo ni	around twin-peaked Futagami
ami sashite	I set the traps,
a ga matsu taka o	and I waited for my hawk—
ime ni tsugetsu mo	and then came the news in a dream![5]

This poem is by Ōtomo no Yakamochi (c. 718–85), one of the editors of the *Man'yōshū*, the oldest extant anthology of Japanese poetry. That, however, was not the only measure of Yakamochi's greatness as a historical figure; the *Man'yōshū* became an archetype for the Japanese spirit and sensibility, and behind his work on it lay a most ambitious purpose.

The *tomo* in Ōtomo signifies a communal social organization—a clan engaged in a specialized profession. In its heyday the Ōtomo clan provided the ancient imperial court with the majority of its technocrats (at one time dominating the military), but it was gradually squeezed out of the centers of power by the rising fortunes of the Soga and later the Fujiwara family.

The Ōtenmon Conspiracy of 866, in which Tomo no Yoshio (a descendant of the Ōtomo) was forced from power in a plot engineered by the Fujiwara, signaled the turning point in the decline of the Ōtomo. As a clan leader during this period of waning power, Yakamochi worked to preserve the fading legacy of the Ōtomo and open a pathway for the future of the clan. In Japanese cultural history, the end of antiquity is marked by the eclipse of the world of the *Man'yōshū*—in which the Ōtomo held sway—by the Fujiwara-dominated world of the *Kokinshū*.

Yakamochi's poem reflects this. Futagami is a mountain in Etchū province (present-day Toyama prefecture), where Yakamochi served as governor. The poem relates how Yakamochi placed nets around the mountain in the hope of catching a prized hunting hawk that he had lost, and then had a dream foretelling its return. A larger vision underlies this story.

At the time a vast national network of provincial temples (*kokubunji*) and convents (*kokubun niji*) was being constructed, headed by Tōdaiji, the temple housing the Great Buddha in Nara. This grand project reflected the increasing power of the Fujiwara within the central government, compared with the decline of the Ōtomo family fortunes, which was becoming more and more apparent. Thus in his poem Yakamochi, like the people of old, is envisioning his hawk in flight and wishing to know how far its spirit might range. The hawk has not yet returned—Japan has grown so much larger than in former times! Nevertheless, his dream says the bird will return, and so he continues to wait. Here is another poem by Yakamochi about a hawk:

yakatao no mashiro no taka o   Keeping in my chamber
yado ni sue kakinade mitsutsu   my arrow-tailed white hawk,
kawakushi yoshimo   I pat and stroke its back—
                                  O the pleasure of it![6]

Clearly hawks held a special significance for this poet. The French philosopher Gaston Bachelard wrote that birds have an "instinct for confidence in the world," which can stimulate "the very impetus of the imagination."[7] It seems to me that Yakamochi must have undertaken the compilation of the *Man'yōshū* with the same imaginative power he invested in his dreams of hawks.

In conclusion, I wish to emphasize that birds were seen as go-betweens connecting *here* and *there*. And like the wind, they were recognized as messengers bearing special information.

CHAPTER 6 FLOWERS

Blossoms on a withered tree

Folk tales give us a rich variety of information regarding the phenomenology of nature in Japanese culture and, beyond that, hidden insights into Japanese ethnology and folklore. As an example, let's look at the well-known story "Hanasaka Jijii" (The Old Man Who Made Withered Trees Bloom).

This story belongs to a genre known as *ko morai setsuwa* (literally, "child-receiving tales"), in which a childless couple wishing for a child is given one through some operation of magic or karma. Other examples are "Taketori monogatari" (Tale of the Bamboo Cutter), in which the infant Princess Kaguya is discovered within a stalk of bamboo; and the story of Momotarō, the Peach Boy, who is born when an old woman discovers a peach floating downriver and cuts it open to reveal a tiny boy. Issun-bōshi (One-Inch Boy) is bestowed upon another childless old couple after they pray to the gods of Sumiyoshi Shrine.

Such folk tales were common because it was once believed that children were not conceived but instead bestowed by mysterious beings transcending human knowledge and understanding. "Hanasaka Jijii" starts with an old couple longing for a child, but then the story takes a slightly different turn. While clearly grounded in the *ko morai* genre, it presents a new development.

Here is how it goes. One day, as the old man and woman set out from their house, they find a white puppy abandoned along the roadside. What they really want is a child, but the puppy is so cute and helpless that they take it home with them and raise it with the love they would have given a human child.

This basic version of the folk tale, with the rescued puppy, is common especially in northeastern Japan, but for some reason, as we move westward through the rest of the country, a number of variants arise featuring different animals: turtles, geese, and so on.

One of the fundamental principles of the folk tale is the substitution of one important element or concept for another. Here, the puppy serves as a substitute for the desired human child. Many stories are built on the principle of satisfying some deficiency or lack with something from a different order or category.

In any case, the old man and woman cherish the puppy as they would a child. They give it the meat of the fish they catch, contenting themselves with the bones, and raise it to be big and strong. One day the man and dog go into the mountains to gather firewood. They come to a place where the dog barks insistently, pawing at the ground. When the man digs in that spot, he finds a cache of gold coins. Amazed, he offers thanks to the gods.

Already the story points to a number of suggestive issues.

The first is going woodcutting in the mountains, an important element in Japanese folklore. The folk tale "Kachikachi Yama" (Crackling Mountain) and the "Tale of the Bamboo Cutter" both have scenes involving wood- or bamboo cutting. The old bamboo cutter is a representative of the "mountain people" (*yama no tami* or *yamabito*). As we saw in chapter 1, "Mountains," such folk developed into the foresters (*matagi*), woodworkers (*kijishi*), hunters, prospectors, and mountain ascetics who created the folkways and popular conceptions of the mountainous regions of Japan. Storylines involving an old man going into the mountains to gather firewood reflect the traditions of such mountain people.

The notion of a dog barking at the place where something is buried also tells us something important. This story template comes to Japan from China and has been analyzed in detail by Sawada Mizuho, a scholar of Chinese literature and folklore, in books such as *Chūgoku no minkan shinkō* (Popular Religion in China, 1982) and *Kishu dangi: Chūgoku yūki no sekai* (The World of Chinese Ghosts and Spirits, 1976).

Shirakawa Shizuka, a noted authority on the etymology of kanji, tells us that the character 書 (meaning "calligraphy" or "book") depicts something being exhumed from the earth, something buried being revealed.

Similar ideas inform the legends surrounding Mount Kōya. In the preceding chapter, I introduced Nibutsuhime (also known as Niu Myōjin) as a female deity associated with mercury who alighted at Mount Kōya, a site rich in deposits of this metallic element. Nibutsuhime ruled over the area with a previously established male tutelary deity, Kariba Myōjin (also known as Kōya Myōjin). Then the scholar-monk Kūkai arrived seeking to establish his great monastic complex, and at that time, the story goes, Kariba Myōjin appeared with two dogs, one black and one white, to lead him to the mountain. According to research by Gorai Shigeru, Kariba Myōjin represents the Inukai clan, whose name literally means "dog keeper."

FLOWERS

In short, dogs, like birds, serve as messengers of the deities. Dogs guide the lost, functioning to free them from the labyrinth of confusion. This is a motif in tales throughout Japan associated with the Inukai clan. The Inukai fostered a belief in *inugami*—"dog spirits," who could possess human beings—a motif later employed in fiction by writers such as Yumeno Kyūsaku in *Inugami hakase* (Dr. Inugami, 1931–32) and Yokomizo Seishi in *Inugami-ke no ichizoku* (The Inugami Clan, 1950–51).

But let's return to the story of Hanasaka Jijii. Delighted by the gold coins, the old man carries them home, and he and his wife place them reverently on their household shrine. At this point, their mean old neighbor appears to borrow live coals for his fire.

This business of borrowing fire is a significant theme in Japanese folklore. It was often used as a pretext for snooping around a neighbor's house; generally speaking, if a neighbor showed up at the door asking to borrow fire, the household would rush about, straightening things up and hiding anything they didn't want seen. Especially in the days before matches, it was not so easy to light fires. So people tried to keep them burning continuously, which made charcoal a valuable commodity, charcoal-making an important occupation, and keeping a supply of charcoal on hand a basic housekeeping rule. Nevertheless, sometimes the fire would go out. Even in the Kyoto home of my youth, in winter my mother would start the day by lighting charcoal on the gas burner and then distributing the live coals to the hibachi used to heat each room.

So live coals were precious, and neighbors frequently shared them with one another, which also gave them an excuse to see what everyone else was up to. It follows that in our story, when the neighbor shows up at their door, the old man and his wife have every reason to be wary.

Of course the neighbor is there because he has somehow learned about the gold coins, which he soon figures out the dog had something to do with finding. He manages to convince the couple to lend him the dog. But the mean old man does not treat the dog kindly; he eats all of the fish and gives the dog only the bones—he's the polar opposite of the sweet old couple. The dog doesn't do anything for him, so he gets frustrated with it and, in a fit of rage, kills it.

The kind old man is heartbroken. He collects the dog's body and buries it in the mountains. Eventually, a stately pine grows out of the grave. This is a motif—transformation into plants—common throughout the world: for example, in Greek mythology, it figures in the stories of Adonis, Daphne, and Narcissus. Adonis was born from a scar in the myrrh tree that his mother, Myrrha, had been transformed into as a result of Aphrodite's machinations. Daphne is transformed into a laurel tree by her father, the river god Peneus, so that she may escape being ravished by the god Apollo. And Narcissus, of course, is turned as a result of his own vanity into the flower that bears his name.

Back to our story. In remembrance of his beloved dog, the old man decides to use the trunk of the pine tree to make a mortar for pounding rice cakes. But the first blow of the pestle produces a gold coin! And with each successive strike, the mortar brings forth more coins. Once again the mean neighbor arrives and convinces the couple to lend him the mortar, hoping to enrich himself. But when he pounds it, nothing comes out except junk. Enraged, he breaks the mortar into pieces and burns it.

The kind old man, duped and disappointed once again, takes the ashes of the mortar home in a basket. But as he is walking, a wind comes up, blowing some of the ashes onto a withered cherry tree—which suddenly bursts into bloom. This strange and wondrous occurrence makes the old man into something of a local superstar.

Rumor of this eventually reaches the ears of the daimyo, who commands the old man to restore to health a cherry tree standing before them. The kind old man scatters some of the ashes on the tree, and it bursts into bloom. This command performance, brilliantly executed, concludes the tale of Hanasaka Jijii.

Narrative principles

"Hanasaka Jijii" features a number of motifs found in Japanese folklore. Examining them in detail, we can discover some of the archetypes common to Japanese narrative.

As mentioned earlier, there are many regional variants of this tale. In some, the dog is a turtle; in the version known as "The Old Man Who Caught Geese," when the ashes fly up on the wind at the end, they bring down a flock of geese; in another variant the couple find an incense box floating in the river, and open it to find a puppy. This last story is somewhat similar to the Momotarō folk tale. By the way, I believe that Momotarō's animal companions—the dog (*inu*), pheasant (*kiji*), and monkey (*saru*)—

represent the Inukai clan, woodworkers (*kijishi*), and a clan associated with either the deity Sarutahiko or the related deity Sarume, respectively.

The envious neighbor who tries and fails to emulate the successes of the protagonist is another common narrative motif. The Muromachi-period illustrated handscroll *Fukutomi sōshi* tells another story of this type.

The story deals with a man living on the outskirts of Kyoto named Fukutomi no Oribe, who excels at a very particular art—farting for the amusement of the aristocrats. For his efforts in this regard, he receives heaps of presents. His neighbor, a poor man known as Bokushō no Tōta, is driven by envy to try to learn the secrets of his technique but is never able to become more than a mediocre flatulist. This all sounds rather preposterous, but there are numerous stories of this kind, and the Edo-period writer, physician, polymath, and painter Hiraga Gennai (1728–80) is renowned for continuing this tradition in his essay *Hōhiron* (On Farting).

Archetypes and recurring motifs appear in numerous other folk tales as well, from Momotarō and Princess Kaguya to Crackling Mountain and Urashima Tarō. In Japanese such stories are known as *monogatari,* which is itself an unusual word. *Mono* means "thing"; *kataru* is "to speak, tell, relate." So we have things that speak—but these "things" can be both material and spiritual. Moreover, they are capable of possessing other things. These possessive entities are free-floating, found anywhere and everywhere, like elementary particles or neutrinos, filling all the gaps and cracks in the universe.

Monogatari are stories about worlds populated by these matter-spirit entities. People in the past no doubt invested far more meaning in, and were more deeply affected by, these narratives than is the case for us today.

Monogatari adhere to a certain set of narrative principles. First and foremost, they were originally transmitted as an oral tradition. Itinerant storytellers would travel from region to region, sometimes even making an appearance before the imperial court. Moreover, the tales spread by these traveling storytellers merged with local traditions to produce variants at the village level. Tales grew and developed through the act of being told in village households; a storyteller—usually an old man or woman—would settle down by the hearth, the family would gather, neighbors might drop by, and the storyteller would say, "Well, how about it?" and launch into a story.

"Well, how about it?" was the storyteller's rhetorical question to the people whom he knew were waiting to hear him. Then, from the moment he said, "Once upon a time," the room and the villagers in it would be transported into a magical realm transcending space and time.

Once they had thus entered the realm of the narrative, the storyteller might insert any number of exaggerations or amusing incidents from his own experience to entertain his audience. This may be the reason old men and women feature prominently in so many folk tales. The narrator—indispensable to the narrative in any case—has been inserted into the story itself.

Structuralist thinkers such as Claude Lévi-Strauss and Roland Barthes were keenly interested in narrative techniques and the process of narrative transmission. In Japan as in the West, narrative archetypes were developed by specialists—either bards attached to ancient royal courts or more humble local storytellers. In Japan the courtly bards are exemplified by Hieda no Are, who memorized the orally transmitted lore that was compiled and edited into the *Kojiki*. Hieda no Are was a member of a clan that specialized in memorizing and preserving prayers and other ritual incantations. The Inbe and Nakatomi were other examples of clans tasked with carrying on the memory of *furukoto* 古言 or 古事—the deeds and words of the past—a word reflected in the title of the *Kojiki* 古事記 (Record of Ancient Matters). In the preceding chapter we encountered *sahegi* as an ancient term for people speaking an unintelligible language. The members of the Saeki clan that emerged from these *sahegi* were specialized regional storytellers who were summoned to the central court. Members of the Saeki clan from throughout the land were always invited to the Daijōsai, the central ritual in the enthronement of a new emperor.

In addition to such official or semiofficial narrative specialists were many others who served as storytellers and conveyors of tradition, notably performing artists and religious practitioners such as those associated with Shugendō. These folk traveled throughout the country, which was a significant factor in their attributes as narrators, since they were exposed to a wide variety of tales. Known as "wandering people" (*yugyō no tami*), they included itinerant monks and *yamabushi* mountain ascetics, the lute-playing narrative chanters known as *biwa hōshi*, and a variety of performing-arts troupes.

Shirabyōshi dancers and courtesans, too, became narrators. And so what we might call regional editorial centers emerged to support the evolution of such grassroots narrative traditions, typically in highway post towns—such as Aohaka in Gifu and Ashigara near Hakone—with large numbers of brothels. Itinerant monks and artists would stop there on their travels and teach the dancers and courtesans stories from all over the country, which the women would remember and pass on. Many were set to music, giving birth to the *imayō* and other popular song traditions.

Another fundamental principle of *monogatari* is that most are based on some sort of structured fictional world. This basic stage setting, which I refer to as a "world model," is central to the story, remaining stable amid changes of scene and perspective. The world model provides a symbolic premise, like the world mountain Sumeru or the world tree discussed in chapter 1, "Mountains," or the idea of a vast river cleaving the world in two.

After first setting out this basic world model, folk tales often go on to mobilize a set of structural oppositions in their plots: old man / old woman; beautiful girl / ugly girl; spiteful older sister / lovable younger sister; mountains/village; heaven/earth; light/darkness; this side / other side of the river; rich man / poor man; king/beggar; god/devil; and so on. Such structural oppositions power countless myths, legends, folk tales, religious scriptures, and works of literature, from *Cinderella* and *Snow White* to *The Red and the Black*, *The Hunchback of Notre Dame*, *The Brothers Karamazov*, *Dr. Jekyll and Mr. Hyde*, and *The Wonderful Wizard of Oz*.

Practitioners of Kabuki theater also speak of "establishing a world" (*sekai sadame*). Kabuki plays are classified by plot into one of several "worlds," each with its own established conventions, so that, for example, works about the Soga brothers belong to one world while *Chūshingura* and related works about the forty-seven ronin belong to another. These worlds can have a "front" and a "back"—for example, the grisly ghost story *Yotsuya kaidan* serves as the flip side of the more noble and heroic tale of *Chūshingura*. Indeed, *Yotsuya kaidan*, which features characters belonging to the same daimyo house as the forty-seven ronin, was originally written as a companion piece (*nibanme*) for *Kanadehon Chūshingura*, and its first staging took the unorthodox step of alternating back and forth between the two works, a few acts at a time over two days, rather than performing them sequentially.

Another narrative device common to folk tales is the scene switch. These stories usually begin—"once upon a time"—with a quick shift of time and space. Next a structural opposition is introduced—for example, in the form of an old man and an old woman: the old man goes to the mountains to cut wood, the old woman to the river to wash clothes. Then the scene switches: "Meanwhile, the spiteful old neighbor . . . ." This simple narrative structure is still quite effective today. Hashida Sugako's immensely popular television drama of the mid-1980s, *Oshin*, draws inspiration from *Cinderella*, while George Lucas's *Star Wars* borrows heavily from Joseph Campbell's research into the common structural underpinnings of the archetypal hero in myths from around the world.

Folk tales also embody something we might call "a yearning for the uncommon." It is this element that makes them so memorable. A classic example is "Sannen Netarō" (The Young Man Who Slept for Three Years). Of an age when he should be working, Sannen Netarō does nothing but sleep, waking only to eat and then sleep once more. This goes on for three years, distressing his elderly parents, until one day he suddenly jumps into action, achieves success, finds himself a good wife, and lives happily ever after. This is the basic pattern: events that would not normally occur, but do. In the story of Hanasaka Jijii, there is an extended series of such extraordinary events: the dog leading the old man to buried treasure, the mortar that produces gold coins, the blossoms blooming on a withered tree.

The uncommon can frequently be gruesome or shocking. "Little Red Riding Hood," as related by Charles Perrault and the Brothers Grimm, is a famous example, but there are a number of Japanese folk tales that seem almost too brutal to tell to young children, such as "Shitakiri Suzume" (The Tongue-Cut Sparrow), "Bunbuku Chagama" (The Magic Teakettle), and "Crackling Mountain," in which the characters are variously maimed or burned alive. The cruelty is part of what makes the story out of the ordinary—though it is also difficult to think of any narrative that does not contain unusual elements.

In relation to the Hanasaka Jijii story, I would like to point out the symbolic importance of the word *saku* 咲く (to bloom), which has its etymological root in the word *saki*. *Saki* is also the root of a number of other words: *saki* 先 (tip, end; future; ahead; beyond), *saki* 崎 (promontory, point), *saku* 柵 (fence; stockade), *saku* 裂く or 割く (to tear, cut, rend), *saka* 坂 (slope, incline), and *sake* 酒 (rice wine or another alcoholic beverage). Its basic sense is a state of accumulated energy that is held back from going any further. This image is clearly present in the first three words listed above. *Saka* is a slope climbing toward a point past which it can climb no more; *sake* expresses the feeling of teetering on the brink of intoxication. *Saku* 咲く, the phenomenon of blooming, occurs at the point at which the energy of the buds can no longer be constrained, and they burst forth, rending their envelopes. *Sakura*, the word for both the cherry tree and its blossoms, no doubt derives from *saku*.

FLOWERS

The Japanese root *saki* resembles the Sanskrit word *sphota* (bursting, opening). The fifth-century Indian philosopher of language Bhartrihari constructed an entire linguistic theory around the concept of *sphota*.

The concept of *saki* is connected to that of *musubi* (join, tie, connect, fruit), because fruit originates in blossoms. Originally *musubi* was compounded from *musu* (to give birth) and *hi* (spirit) and meant to generate spiritual power. Hanmura Ryō's epic fantasy novel *Musubi no yama hiroku* (The Secret History of Mount Musubi; 1973), winner of the first Izumi Kyōka Prize for Literature, is the saga of the Hi family, which has transmitted secret techniques for generating supernatural powers down through the ages. The Hie or Hiyoshi in Mount Hiei in Kyoto, the Sannō Hie Shrine in Tokyo, and Hiyoshimaru, the birth name of the warlord Toyotomi Hideyoshi, denotes a site rich in the spiritual power of *hi*.

From this original sense of generating spiritual power came the sense of *musubi* 結び as a connection or bond, which in turn led things that can be tied or bound to be imbued with symbolic significance. In chapter 3, "Deities," we talked about the ways in which ropes, cords, or paper could be tied or folded to form *himorogi* and *shimenawa* to demarcate sacred spaces. Eventually the concept of *musubi* came to be seen as residing in everything from the tying of hair ornaments and kimono cords to the wrapping of packages, weaving of horses' reins, and even the shaping of rice balls (*omusubi*) by hand. Japanese delight in such resonances among disparate forms.

The words for son (*musuko*) and daughter (*musume*) are also related to *musubi*: *musuko* derives from *musu hiko* ("newborn prince") and *musume* from *musu hime* ("newborn princess"). When a man and woman form a couple, the verb *musubareru* 結ばれる (to be joined, united) is used. When this is formalized, we have an engagement (*yuinō* 結納) and marriage (*kekkon* 結婚), using the same kanji and again stressing the sense of tying, joining, binding. This basic sense of *musubi* pervades Japanese culture.

Linking a chain of forms and other associations in this manner is known as magical thinking or associative thinking, and Japan is certainly a land in which such resonances having to do with *musubi* have proliferated.

The Japanese perspective on nature

Of all the seasons, the Japanese have always had particular regard for spring, when the flowers first bloom. And if spring is important, so is the winter that precedes it. *Fuyu* (winter) comes from the archaic verb *fuyu* 殖ゆ,

meaning to increase or grow, and signifies a period in which the spirit and energy of life and nature are gathering momentum for the swelling (*haru* 張る) buds of spring (*haru* 春).

Then comes summer, the season of growth, followed by autumn, the season of harvest, when seeds are set aside to be planted again in spring. This is the annual cycle in Japan and in every agricultural society. The cycle of flowering, fruition, and harvest is reflected in views of society and of life in general. Phrases from everyday speech—"Soon it'll be your time to bloom," or "Well, somehow it just didn't bear fruit"—suggest that we still think about life in these terms.

In Japan, this continual shifting of energy through the seasons has nurtured a sense of evanescence or impermanence (*utsuroi*). Another way of looking at these shifts would be to say that in the energy cycle between *ke* (the everyday, the mundane) and *hare* (the sacred), winter represents *ke* and spring represents *hare*. This cycle of *ke* and *hare* is fundamental to Japanese folkways. I will return to the concept of *utsuroi* in the "Time" chapter.

In Japan we like to think of ourselves as having a profound love of nature and the cycle of the seasons, but is this really so?

Today in Japan it seems like there is a flower shop on almost every street corner, but for the most part the plants they offer are cultivated, not gathered from the wild. Seeds are frequently imported, and the shops are full of flowers of European or North and South American origin, many grown in hothouses. Do we conceive of these as "nature," or simply as "flowers"?

We are surrounded by a flood of "ersatz nature." Concrete that is molded and stained to resemble wood is used in construction; sushi and box lunches are garnished with plastic leaves; phony wood grain is printed on fire-resistant wallpaper and on styrofoam food containers at convenience stores; the list goes on and on. Doesn't this reveal something about our feelings toward nature?

For some time there has been a debate over whether the Japanese actually love nature or are content with the appearance of nature.

Susan Sontag, author of *Against Interpretation* (1966) and *Illness as Metaphor* (1978), once remarked on the gaudy artificial cherry blossoms decorating Japanese shopping streets and the floral patterns featured on the white crockery and ceramics in department stores, saying that it seemed that the Japanese love of nature was really love for the "semi-natural." The architectural historian Bernard Rudofsky, author of *The Kimono Mind* (1965), was quite fond of how the Japanese find ways of enlivening the smallest spaces, such as the entryways and window-sills of apartments and townhouses, with potted plants and flowers—but also observed that the immensity of nature in the wild is not something that really suits the Japanese.

It is certainly true that we have not devoted a great deal of thought or feeling to the stronger, harsher aspects of nature. There are haiku that mention strong winds flattening the crops in the fields, and hand-scrolls that depict thunder and lightning, but for the most part we have focused our attention on the gentler, more intimate aspects.

Flowers and shrubs enliven a lane in Tsukishima, an island in Tokyo Bay built on reclaimed land in 1892.

haru no no ni	To the fields of spring
sumire tsumi ni to	to pick violets I came—
koshi ware so	I who in fondness
no o natsukashimi	for those fields could not depart,
hitoyo nenikeru	but stayed and slept the night.[1]

(Yamabe no Akahito)

ominaeshi	Go gather sprigs
akihagi taore	of ladyflower and bush clover
tamahoko no	for my dearest child
michiyuki zuto to	who begged me for a gift
kowamu ko ga tame	from my journey.

(Ishikawa no Okina)

wa ga yado ni	How impatient I grow
makeshi nadeshiko	to see the bloom
itsu shika mo	on the wild pink
hana ni sakanan	planted in my garden
yosoete mo mimu	for I shall think of it as you.[2]

(Ōtomo no Yakamochi)

These three poems from the *Man'yōshū* show us that from very early times people set out for the mountains to view wildflowers, pick them, and express their feelings through them, and that they also planted seeds to grow in their gardens. Yet at the same time there is no poetry that closely describes flowers in terms of how they look or how they grow. Rather than immersing themselves in nature, the ancient Japanese seem to have contented themselves with brief excursions to pick a few grasses and flowers. Oftentimes they also brought those wildflowers back from the mountains to cultivate at home, as in the poem by Yakamochi.

As a result, many scholars have argued that Japan never really developed an objective outlook on nature or a perspective embracing a rigorous examination of natural forms. Even Sontag's and Rudofsky's assessments were somewhat more charitable than this.

The development of rational scientific thought in Japan would have to wait until about the middle of the Edo period; the first objective, detailed illustrations of plants and animals emerged during the era of shogun Tokugawa Yoshimune (r. 1716–45), around the same time as the creation of what are now the Koishikawa Botanical Gardens. About this time, Japanese botany finally freed itself from the study of plants associated with traditional Chinese medicine (honzōgaku).

Pioneers in the objective study of the natural world included Kaibara Ekiken, whose passionate pursuit of a classification system for Japanese flora resulted in Yamato honzō (Medicinal Herbs of Japan; 1709), Inō Jakusui, who compiled Shobutsu ruisan (A Classification of All Things) under the patronage of Maeda Tsunanori, daimyo of Kaga, and Ono Ranzan, originally of Kyoto, who authored Honzō kōmoku keimō (Clarifications on the Bencao gangmu, 1803–6). All of these scholars were of a generation somewhat previous to the great Swedish botanist Carolus Linnaeus (1707–78). Kimura Yōjirō, author of Nihon shizenshi no seiritsu (The Formation of Natural History in Japan; 1974) and Edo-ki no nachurarisuto (Naturalists of the Edo Period; 1988), has written that without the influence of Chinese honzōgaku and the instruction offered by the German botanist Philipp Franz von Siebold during his residence in Nagasaki in the 1820s, serious scientific examination of the natural world might not have commenced in Japan.

But while it may be true that rigorous written observation of nature started comparatively late in Japan, how is observation of nature to be defined in the first place? Must observation be recorded in writing in order to be counted rational? Are careful observation and perception alone insufficient to develop a perspective on the natural world?

The recorded observations of scholars like Inō Jakusui and Ono Ranzan gave birth to Japanese natural history, and I personally am quite inspired by the flourishing of Edo-period science that these men pioneered. Even so, it seems to me that there was no great deficiency in the Japanese view of nature before their time in the late eighteenth century.

Let's shift focus for a moment and have a look at flowers and plants from the perspective of the natural sciences. I want to give a sense of the range of ways that nature may be observed from this vantage point. I should add that the great majority of people in the West, including Sontag and Rudofsky, have not always been accustomed to looking on flowers scientifically in the ways that I am about to describe. Thinking scientifically is a challenge, no matter where you are from.

The wonder of plants

Plants are highly developed photochemical organisms. They possess mechanisms for using light energy to synthesize carbon dioxide and water into glucose and starches for energy storage. We learn this much in elementary or middle school.

In what way do plants and human beings most resemble each other? One answer might be that both stand erect. But there is an even closer resemblance: chlorophyll in plants and heme groups inside the hemoglobin in human blood have an almost identical chemical structure, a porphyrin ring. The only difference is that in a heme group the ring is built around a central iron ion, while in chlorophyll the central ion is magnesium.

Plants function as an amazing respiratory apparatus. They have two different modes of respiration. One is the assimilation of carbon dioxide through photosynthesis, while the other is similar to our own: taking in oxygen and expelling carbon dioxide gas. This makes me think that all life must once have possessed these two types of respiration, until the appearance, at some point in evolutionary history, of life forms using only the oxygen–carbon dioxide cycle—animals, in other words. If this is the case, we animals seem incomplete by comparison.

Plants are also marvelous chemical laboratories. They possess amazing catalytic properties—the capacity for facilitating certain types of chemical reaction. Their ability to generate glucose and chlorophyll is itself evidence of the internal systems they carry for regulating chemical reactions.

Plants are also specialists in thermodynamics. In most plants, the flowers have the highest temperature, while the leaves and stems are somewhat cooler. This not only helps the plant regulate its own internal temperature balance but also makes the flower an appealing bed for insects, which are quite sensitive to temperature differentials and are thus drawn to its warmth. This regulation of temperature on the part of plants dovetails neatly with the mechanisms insects have for sensing chronological and environmental cues of the sort we covered in the previous chapter.

Moreover, the thermodynamic balance maintained by different species of plants is subtly varied, attracting different insect species. In a way, flowers are like beacons broadcasting information in the form of temperature.

Plants are also brilliant architects. There is a variety of water lily, *Victoria amazonica*, whose leaves are large enough to bear the weight of a human being yet are each supported underwater by only a single slender stalk. Great trees with complex canopies of branches also begin by growing from a single trunk. What is it that enables such a structure?

As architects, plants have two hidden advantages. One is that trunks and stems are made up of pipelike stuctures (xylem)—in other words, parts with a hollow-core design that is quite strong. The second is the zigzag or wave pattern of their growth. It is impossible to place weight on a single sheet of paper stood on end, but if the same sheet is folded like a fan into a vertical wave pattern it can actually support significant weight. Sir Joseph Paxton's famous Crystal Palace design for the Great Exhibition of 1851 in London, which attracted more than 600,000 visitors, was inspired by the internal structure of the leaves of the giant water lilies mentioned above. In the twentieth century, the Crystal Palace influenced architect Buckminster Fuller in his creation of the geodesic dome.

Plants are also masters of spatial geometry. Their leaves are structured based on principles of geometric division, in addition to which the growth patterns of the branches and leaf veins are determined so that they occupy the maximum area possible. Every plant is engaged in a miraculous geometric plotting of the surrounding space. In the 1970s, the maverick mathematician Benoit Mandelbrot applied the concept of "fractal structure" to such patterns.

In the nineteenth century, the German psychologist and physicist Gustav Theodor Fechner made an aesthetic discovery inspired by plants. He experimented with showing large numbers of people a series of rectangular shapes with different height-to-width ratios and asking them to choose the "best" one. After testing hundreds and then thousands of people, he found that the vast majority preferred the proportion 1.62—commonly known as the "golden section," or golden ratio. The branching pattern of most plants follows this ratio.

Even more astonishing, and less known, are a number of what we might call "superscientific" capacities of plants.

Say we have two potted plants of the same variety. One is about to bloom; the other is still just budding. If the conditions are right, the second will speed up and open its flowers at the same time as the first. Even though they are in different pots and in no way physically connected with one another, the two will frequently bloom at the same time.

Also, if you put several ripe apples in a box with unripe apples, the unripe apples will begin to ripen almost immediately. Veteran growers are aware of this, and also the corollary: if you ship boxes full of ripe apples, there is a high risk that the entire box will go bad in transit—it is better to mix ripe and unripe in each box. One researcher has discovered that ripe apples give off a significant quantity of ethylene gas, which may signal the others to ripen. This is known in scientific terminology as a "contingent system." Plants seem to have some sort of threshold mechanism that helps them synchronize with one another.

All of these biological capacities of plants that we have been looking at are built into them for the instant, after flowering and fruition, when they release their seeds in order to reproduce. This process of seed dispersal is another engineering marvel.

In some plants the mechanism is based on pressure. A flower bud can have an internal pressure of nearly two atmospheres. The seeds it produces may be subject to double that pressure, in other words nearly four atmospheres. A car tire is normally inflated to about two atmospheres, so four atmospheres is considerable. This pressure pushes the seeds against the outer covering of their fruit, which eventually ruptures, releasing them.

Seed dispersal occurs in a variety of other ways as well. In the dandelion, the seed is not ejected by force but remains attached to its fruit, the top of which becomes the fluffy head that carries the seed on the wind; the seeds of other wind-dispersed plants, like the maple, act something like parachutes when expelled. Some seeds, like those of the dandelion, fall straight and vertical to the ground at the end of their descent; but most spin merrily, like a propeller, as they fall—in other words, their descent is helical. The hydraulic apparatus of the stem and the growth pattern of the roots also have helical structures.

There are many more wonderful things about plants. The need to assimilate great amounts of water in order to survive has made them skillful hydraulic engineers. And many of them are talented colorists as well, going through an entire spectrum of color gradations from black and brown seeds to a rich variety of greens in the stems and leaves, a riot of shades and hues in the flowers, and then back to black and brown once more.

It is often said that the life of a flower is short, but in that brief span between birth and death the energy packed into those tiny seeds manifests in a vibrant panoply of color.

My basic aim in presenting these topics has been to illustrate that a full scientific accounting of plants involves an almost unending succession of perspectives. Simple observation of nature will not necessarily reveal all the secrets of the plant world, and external appearances can lead to mistaken conclusions. The scientific gaze must be connected to a broader worldview; analysis of individual elements, no matter how accurate, is by itself not science. One of the problems with contemporary science is that not enough connections are being made between discrete findings, because scientists have restricted themselves to what fits the rational scientific paradigm in their particular fields. Without a worldview to inform it, science is at risk of becoming nothing but a soulless exercise.

It is for this reason that I reject the notion that there is something deficient in the Japanese view of nature. When a scientific perspective is necessary, we've been able to rise to the occasion, as Inō Jakusui and Ono Ranzan did with their observations of nature in the Edo period, and others of their time in fields including astronomy and mathematics.

Observation and analysis are not the only ways to appreciate flora. Since ancient times, Japanese have embraced and been fascinated by the transformations of the plant world. We might even say that this is what lies behind the particular regard they have always had for flowers. To quote the *Kadō zensho*, a 1717 treatise on flower arrangement (ikebana), "Flower arrangement originates from a representation of the primal energy of heaven, earth, and nature." And in *Ikenobō Sen'ō kuden* (Sayings of Ikenobō Sen'ō) from the mid-sixteenth century we find the following passage: "Those who practice the Way do not merely view the grasses and trees, open their hearts, reflect on the changing seasons, and find momentary pleasure. In the presence of the wind that scatters the blossoms and causes the leaves to fall, they are able to glean the seeds of enlightenment."

The flower of Noh

hana no iro wa	The color of the flowers
utsuri ni keri na	has faded—in vain
itazura ni	I grow old in this world
waga mi yo ni furu	lost in thought
nagame seshi ma ni	as the long rain falls.[3]

This famous poem by Ono no Komachi appears in the collection *Hyakunin isshu* (One Hundred Poets, One Poem Each). It contains two crucial *kakekotoba*, or "pivot words." The first is *furu*, which can be read here as both rain falling and time passing; the second is *nagame*, which can signify both "long rain" and "to gaze pensively." Ono no Komachi is clearly using the flowers as a metaphor for herself.

Just as the flowers gradually lose their vibrant color, Komachi is aware that she is aging. The perception of the changing seasons overlaps with that of the passing years to produce a sense of the impermanence of life known as *utsuroi*.

In a sequence of linked verses composed in the summer of 1690, the haiku poet Bonchō wrote,

samazama ni	In countless ways
shina kawaritaru	I have known the vagaries
koi o shite	of being in love.

To this Bashō provided the following response:

ukiyo no hate wa	In this floating world of ours
mina komachi nari	all must meet Komachi's end.[4]

In this verse, Komachi becomes synonymous with the fate that will befall us all, a symbol of the ephemerality—*utsuroi*—with which the Japanese regard the flower.

This vision of Komachi has proven to be enduring, embodied in works such as the Noh play *Sotoba Komachi* (Komachi and the Grave Marker) by

Kan'ami (1333–84). The protagonist is Komachi, a withered old beggar woman of nearly a hundred years. She is resting with her hands on an ancient stupa in the southern outskirts of Kyoto, beyond the Rashōmon gate, when a pair of traveling monks from Mount Kōya happen upon her.

After some exchange of words Komachi begins to tell them of her past. When she was in the full flower of her youth, a young nobleman named Fukakusa no Shōshō began courting her. She made him promise to visit her for one hundred nights before she would return his affections, and for ninety-nine nights he came. But on the final night he did not appear, for he had died from the emotional strain of attempting to fulfill this vow to her. Whether possessed by the anger and misery of the young nobleman or by her own grief and sadness, Komachi suddenly begins to dance, and her voice alters to that of a man. A dialogue begins between the spirit of Fukakusa no Shōshō, which has taken over her body, and the monks from Mount Kōya. Eventually Komachi recovers herself and attains enlightenment. The compassion of the Buddha is essential to freeing her from the malevolent spirit embodying the karma of her past.

Sotoba Komachi presents a fine example of a category of Noh dance referred to as *utsuri-mai*, in which the dancer is possessed by or takes on the persona of another. It adeptly employs a version of the Ono no Komachi legend that was popular in medieval times to speak of the fate of women, the evanescence of flowers, and the fragile and transitory nature of human life. Mishima Yukio would offer an updated version of this play in his *Kindai Nōgakushu* (Modern Noh Plays, 1956), later memorably performed by Miwa Akihiro in 1996. A number of other Noh plays offer well-crafted takes on the Komachi story—*Kayoi Komachi* (The Courting of Komachi), *Sekidera Komachi* (Komachi at Sekidera), *Ōmu Komachi* (Parrot Komachi), and *Sōshi-arai Komachi* (Komachi Washes the Manuscript)—a clear indication of the many ways in which the vicissitudes of Komachi's life have been used to express the Japanese sense of *utsuroi*.

It goes without saying that the "flower" embodied by Komachi is not an actual flower but the flower of life itself, the flower of the spirit. And it is this flower that Kan'ami and his son Zeami (c. 1363–c. 1443) sought to capture in the Noh drama and that became a central concept in their aesthetic.

Zeami's *Fūshi kaden* (Teachings on Style and the Flower; also known as *Kadensho*) and *Kakyō* (Mirror to the Flower) are splendid treatises on this aesthetic. No other work succeeds to this degree in distilling the essence of the Japanese phenomenology of nature into their very titles, and the writing is inspiring in its perfection. There is much here I would like to share, but I will be brief.

Zeami is said to have stressed the quality of *yūgen*, but that quality is in fact quite difficult to grasp. Zeami stated that Fujiwara no Shunzei (1114–1204) captures the essence of *yūgen* in the following poem:

mata ya min	Will I ever again
Katano no mino no	seek cherry blossoms
sakuragari	in the royal fields of Katano?
hana no yuki chiru	Flowers of falling snow,
haru no akebono	early dawn in spring.[5]

Here, Shunzei recalls an unforgettable excursion to the mountains in days gone by to view the cherry blossoms. After a night of revelry, the blossoms fell like spring snow as the new day dawned; would that he might experience the same sight again! Shunzei relives this dreamlike scene, nurturing it in his mind and letting it take on a power that enriches his quiet contemplation of the sight he once beheld. This, then, is an example of the sophisticated layering and overtones (*yosei*) of which Shunzei was master.

So now we have some sense of what Zeami meant by *yūgen*, but something still seems to elude us. Does *yūgen* refer to the dreamlike or illusory landscape, or to the mind that perceives it? In *Fūshi kaden*, Zeami gives a brief and somewhat surprising list of entities that innately possess *yūgen*: "Among humans, imperial consorts and ladies-in-waiting, courtesans, rakes, and handsome men; among plants, the various types of flowers." So flowers are expressions of *yūgen*, which seems understandable enough, but so are women of the nobility, courtesans, and handsome ladies' men. What does this mean? Is the *fūshi* 風姿 (appearance, demeanor, manifestation) of *Fūshi kaden* meant to point to that of human beings?

Zeami makes a similar statement in *Kakyō*, in which he stresses that "in the art of Noh in particular, the manifestation of *yūgen* is of the first importance." He then elaborates:

> In what sort of place, then, is the stage of *yūgen* to be found? Let us begin by examining the various classes of people on the basis of the appearance they make in society. May we not say of the courtiers, whose behavior is distinguished and whose appearance far surpasses that of other men, that theirs is the stage of *yūgen*? If such is the case,

then their dignified appearance represents the essence of *yūgen*. From this we may see that the essence of *yūgen* lies in a true state of beauty and gentleness. . . . The actor should realize that *yūgen* is attained when all of the different forms of visual or aural expression are beautiful. It is when the actor himself has worked out these principles and made himself their master that he may be said to have entered the realm of *yūgen*.[6]

Zeami clearly sees the behavior and deportment of the nobility as the model for *yūgen*. Here we must recall the circumstances surrounding the growth of Noh from *sarugaku*, a performing tradition developed by Kan'ami's Yūzakiza and other troupes in the Yamato region. Seen by contemporaries as lower class—"an occupation for beggars"—*sarugaku* nonetheless won acceptance in the capital thanks to the patronage of the third Ashikaga shogun, Yoshimitsu; having done so, however, it was necessarily called upon to incorporate the customs and manners of the aristocracy.

But this was not all. In the perception of the "flower" in the graceful demeanor of noblewomen and courtesans and the association of the elusive quality of *yūgen* with it, we may also sense a broader historical current— the gradual transition, in the Kitayama culture of the late fourteenth century, of the *yūgen* originally articulated as a matter of emotional "overtones" (*yosei*) in the era of Fujiwara no Shunzei and Kamo no Chōmei into a nostalgia for the courtly elegance of the past.

With the flower of *yūgen*, Zeami sought to link the flowers of nature to the flowers of humanity. This "flower" was a flower of sensibility and perception, a flower of character and refinement, and, in Zeami's famous formulation, a transitory or seasonal flower (*jibun no hana*).

The flowers of Zeami have exerted wide-ranging influence upon later generations. The idea that there is only a brief period of flowering in any human life, the perception of the innocent beauty of youth as that flower, and the notion that the true "flower" blooms in the human heart and mind—all of these stem from the same source.

The genealogy of flowers, birds, wind, and moon

Kan'ami was the first to pursue the concept of the flower in the art of Noh, though he went no further than to conceive of it as something exquisitely rare that was to be achieved through a lengthy process of repeated practice and performance. Zeami deepened this thinking, believing that the "flower" could be made to bloom at any time, and calling this level of artistic accomplishment "the flower of truth" (*shōkafū* 正花風). This formulation satisfied him for a while, before he went on to posit three further possible stages of artistic development.

The first stage of higher development he called the "flower of stillness" (*kankafū* 閑花風), by which he meant a style that had rejected superficial beauty to reveal a fleeting glimpse of something "colder" and more profound. As I will explore later in more detail, the "flower of stillness" shares a similar sensibility with *hiesabi* ("chill melancholy"), a quality advocated by the linked-verse master Shinkei (1406–75). The second stage was "the flower of supreme profundity" (*chōshinkafū* 寵深花風). This stage was one of great subtlety, in which even the most eccentric and even heretical performance might be delivered with dignity and grace and be seen as having great beauty. Another name for this stage was *ran'i* 闌位, in which the character *ran* signifies something that has reached its apogee and is about to decline; this is a phase of sharply honed, risky artistic development.

Above these, Zeami placed a final rank—the highest of his nine stages (or ranks) of attainment in the art of Noh—called "the flower of the miraculous" (*myōkafū* 妙花風). This level transcends all notions of beauty and ugliness, good and evil, and all efforts to evaluate or criticize. It is something close to the concept in Kegon Buddhism of "the Dharma world of the unobstructed mutual interpenetration of all phenomena" (*jiji muge hokkai*)—a mysterious and perhaps purely ideal or ideational realm. (We will take up Kegon philosophy in the next chapter, "Buddhas.") Zeami's unfaltering pursuit of the flower is permeated by both the Buddhist perception of impermanence and the Daoist concept of *wu wei* ("non-action," or "effortless action").

Zeami was attempting to take Japanese culture to its very limits. In his final years Zeami lost the patronage and support of the Ashikaga shoguns and was exiled to Sado Island, ultimately failing in his efforts to give shape to his theoretical ideas on stage. But that only speaks to the vastness of his vision, the inheritance and transformation of which by later generations would become the determining factor in the evolution of the phenomenology of nature in Japanese culture. The heirs of Zeami's legacy ranged from the poet Shinkei and the scholar Ichijō Kaneyoshi (1402–81) to the Zen master Ikkyū, the Noh master Konparu Zenchiku (1405–70?), the ikebana master Ikenobō Senkei (fl. 1457–66), and the *renga* poet Sōgi (1421–1502);

the tea masters Murata Jukō (1423–1502), Takeno Jōō (1502–55), and Sen no Rikyū (1522–91); and finally the Edo-period haiku poets Bashō and Ryōkan.

Was this realm of "the flower" an invention of Zeami's? There were many original elements to his vision, but one poet had prepared the way for him: Saigyō (1118–90), who initiated the spirit of reveling in birds, flowers, wind, and moon and showed others the way to live a life imbued with a deep sense of play amid the phenomena of nature. Saigyō was the first poet who proved capable of pursuing the symbolic significance of the flower in the Japanese context. One could say it all began with this man, though Saigyō himself revered the poet Nōin (Tachibana no Nagayasu, 988–?), who preceded him by about a century.

The artistic and philosophical lineage that originates with Saigyō runs through the poets Fujiwara no Shunzei and his son Teika (1162–1241), the poet and essayist Kamo no Chōmei (1156?–1216), and the poet and historian Jien (1155–1225) to the Zen master Dōgen (1200–53) and the Pure Land tradition of Ippen (1239–89)—then onward through the poet and essayist Yoshida Kenkō (c. 1283–c. 1352) to Nijō Yoshimoto, Kan'ami, Zeami, and Shinkei. This is the genealogy of the phenomenology of nature in Japanese literature down to the end of the medieval period.

In secular life Saigyō was known as Satō Norikiyo; he was from a warrior family of the Fujiwara clan that traced its lineage back ten generations to Fujiwara no Hidesato (also known as Tawara no Tōta and famous in popular lore for his alleged conquest of a monstrous centipede). In his youth he is said to have served with distinction in the Northern Guard (*hokumen no bushi*) of the retired emperor Toba and to have been an adept at *kemari*, a kickball game popular among the nobility of his day.

But in the spring of his twenty-third year, he suddenly bade farewell to his wife and daughter to become a Buddhist priest. Those who knew him were astonished by his decision, and we still do not know the motive for it, though a variety of theories have been proposed, from a failed love affair to the death of someone close to him.

Having thus abandoned secular life, Saigyō wandered for a time from one temple or hermitage to another before returning from a journey to Mutsu in northern Japan to take up residence in the great monastic complex at Mount Kōya—"entering the mountains" in the sense described in chapter 1. From the perspective of his times, this was also a case of a member of the warrior class embracing the tradition embodied by Mount Kōya and its famous Kōya *hijiri*—traveling priests who were sent forth to practice and preach throughout the land. Although Saigyō probably did not engage in much religious practice, he adopted the itinerant life of a Kōya *hijiri* to travel about the country composing poetry.

The poetry he composed was remarkable. Yet at the time, only a few discerning individuals such as Fujiwara no Shunzei and the brothers known as the Ōhara no Sanjaku ("three Jaku of Ōhara"; Jakunen, Jakuchō, and Jakuzen) gave his work the deep respect it deserved.

Saigyō was not without social connections, but neither was he a celebrated person of his day. He had removed himself from the main currents of his times and the life of the capital to the secluded world of Mount Kōya, but once there he scarcely engaged in the Buddhist religious practices that were supposed to be the point of abandoning secular society. He was a "disappearing man," an enigma to all.

Indeed, the warrior-monk Mongaku (1139–1203), who features in several chapters of *The Tale of the Heike*, openly disapproved of Saigyō for his lack of commitment to religious practice and threatened to strike him if they ever met. Yet when Saigyō eventually visited Jingoji temple, where Mongaku was abbot, Mongaku quickly changed his mind and received him with courtesy, apparently impressed by Saigyō's stance of emptying the self through the act of travel. Mongaku recognized in Saigyō a true outsider.

A poem is an arrangement of words born out of emptiness, without tangible form, an embodiment of mutability. It does not seek "truth" but instead expresses mutability in ways that are themselves ephemeral. Only the heart and mind of the poet are capable of apprehending this emptiness. Yet once formed into words, a poem can be written down, making visible the invisible—and so the thirty-one syllables of the *waka* poem return anew to its author.

As this process is repeated, the poem and the mind merge with one another, until all that is left is the resonating energy of the scene the author was envisioning when he composed the poem. The phenomenology of nature resides in this resonance of scenic energy, or *keiki*.

That is the heart of Saigyō's poetry. By emptying the self, he reaches for the something that slips in from the cracks of that void. He has little to gain even should he be able to grasp it, but in any case, it is all that is there. Such is the fleeting reverberation we sense in his poems—the refined sensibility (*suki*) that comes when attachment and clinging are exhausted.

Saigyō chose the life of the outsider. It's true that he was in a sense an itinerant mendicant, as Gorai Shigeru and Mezaki Tokue have written. But more fundamentally, his way of life was founded on emptying out his substance and assembling all the "useless" bits generated from that emptiness into thirty-one syllables of verse: 5-7-5-7-7.

Saigyō's flower

With the advent of Saigyō, flowers in Japan became a matter of the heart and mind.

In the era of the *Man'yōshū*, people were drawn to the life force embodied in flowers and to the mystery of their blossoming. And so flowers were perceived in spiritual terms, resulting in a vision of them, unique to antiquity, as a manifestation of *makoto* (honesty, truth, sincerity). Later, this perception underwent a kind of individuation on the part of figures such as Ono no Komachi, turning the flower into an emblem of the transitory and evanescent.

With the transition from aristocratic to warrior culture, flowers became strongly associated with the brevity of human life, as exemplified by tragic heroes such as Minamoto no Yoshitsune. Yoshitsune's life is almost always likened to cherry blossoms, as in the classic Kabuki play *Yoshitsune senbon zakura* (Yoshitsune and the Thousand Cherry Trees). With this development, flowers took on a masculine signification, inspiring not *aware* (pity, compassion) but *appare* (admiration, awe). It is at this point that Saigyō appears on the scene. Viewed in this context, the fact that Saigyō had been a member of the palace guard, the prototype for the culture of the warrior, assumes great significance.

Saigyō's flower was neither that of Komachi nor that of Yoshitsune. His was a flower of wandering, of obsession, of refined taste, of impermanence, and of a heart tempered by suffering.

Yoshinoyama	Since the day I saw
kozue no hana o	Mount Yoshino's
mishi hi yori	blossoming treetops
kokoro wa mi ni mo	my body's in one place
sowazu nariniki	my heart in another.[7]

hana mireba	Viewing the cherry blossoms
sono iware to wa	I cannot really say why
nakeredomo	But deep in my heart
kokoro no uchi zo	I suffer.
kurushikarikeru	

hana ni somu	Why should my heart
kokoro no ika de	still harbor
nokoriken	this passion for cherry flowers
sute hateteki to	I who thought
omou waga mi ni	I had put that all behind me?[8]

negawaku wa	My wish is
hana no shita nite	to die in spring
haru shinan	under the cherry blossoms
sono kisaragi no	on that day in the Second Month
mochizuki no koro	when the moon is full.[9]

These poems contrast Saigyō's feelings upon viewing the cherry blossoms with a self that would not normally be overcome by such emotion. The first presents a state of mind unique to Saigyō. Would anyone viewing the cherry blossoms at Yoshino really be so likely to feel this sight had fundamentally altered their personality, or to suffer from that day forward because their body and heart had parted ways? Saigyō did, and not just once or twice; this was a pain he carried with him for quite some time. In the second poem he states that he cannot explain why he suffers so. But what, exactly, is this feeling?

I've read poems about flowers by Hölderlin and Wordsworth and Whitman, but never have I come across one that addresses an unfounded feeling of suffering upon viewing a flower. There are poems that associate flowers with the anguish of love or the questioning of God, but those in which flowers inspire a fundamental existential anxiety are rare indeed. If we speak of the moon rather than flowers, then we can say that the Symbolist poet Jules Laforgue (1860–87) sings of such despair upon viewing the moon. And in the visual arts, we have the flowers of Odilon Redon (1840–1916) and Georgia O'Keeffe (1887–1986). But these are special cases—not the norm in Western culture.

The fourth poem is one of Saigyō's best known, written when he was only twenty-five or twenty-six, yet clearly hinting that he already linked the themes of flowers and death. When Saigyō did die, it was on the sixteenth day of the second month of Kenkyū 1 (1190)—a bit early for the cherry blossoms, but under a full moon. This made an impression on the literati of his day, including Jien and Shunzei, who were moved by the apparent fulfillment of the wish expressed in his poem.

hanami ni to	Wanting to see the blossoms
muretsutsu hito no	people come in droves
kitaru nomi zo	to visit—this alone
atara sakura no	regrettably
toga ni wa arikeru	is the cherry tree's fault.[10]

oshimarenu	Though unmissed
mi dani mo yo ni wa	I persist in this world;
aru mono o	how contrary, then, are the cherry blossoms,
ana ayaniku no	which scatter
hana no kokoro ya	though no one wishes them to go.

morotomo ni	Blossoms,
ware o mo gushite	when you scatter,
chirine hana	take me with you too!
ukiyo o itou	My heart is oh so weary
kokoro aru mi zo	of this cruel world.[11]

haru fukami	Spring deepens
eda mo yurugade	and the blossoms fall
chiru hana wa	from the unmoving branches
kaze no toga ni wa	surely this is not to be
aranu naru beshi	blamed upon the wind.

nagamu tote	Gazing at them,
hana ni mo itaku	I've grown so very close
narenureba	to these blossoms,
chiru wakare koso	to part with them when they fall
kanashikarikere	seems bitter indeed![12]

At first glance, these seem to be very dark poems. As in the set of poems quoted earlier, suffering, world-weariness, and sadness are central themes. Yet Saigyō also tells us that such things are to be blamed upon neither the cherry trees nor the wind.

So these are not necessarily poems of despair. Rather, they suggest some sense of deficiency on the part of Saigyō himself—a deficiency he observes from the point of view of the blossoms. What is it that is missing? A sense of meaning or purpose (*haka*) to life. He can no longer do anything to recapture it, but when he encounters the cherry blossoms, he is also made to encounter the purpose he can no longer possess. This absence of purpose (*haka ga nai*) is at the root of the feeling of the transitory (*hakanai*) nature of existence. This is what these poems say to us.

kokoroetsu	I see what I should do—
tada hitosuji ni	without fail
ima yori wa	from now on
hana o oshimade	I will not regret the falling blossoms
kaze o itowan	but resent the wind.

aoba sae	Once I see
mireba kokoro no	the new green leaves
tomaru kana	my heart may take to them too—
chirinishi hana no	if I think of them as mementos
nagori to omoeba	of blossoms that scattered.[13]

harukaze no	When I dream of
hana o chirasu to	spring wind
miru yume wa	scattering cherry blossoms
samete mo mune no	my heart stirs
sawagu narikeri	even after waking.[14]

I am especially fond of this last poem. The blossoms scattering in the spring wind and himself, seeing them; the dream of blossoms reaching their end and himself, awakening from that dream and knowing it too has gone—all melt into one another and pass on, the boundaries between them gradually erased. The poem expresses that half-waking state—*yumeutsutsu*—when dreams and reality intermingle. In it, I think we see two Saigyōs: one who wishes never to wake from this blending of dream and reality, and another who cannot suppress the stirring of the heart that he feels on waking.

In this stirring of the heart we see the true source of Saigyō's suffering. The pathos of the flower lies in his inability to achieve a perfect dreamlike union between self and flower. Although he wandered in pursuit of this unity, he remained unfulfilled; a boundary still kept him from identifying totally with the flower. And this was a source of deep dissatisfaction to Saigyō to the very end of his days.

The genealogy of impermanence

An enduring current of impermanence (*mujō*) flows through the work of Saigyō, providing evidence of how the Japanese sense of impermanence had begun to diverge from Buddhism itself. What I mean here by "impermanence" is the transitory and fleeting flux of *keiki*—the energy inherent in the landscapes of the heart and mind. This perspective on impermanence has been little addressed by critics after Kobayashi Hideo (1902–83), much to my disappointment.

The Japanese sense of impermanence, as we've already seen, has clear origins in the frequent mythological references to journeys to an eternal land (Tokoyo), as well as in Prince Shōtoku's remark that "The world is folly. Only the Buddha is real," which appears on the Tenjukoku Shūchō Mandala commissioned after his death in 622 and today owned by Chūgūji temple.

The poets of the *Man'yōshū* also gave frequent voice to the sense of impermanence.

kora ga te o	Makimuku Mountain
Makimukuyama wa	will be there forever
tsune ni aredo	but never again will I be able to see
suginishi hito ni	the one who has passed away
yukimakame yamo	and cradle my head in her arms.

This poem by Kakinomoto no Hitomaro contrasts "forever" (*tsune ni*) with "passed away" (*suginishi*), expressing what might be called the typical concept of impermanence among the *Man'yōshū* poets—that nature is eternal, but human life is ephemeral. Consider the following poems:

yo no naka wa	Each time I realize
munashiki mono to	the transience of
shiru toki shi	this world,

iyoyo masumasu	the more, the harder
kanashikarikeri	I am struck with sadness.[15]

(Ōtomo no Tabito)

yo no naka o	Now at last I learn
tsune naki mono to	that the world in which we live
ima so shiru	is ephemeral—
Nara no miyako no	now that I see it fade away
utsurou mireba	the royal city of Nara.[16]

(Tanabe no Sakimaro)

Here, *yo no naka* (the world), *munashi* (transience), *tsune naki* (ephemeral), and *utsurou* (fade away) are associated with one another, suggesting that the concept of the impermanence of human life was widely held, at least among a segment of the nobility. *Munashi* should also be understood as "fruitless" (*minashi*).

This ancient perspective on impermanence is also reflected in the presentation of Daoist thought in Kūkai's allegorical *Sangō shii ki* (Principles of the Three Teachings, 798) and in the language of his long poem *Yuzan bosen shi* (Encounters with Mountain Sages), such as the line from its preface that speaks of his intention to "represent impermanence by the things of this world" (*mujō o keibutsu ni hishi*). In general, such ways of thinking would be absorbed into the Heian Buddhist concept of impermanence— into the idea, in simplest terms, of impermanence as mortality, which we find in the vision of the six realms of existence depicted in Genshin's *Ōjōyōshū* (Essentials of Rebirth in the Pure Land, 985).

Yet this Buddhist sense of impermanence was given little theoretical discussion and instead remained largely intuitive or impressionistic, as expressed in the famous *iroha uta* poem that employs forty-seven of the forty-eight characters in the kana syllabary and that has long been used as a mnemonic for learning kana:

iro ha ni ho he to	iro wa nioedo chirinuru o
chi ri nu ru wo	waga yo tare zo tsune naran
wa ka yo ta re so	ui no okuyama kyō koete
tsu ne na ra mu	asaki yume miji ei mo sezu
u (w)i no o ku ya ma	
ke fu ko e te	
a sa ki yu me mi shi	
(w)e hi mo se su	

The colors blossom, scatter, and fall.
In this world of ours, who lasts forever?
Today let us cross over the remote mountains of life's illusions,
and dream no more shallow dreams nor succumb to drunkenness.[17]

The *iroha* poem was written around the turn of the tenth century. Its authorship is uncertain: it has been attributed to Kūkai and also to Kakuban (1095–1143), an unconventional monk associated with the temple Negoroji and credited with the revival of esoteric Buddhism more than two centuries after Kūkai. Neither of these attributions are accepted by scholars of the Japanese language, as in Kūkai's era the system of Japanese pronunciation was still unstable.

The poem was instead probably the result of a lengthy editorial process within the Shingon sect of esoteric Buddhism founded by Kūkai. The content references a famous *gatha* from the *Nirvana Sutra*, "All things are impermanent / This is the law of birth and death / When birth and death are done with / The bliss of nirvana is realized,"[18] setting the basic idea to the rhythm of the *shōmyō* chanting that was a key element of Shingon practice. For a more detailed account, see my book *Kūkai no yume* (Dreams of Kūkai, 2005).

Iroha is sometimes written 色葉 ("colored leaves"), signifying both the leaves of plants and the shadings of language itself (*kotoba* 言葉, or "the leaves of speech"). In this we see a concept of language grounded in a uniquely Japanese sense of the impermanence of plant life, an image that suggests words glittering and glistening like the leaves of trees in sunlight. Another phrase—*man'yō kebutsu* 万葉化仏, "the myriad leaves become buddhas"—suggests the miraculous quality of this phenomenon.

Resonant with this image of colored leaves, the *iroha* poem subtly sings of the vicissitudes of life and the impermanence of all things. I sometimes find myself humming the melancholy tune of "Iroha" by my friend Stomu Yamash'ta, which always puts me into a kind of reverie.

The impermanence of the *iroha* poem and of the *Nirvana Sutra* would eventually mingle with the sensibility of courtly elegance (*miyabi*) arising during the era of the Fujiwara regency to create something quite unique. *Miyabi* derives from the verb *miyabu*, which meant "to adopt the manner of the palace." In the period when the Fujiwara held sway and their courtly culture increasingly dominated a capital over which towered the great temple complexes of Hosshōji and Hōjōji, the sensibility embodied in the *iroha* poem—"the colors blossom, scatter, and fall"—gradually and subtly permeated society. One of the hallmarks of this courtly culture was a sophisticated, aristocratic feminism: predicated as it was on patriarchal polygamy and male erotic liberty, this culture was admittedly quite unequal and constrained women in many ways, but also gave them considerable freedom to express themselves in cultural pursuits.

Another factor behind the emergence of this "metropolitan style" was the spread of millenarian *mappō* thought and the resulting descent of "mountain Buddhism" into the streets of the capital, as mentioned in chapter 1.

In 1052 the eschatological theory that Japan had entered *mappō* ("the latter days of the Dharma," a period of degeneration of the Buddhist teachings believed to have commenced a thousand years after the death of the historical Buddha) caused great anxiety among the Japanese nobility, spurring their desire to be reborn into the Pure Land of Amida Buddha and encouraging them to practice the *nembutsu*, or recitation of Amida's name. The watchword catchphrase of the day was *onri edo gongu jōdo* ("desire to leave this impure world and enter into the Pure Land"). To put it simply, in the eighth and ninth centuries the energy of ancient Japan was swept into the seclusion of the mountains, but from the eleventh century onward, it descended once more on the imperial capital.

The itinerant Pure Land priest Kūya (903–72) was representative of this phenomenon. Buddhist priests like him were known as *ichi no hijiri* ("holy men of the marketplace")—the nuance being that they embodied the energy of ancient times and brought it to the streets of the metropolis. Before this, the *hijiri* who made up part of the itinerant population (*yugyō no tami*) mentioned earlier in this chapter would rarely enter the cities. For one thing, these Japanese "holy men" (the word for whom derives from *hijiri* 日知り, "those who know the sun," a reference to their mastery of astrology and the calendrical arts) had their origins as the wise elders of rural communities.

A succession of calamities exacerbated the situation in the capital: fires at the imperial palace and outbreaks of epidemic disease. The aspiration for rebirth in the Pure Land intertwined with a world-weary resignation. Women fixed their inward gaze upon *aware*, the pathos of life, to the extent that even the poet Izumi Shikibu (976–1030), known for her uninhibited love affairs, was led to reminisce in her famous diary about the days she had spent "distraught and saddened by the transience of this world, more fleeting than a dream."

Men felt this, too, and frequently came to depend on words such as *yosei* ("overtones" or "resonance") to express it, as we see in Mibu no Tadamine's *Wakatei jisshu* (Ten Varieties of Japanese Poetic Style), for example. An epitome of this sensibility was the aforementioned Fujiwara no Shunzei, the leading light of the twelfth-century literary world, and his son Teika. Shunzei strove to express in the "overtones" of his poems the fluctuations of *keiki*.

These poets concentrated on a psychological or spiritual approach to poetry, and they developed a new style characterized by what Teika described as *ushin* (conviction of feeling; literally, "possessing heart"). Here we may see *aware* already shifting into a sensibility prizing poetic resonance (*yosei*), emotional depth (*ushin*), and another quality admired by Teika, *yōen*, which might be translated as "ethereal beauty." Yet at this point, the sense of impermanence had not yet grown overwhelming, though as in the diary of Izumi Shikibu, distress over the fleeting nature of life had become more common. The real shock to the courtly system of values was the rise of the warrior class.

It was at this juncture that Saigyō appeared on the scene. This twenty-three-year-old soldier in the Northern Guard abandoned secular life and took monastic vows in 1140. The Hōgen and Heiji disturbances followed less than twenty years later; Taira no Kiyomori became grand minister of state when Saigyō was fifty-two. In 1190, the year of Saigyō's death, Minamoto no Yoritomo was consolidating his victory over the Taira and laying the foundations of the Kamakura shogunate.

Another development of this period that cannot be overemphasized is the spread of the *hiragana* syllabary, often referred to as *onnade*, or "women's writing." Widening use of the supple kana script had a profound connection to the spread of feminine culture and of poetry. A range of new techniques for making decorative papers displayed kana calligraphy to full advantage and stirred the subtle sensibilities of the court nobility. The feelings of *aware* and *hakanashi* that contributed to the concept of impermanence were thus given more powerful visual representation.

From impermanence to aesthetic refinement

The following years radically altered Japanese society. In particular, the establishment of the Kamakura shogunate would spur many changes in the aesthetic consciousness of the Japanese people. The turbulent spread of Kamakura Buddhism—from the Zen of Eisai and Dōgen to the Pure Land teachings of Hōnen and Shinran and Nichiren's focus on the *Lotus Sutra*— as well as the birth of a warrior aesthetic out of the heroic conflict of the Minamoto and Taira clans were all part of these developments. A "new wave" arose in the world of Shinto, characterized by an amalgamation with Buddhism and the identification of Shinto *kami* as avatars of specific members of the Buddhist pantheon (*honji suijaku*). Narratives of the rise and fall of the Taira that would eventually produce the epic *Tale of the Heike* were already being composed.

And from the perspective of the flower, as noted earlier, the feminine flower of *aware* was transformed into the masculine flower of *appare*, as typified by the legends that grew up around the tragic figure of Minamoto no Yoshitsune. This would feed into the later ideology and aesthetic of *bushidō*, as encapsulated in the saying "among flowers, the cherry; among men, the warrior" that equated the short but glorious lives of the samurai with cherry blossoms.

With regard to poetic style, the period was shaped by the compilation of the *Shinkokinshū* (New Collection of Poems Ancient and Modern), commissioned by the retired emperor Go-Toba and completed in 1205. Incidentally, in his final years Go-Toba also authored an unusual religious tract entitled *Mujō kōshiki* (Sermons on Impermanence).

The circumstances of the times produced a flood of individuals proclaiming their renunciation of the world, or *tonze*. Unlike in earlier times, this did not mean merely taking Buddhist vows and entering monastic life, but rather involved recognizing the impermanence of the things of this world and keeping that sense alive in an embrace of an aesthetic sensibility (*suki no kokoro*) keyed to the phenomenology of nature.

As I have touched on in chapter 3, "Deities," and elsewhere, the aesthetic sensibility of *suki* is rooted in the *susabi* (wildness) personified by the "rough god" Susanoo. Saigyō was perhaps the leading representative of this *suki*, but he was also joined by many other contemporaries, including the three Jaku of Ōhara (the brothers Jakunen, Jakuzen, and Jakuchō), whom he deeply respected; Fujiwara no Shunzei; Jien, author of the historical work *Gukanshō*; and Shunzei's son Teika. Later, Kamo no Chōmei,

Yoshida Kenkō, and even religious figures such as Dōgen and Ippen would help pave the way from impermanence (*mujō*) to aestheticism (*suki*). And Zeami would eventually channel these currents into an aesthetic of *yūgen*.

Kamo no Chōmei was the first, after Saigyō, to articulate a philosophical vision of the shift from impermanence to aestheticism. Disappointed in his life's ambition to be appointed to a major position at the Shimogamo Shrine in Kyoto, where his father had been the superintendent, he retired from the world and secluded himself in a hermitage at Hino, in the hills southeast of Kyoto.

In *Hōjōki* (An Account of a Hut Ten Feet Square, 1212) Chōmei writes, "Surely it is best to make friends with strings and woodwinds, blossoms and the moon,"[19] steeping himself in the life of the aesthetic recluse communing with the phenomena of nature. A certain ironical outlook can be detected in a way of life that included repeated readings of Genshin's *Essentials of Rebirth*. An episode about him in a collection of didactic stories, *Jikkinshō*, stresses a view of him as someone who failed in his life's plans, commenting, "he had desired to become a shrine official, but when this was not fulfilled, he grew resentful of the world and withdrew from it."

In the essay collection *Mumyōshō* (Anonymous Notes) Chōmei explains the concept of *yūgen*, writing that its importance lies in "overtones that do not appear in words and an atmosphere (*keiki*) that is not visible in the formal aspects of the poem."[20] As one example of *yūgen*, he posits an autumn evening in which the sky shows no particular color and makes no sound, and yet one is somehow moved to tears. As I have mentioned before, one of the themes we are pursuing in this book is precisely this mysterious power of the landscape, or *keiki*.

Yoshida Kenkō (c. 1283–c. 1352) would take Chōmei's invisible *keiki* even further, and with more thoroughness. Kenkō was another aristocratic runaway—but in contrast to Chōmei, who was past fifty when he took up the eremitic life, Kenkō was still in his early thirties when he secluded himself in Shugakuin and Yokawa (both part of the network of temples on and around Mount Hiei), and in his forties when he built the hermitage on Narabigaoka hill where he wrote his famous *Tsurezuregusa* (Essays in Idleness). Perhaps this is why he seems to have been more firmly grounded in his thought—and why he was able to set the point of departure for the medieval exploration of the phenomenology of nature. This sensibility is clearly expressed in the following passage from *Tsurezuregusa*:

FLOWERS

Are we to look at cherry blossoms only in full bloom, and the moon only when it is cloudless? To long for the moon while looking at the rain, to lower the blinds and be unaware of the passing of spring—these are even more deeply moving.[21]

Kenkō was completely committed to an aesthetic that focused on the heart, not on material things. He wrote scornfully of the crowds filling the stands erected for the procession of the Aoi Festival in Kyoto, "All they are interested in is what they can see."[22] Kenkō's own way of appreciating the festival was to take in the silence of the streets after it was over and recall the procession that had passed by: "You realize, with a pang of grief, that life is like this. If you have seen the avenues of the city, you have seen the festival."[23] Perhaps he overdoes it a bit here, but he is convincing, nonetheless.

In this way, the contributions of Saigyō, Shunzei, Teika, Chōmei, and Kenkō provided Zeami with the basis for developing his aesthetic of *yūgen*. As noted earlier, however, Zeami died before completing this work. It was Shinkei who would take things one step further.

Shinkei (1406–75) was a Buddhist cleric and master of linked verse at the temple Jūjūshin-in in the Higashiyama area of Kyoto. Although he eventually rose to a middle rank (*gon no daisōzu*) of the priesthood, he remained more interested in embracing the aesthetic of *yūgen*, which he had studied under the monk-poet Shōtetsu of the Reizei school, and devoting himself to aesthetic pursuits. The imperial *renga* anthology *Shinsen Tsukubashū* contains 123 verses by him, more than by any other poet. An intimate of Hosokawa Katsumoto, commander of the Eastern Army in the Ōnin War (1467–77), Shinkei became a close eyewitness to the events of this conflict. The destruction it wreaked upon the capital disgusted him, and in his later years he wandered the Kantō region of eastern Japan, eventually passing away at a hermitage in the foothills of Mount Ōyama in Sagami province (present-day Kanagawa prefecture). In other words, he was an itinerant *renga* master who lived—and died—on the road. Shinkei's *Hitorigoto* (Solitary Ramblings, 1468) contains this startling observation:

Nothing is more exquisite than ice. The stubbled fields of early morning, with needles of ice formed where sleet has glazed the cypress bark of the roof, or the dew and hoarfrost frozen upon the withered grasses and trees of the meadow—what is there to match this loveliness, this beauty.[24]

This paean to the beauty of ice offers a unique perspective that would later come to be known as *hiesabi* ("chill and aged," "chill melancholy"). Although he aspired to be, Zeami was never this cool. It was Shinkei who broke that barrier. In *Sasamegoto* (Whisperings) he offers the following dialogue:

> Question: Once a renowned poet was asked how a person should go about composing a poem. He replied:

> kareno no susuki　　Pampas grass on the withered moor,
> ariake no tsuki　　　the moonrise at dawn.

> Answer: By this he meant that one must turn at heart to what is unspoken and awaken to and grasp the chill and desolate (*hie-sabi*). The verse of the person who has fully attained the realm of mastery is wholly of this cast.[25]

Here Shinkei urges his readers to pay attention to what is unsaid, expose their hearts to cold and loneliness, and thus transcend their limitations. Saigyō never quite managed to erase the boundaries. Chōmei had a sense of history, but that was because he hung on to an awareness of boundaries, and not because he had transcended them. Zeami remained bound by the barriers of class, and so was exiled to Sado once he lost the patronage of those in power. It was Shinkei who finally broke through to this cold and austere vision of beauty—a beauty absent from the Kitayama culture of Yoshimitsu and Zeami.

Shinkei's *hiesabi* was acquired by the Japanese after the historical turning point of the Ōnin War and the late-fifteenth-century Higashiyama culture that it inspired, at a time when dry landscape gardens were just beginning to make their appearance. It is, I think, the ultimate expression of the phenomenology of nature in our culture.

CHAPTER 7 BUDDHAS

Asian Buddhas

The Japanese word for buddha, 仏 (pronounced *hotoke* or *butsu*), developed through a series of euphonic changes as the Sanskrit term migrated to Japan via the Chinese language. *Hotoke* began with the Sanskrit *buddha*, which the Chinese originally rendered phonetically with the characters *fotu* 仏図, *futu* 浮屠, or *futu* 浮図. In the Chinese dynastic histories, Buddhism was originally called *futuzong* 浮屠宗 (the sect of the Buddha). Japanese pronunciation turned *futu* into *hotoke.*

Buddhism in Japan is traditionally said to have been the result of a three-country transmission from India to China to Japan, and it is worth noting that the word that can be rendered with the single kanji 仏 traveled all the way across Asia. This three-country transmission is an indispensable perspective when considering the origins of Japanese culture. (A fourth country, Korea, should be added to this line of transmission but was omitted from the traditional reckoning.)

Many common expressions in Japan mention buddhas. For example, *hotoke no yō* (like a buddha) means that someone is gentle and kind, which is perhaps derived from the gentle visage of buddhas in religious iconography. The word *butchōzura* ("Buddha-face") suggests impassiveness or inscrutability. *Hotoke ni naru* (to become a buddha) means to die, and *hotoke-san* is a colloquial way of referring to a corpse or to the dead.

What manner of man was the historical Buddha? Strangely enough, while Japan is nominally a Buddhist country, most Japanese probably have a better notion of the life of Christ than they do of the life of the Buddha. To understand Buddhism, we really have to take a look back at the Buddha himself. This is, however, more difficult than one might think.

The teachings of the Buddha, like those of Christ, were written down and edited by his followers into sacred texts. But unlike in the Christian tradition, the disciples of the Buddha who studied with him in the sixth century BCE (referred to as the Ten Principal Disciples) did not leave any written records. It was several generations later that the first serious attempts were made to put the teachings into written form. These texts—the sutras—were originally written in the Magadhan dialect of eastern India, then in the Pali language of western India, and then finally translated into Sanskrit. After this canon became established, the sutras were translated into various Central Asian languages, including Tibetan, and into Chinese. The Chinese texts (including some that also passed through the Korean language) were then transmitted to Japan. Principal texts such as the *Lotus Sutra* (J. *Hokkekyō*), the *Flower Garland Sutra* (J. *Kegonkyō*), and the *Heart Sutra* (J. *Hannya shingyō*) all came to Japan from China.

Another reason that it is difficult to speak of the life of the Buddha is a proliferation of Jātaka tales—stories of the previous lives of the Buddha in human and animal forms—which have little to do with the actual life and thought of the Buddha but have become confused with them. A number of these are found in *Konjaku monogatari* (Tales of Times Now Past), a late-Heian anthology.

Let's consider the context from which the Buddha emerged. Imagine the Indian subcontinent around 2500 BCE. To the north lie the Himalayas and what is now Nepal, and to the east, the Ganges River flowing southward. To the west lie the Arabian Sea, the Gulf of Oman, and the Persian Gulf, into which flow the Indus and Tigris-Euphrates rivers. To the northwest lie the Caspian Sea and the Black Sea.

First, let's focus on the triangular region bounded by the Black Sea, the Caspian Sea, and the Persian Gulf, which is essentially the birthplace of world civilization. The Nile and Yellow River valleys are also regarded as origin points for civilization, but, based on evidence such as the geographical distribution of wild wheat, Western Asia seems to be where the basic requirements of civilization—chiefly the cultivation of grain and the emergence of settled agricultural communities—were first achieved. This was where the Sumerian civilization arose; one of its oldest cities was Ur.

The spark of civilization ignited in Western Asia flowed eastward over two principal routes. The first route was used by a nomadic herding people known as the Scythians, who originated north of the Caspian Sea. The Scythians moved eastward across Asia along the southern edge of Siberia, pushing local tribes and peoples such as the Tungus east as well, and eventually transmitting their influence to Japan via the Korean peninsula. Other nomadic peoples migrated in a similar fashion through what is now Mongolia along the so-called Steppe Route, a precursor to the Silk Road.

The other major route is more closely related to our topic of Buddhas and involves the Indo-Aryan peoples, whose origins remain unclear but whose migration from what is now Iraq and Iran into India stimulated the birth of Indian civilization. Other civilizations had developed centuries earlier in the Indus and Tigris-Euphrates river basin, but the migrations of the Indo-Aryans changed everything.

In India, the period beginning with the Indo-Aryan migrations is known as the Vedic period. The Vedas are a large canon of religious and liturgical texts compiled by the Brahmanic priesthood of ancient India. If we date the Indus Valley civilization from about 2500 BCE, then the Vedic period begins around 1500 BCE.

From this time forward, Asia underwent a major transformation. In other words, if we could know what sort of culture these Indo-Aryan peoples brought with them, it might reveal a great deal about the early days of these ancient civilizations. Unfortunately, research into these early migrations, based on comparison of the characteristics of Vedic culture with those of earlier city-states such as Mohenjo-Daro, is still in its infancy.

The Indo-Aryans instilled in the indigenous peoples of the Indian subcontinent new religious concepts that would eventually merge with Dravidian religion and ideas.

Escape from samsara

One of the central concepts that the Indo-Aryans introduced was samsara, the cycle of death and rebirth, or, to put it more simply, the idea of life after death. The belief was that future rebirth was determined by one's actions in the present life. During the era of the Upanishads at the end of the Vedic period, samsara became associated with the concept of karmic retribution.

Two possible courses of this cycle of death and rebirth were imagined. The first was "the path of the ancestors," which awaited those who had observed proper rites and rituals, performed good works, and were generous and charitable. When such people died and were cremated, it was believed that their spirit would first travel to the moon, then fall as rain upon the land to be absorbed by the roots of plants. If eaten by a man, they would form sperm, enter a woman's womb, and be reborn. An alternative path was "the path of the gods" followed by ascetics performing austerities in the wilderness. After death they, too, would be cremated, but would ascend to heaven out of the flames, and after passing through various worlds would eventually reach the realm of Brahma, where they would remain.

Others would follow neither of these paths. This was the fate of the majority, those who had not done much with their lives and so were trapped in the nightmare of not knowing where they might end up in their next life. Their perpetual circling through rebirth in what came to be known as "the three worlds and six realms" gave rise to the Japanese expression "no home among the three worlds" (*sangai ni ie nashi*).

The peoples who came to India were nomads, having no fixed abode; their lives had been a series of journeys. They were well aware of the unknowability of when or where death would come; this was something they simply accepted. What animal they might be reborn as did not concern them. For city-dwellers, who were primarily indigenous, the idea of being reborn as an animal after death was frightening and presented the issue of what could be done to escape such a fate. This escape would later be called *vimokṣavimukti* (J. *gedatsu*), meaning liberation, release, or salvation.

With the arrival of Vedic culture in India, Hinduism was born. Hinduism in turn gave birth to the caste system, including the aristocratic Brahmin caste. At the time of the Buddha's birth—around the sixth century BCE—the Brahmins dominated politics, economics, and the lower orders of the caste system. Their sense of privilege extended to the conviction that only their own liberation was of any importance.

It was at this juncture that six revolutionaries—later known as the Six Heretical Teachers—appeared. They criticized the techniques, including meditation, used by the Brahmins in their search for liberation and offered their own teachings and methods, which emphasized rigorous ascetic practices. Under this influence, the Brahmin religion entered an era of asceticism.

This was the era into which Siddhārtha Gautama, later known as Shakyamuni Buddha, was born. The Shakyas were a clan that ruled the Kapilavastu region in northern India. Siddhārtha was a prince of this clan, and a Brahmin.

The sixth century BCE, when the Buddha was born, was a critical period in world history. It was the time of Pythagoras and Heraclitus in Greece, of Isaiah in the Judaic tradition (specifically, Deutero-Isaiah, or Second Isaiah), of Confucius and Laozi in China. Somewhat later we have Zhuangzi in China, and Zoroaster in Persia. All over the world, great sages arose who would have enormous influence on the history of the human race. The

German philosopher Karl Jaspers has called this the "Axial Age" of humanity. Why did this synchronicity occur?

The geographer Suzuki Hideo at the University of Tokyo offers one hypothesis, charting the influence of temperature on civilization. Throughout the history of the planet, he argues, surface temperature has increased and decreased in repeating wavelike cycles. Periods of rising temperatures are called hypsithermal, and one of these warmer periods occurred in the fifth to seventh centuries BCE, a time of great advances in human consciousness when sages and great teachers appeared in the world. I will simply note that at the time the Buddha appeared near the headwaters of the Ganges River, similarly courageous individuals armed with great philosophies were proclaiming revolutionary ideas in other parts of the world.

From asceticism to meditation

The name Siddhārtha means "one who has attained his goal." As is typical in the life stories of sages and holy men, we are told he was a beautiful child, his body golden. Showered with love, he was educated as befitted a prince in both the intellectual and martial arts and grew to be a fine young man. But he was a sensitive and perceptive individual and became deeply concerned by the question of why people must die. He began to ask whether there might be a greater purpose to human life. This was a question that almost all members of the aristocracy of his day at least entertained at some point, though most of them did nothing more than consult the priests and be reassured by the orthodox answers they received. Siddhārtha was not satisfied with such explanations.

Siddhārtha was so loved and coddled by his parents and all of his retinue that he had never set foot beyond the palace. He was also allowed to indulge himself as much as he liked with concubines. But his doubts and questions about life continued to grow, and he began to desire to see what the world outside the palace was like. And one day, he found the opportunity to do so.

Accompanied by an attendant, he departed from the east gate of the palace, where he almost immediately came across an old man on the verge of death. This was his first face-to-face encounter with the reality of old age and death. Deeply shocked, he returned to the palace. He then exited from the west gate and encountered a sick man. Then, at the south gate, he ran into a funeral procession and saw a corpse, as still as a stone. In short, setting foot outside three of the four gates of the palace, Siddhārtha was confronted with the essentially painful nature of human life.

This episode of the Four Gates is treated as the first important event in the life of the Buddha. In his poem "Ame ni mo makezu" (Strong in the Rain), the Japanese poet Miyazawa Kenji portrays his ideal self as a person who, when there is a sick child in the west, goes to care for it; when a person is dying in the south, goes to say there is nothing to fear; and so on. Siddhārtha's encounters at the Four Gates clearly underlie this famous poem. Miyazawa was a fervent believer in the *Lotus Sutra*; he would later write the poem "Namu *Saddharma Puṇḍarīka Sūtra*" (Sanskrit for "Hail to the *Lotus Sutra*").

But what of the north and final gate? There, Siddhārtha met a gaunt and ragged ascetic about to leave on a pilgrimage. Something in the ascetic's demeanor suggested a sense of purpose and determination. Seeing this, Siddhārtha knew for the first time the path he himself would choose, and he left from the gate to engage the world outside the palace.

This is the story relating Siddhārtha's motivation for leaving the comforts of home and family to begin his quest for liberation; it was from here that he started on the path toward enlightenment and buddhahood. He first entered a community of other ascetics who followed a rigorous practice involving severe fasting and other mortifications of the body.

At that time in India, there was a holy man named Mahāvira, the great propagator of Jainism, and one of the Six Heretical Teachers mentioned earlier. In my youth, there was a time when I was more enchanted by Mahāvira than the Buddha. I once spent an entire night talking with the writer Haniya Yutaka (1909–97) about Jainism. Mahāvira was an uncompromising ascetic who went about completely naked; the Sanskrit word for this practice, "sky-clad," later became the name of one of the two principal sects of Jainism, Digambara. The practices of Mahāvira and his followers were at the cutting edge of asceticism in those times.

Siddhārtha found that no manner of austerity relieved his suffering, and after six years of diligent training he had gained nothing. His vital energy completely exhausted, he collapsed. His body was emaciated, his hair wild. A milkmaid named Sujata from a nearby village passed by, saw his plight, and offered him milk to restore his strength. Whether or not this actually happened, it describes Siddhārtha regaining the strength of his body and mind after punishing ascetic practice. This image of the bearded, emaciated Siddhārtha is known in iconography as "Buddha emerging from the mountains"—the mountains signifying ascetic retreat.

After regaining his strength, Siddhārtha then sat down to meditate beneath an *aśvattha* tree—which would later be known as the bodhi tree, or tree of enlightenment (its Latin name is *Ficus religiosa*). A member of the mulberry family, the *aśvattha* is common throughout northern India. Regarded as sacred from the Indus civilization onward, it is described in the Atharva Veda as "an abode of the gods"; it was, we might say, a world tree for the contemplation of immortality. Under this tree, Siddhārtha sought the mental state he had been unable to achieve through austerities—his original self, the state beyond selfhood. Restored to a pristine body and mind by the milk Sujata had given him, he entered into meditation beneath the tree, and one night, under a full moon, he attained enlightenment.

This initial breakthrough to enlightenment was his awakening as a buddha, and what is called in Japanese "attaining the Way" (*jōdō*). For the Buddha, enlightenment was something visited upon him as a kind of blessing. He did not initially think of it as something he should teach others. But at that point—no doubt a story added in later times—Brahma, the highest deity in the Hindu pantheon, appeared and told him, "This enlightenment is not yours alone. You must teach others your thought and what you have realized." This encounter resembles the story of Yahweh speaking to Moses from the burning bush.

Taking Brahma's message to heart, the Buddha set out to deliver his first sermon, or, as it is known in the Buddhist tradition, "the first turning of the wheel of the Dharma." His destination was the Deer Park at Sarnath, on the outskirts of Benares, a place well known at the time as a haven for religious practitioners of all kinds. There the Buddha met a number of former acquaintances from his years as an ascetic. They had regarded him as someone who had fallen away from the ascetic path, but upon meeting him again they were struck by his newfound dignity and strength and asked him to teach them what he had learned.

News of the Buddha spread rapidly, and the number of his followers grew steadily. Holy men brought their own followers to listen to the Buddha's teachings. Thus the group around the Buddha expanded, gradually developing into what became known as the sangha, the community of practitioners. This was the first Buddhist religious organization, resembling the twelve apostles of Jesus and the community formed by his early followers.

The Buddha, accompanied by a small number of his disciples, began to travel among the various states and kingdoms of northern India, bringing his message to the people. This group, having renounced family life, had no fixed abode and led a life of travel and teaching. But during the rainy season they would make a temporary camp in the vicinity of a village or town. The dwellings they made for this purpose would eventually develop into *vihāra* (J. *shōja*), or monastic residences. Later, kings and rich merchants endowed such monasteries as a form of charity. Two of the most important were the Venuvana and the Jetavana monasteries.

The Jetavana monastery was endowed by Sudatta, a wealthy lay follower of the Buddha, whose generosity was so legendary that he became known by the name Anathapindika—literally "almsgiver to the helpless." An alternative name for Jetavana was "Anathapindika's Garden in the Jeta Grove"; transliterated into Chinese characters and abbreviated, this would become Gion in Japanese, serving as both the Japanese name for the Jetavana monastery in India and the name for an important shrine and the district surrounding it in the capital of Kyoto. It was around these early monasteries that Buddhism as a religion was born; historians of religion have described this period of its development as "original" Buddhism.

As the sangha expanded and this original Buddhism began to take on a more mature form, the Buddha's health began to decline, and he approached the end of life. In Japanese the Buddha's death is referred to by such terms as *nyūmetsu* ("extinction") or *nehan ni hairu* ("entering nirvana"), nirvana being a Sanskrit word that originally meant the extinction of suffering—not death. However, since death is also the extinction or blowing out of the spark of life, nirvana came to be associated with that as well. And so the life of the historical Buddha came to an end.

If I had to sum up the thought of the Buddha in a single phrase, I would not hesitate to say, "insight into interconnectedness," or a deep understanding of what we call *engi* in Japan.

Siddhārtha attained enlightenment under the bodhi tree, was told by Brahma that he must go forth and teach his realization, and began to walk the great path of the Buddha. When he did, he began to become aware that his personal experience of enlightenment and his own thoughts brushed against what might be called connections or links in the outside world. Outside and inside were inextricably intertwined. His intense realization of this fact formed the core of his thought.

Say we have a glass of water. At first glance, the water seems to simply sit there in the glass, but in reality, physical processes are taking place, such as evaporation and condensation, that make it possible to say the water is actually entering and leaving the glass moment by moment. If the glass were filled with liquid helium, it would be easier to see it spilling over the lip of the glass and into the surrounding environment.

This is the concept of *engi* (Sk. *pratītyasamutpāda*), of interconnectedness—or "interdependent co-origination"—in Buddhism. Completely unrelated entities can, through the power of mediation, through an uncanny fluidity, overflow their boundaries to interconnect with one another. What appear to be external relationships and connections are actually internal; apparently internal links and relations are in fact external. The basis for the Buddha's teaching may be found here in this sense of the interrelationship or interdependency of all phenomena.

The nucleus of the Buddha's experience, on the other hand, was meditation (Sk. *dhyana*, J. *zenjō*) and the concentration of awareness (Sk. *samādhi*, J. *sanmai*) that arose from it—the ideal mental states that led to his enlightenment. If we compare *zenjō* and *sanmai* with *engi*, then we can say that meditation would seem to produce a state pleasurable to the individual, while *engi* is something quite different: the pleasure of becoming one with something other than the self—a principle of unconscious sympathy, resonance, identification. Meditation and interdependence form the opposite poles of the Buddha's experience and thought.

Moreover, while it is a perception that seems likely to have antedated him, the Buddha is regarded as having been thoroughly uncompromising in his assertion in the First Noble Truth that "life is suffering." We see this in allegorical form in his excursions from the gates of his father's palace to encounter what all human beings must encounter: the pains of sickness, old age, and death.

The compassion of the bodhisattvas

Following the death of the Buddha, the original Buddhist religious community divided into factions, as one might expect. That even the original sangha of the Buddha would generate such schisms is a testament to the human capacity for discord, rancor, and the competition for dominance.

The first schism was between a conservative group known as the Sthavira Nikāya ("sect of the elders") and a progressive group called the Mahāsāṃghika ("the great sangha"); their rift marked the beginning of what would later become the major division in Buddhism, between

Theravada Buddhism and Mahayana Buddhism. (Note that Theravada is sometimes referred to as Hinayana, a derogatory name meaning "lesser vehicle," in contrast to the "greater vehicle" of Mahayana.)

In the third century BCE, as the organizers of the early Buddhist sangha were beginning their activities, Ashoka, the powerful ruler of the Mauryan dynasty, took a particular interest in Buddhism and began dispatching missionaries far and wide. As a result, the religion spread through almost all of what is now India, but as it did, its teachings became formulaic and corrupted. It was in this context that internal schisms occurred within the sangha, producing the two main traditions of Theravada and Mahayana, which carried on an extensive ideological conflict with one another. These disputes gave rise to a vast body of interpretive and explanatory literature known as the Abhidharma ("special teaching"). They also led to further divisions of the sangha, particularly in the so-called Sect of the Elders.

One of the most powerful of these factions within the Sthavira Nikāya was the Sarvāstivāda ("the theory that all exists"), which produced a highly abstract body of thought that was quite compelling, but that also strove so hard to maintain fidelity to the original teachings of the Buddha that it grew overly philosophical and complex. Another sect was the Vibhajyavāda ("defenders of what is to be differentiated"), which opposed the Sarvāstivāda on many points. This sect later established a stronghold in Sri Lanka, and from there it developed into the form of Theravada Buddhism that would spread throughout Southeast Asia.

In reaction to these philosophical developments, a movement for greater unity and integration arose that eventually grew into the Buddhist tradition known as Mahayana. The rise of Mahayana Buddhism was occasioned by something that occurs in almost any age: a call to go "back to basics." At the time, the Buddhist sangha included both *shravakas* (monastics) and *pratyekabuddha* ("lone buddhas"), who practiced in the mountains and forests. Both sought to become arhats, holy men who had gained insight into the true nature of existence. The reformists in the Buddhist sangha began calling for a return to the Buddha's original teachings. They declared that the goal of religious life and practice should be to become living buddhas.

In China and Japan, the earliest disciples of the Buddha to walk the holy path are known as the Sixteen Arhats, and the participants in the First Council of the Buddhist sangha are called the Five Hundred Arhats.

Collective images of these arhats, each rendered with uniquely individual features and expressions, are enshrined at many Zen temples in Japan including inside the main gate of Tōfukuji. The Japanese image of the arhat in a non-idealized, deeply human form is reflected in these imaginative and often playful images.

What distinguishes Mahayana Buddhism from Theravada Buddhism can be distilled into the Mahayana concept of the bodhisattva.

A major landmark in the emergence of Mahayana Buddhism was the compilation of the Prajñāpāramitā sutras, a collective term for the *Mahāprajñāpāramitā Sutra* and some forty other sutras on the subject of prajna (supreme or transcendental wisdom) that followed it. The establishment of this corpus of teaching, around the beginning of the Christian era, divided the Theravada and Mahayana traditions and was an epochal event in the history of East Asia. The two fundamental teachings in this literature concerned prajna and shunyata, or "emptiness."

In Mahayana Buddhism, the material and mental phenomena having to do with humans and the world are believed to contain six dimensions of "perfection," or paramitas. The name of the historic Kyoto temple Rokuharamitsuji means "The Temple of the Six Paramitas."

Prajna, commonly translated as "wisdom," is one of the Six Paramitas. But what sort of wisdom is prajna? This is difficult to explain, but we can begin by saying that it is the knowledge that was attained by the Buddha when he realized the mutual interdependence of all phenomena. By extension, it means the capacity for deep insight into the principle of impermanence as understood by Buddhism, and beyond that, a knowledge so transcendent that it surpasses our capacity to put it into words.

So is prajna something like Michael Polanyi's concept of "tacit knowledge"[1]—a deep level of understanding that is difficult to articulate in language? Not really. "Tacit knowledge" refers to knowledge expressed but not codified, while prajna is an archetypal wisdom that transcends its own archetype and thus can be transmitted only in silence.

Meanwhile, "emptiness" or shunyata is a concept of freedom transcending all phenomena and constraints, resembling what the Greek philosopher Epicurus called ataraxia. But ataraxia denotes a mental state of equanimity or imperturbable freedom, while in the era of the Prajñāpāramitā sutras, shunyata focused more on how "emptiness" could and should be apprehended.

Imagine, for example, a garden in which there is no ox. The absent ox is "empty," but I am here to perceive this emptiness. Then, to the emptiness of the absent ox and my perception of that emptiness must be added another layer perceiving all of this as empty. This is the emptiness of shunyata, in which all phenomena are empty of self-nature and interdependent.

We've slipped into rather deep water here, but suffice it to say that the Mahayana monks who preached the doctrines of prajna and shunyata would eventually come to be referred to as bodhisattvas.

What was the way of thinking defined by the bodhisattvas? The core of it was that enlightenment should not be a purely individual matter; one's own process of awakening must be accompanied by works and teaching aimed at the salvation of others. This was something slightly different from preaching religious doctrine; the bodhisattvas had already gone beyond such activities. Listening to someone expounding dogma or reading the scriptures was of little use. One needed to seek out the monks already recognized as bodhisattvas and train with them.

The Sanskrit word *bodhisattva* is a compound of *bodhi* (enlightenment) and *sattva* (sentient being). "Sentient being" refers to living things possessing mind or consciousness, as opposed to other elements of the natural world—mountains and rivers, plants and trees—that do not. A bodhisattva is thus a person who possesses a mind that seeks enlightenment.

Such awakened individuals exist in any age and any culture. And word of them gets around. Other people want to meet these "spiritual superstars," and the ardor they feel increases the popularity of the bodhisattvas by leaps and bounds. First you have the Beatles, soon followed by a wave of other rock musicians aspiring to be the Beatles. At a certain point this creates a prototype for the rock star (or bodhisattva). The next generation buys the recordings of these rock stars, goes to their concerts, practices their songs and styles. And before you know it, rock music has spread throughout the world. This sort of charismatic effect was one of the secrets of the rapid diffusion of Mahayana Buddhism, and why many of the Mahayana sutras are filled with passages praising the virtues and merits of the bodhisattvas.

Largely in the first and second centuries of the Common Era, after the initial compilation of the Prajñāpāramitā sutras, Mahayana Buddhism inspired a new wave of sutra production that gave birth to the *Lotus Sutra*, the *Flower Garland Sutra*, the *Nirvana Sutra*, and the *Vimalakirti Sutra*, among others. All of these sutras are grounded in a fundamentally similar worldview but vary according to the character and personality of the bodhisattvas that feature prominently in them.

Moreover, these sutras are written on an epic scale. Shaped around the bodhisattvas that star in them, they are united in their attempt to convey the extraordinary, all-embracing quality of the bodhisattvas.

With the legendary lives of actual bodhisattvas as a model, a number of ideal bodhisattvas were generated. Of these ideal bodhisattvas, Avalokiteś-vara (J. Kannon) has perhaps played the broadest role.

The first images of Avalokiteśvara were created in about the fifth century in the vicinity of Sarnath in northern India. Different iconographical treatments arose, beginning with the Blue-Throated Avalokiteśvara and, by the sixth century, such variations as the Eleven-Headed Avalokiteśvara. In other words, from the beginning Avalokiteśvara was a "bodhisattva of transformation," taking on a variety of forms and guises.

The concept of Avalokiteśvara as a bodhisattva of transformation was canonized in a chapter of the *Lotus Sutra* devoted to Avalokiteśvara that gained popularity as a stand-alone sutra known in Japan as the *Kannonkyō*. The *Kannonkyō* describes the "skillful means" that the bodhisattva uses to save sentient beings, appearing to them in manifestations appropriate to their condition and level of understanding. This image had immense appeal, making Avalokiteśvara the most popular of all bodhisattvas and encouraging a diversity of iconographic representations. Aside from the standard form, known as Shō Kannon (Holy Kannon) in Japanese, popular versions included

Jūichimen Kannon (Eleven-Headed Kannon), Fukūkenjaku Kannon (Kannon of the Unerring Lasso), Senju Kannon (Thousand-Armed Kannon), Batō Kannon (Horse-Headed Kannon), Nyoirin Kannon (Kannon of the Jewel and Wheel), and Juntei Kannon (Kannon of Purity). Sets of six out of these seven (varying according to school) were venerated as the Six Kannon.

The *Lotus Sutra* is not the only canonical text containing descriptions of Avalokiteśvara. In the *Flower Garland Sutra*, Avalokiteśvara is described as residing on Mount Potalaka (J. Fudaraku), giving rise to a belief that this was the Pure Land of the bodhisattva. And

Thousand-Armed Kannon, eighth century. Tōshōdaiji temple, Nara.

BUDDHAS

in the *Sutra of Immeasurable Life* (*Longer Sukhavativyuha Sutra*; J. *Muryō-jukyō*) Avalokiteśvara is described as one of the attendants of the Buddha Amitābha (J. Amida). As a result, in many temples in Japan, a standing or seated image of Amida is flanked by images of the bodhisattvas Kannon (on the right) and Seishi (on the left)—forming a trinity representing the Western Paradise.

Emptiness, the middle way, and impermanence

It was during the spread of Buddhism in the second and third centuries that the great philosopher Nāgārjuna was born. Nāgārjuna was a Brahmin from south India, rumored to have been skilled in magical arts, including the ability to make himself invisible, like a ninja. In his youth he is said to have used these powers to entertain himself and indulge in sensual pleasures (invading the palace to have his way with the women there, for example). But eventually, perhaps as some divine punishment, he lost the ability to enjoy these illicit pursuits, had a complete change of heart, and became a Buddhist monastic.

He began to devote himself to the study of Buddhist teachings, reading everything he could find. Eventually he realized that while Theravada Buddhism offered plenty of theory, it would not enable him to attain buddhahood itself. He turned to the concepts of shunyata and prajna and developed a philosophy of the "middle way" that became the foundation for a significant school of Buddhist thought known as Mādhyamika.

Nāgārjuna's philosophy was based on a logical construct known as the tetralemma, or fourfold negation. A dilemma is a logical method based on the denial of two separate propositions. It is not as negative as is commonly thought; by denying rather than adhering to either of the two original propositions, one finds a way forward. It is actually an affirmation of sorts. The trilemma is a triple negation: not A, not B, but neither not-A nor not-B.

Eventually, Nāgārjuna found both the dilemma and the trilemma to be insufficient. With the tetralemma—piling on a fourth negation—he eliminated logic itself. Or perhaps we could say that by negating logic, he broke through to a new and more transcendent logical system.

For example, take these four propositions: I exist. I do not exist. I both exist and do not exist. I neither exist nor do not exist. This completely and totally reduces all objects of language to their vanishing point; this is the transcendental logic Nāgārjuna created. The disappearance of logic itself at the vanishing point is in fact shunyata, or emptiness, and the ability to stand in that position is the middle way or middle path.

This manner of thinking regarding emptiness and the middle way would have a far-reaching impact on Buddhism, becoming one of the foundations of Mahayana thought not only in India but also in Tibet and China.

In sixth-century China, the Tiantai (J. Tendai) Buddhist master Zhiyi added the concept of "provisional existence" (C. *jia*, J. *ke*) to Nāgārjuna's emptiness and middle way and, on the basis of this "threefold truth," created a fantastic, dazzling logical and theoretical system that was captured in *Mohe zhiguan* (The Great Calming and Contemplation), a treatise based on his lectures that also addresses the fundamentals of Buddhist meditation (*zhi* and *guan* being the Chinese for *śamatha* and *vipaśyanā*, two essential meditation practices).

With the emergence of the Madhyamika school from within Mahayana Buddhism, other schools and sects were also energized. The influential Buddhist scholar Vasubandhu, author of the *Abhidharmakośakārikā* (Verses on the Treasury of the Abhidharma), lived during this time. Hinduism, which had been losing ground to Buddhism, also began to show new life with vigorous sectarian debate among the Six Philosophical Schools, laying the groundwork for the great achievements of Indian thought in the fifth and sixth centuries. I highly recommend the religious scholar Kimura Taiken's brilliant book, *Indo roppa tetsugaku* (The Six Schools of Indian Philosophy), for further study on this subject.

After this, however, Buddhism and Hinduism in India (with the exception of some esoteric sects) headed into a gradual decline—just as Islam emerged as a vital force and began its journey to the east.

The arrival of Islam, like the earlier Western Asian civilizations, reached India in successive waves. Indian Buddhism became a paradise for heterodox sects, and in medieval times yoga and other therapeutic practices, as well as Tantric Buddhism and Hinduism, flourished as mainstream Buddhism gradually lost its original vigor and power.

Kegon and Zen

So where did Buddhism go from there? Eastward, to Central Asia, Tibet, and China, and to Southeast Asia. If not for the rise of Islam in Western

Asia, Buddhism probably would have reached Europe as well. If it had, there would have been a direct confrontation between Christianity and Buddhism, and perhaps a Christian Buddhism would have emerged.

I say this because it has been acknowledged that a number of Buddhist elements—literary rather than religious—found their way into the Arab world in the stories of *One Thousand and One Nights*, and a Buddhist influence can also be detected in many European legends and folk tales. In his book *Ōgon densetsu to buddaden* (The Golden Legend and the Lives of the Buddhas, 1992), the popular historian Harada Minoru offers a variety of fascinating evidence demonstrating the incorporation of Buddhist stories into European medieval narratives of the lives of the saints.

So from the fourth to the sixth century, Buddhism crossed Central Asia and flowed into China, permeating society in the period from the disintegration of the Han dynasty through the era of the Northern and Southern dynasties.

In China the teachings of the various Indian Buddhist sects were initially scrutinized, compared, and appraised, both with one another and with the established traditions of Confucianism and Daoism. Buddhism began to take root in specifically Chinese form around the end of the fourth century, when the monk Huiyuan formed a Buddhist association called the White Lotus Society on Mount Lushan. This would eventually develop into the Pure Land sect, creating the earliest climate for a distinctly Chinese Buddhist culture.

In the sixth century with the Tiantai master Zhiyi and in the seventh century with Xuanzang, the great scholar and translator of the Buddhist canon, there was something of a "back to basics" movement seeking the Indian roots of the teachings. This had the effect of stimulating a full-fledged flowering of uniquely Chinese forms of Buddhism. Xuanzang's and Yijing's travels to India were of great significance in this sense.

There was also a reverse flow of influence from India to China. Buddhism was waning in India, and many outstanding Buddhist clerics left India for Central Asia and, ultimately, China. Utopian models of Buddhist communities, such as Dunhuang, sprang up along the route. The situation resembled one that would occur in later times, when the declining fortunes of Buddhism in China resulted in many Chinese Buddhist monks crossing the sea to Japan.

One of the Indian monks who made his way to China around the middle of the fifth century was the Chan (J. Zen) master Bodhidharma, though it was not until the seventh century and the era of the sixth Chan patriarch in China, Huineng, that Bodhidharma's teachings would become firmly established in China. The seventh century was also when Buddhist teachings from South India based on the *Flower Garland Sutra* reached China, and the great Chinese teacher Fazang of the Flower Garland (C. Huayan, J. Kegon) school strove to adapt them to the Chinese situation.

Esoteric Buddhism (C. Mijiao or Mizong; J. Mikkyō) was the final form to arrive in China, brought by the Indian masters Śubhakarasiṃha, Vajrabodhi, and Amoghavajra. The latter proved especially capable of taking the esoteric teachings he had learned from Vajrabodhi and interpreting them for a Chinese audience, and they soon spread throughout China.

Summing up these rather complex and multifaceted developments in Chinese Buddhism, we might say that Buddhist teachings flowed into China along three main routes: the Huayan route, the Chan route, and the esoteric route. In actuality the three were preceded by the *Lotus Sutra* route (of Tiantai Buddhism) and the Pure Land route (of Huiyuan), both of which I touched on earlier. The concept of the Pure Land and the central importance of the *Lotus Sutra* are widely seen as the foundations for everything else in Buddhism.

The Huayan route ran over the Silk Road, traversing Central Asia to reach China. The Chan route followed what we believe to have been Bodhidharma's itinerary, by sea from south India to the port of Hangzhou, then up the Yangtze River and from there to Luoyang, capital of the Northern Wei dynasty. The esoteric route probably used both the Central Asian and maritime routes.

Huayan teachings had the most significant impact on Chinese culture. Chan was focused on the individual attainment of enlightenment, and esoteric Buddhism was aimed at awakening to hidden or secret truths. In contrast, the nature of Huayan thought was to address the universe as a whole—seeing the entire universe as a comprehensive network. Having entered China, the two streams of "global" Huayan and "personal" Chan would collide and combine with one another.

Thus, in the early stages of its development, Chinese Buddhism was confronted with the unusual challenge of having to integrate Huayan and Chan. This meant that esoteric Buddhism, which came into China later, was left with no other way of deepening its world of thought than to attempt to transcend this amalgam of Huayan and Chan.

The world of mutual interpenetration and non-hindrance

The classic exposition of the Huayan worldview is contained in the *Mahāvaipulya buddhāvataṃsaka sūtra* (The Great and Extensive Sutra of the Buddha's Flower Garland), or, as it is commonly known, the *Flower Garland Sutra* (Sk. *Avataṃsaka sūtra*, C. *Huayanjing*, J. *Kegonkyō*). As suggested by its title, this sutra is concerned with buddhahood. The full title of the *Lotus Sutra*, by comparison, is the *Saddharma puṇḍarīka sūtra*, literally, the "Sutra on the White Lotus of the Sublime Dharma," reflecting its primary aim of expounding the dharma. In the Buddhist canon, different sutras clearly focus on different purposes.

In its Chinese translations (several of which exist), the *Flower Garland Sutra* is enormous, running from forty to eighty volumes depending on the version. Based on the concept of "the myriad leaves [all phenomena] become buddhas" (J. *man'yō kebutsu*), this sutra describes buddhas as being present everywhere, in every pore of the skin of every creature. Uniting these innumerable avatars was the immense and all-encompassing dharma-body of the sutra's central, cosmic buddha, Vairocana (J. Birushana).

The Great Buddha of Tōdaiji in Nara is a classic rendering of Vairocana Buddha. The Sanskrit name means "Buddha of All-Pervading Light," and Huayan thought is constructed around this central illuminated being.

The longest version of the *Flower Garland Sutra*, comprising thirty-nine chapters in eighty volumes, begins with the Buddha awakening to enlightenment under the bodhi tree, at which point light begins to emanate from his mouth, and the bodhisattva Samantabhadra (J. Fugen) enters samadhi (deep concentration) to announce that preparations for the advent of the principal subject of the sutra have been completed. With this, buddhas from throughout the universe assemble, and Vairocana Buddha makes a grand entrance to commence a discourse on the Huayan worldview. This is the prologue to the sutra proper; it takes up the first six chapters of the text, setting a quite leisurely pace.

In chapters 13 and 14, Mount Sumeru is depicted and Indra (J. Taishakuten) appears; by chapter 19, we reach the Yāma heaven. The text gradually becomes theoretically richer, and in chapter 26 commences a famous discourse on the ten "grounds" or stages of the bodhisattva's practice and development, keyed to the ten perfections (paramitas). From this point onward the Huayan secret teachings are revealed one after another. Chapter 36, "Samantabhadra's Practice," speaks of the profoundly providential nature of the complete and perfect teaching. The sutra finally reaches its logical climax in chapter 37, "The Manifestation of Buddha," a magnificent and subtle exposition of the fundamental innateness and identity of the manifestations of the Buddha. The final chapter, "Entering the Dharma Realm"—comprising about a quarter of the length of the entire *Flower Garland Sutra* as well as circulating as a sutra in its own right, known as the *Flower-Array* (*Gaṇḍavyūha*) *Sutra*—is a kind of spiritual bildungsroman in which the disciple Sudhana travels to visit fifty-three "wise advisors" in his quest for enlightenment.

The sutra is thus of breathtakingly heroic scope. And I might mention in passing that Japan's famous Fifty-Three Stations on the Tōkaidō Road—the series of post-station towns created in the Edo period to link the shogunal capital of Edo with the imperial capital of Kyoto—was based (at least numerically) on Sudhana's visits to his fifty-three spiritual mentors.

If the central concept of the *Flower Garland Sutra* were to be summed up in a single phrase, it would be "mutual interpenetration and non-hindrance" (J. *yūzū muge*). In colloquial Japanese this phrase has come to mean "versatile," or "flexible," which makes it sound rather sloppy and careless, but that is simply because we have been using it in a sloppy way. It is actually a profound teaching.

Imagine an infinite number of mirrored spheres glittering in the light. Arrayed in all directions, endless, each of these spheres reflects each of the others, producing an utterly indescribable chain reaction of illumination. This image, which appears in the *Flower Garland Sutra*, is called "The Diamond Net of Indra." The concept of *yūzū muge* refers precisely to this realm of mutual reflection—a realm of complete and perfect boundlessness (*muge* means without defect or hindrance; that is, our mirrored spheres have no scratches). Its apotheosis is the *jiji muge hokkai*, a transcendental "dharma-realm" in which all phenomena freely and flawlessly exist in mutual interdependence.

What is this dizzying image of a network of mirrored orbs of light trying to tell us? That in the smallest particle of dust the entirety of the world is reflected; that in the smallest unit the relations of the whole are contained.

This is what might be called the end point of a hyperholonic system, borrowing the concept of the holon as articulated by the biologist Ludwig von Bertalanffy, founder of general systems theory, and Arthur Koestler, who wrote *The Ghost in the Machine* (1967). Holon is the name given to self-reliant individual parts of a system that, even if removed from it, would still show the influence of their relationship to the whole. The biophysicist Shimizu Hiroshi has been using this concept in his research into biological information systems that he calls bioholonics.

The *Flower Garland Sutra* also stresses a concept called *shōki* 性起 in Japanese (or *xingqi* in Chinese), meaning something like "naturally arising," or "arising from intrinsic nature." According to this view, human beings are all intrinsically endowed with buddha-nature, and the existence of a given individual in a certain place and time is in itself a realization of buddha-nature. All things possess the capacity to realize truth, as encapsulated in the phrase *kyotai zenshin* 挙体全真 (made up of the words for "body" and "complete perfection"). This is the basic idea of *shōki*, which may be described as one of the core concepts of Huayan thought.

The Huayan hyperholonic system is the result of an infinite replication of *shōki*. This is described as "mutual identity and mutual penetration" (C. *xiangji xiangru* 相即相入, J. *sōsoku sōnyū*), or "mutually variable and mutually interrelated" (C. *xiangyi xiangru* 相移相入, J. *sōi sōnyū*): a world whose constituent elements transcend the boundaries and divisions separating them to freely intermingle with one another. If this sounds like a total free-for-all, that's because it is.

Huayan thought was rendered in an intensely difficult and meticulous process of translation from Sanskrit into Chinese. The result was subtle, elaborate, and multilayered—but also quite difficult to comprehend. The philosopher Tsuchida Kyōson once compared it to Husserl's phenomenology. For a more detailed introduction, see Kamata Shigeo's *Kegon no shisō* (Huayan Thought, 1982) and other writings. Kamata passed away in 2001, but he remains the preeminent Japanese scholar of Huayan. I would also recommend Matsuyama Shuntarō, a scholar of Indian philosophy, for a far-reaching discussion of Huayan imagery. I will touch later on the role that this Huayan worldview played in ancient Japan, when I believe Huayan thought was used only in superficial ways.

The Chan route

For the Chan route of Buddhism into China, let's begin with Bodhidharma's arrival in Luoyang in the sixth century. At the time the temple Yongningsi in Luoyang was said to have the most splendid nine-story pagoda in the world. It stood for only fifteen years before being lost to fire, but during that time it towered over the city and drew visitors from many countries. One day, or so the story goes, there appeared among the crowds thronging the temple a ragged, wild-haired, sturdily built blue-eyed man, weeping unashamedly. This is our first glimpse of Bodhidharma in the Chinese chronicles.

These sources describe Bodhidharma as a *huseng* 胡僧, or "Persian monk," perhaps because of his blue eyes or ruddy face. I personally doubt Bodhidharma was Persian; most likely he came from south India.

In any case, this "Persian" monk Bodhidharma stood in the streets of Luoyang, gazing up at the pagoda of Yongningsi and weeping profusely. Why? No one knew. Bodhidharma then left Yongningsi and entered the Shaolin Monastery at Songshan, not far away. There he sat in meditation, facing a wall, for nine years.

This must have been quite shocking to people of the time. Buddhism was seen as an effective method for seeking liberation from the cycle of birth and death through awakening to the conditioned nature of all existence and attaining nirvana—but all this big blue-eyed monk did was sit staring at a wall. It's no surprise that they wondered what he was up to. Bodhidharma's style of seated meditation, later known as *biguan* (J. *hekikan;* "wall-gazing"), was the precursor of zazen.

The first disciple to come to the wall-gazing Bodhidharma was Huike, who is said to have stood in the snow for days outside Bodhidharma's meditation chamber vainly trying to convince Bodhidharma to accept him as a student. Seeing that this was of no avail, to prove his seriousness of intent, the iron-willed Huike severed his own left arm and flung it before Bodhidharma.

Although his practice is frequently described as "wall-gazing," that was not what Bodhidharma was about. Yanagida Seizan, an intellectual historian with a profound knowledge of Zen, says that "*hekikan* is not staring at a wall; it is the wall looking back." We think of Bodhidharma facing the wall in meditation, staring fixedly at one point on the wall for nine years—but in fact, his practice was to be seen by the wall, or to discover that the wall could in fact see him. This was what powered the development of his meditation.

So what arose from Bodhidharma's sitting? A collision between the central concepts developed within the cultural spheres of India and China. Broadly speaking, India had given form to the concept of "emptiness," while China had cultivated the concept of *wu* (J. *mu*), which we might call "negation." From the origins of philosophical and folk Daoism onward, the Chinese have always embraced the concept of *wu*.

Wuwei ziran 無為自然 ("effortless and natural") has been a Chinese ideal from ancient times. The Daoists longed for a life spent "taking a reclining journey amid mountains and rivers" (*shanshui woyou* 山水臥遊), or living in harmony and friendship with nature, as we saw in the chapters "Mountains" and "Paths." In other words, the Chinese approached the Indian concept of nirvana not from the perspective of "emptiness" but from the Daoist concept of *wu*.

Until the fifth or sixth century, the concepts of emptiness and negation did not really meet face to face. Then Huayan thought reached China, Chan came into being, and the two concepts began to bump up against one another, both in the external realm of national ideology and the internal realm of personal philosophy. At the national level the notion of creating a theocratic state based on Huayan teachings arose; on the personal level a Chan-influenced religious subjectivity was born. Furthermore, Bodhidharma's uncompromising meditative practice offered the possibility of new interactions between the Indian and Chinese civilizations through these central concepts of emptiness and negation.

As noted earlier, the Chan Buddhism founded in China by Bodhidharma did not really take root there until the late seventh century and the era of its sixth patriarch, Huineng. Meanwhile, a variety of different meditation practices and techniques entered China. One of these was the Oxhead school, founded by Farong (594–697) on Mount Niutou (Oxhead Mountain); others mingled Chan and Huayan teachings.

A number of different schools of Chan developed. The acceptance of the lineage of transmission from Bodhidharma as orthodox came only after a protracted and serious struggle. This struggle reflected the opposition that arose between the southern schools, which believed in "sudden" enlightenment, and the northern schools, which believed in "gradual" enlightenment. The southerners were said to favor a rapid, clever approach; the northerners, a slower, more methodical sweeping away of delusions. Southern Chan believed the purity of one's original nature could be realized in a flash of sudden insight; Northern Chan believed that same original nature would be revealed by gradually clearing away what obscured it.

However, as time would tell, it was only the southern school that developed, as a result of a revival engineered by Huineng. The robust Chan tradition that began with this revival would later produce a number of different sects and schools. The Rinzai (C. Linji) sect brought back to Japan by

Eisai (1141–1215) and the Sōtō (C. Caodong) sect brought back by Dōgen (1200–53) were originally part of this development of Chan in China.

The Buddhism that reached Japan

The Huayan, Chan, Pure Land, and Tiantai traditions were all part of what might be described as the northern transmission of Buddhism. In contrast, esoteric Buddhism belonged to a southern transmission that made its way slowly up from Southeast Asia, picking up various folk beliefs and an accretion of local spirits and deities along the way while adding to this mix the fruits of the Indian and Chinese civilizations. All of these different northern and southern Buddhisms, this heady and diverse mixture of thought and belief, would eventually arrive in Japan.

Buddhism is typically thought of as being transmitted through the sutras comprising the Buddhist canon, but there has always been an esoteric transmission as well. And interestingly, from a historical perspective, there has always been something of a gap between the two. By observing this gap, we can gain insight into why the scriptures were written, and why secret transmissions arose. The struggle among national and personal, major and minor ideologies come into view; so do questions of what was suppressed or repressed by state-centered ideologies, and what manner of religious hierarchies were established.

Next, I would like to look at the development of Buddhism in Japan while also examining this conflict between major and minor ideologies.

Buddhism was formally introduced to Japan sometime between 530 and 552 CE during the reign of Emperor Kinmei. However, esoteric teachings had reached Japan before that time. I believe we can trace Buddhism entering Japan by three different routes: Kegon (Huayan), Mikkyō (esoteric), and Zen (Chan).

Esoteric teachings developed in Japan as part of ascetic practices in the mountains, which later came to be called Shugendō. These various forms of esotericism are known as *zōmitsu*, or "mixed esotericism," to distinguish them from the orthodox schools of esoteric Buddhism that were introduced later, such as Tendai and Shingon. The transmission of *zōmitsu* from the continent to Japan was completely different from that of Mahayana Buddhism; we can assume it was highly personalized and adapted to the individual's temperament and character.

Although Zen teachings are usually said to have been promulgated by Eisai and Dōgen in the Kamakura period, there is reason to believe that a different and more personal type of Zen came to Japan as early as the time of Prince Shōtoku in the early seventh century. The rejection of the world conveyed by Prince Shōtoku's statement, mentioned earlier, that "The world is folly. Only the Buddha is real" certainly has the ring of Zen.

But there is no doubt that the early history of Buddhism in Japan was dominated by the Kegon teachings. It can even be said that the acceptance, establishment, and gradual decline of Kegon Buddhism reflects the history of ancient Japan.

In Japan there was of course an indigenous religion. Whether this constituted a religious worldview or not, it was polytheistic and probably deeply tinged with elements of animism and shamanism. While this polytheistic sensibility was uniquely Japanese, it was also significantly influenced by folk Daoism, as I suggested in chapter 3, "Deities."

But it was still too early to integrate reverence for the kami with the policies of the state. Instead, the kami worship of the Mononobe clan was pushed aside by the Soga clan in their strategic deployment of the newly arrived Buddhist system. Believed to be descendants of Nigihayahi, a legendary figure who was said to have ruled the Yamato region before the establishment of imperial rule, the Mononobe were a clan of ritualists who had dominated religious affairs at court. The Soga, who supplanted them, were the leaders of the Buddhist faction, from whose embrace of the faith "were created the beginnings of the Buddhadharma," in the words of the *Nihon shoki*. This is the history we learn in school.

But in fact, the world of the indigenous deities was not destroyed at a stroke; although scattered, these deities were incorporated into the mixed esotericism of the mountain folk and itinerant artists who would contribute so much, from the grassroots, to the history of the performing arts in Japan, as touched on earlier in chapter 1, "Mountains."

Having secured the main stage of Japanese religion, Buddhism dramatically increased its power with the ascendancy of Fujiwara no Fuhito and his clan and the establishment of the imperial capital at Fujiwara. The Fujiwara clan was a separate lineage from the imperial house, but by marrying their daughters into the imperial line—and backed by the newly arisen power of Buddhism—its members began to control a number of the emperors. One of them was Emperor Shōmu (r. 724–49).

Emperor Shōmu is generally credited with introducing Kegon to Japan, though it was probably the Fujiwara clan behind him that played the central role in the process. Their strategy was to create a powerful Kegon network throughout the Japanese archipelago by establishing provincial temples (*kokubunji*) controlled from a head temple, Tōdaiji, in Nara. This was modeled on a system established in China by Empress Wu Zetian of the Tang dynasty, based on an ideology derived from Huayan Buddhism. The construction and "eye-opening," or dedication, of the Great Buddha of Tōdaiji became a national project.

The Kegon worldview, originally intended to preach the universe of Vairocana in which every leaf contains a buddha, had been diverted for use as a state ideology benefiting the Fujiwara clan.

We do not know precisely how the Fujiwara clan and Emperor Shōmu incorporated Kegon into the Japanese state, but the story probably went something like this. A Buddhist group called Haedong on the Korean peninsula were associated with the Hwarang, a group of young Korean aristocrats who held the Huayan (K. Hwaeom) worldview and venerated Maitreya, the buddha of the future. Members of the Haedong Hwaeom crossed the sea to Japan one after the other, establishing a beachhead in the Kawachi region of present-day Osaka prefecture, where they built a temple called Chishikiji, occasioning an important turning point in ancient Japanese history— for one day, Emperor Shōmu and his retinue visited this temple, becoming probably the first Japanese to be made aware of Vairocana Buddha.

To the Japanese of the time, Vairocana Buddha must have seemed like a visitor from outer space, shocking and imposing, a powerful alien god. The members of the Fujiwara clan thought to themselves, "If we worship such a god, we can rule Japan."

But the Kegon world peaked at this point and then began to decline. The Kegon state crafted by Emperor Shōmu and the Fujiwara laid out an impressive nationwide network of provincial temples, but as a ruling ideology produced no significant further developments. The national project fizzled. Why? This is an important point to consider in recounting the story of Japanese Buddhism.

Japan's mystery zone

In the temple complex of Tōdaiji there is a structure called the Hokkedō

(Lotus Hall), more popularly known as the Sangatsudō (Hall of the Third Month). Enshrined there is a marvelous statue of Fukūkenjaku Kannon. At nearly 3 meters in height, it looms surprisingly large within the modest interior of the Sangatsudō.

This image of Fukūkenjaku Kannon can be viewed by the public, but concealed directly behind it is a secret image of Shukongōjin ("Vajra-wielding deity"). I served as the editorial director of the eighteen-volume *Nihon bijutsu bunka zenshū* (Art Japanesque; 1982–84) published by Kōdansha, which afforded me the opportunity to see a variety of secret Buddhist images from all over Japan, but even so, I missed the chance to view this one of the Shukongōjin—an image completely unrelated to the Kegon teachings upon which Tōdaiji was founded. As one might guess from his rather forbidding name, this thunderbolt-wielding deity was not a buddha but an Indian god of war. So what was an icon of this type doing at Tōdaiji?

All four sons of the powerful courtier Fujiwara no Fuhito died of smallpox. His grandson Fujiwara no Nakamaro carried out Fuhito's plan to break the power of the Ōtomo clan and of Tachibana no Moroe, leader of the Tachibana clan—thus taking control of the project to construct Tōdaiji. The first order of business was to secure the necessary land, except that the area where Tōdaiji now stands was already a stronghold of esoteric practitioners. Notable among them was the monk Rōben, who lived in a small temple he had established called Konshuji. Rōben was a devotee of radical sutras such as the *Fukūkenjaku Kannon-kyō* and the *Jinpen Kujaku Myōō-kyō*, believed to contain esoteric formulas for achieving identification with specific deities. Some pretty wild tales surround Rōben, including the legend that as an infant he was carried off by an eagle and deposited at the top of an immense cryptomeria tree. In any case, the deity that Rōben was privately worshipping at this site was none other than Shukongōjin.

Buddhist iconography is basically divided into four classes of beings: buddhas (J. *nyorai*), bodhisattvas (J. *bosatsu*), wisdom kings (J. *myōō*), and devas (J. *ten*). The *nyorai*, the pinnacle of the pantheon, include figures such as Shaka (Sk. Shakyamuni), Yakushi (Sk. Bhaiṣajyaguru), and Dainichi (Sk. Mahāvairocana). Bodhisattvas we have discussed previously; although they have compassion for the masses, they are not yet buddhas themselves. The wisdom kings, such as Fudō and Gundari, are primarily associated with esoteric Buddhist iconography and are originally Indian deities that were absorbed into Buddhism. The devas are a large category, thought to be vestiges of Buddhism's clash with Brahmanism and Hinduism. They include the Ashura, the Twelve Heavenly Generals, the Twenty-Eight Guardians, Bonten, Taishakuten, and so on, and are believed to reside on the upper reaches of Mount Sumeru. The buddhas, bodhisattvas, and wisdom kings have little to do with Mount Sumeru, but for some reason the devas came down from the mountain and assumed a role in Buddhist iconography.

The world of esoteric Buddhism had from the beginning incorporated a variety of folk beliefs and practices from southern India and Southeast Asia, so Rōben's veneration of Shukongōjin was by no means unusual. Still, even though the land that Rōben lived on was needed to build Tōdaiji, such beliefs could not very well be openly associated with the state-sponsored Kegon project.

The solution that Fujiwara no Nakamaro proposed was to appoint Rōben abbot of Tōdaiji. That is, he offered Rōben power and status in exchange for his cooperation, and he turned a blind eye to his more exotic esoteric beliefs. Nakamaro also enlisted the popular monk Gyōki to mobilize manpower for this national project.

In any event, this was how the strange image of a god of war came to be enshrined at Tōdaiji. This alone, of course, would not undermine the foundations of the Kegon state. But there were other developments afoot.

The Nara basin is surrounded by mountains—Ikoma, Futakami, Katsuragi, Kongō, and Yoshino, and from there southward to Mount Kōya and Kumano, and eastward to Ise. These mountains have served as a kind of magical mystery zone of Japanese culture from ancient times.

The region occupying the plain spreading out from the foothills of these mountains is known as Yamato, written 大和 in modern Japanese but originally meaning "mountain gate" (山門), or "mountain door" (山戸). Yamato was home to the capital of Heijō, where the present-day city of Nara is located. On the other side of the mountains, looking northward, lay the region of Yamashiro 山背 ("back of the mountains"), later written 山城— what is now the southern part of Kyoto prefecture and the city of Kyoto. Yamato and Kyoto formed a pair, separated by this magical mystery zone of mountains. I might add that the word for "port," *minato* 港, originally meant "water gate" (水門), or "water door" (水戸).

This magical and mysterious mountain region was in those days inhabited by bands of young and earnest mountain ascetics, students and practitioners of *zōmitsu*, the "mixed esoteric" tradition. They were adepts of the type of mysticism practiced by Rōben. They were also essentially freelancers, practicing without authorization or regulation, and immune to the lure of the grand temples of the Six Sects of Nara and the forms of Buddhist thought and ritual headquartered there. We might call them Buddhist hippies. And they were scathingly critical of state Buddhism.

This renegade movement eventually undermined the national project of Tōdaiji. From time to time the government attempted to suppress the mountain ascetics. But they were undaunted, and mounted a counterattack on the decadence of state-sponsored Buddhism. From among their ranks appeared the leaders of a new age of Buddhism: Saichō (767–822) and Kūkai (774–835).

But Saichō and Kūkai did not take immediate action. They were not ready, either philosophically or in terms of their Buddhist practice. Both crossed the sea to study in China, driven by a desire to connect with a more dynamic form of Buddhism than that offered by the conservative Nara sects, and they brought back with them a genuine esoteric Buddhism that could supplant both the heterodox magic of the *zōmitsu* tradition and the Kegon orthodoxy. Later, in his treatise *Himitsu mandara jūjū shinron* (Secret Mandala of the Ten Stages of Mind), Kūkai would describe ten stages of spiritual development, of which the eighth was the worldview represented by the *Lotus Sutra*, and the ninth, the Kegon worldview of the *Flower Garland Sutra*. The final and tenth stage he assigned to esoteric teachings and the Pure Land of the Mahavairocana Buddha.

This treatise was significant in that it simultaneously provided the first comprehensive introduction of Kegon philosophy to Japan and proclaimed esoteric Buddhist thought to be superior. In effect, it launched a twofold attack on the superficial and formulaic state-sponsored Kegon Buddhism that had appeared in the Tenpyō era (729–49), finding fault in the Japanese adoption of the Kegon teachings and also in the teachings themselves. As we can see, then, the early days of Buddhism in Japan were tempestuous, reflecting its arduous journey across Asia.

It would take until the Kamakura period for Japanese Buddhism to become truly "made in Japan." With the merging of Shinto and Buddhism in the concept and practice of *honji suijaku*, which saw Japanese deities as localized avatars of the buddhas and bodhisattvas, Japan's indigenous religion was intentionally fused with esoteric Buddhism.

Japanese Buddhism, as distinct from Indian or Chinese Buddhism, might thus be called the product of a Japanese "editing" of Buddhism. The unique characteristics of that editorial process would become more clearly visible as the Japanese sense of "time" developed—for it was through Buddhism that the Japanese sensibilities of impermanence (*mujō*) and ephemerality (*hakanasa*) were given a solid foundation.

CHAPTER 8   TIME

Musical experimentation

In 1955 Karlheinz Stockhausen (1928–2007) composed what is often cited as the first masterpiece of electronic music—*Gesang der Jünglinge* (Song of the Youths)—working in Cologne with a team of young technicians at the world's first electronic music studio. At the time, Stockhausen declared that music is a spatial art, overturning the conventional wisdom that it is a temporal art.

Much of contemporary music has advanced by incorporating spatial concepts. Twentieth-century composers attempted to free themselves from the constraints of traditional classical music, expanding the very concept of music. By the late 1950s there was a flood of new experimental work.

In 1958 Edgard Varèse (1883–1965) created *Poème éléctronique*, an electronic music composition for the Philips Pavilion at the World's Fair in Brussels. Le Corbusier (1887–1965) designed the pavilion, which also featured *Concret PH*, an electronic work by the Greek composer, mathematician, and architect Iannis Xenakis (1922–2001). For *Poème éléctronique*, both mono and stereo tape were used, combined onto 35mm tape to synchronize with a film and lighting changes.

In France Pierre Schaeffer (1910–95) developed a form of music known as *musique concrète*, which drew on sound techniques from radio and film. Pierre Boulez (1925–2016), Xenakis, Stockhausen, Varèse, and others were attracted to the Groupe de Recherche de Musique Concrète, founded by Schaeffer in 1951, and its electroacoustic music studio in Paris.

In Japan Takemitsu Tōru (1930–96) incorporated elements of traditional Japanese instrumentation, including the shakuhachi flute and the instruments used in Gagaku court music. American composers like Aaron Copland (1900–90) also connected with their folk traditions. And then came John Cage (1912–92), bringing with him the sound of silence.

Quite a while ago I visited Cage in New York City, on which occasion he talked at length about haiku. Cage and Merce Cunningham (1919–2009), the avant-garde dancer, were life partners and collaborators. On the day I was there, toward the end of November, Cunningham and Cage were in the kitchen making an omelet. Kosugi Takehisa, a musician and composer who was involved with Yoko Ono in the early Fluxus movement, was also present.

Cage suddenly said, "Seigow, listen! It's the hot water!" Most of the older buildings in New York are heated by radiators. When the hot water flows into the coiled tubes of the radiator pipes, it makes a variety of intriguing sounds: gurgles, growls, and clangs form a unique music. Cage very much enjoyed listening to this water music.

For Cage, music encompassed noises made by three-dimensional objects within space—including the sounds that sometimes unexpectedly cropped up at particular points in space. He considered all sound to be music, and music to be the "organization of sound." On the front lines of the music revolution of the 1950s, Cage referred to his technique of attempting to grasp this type of music as "chance operations."

Across the Atlantic, the Beatles were emerging out of the industrial towns of Liverpool and Manchester, and the port city of Hamburg. Baptized in the contemporary sound of early American rock, they were shouting out their own fresh musicality in the form of what was dubbed the "Liverpool Sound." In the late 1960s, Stockhausen had a significant influence on the Beatles. In my youth I went from Stockhausen to Cage, Xenakis, and Boulez to the Beatles. In the flow of that experience, I never once thought of music as time.

Rather—and this is especially true for the post-Beatles generations, I think—I experienced it more like a shower falling over me in a particular space, or like a volume that could be felt physically, corporeally. It was as if the music had both mass and vibration, as if it were the beat itself.

So at this point, I came to question whether there really was any basis to the long-cherished belief that music is the art of time. In fact, musicians and composers also grappled with this problem and created a variety of works addressing the issue of whether music is a spatial or temporal medium—spawning experiments in "chance music," "chance operations," "furniture music," "ambient music," and so on.

I had just entered Waseda University in the early 1960s when Merce Cunningham and John Cage performed as part of a series of experimental music concerts at Sogetsu Hall in Tokyo. The evening, which also featured Yoko Ono lying atop the piano and an appearance by the youthful Takahashi Yūji, was unsettling and caused quite a stir. When Takahashi came out to play, all he did was fiddle for a while with the piano chair, sounding the keys from time to time but otherwise maintaining strict silence.

The point was to proclaim music as a visual as well as auditory experience, to send out a strong message that the entire previous history of music must be rejected. But for people who had come to listen to music, the result was intense boredom. When I later met Takahashi, who had returned from New York, and had the opportunity to listen at length to his meticulous methods of composition, reminiscent of genetic engineering or the geometry of chromosomes, I realized what an inspired performance of "furniture music" that recital at Sogetsu Hall had been.

Through such encounters with avant-garde music in my youth, I was able to experience viscerally the transition from time-based to space-based music. Still, if you were to ask me whether music is therefore space itself, I don't think I could give you an answer. And I would be even less confident of my ability to answer the question of what had happened to time in this type of music.

The discovery of time

How is time produced? Does sound arise in tandem with time?

When we ponder the relationship between sound and time, one of the first issues we encounter is repetition. Tick-tock goes the metronome as its arm swings back and forth; this repetitive sound and motion seem as if they could be the source of time in music. Conventional wisdom would tell us this is so. Set to a specific range of motion, the metronome appears to repeat a perfect cycle. But does it really? We would need another metronome to verify this—without it, we cannot really measure "time."

Humans have always been aware of time in some sense. The concept of time in ancient Egypt or ancient India was highly developed and distinctive. In today's world most of us do not even think to doubt the certainty of time. But there are also those who have taken up a new perspective by questioning time and studying it.

It is said that the Nile helped foster a sense of time in ancient Egypt. The flooding of the river was cyclical, fertilizing the land and contributing to bountiful harvests. But this characterization of the Nile as the cradle of ancient Egyptian civilization still does not really address the issue of time. It overlooks an important point, which is that the ancient Egyptians did not, in fact, discover time by observing the Nile floods.

The flooding of the Nile was significant, but what was of crucial importance was that the flood cycle happened to coincide with the cycle of the appearance of the star Sirius in the eastern sky. This was when time really began in ancient Egypt, and it provides an interesting clue in developing our temporal theory. The perception of a single cycle is in itself probably insufficient for the perception of time. Another cycle must be encountered that converges with the first.

The year begins with the appearance of Sirius in the sky; 365 days later, Sirius rises again. Precisely at that time, the Nile floods. And here we encounter one of the most important concepts underlying time: "pairing." For time to exist, at the very least a pairing of phenomena, or a pairing of cycles, is required. It is the encounter between the elements in these pairs that gives birth to the idea of time. The phenomenon of the Nile flooding is not time. The repetition of Sirius's appearance in the sky is not time. But when we discover that these two phenomena coincide, then our understanding of time is born.

We can also consider time from a somewhat different vantage point: a macroscopic view that sees the movement of the entire universe as Mother Time.

In the chapter "Deities" I write of the Big Bang and the expansion of the universe and matter that has taken place since that event. From this perspective, you might say that tracking the direction of this expansion is our way of measuring time. At present the universe is still pretty young, so there's probably nothing wrong with thinking that the vectors of matter and time overlap. But as the universe ages, if it begins to shrink even a little bit—what then? The movement of matter will become unpredictable, and we will have to conceive of the direction of time as something more complex and diverse. A standard clock would be useless. We'd need something more like the soft clocks in a Dali painting.

In other words, we conceive of time as unidirectional merely because that is how we have come to understand it within the prescribed limits of the evolution of our universe; it may have nothing to do with the real nature of time.

Of course, if we think of it in this way, then there is no way we can really grasp the true nature of time in the universe. And we may wonder what is the point of such mental exercises.

Even so, scientists engaged in the study of difficult phenomena such as thermodynamics and entropy—and here I will spare you the details—are currently striving to discover the sort of minute discrepancies or incongruities in time that I have just suggested, and to answer the question, as well, of how they relate to the fundamental thermodynamic equilibrium supporting the phenomenon of life as we know it.

Time, West and East

In 1960 Erwin Panofsky published *Renaissance and Renascences in Western Art*, a classic. Reading that book as a young man gave me my first real understanding of what the Renaissance was all about. Panofsky emphasizes that the Renaissance was not purely an age of humanism and progress. Other scholars such as Frances Yates, Wylie Sypher, and Wayne Shumaker followed his lead, shedding considerable light on the darker corners of the Renaissance, recognition of which is now axiomatic.

In "Father Time," originally published in 1939 and reprinted in 1962, Panofsky wrote about the changing European conception of time. In addition to Chronos, the personification of time as past, present, and future, the Greco-Roman world had two concepts of time: *kairos* and *aion*. *Kairos* signified fleeting opportunity or the critical moment; *aion* was unbounded time, eternity. The two conceptions of time remained embedded in European thinking from Greek antiquity up to the Renaissance, when this duality collapsed.

Panofsky's meditation on time was confined to the sphere of European culture. *Kairos* and *aion* may have collapsed in Europe, but they lived on in Eastern cultures. Not only that, but the idea I discussed earlier that time can be perceived only through the intersection of two different cycles is itself a very European notion, and one that is not completely convincing to the Asian mind.

Nakamura Hajime, the great scholar of Indian philosophy, has written that in India time is seen not as dynamic but as static, and the idea of Heraclitus that "one cannot set foot in the same river twice" would be rejected.

In India the river would be seen as a universal, unchanging presence. No matter when you set foot in it, this universal river remains the same. This is not Heraclitus's famous formula *panta rhei* (everything flows; everything changes).

Nakamura explains the reason for this as having to do with the structure of classical Indian languages such as Sanskrit, which have no word corresponding to "to become"; to express such an idea it must be turned into an aspect of "to be." In other words, becoming is simply a different form of being. From this we can elicit one of the fundamental characteristics of Indian philosophy that I was unable to touch on in the "Buddhas" chapter.

Indian philosophy conceives of temporal existence as three different states: appearance, continuity, and extinction. Moreover, all three states are regarded as static. Changes expressed by dynamic verbs in the European languages are always perceived in India as a succession of static states. I think you can see how the Buddha and the philosophy of Nāgārjuna could have emerged from this context.

Here is an example. As noted in the preceding chapter, the historical Buddha was born in Lumbini, reached enlightenment under the bodhi tree at Bodh Gaya, and entered his final nirvana at Kushinagar. Naturally, all of these events occurred in different years. But in India all are commemorated on a single day in the month of Vaisakha (April or May by the Western calendar). Apparently, there was no interest at all in marking the temporal separation between the events. This sense of time is also evidenced by the nearly complete absence of reliable dating in the Indian chronicles.

Dariush Shayegan (1935–2018), a philosopher at Tehran University, has pointed out that neither Persian, Arabic, nor Sanskrit has a term corresponding to "subjectivity." Societies communicating in such languages do not readily accept thought premised on separating inside and outside, religion and philosophy, and scientific analysis and subjective contemplation. According to Shayegan, such languages simply distinguish between the universal and the particular.

But what about Japan? The Japanese consciousness of time is based on the concept of *utsuroi*. *Utsuroi* means changing or shifting, like the changing seasons, or the shifts from light to darkness, and from darkness to light; the changes and transitions in the course of a single day, or the course of a human life. Without grasping this concept of *utsuroi* we cannot grasp time in Japan. So I would like to reflect in a bit more detail on this subject.

The philosophy of *utsuroi*

The word *utsuroi* comes from *utsu*, which means empty, hollow, or void.

A number of words derive from or relate to this root: *utsuro* (empty, hollow), *utsubo* (quiver for arrows), *utsuru* and *utsusu* (intransitive and transitive forms of verbs that carry a host of different meanings depending on context and the kanji used to write them, as discussed below), *utsusemi* or *utsushimi* (this mortal world and its inhabitants), *utsuwa* (vessel or container), and others. The verbs *utsuru* and *utsusu* are particularly important because they refer to concepts as disparate as moving, shifting, or passing; transferring, copying, or recording; and projecting or reflecting—all of which share the same root. This makes for a remarkable associative network of images.

Think about it for a moment. If *utsuru* 移る (to move, shift), *utsuru* 写る (to record or capture an image), and *utsuru* 映る (to reflect or project) are all the same word, then the actions they denote can be thought of as a series—as something shifts or changes, this is pictured in the mind, which then projects this perception back into the external world. This suggests that the phenomenology of nature that is the principal theme of this book is the product of a seamless succession of images that are by turns captured and reflected.

But why did this continuous succession come to be expressed in language that draws on the root meaning of *utsu*—that is, empty, hollow, void? To understand this, we must know that in ancient and medieval Japan, things possessing these properties had great significance.

As I've mentioned before, our ancestors used clapperless hollow bells called *sanagi* and other types of bells to pacify the spirits of the dead or to elevate their own consciousness. A *sanagi* was an empty vessel, and its very emptiness encouraged the notion that something might be fostered within it. In other words, from "empty" things, something else might grow.

An ancient type of boat, the *utsurobune* or *utsubobune* ("hollow boat"), was made from hollowing out a giant log. It was used by the prehistoric seafaring peoples who reached Japan, and its design was most likely from Southeast Asia or Polynesia. The Ama no Torifune ("heavenly bird-boat") mentioned in chapter 5 was probably such a boat, hollowed out of camphor wood. It was a hollow spirit-vehicle, a treasure boat.

The image of the hollow boat was associated in the minds of the ancient Japanese with the hollows of trees—which were also empty and void and thus contained the potential for nurturing something new. The folk tale "Taketori monogatari" (Tale of the Bamboo Cutter) is based on such an image; it begins with Princess Kaguya being born out of the hollow of a stalk of bamboo. And in the beginning of *Utsuho monogatari* (The Tale of the Hollow Tree; late tenth century), Japan's oldest extended work of narrative fiction, the protagonist, Nakatada, is raised by his mother in a hollow tree in the hills of Kitayama on the outskirts of Kyoto. There, she teaches him the secrets of playing the zither that her father, Toshikage, had mastered after being shipwrecked on a mission to China many years before. This storyline seems to indicate the existence of earlier lore from various parts of Japan of people who were raised in a tree hollow or who gained special skills and power from coming into contact with one.

Such images were further associated with the idea that someone riding in something that suggests a boat or hollow object would be endowed with special powers and abilities, leading us to the story of Issun Bōshi riding in a bowl for a boat with a chopstick as his paddle, or Momotarō floating downstream inside his peach.

In this manner, "empty" things and "empty" places became paired concepts that ranged freely over the terrain of Japanese myth and legend. Or to put it another way, the emptiness or void of *utsu* served as the mold out of which other images were born. Here it becomes clear that *utsu* is also a generative vessel for time itself. *Utsuroi*, the shifts and changes of time, is the movement of the empty things born from empty places.

I might add that the Jungian psychologist Kawai Hayao has proposed the unique hypothesis that the most fundamental aspect of the structure of Japanese myth as told in the *Kojiki* and *Nihon shoki* is "hollow-centeredness,"[1] a central nothingness or void created by the absence of a powerful central deity.

The vessel giving birth to time

In Japanese the word *toki* (time) does not mean clock time. It refers to the passage of time or to a span of time—in other words, *utsuroi*. Consider the following examples:

yo no naka no	The way of the world—
ukeku tsurakeku	how hateful and harsh it is!
saku hana mo	Flowering petals
toki ni utsurou	fade with time and lose their bloom,
utsusemi mo	and the life of man
tsunenaku arikeri	passes in mutability.[2]

(Ōtomo no Yakamochi)

imo ga mishi	Flowers are in bloom
yado ni hana saki	in the garden that she knew,
toki wa henu	and time goes by;
wa ga naku namita	but still there has been no drying
imada hinaku ni	of the tears I shed for her. [3]

(Ōtomo no Yakamochi)

o no kami mo yurushi tamai	The god allows us and the god-
me no kami mo chiwai tamaite	dess gives us favor,
toki to naku kumoi ame furu	they uncover the peaks of
Tsukuhane o saya ni terashite	Tsukuba in the sun,
	which were veiled with timeless
	clouds and rain . . . [4]

(Takahashi no Mushimaro)

toki narazu	That this young girl
suginishi kora ga	who passed before her time
asatsuyu no goto	should, like the morning dew . . .
yūgiri no goto	should, like the evening mist . . .[5]

In *Utsuho monogatari*, the empress dowager speaks the following line after her sixtieth birthday celebration: "Living as I do in ignorance of the times, I had not realized how many years and months had passed."

In the chapter "The Broom Tree" of *The Tale of Genji*, we find the following remarks: "So you see, I have no faith in the obvious show of affection that a woman may sometimes [*toki ni atarite*] put on."[6]

Toki, as it appears in these passages, is not indicative of a single, fixed moment, expressing instead a range or flow of time. The first poem by Yakamochi is particularly important for its association of the passage of time (*utsuroi*) with mutability or impermanence (*mujō*). Mushimaro's *toki to naku* indicates an indeterminate timelessness; *toki ni atarite* in *The Tale of Genji* means "according to the occasion," translated here as "sometimes."

Of course there are also many places in classic texts where time is given more precise, clocklike specificity, but in general we may think of people in ancient and medieval Japan as using "time" in a broader sense—in other words, they delimited it in looser spans and also regarded it as malleable, capable of both expansion and contraction.

An even more telling example in this regard is the expression *toki nashi* (literally, "there is no time"), which could mean a variety of different things. In the following two poems from the *Man'yōshū*, it is used to mean "ceaselessly":

Miyoshino no	In fair Yoshino
Mimiga no mine ni	on the peak of Mimiga
toki naku so	without a season
yuki wa furikeru	snow falls, as I well recall,
ma naku so	without interval
ame wa furikeru	rain falls, as I well recall. [7]

(Emperor Tenmu)

uchiwatasu	Gazing across the fields
Taketa no hara ni	at Taketa I hear the cranes
naku tazu no	ceaselessly crying:
ma naku toki nashi	not a space, not a moment
wa ga kouraku wa	of pause in my longing. [8]

(Lady Ōtomo of Sakanoue)

Moreover, it is important to note that in both of these poems the words *toki* 時 and *ma* 間 (space) are used almost interchangeably. In modern speech we would not regard these two as having the same usage, though it's also true that in the word *jikan* 時間 (time) we combine them without giving it much thought. In ancient times, however, people might use *toki nashi* in situations where modern Japanese would say *ma mo naku,* to mean "soon," or "in a moment."

It seems to me that in Japan time has been what might be called a portable concept: seen not as existing independently, in its own right, but shifting and changing in affiliation with some other thing. This is hinted at by the power of the vessel or container (*utsuwa* 器) in Japan.

There is a traditional wooden container called a *hokai*, usually written 外居 or 行器. It was used to transport food when traveling, like a modern bento box, but it was larger, rounded and barrel-like, similar to the bamboo steamers used in many parts of Asia to make buns or dumplings.

The *hokai* was originally a ritual vessel. Bedecked with a *sakaki* branch and *gohei* streamers, it might contain a sacred presence. Its prototype was a dish of simple unglazed earthenware known as *kawarake*. In the hills surrounding Kyoto there are a number of lookout points from which tossing small plates of this type is a traditional amusement. This, too, has ritual origins.

The *hokai* as ritual vessel was not for placing something inside, but rather for inviting something to enter—a receptacle for a revelation or some other thing deserving attention—that is to say, for powerful information. But if you gave it some kind of stimulus, it might share that power with you. So people began putting their precious food in it, which became a common practice.

Ogata Kōrin, lacquer writing box decorated with the *yatsuhashi* (eight-planked footbridge) and iris motif, eighteenth century. Collection of Tokyo National Museum. Photo: TNM Image Archives.

But in fact it was also fine to put nothing in it. Why? Because it contained sacred time.

The *hokai* was portable. In theory, you could carry it anywhere. It was like a magic box from which one could always receive energy—a mobile shrine or portable sacred space (*himorogi*). In the chapter "Deities," I cite this poem by Sugawara no Michizane:

kono tabi wa	On this journey
nusa mo toriaezu	I have no silk streamers to offer up.
Tamukeyama	Gods, if it pleases you,
momiji no nishiki	may you take instead this brocade
kami no mani-mani	of Mount Tamuke's autumn colors.

I then pointed out that in those days, travelers carried with them a small bag of finely cut strips of cloth or paper to offer the roadside deities on their journey. This custom was one version of the ritual for which *hokai* were originally used.

What I have said so far should be fairly straightforward as long as we understand that the *hokai* was a type of sacred or magical vessel. But there was also a word, *hokahi*, that closely resembled *hokai* and that referred to the celebration of the gods in order to receive their blessings and, by extension, the prayers or incantations addressed to the deities for this purpose. Over time, these two words blended into one word, *hokai*.

This brings us to an even more important secret. *Hokai* and *hokahi* are both nominalizations of the verb *hokau* 祝う, to supplicate, revere, or celebrate: actions that typically require a consciousness of *hoka*—the other, the external, the separate, the different.

In kanji, *hoka* is represented by 外 or 他; in classical Japanese, it is written usually with the former, which carries a strong sense of external or outside. So the question then becomes why this direction of *hoka* should be relevant.

But before we ponder that, we need to examine another complex matter, that of the group of people bearing the name *hokaibito*, who played a significant role throughout ancient, medieval, and even early modern history in Japan.

Hokaibito were beggars or mendicants. In *Kokubungaku no hassei* (The Origins of Japanese Literature; 1923), Orikuchi Shinobu calls them the original itinerant performers. They were drifters who gave shape to the fundamental forms of the Japanese performing arts. They were also a group of people who had a unique capacity to receive things wherever they went.

And that is not all. If we see the terms *hokai*, *hokahi*, and *hokaibito* as overlapping, then this act of receiving on the part of these itinerant travelers represented a sacred or ritual activity, or it stood in for one. It announced to the villagers the advent of spring (*haru*), which was also a time of sacredness (*hare*).

External time

We are now arriving, I think, at the most important part of this book. And the issue at hand is the meaning and significance of the concept of *hoka*.

First, let's look at the following poem by Kakinomoto Hitomaro (662–710).

ie ni kite	Returning home
wagaya o mireba	and looking about my house
tamadoko no	in our bedchamber
hoka ni mukikeri	I find my wife's wooden pillow
imo ga komakura	turned to face away.[9]

Here *hoka* clearly means "outside"—and not merely outside, but "other." An "outside" pointing in a certain significant "other" direction, one I've mentioned many times already: *mukō*, "there," as opposed to "here."

In the poem, Hitomaro returns home after being away at some important place, and he finds the pillow that belonged to his wife (who has died) facing a direction "outside" where he has been. He does not specify the direction of this "outside"; rather, he suggests that where it does *not* point is the locus of what is important and valuable.

In other words, by suggesting what is outside or other, what is central and important is automatically suggested as well; and indeed a style of expression is created in which it is *only* by suggesting what is external that someplace important may be indicated.

We all have a sense of some sort of direction that we can express only as being "elsewhere." A place different from where we are, outside our house, across the river, beyond the hills, in the distant skies. Today, this "elsewhere" might be outer space. It is a place unknown to us.

Hoka is this unknown space. And to have it offers us a kind of relief. Why? Because we can imagine it to be an unreal space where our everyday responsibilities do not apply and a different flow of time pertains. Buddhism called it the Pure Land, a fragrant realm filled with ethereal music. The Daoists called it the Realm of the Immortals or the Peach Blossom Spring, and they imagined it as a place of eternal life.

Indeed, every people and nation in history have posited this sort of *hoka*. Arcadia, Utopia, Atlantis, Heaven, Hell, El Dorado, the Garden of Eden, the Kunlun Mountains, Mount Penglai, Shambhala, Mount Sumeru, Mount Fuji, the Pure Lands of Kannon and Amida: all of these are *hoka*, outside, other. Not only that: for children, the other side of the river, the edge of the neighborhood, the vacant lot over in the next village, the high school where the bigger kids go, the destination of the train—all of these are *hoka*. During the Edo period, the pleasure quarters and the theaters were *hoka*.

As I touched on briefly in chapter 2, Japanese folklore studies employs the term *marebito* (稀人 or 客人) for people who arrive from *hoka*—"outside" or "elsewhere." *Marebito* were aliens, strangers. But because these strangers were believed to come from *hoka*, which was imagined as a peaceful and stable "other" realm, they were also seen as divine guests or visiting deities (*marōdogami* 客神). This is the archetype of the *hokaibito*.

So we entertain these divine visitors. They've come from "elsewhere," so we treat them to items from "here," and regale them with songs and dances from "here." But not just anyone can host and entertain such guests. At some point, entertaining becomes the role of professionals—and this is how the performing arts are born.

Such hosting and entertainment also acquire a certain sequence and set of procedures. Decorations, costumes, and manners of performing all become established. This is the birth of the festival.

All of this moreover requires planning and preparation. Getting people in the proper mood is essential. So there are various anticipatory rituals; markers are provided for the awaited deities. This is the origin of the *himorogi*, or sacred enclosure, and the *yashiro*, or shrine.

Most of us in Japan still have a vague sense of all this as we prepare for the New Year's holiday season, and indeed many of these kinds of rituals and practices are still observed in various regions. In the past, *hokaibito* were actually invited to households as part of the New Year celebration. *Hokau* means to celebrate; *hokaibito* thus means something like "celebrants"; and *hokai* was the container holding food and other gifts that was offered to these itinerant performers in front of each house as they went from door to door.

It seems to me that the origin of the Japanese concept of time can be found in *hoka*. Time has never been something that resided in a particular moment "here"; it flows to us from "elsewhere" (*hoka*) and flows back there again. By and large, this flow corresponds to the passing (*utsuroi*) of the four seasons. That is how we think of time in Japan.

Unless we are prepared, this time that flows in from outside will simply slip away again, so somewhere between "here" and "there" we must provide empty vessels of some kind to serve as interfaces for capturing time and information. These vessels eventually took a portable form, one that could moreover be easily readied by any household, as food dishes. This is not to say that all dishes exhibited the power necessary to serve as such an interface; instead, special pieces were set aside in a cupboard or storage chest and brought out at appropriate times for guests. These were the vessels (*utsuwa*) that served as hollow receptacles for time, and that would eventually lead to the teabowls of Raku potter Chōjirō (1516–92) and tea ceremony master Sen no Rikyū (1522–91).

The emergence of *ma*

umare umare	Born, born,
umare umarete	born, born again,
sei no hajime ni kurashi	the beginning of life is dark to us;
shini shini	dying, dying,
shini shinde	dying, dying yet again,
shi no owari ni kurashi	the end of death is dark to us.

These are the words of Kūkai, from the opening passage of his treatise *Hizō hōyaku* (Jeweled Key to the Secret Treasury; c. 830). The beginning of existence is obscure to us, as is its end. No gaze can penetrate them.

We exist in the space between (*aida*). This "between" is the only place we have to exert our energies, but what exactly is this space between birth and death? It is many things. Innumerable things. It is all we know of space and time. Everything is "between." There is nothing that is not "between."

The psychiatrist Kimura Bin (b. 1931) posits *aida* as the most important relational state in the Japanese psychology. Similarly, the sociologist Hamaguchi Eshun and the management professor Itami Hiroyuki employ the terms *kanjin shugi* (contextualism) and *jinpon shugi* (human-capital-ism), respectively, to characterize the Japanese. In short, Japanese value interrelationships in virtually every context.

In Japanese cultural history, this idea of the "between" has been called *ma* 間, bringing to it yet another perspective. *Ma* is a uniquely Japanese concept, and one that is difficult to explain—especially to non-Japanese.

But the word became known to some extent to intellectuals and artists around the world in 1978, when the exhibition *MA: Space/Time in Japan*, conceived and directed by architect Isozaki Arata, opened to explosive acclaim at the Musée des arts décoratifs at the Louvre in Paris. This was the first exhibition to introduce Japanese culture to an overseas audience using contemporary methods. It began with a corridor of photos of Japan by Shinoyama Kishin, followed by a teahouse entryway by the master carpenter Nakamura Sotoji. After displays of tea ceremony spaces, viewers arrived at a room with a small aluminum Noh stage designed by Isozaki, next to which sat nine figures of monks crafted by the sculptor and doll maker Yotsuya Simon and dressed in costumes by the fashion designer Miyake Issey. The room played host to a variety of performance programs, including music by Takemitsu Tōru, a Butoh dance choreographed by Hijikata Tatsumi, and a dance work staged by Suzuki Tadashi; the dancer Tanaka Min gave his first overseas performances here, immediately propelling him onto the world stage. Beyond this space, the route led into more galleries with exhibits by the interior designer Kuramata Shirō and the sculptor Miyawaki Aiko, among others. I myself was involved as the editorial director for this project. The result was that *ma* has become an internationally recognized concept.

The image of *ma* is more likely to be understood when packaged artistically in this way; indeed, it was precisely this artistry of *ma* that inspired such delighted astonishment in the architect Bruno Taut when he saw the Katsura Detached Palace for the first time in the 1930s. The photographer Jūmonji Bishin has published work exploring *ma* at this famous site.

Nevertheless, it is surprisingly difficult to put the feeling of *ma* into words. This is because *ma*, while principally a spatial concept, is also deeply associated with time.

The common view of *ma* traces it back to its early usage as an architectural term denoting the interval between posts in a building's framing, roughly similar to "bay" in English. In this usage, *ma* was clearly spatial in nature.

For example, one passage in the *Sarashina nikki* (*Sarashina Diary*; c. 1059) describing the dismantling of a single span (*hitoma*) of the bridge at Seta uses *ma* as a counter for spans in conjunction with the prefix *hito-* for "one." In the "Utsusemi" chapter of *The Tale of Genji* one of the characters pounds on the shutters at the south corner of a room (*minami no sumi no ma*) to gain entrance. And a passage in *Utsuho monogatari* speaks of four mortars set up in "one section" (*ma hitotsu*) of the room. In all three cases, the reference is to an interval between posts or pillars. But *ma* soon also came to be used for the space enclosed by the pillars: a room. This is the sense of the word we find in *Makura no sōshi* (*Pillow Book*; 1002) when Sei Shōnagon writes of her displeasure at people congregated around a charcoal brazier in "the next room" (*tsugi no ma*).

At first this *ma* denoted a space demarcated by movable partitions, folding screens, or other portable dividers. But then these temporarily defined spaces gradually evolved into more permanent "rooms": *tsugi no ma* came to refer to an antechamber, a *kokonoma* ("nine-*ma* room") was a sizable reception area, and the tokonoma became a formal alcove for the display of artworks.

This evolution, from the intervals between posts to the rooms of a building, is how *ma* is most commonly explained—yet when I looked into it, I found that the word had been used even earlier, and had not necessarily been predicated on the domestic spaces of the Heian court. For example, consider the following lines in a poem in the *Man'yōshū* by Takahashi no Asomi, c. 744:

asagiri no	As in morning mist
ō ni naritsutsu	you faded into a distant blur
Yamashiro no	slowly receding
Sagarakayama no	into the mountains, the valleys
yama no mani	between the mountains
yukisuginureba	of Sagaraka in Yamashiro.[10]

In the fifth line the kanji 際 (meaning edge or verge) is read *mani* 間に, indicating that *ma* was already being used to convey the image of the boundary or demarcation between two spaces. This would evolve into the usage we see in the last line of the following poem, also from the *Man'yōshū*:

Ki no kuni no	Gazing out
Saika no ura ni	from the shores of Saika
ide mireba	in the province of Ki
ama no tomoshibi	I see the torches of fishermen
nami no mayu miyu	flickering amid the waves.[11]

And from there it would shift in sense to give rise to the word *mani-mani*, meaning to follow along with the movements or will of another, used in expressions like *nami no mani-mani* (at the mercy of the waves), or—returning once again to the poem by Sugawara no Michizane—*kami no mani-mani* (gods, if it pleases you). It seems that *mani* signified a small gap or crack and also functioned as a kind of unit of measure. So from early times, *ma* has had a number of interesting linguistic uses.

If *ma* was a gap or crack, or the interval between posts in a building, then surely it was a spatial concept? Not necessarily. *Ma* had a temporal aspect from the very beginning, and that is what complicates matters. Turning once more to the *Man'yōshū*, we find examples such as the following:

mina no wata	Upon the locks that glistened
kaguroki kami ni	black as the gut of the *mina* snail
itsu no ma ka	in an unknown hour
shimo no furikemu	a winter of white frost descends.[12]

(Yamanoue no Okura)

yūyami wa	In the twilight darkness
michi tazutazushi	indistinguishable is the road
tsuki machite	wait until the moon-rise, and go,
yumase waga seko	that I may see you, my dearest,
sono ma ni mo mimu	even for that while! [13]

(Ōyakeme)

In the first poem, *ma* in the third line is written 麻 (literally, "hemp"), but clearly signifies a specific period of time. In the second, *ma* 間 in the last line refers to the duration of an activity. So there was definitely a temporal sense to the word *ma*.

In addition, *ma* was a term of art in Gagaku and Bugaku, traditional Japanese court music and dance. It was similar to the idea of a beat (*hyōshi*) but could also refer to the subtle space, or interval, between beats. *Ma* was especially strongly associated with percussion; in passing, I might note that *uchiawase*, a common word for a meeting or conference in contemporary Japan, is made up of the verbs *utsu*, "to strike," and *awaseru*, "to match," and originates from the sessions that drummers held to coordinate their timing, focusing on working out the *ma* between their beats.

We might go further and even say that in Japanese cultural history *ma* as a concept was confined to neither the spatial nor temporal realm. *Ma* was applied to all kinds of contexts and situations, spawning a broad range of colloquial expressions—*ma ni au* (to be on time; to be sufficient), *manuke* (a fool, an idiot), *machigai* (an error or mistake), *ma o motaseru* (to buy time; to stall), and so on—and extending the influence of its image into almost all aspects of life and the Japanese temperament.

In *Essays in Idleness* there is a section dealing with the technique of playing the transverse flute in which we find the following passage: "However, between the fifth [hole] and the one above it there is no intermediate scale. What's more, the distance between them is the same as the other holes, which creates an unpleasant-sounding interval."[14] "Distance between them" in the original is *ma kubaru koto*, literally "the distributing of the *ma*"—so then *ma* was conceived as something that could even be distributed or parceled out.

A one-sided world

In 1980 I published the book *Ma no hon* (The Book of Ma) based on my dialogues with Leo Lionni, a children's author and illustrator known for *Swimmy* (1964) and other books. Lionni was also active in the Aspen International Design Conference.

Our talks grew out of Lionni's fascination with the concept of *ma* in Japanese culture. One of the things I tried to stress in the course of our conversation was that *ma* not only was the space or interval between A and B, but also included the individual movements or tendencies of both A and B. Moreover, while A and B were each individual entities, they also tended toward forming a larger unity. Before discussing this further, I need to address the early history of this concept of *ma*.

The word *ma* did not start out meaning "between" in prehistoric and early ancient times. Initially, it was written with the kanji 真, which is used in modern Japanese in compounds such as *shinken* 真剣 (serious, earnest), *shinri* 真理 (truth), and *shinsō* 真相 (facts of the matter), denoting what is true, real, or genuine.

For ancient people, *makoto* (真事 or 真言), meaning truth in word or deed, was the most fundamental concept by which they lived. The Chinese studies scholar Fukunaga Mitsuji has famously argued that this sense of *ma* 真 came from the Daoist notion of *zhenren* 真人 (J. *shinjin*)—the "true" or "genuine" person—but I will refrain from getting deeper into that now.

In any case, *ma* 真 was a central concept in ancient Japanese culture. And here we must note that it also implied "two"—not the ordinal number two that comes after one, but the pair created by the fusion of two discrete units. Each of these two parts making up a unified pair was called a *kata* (part, piece, half). Each *kata* combined with the other to arrive at *ma* 真: the true, the real. *Ma* 真 therefore contained these two parts within itself.

So what happens if we remove the parts to examine them? That provisional state, with both parts placed side by side, is *ma* 間 (in its sense of interval or space): the subtle separation arising between two related parts.

The foregoing is my hypothesis regarding the process by which the concept of *ma* 間 was developed in ancient and medieval times. Here I might note that two more streams emerged from this flow from *ma* 真 to *ma* 間.

One posited *ka* 仮 (provisional, temporary) as the antithesis of *ma* 真 (true, genuine). This appears in the distinction that was made between *mana* 真名, the old term for kanji, and *kana* 仮名, the Japanese phonetic syllabaries. The sense was that *ma* was formal and proper, whereas *ka* was somewhat casual or informal. The name katakana 片仮名 for one of the two syllabaries probably came from the sense of parts (*kata*) of a pair discussed a moment ago.

The other stream, one which I will not go into great detail, led in calligraphy from *shin* 真 (formal script) to *gyō* 行 ("running" script, semi-cursive) and *sō* 草 ("grass" script, cursive), which are considered to be progressively less formal. This *shin-gyō-sō* hierarchy of formality came to be applied to a number of different cultural pursuits, such as the tea ceremony.

Of course the three elements in *shin-gyō-sō* did not always emerge in that order. As historian Murai Yasuhiko has pointed out, in many instances the *sō* form developed out of *shin* first, and then the *gyō* form arose to fill in the gap between the other two extremes. For example, in the culture of the tea ceremony and its related ceramics, imported Chinese tea ware was originally regarded as *shin*; next, the opposite end of the scale, native Japanese ceramics, became *sō*; and finally the intermediate *gyō* designation was assigned to the Korean and Korean-style wares that gained popularity in the sixteenth century.

In all of these cases, *ma* or *shin* 真, connoting unity or genuineness, is the consistent antithesis of *ka*, *gyō*, or *sō*.

One is an odd number, and two is even. The whole numbers form a continuous sequence alternating even and odd. In physics, which mathematically analyzes the structure and tendencies of matter, the terms odd and even are used to describe a fundamental property of matter called parity.

In the late 1950s there was a major discovery concerning parity involving the element cobalt 60.

Until that time, it was believed that all forms of matter maintain parity—basically, bilateral symmetry at the level of molecular bonding. This meant that the arrangement of molecules that make up matter preserves a balance between both of its sides. As we know from chemical formulas, the structure of organic compounds is based primarily on molecules made up of different arrangements of hydrogen, carbon, oxygen, and other atoms, with each molecule providing "arms" with which to link to their opposite numbers to form a balanced whole.

It was believed that any molecular structure, if one could hold it up to a mirror, would demonstrate this fundamental bilateral symmetry. Moreover, this was thought to be true at the level of elementary particles as well. The conservation of parity was a hypothetical law of particle physics. But two physicists, Lee Tsung-Dao and Yang Chen-Ning, proposed an experiment investigating the radioactive decay of the element cobalt-60, which, it was discovered as a result, emitted beta particles asymmetrically—and thus did not conserve parity. This discovery of what came to be called "parity violation" won Lee and Yang the Nobel Prize for Physics in 1957.

Parity violation means that in the final analysis, matter behaves asymmetrically. Or, to put it another way, material phenomena are governed not by the "evenness" of symmetry but rather by "oddness." So let's turn to a discussion of "odd," which implies asymmetry—*kata* 片 in Japanese. As we take a look, we will find that the eruption of asymmetry is something that occurs in the cultural sphere as well as in the realm of physics.

Ancient Japanese society was characterized by symmetry. The centralized *ritsuryō* system established the structure of the imperial state; symmetry governed the grand buildings of the court and the gridded layout of the great streets and avenues defining the capital, first at Heijōkyō (Nara) and then at Heiankyō (Kyoto).

Likewise, on examining the artifacts of Hakuhō and Tenpyō culture (mid-seventh to mid-eighth century) housed today in places like Kōfukuji temple and the Shōsōin Repository, both in Nara, we will find most of their designs and motifs characterized by an attention to bilateral symmetry.

But as the *ritsuryō* system began to disintegrate, so did this symmetry. Designs and motifs became less balanced. In Heiankyō, the western (right) half of the capital declined as the eastern (left) half flourished. The solid and orderly world of kanji began to crumble with the appearance of the more supple and fluid kana.

In the art of calligraphy, paper decorated with *suminagashi* ink marbling, which completely broke with symmetry, came to be prized. The historian Hayashiya Tatsusaburō called these shifts "a transition from a world of bilateral symmetry to a world of bilateral competition." A clear example is the cultural phenomenon known as *awase*, meaning "matches" or "competitions."

These events took many forms, from matches involving poetry, painting, or incense to those concerning collecting and exhibiting flowers, grasses, shells, and so on. There were matches to see who could find the longest iris roots or put together the finest garden plantings. Participants were divided into "left" and "right" teams, with judges placed to determine which side was superior. This was the advent of a "bilaterally competitive" culture.

Even so, while the two sides might compete in these *awase*, a sense of balance was still maintained. These were refined and polite entertainments. In the garden competitions the contestants might deliberately release crickets and make use of props or costumes to bring a sense of the seashore or mountains to their creations; above all, a sense of *miyabi*, or courtly elegance, was valued. Decorum reigned.

But as the balance of power in society shifted to the warriors, things grew rougher and more masculine. Animal matches became popular: dogfights, cockfights, and so forth. The chronicle *Taiheiki* notes that the regent Hōjō Takatoki (1304–33) was so inordinately fond of dogfighting that he held matches twelve days out of each month. Cockfights originally had a divinatory aspect, but they also became a popular sport, and during the Kamakura shogunate (1185–1333) the third day of the third month was made an official cockfighting day.

In short, things gradually became more extreme. And not just extreme: people began to compete and revel in oddity (*ki* 奇). This sense of oddity or eccentricity marks a major turning point in the transition to the next phase of Japanese culture. Those who cultivated eccentricity were said to "lean" (*katamuku* or *katabuku* 傾く) toward it, eventually giving rise to the term *kabuki* 傾奇.

The essence of the *kabuki* ethos was the rise of the "culture of the odd" over the "culture of the even"; of the provisional culture of *kata* 片 over the orthodox mainstream culture of *ma* 真. It was a cultural sensibility born of the dynamic breaking of the paired balance that, as I explained earlier, was inherent in the concept of *ma* 間.

This phenomenon would undergo a revival in a later era, when the literati of the Edo period (1600–1868) brought new attention to the strange and eccentric as an aesthetic value. For example, the artist and poet Gion Nankai (1677–1751) argued in an essay in *Shōun sango* (Cupfuls of Words from the Clouds of the Xiang River) that the taste for oddity was an "illness." Nankai was one of the finest Edo-period practitioners of Chinese-style poetry and an early defender of the literati style of painting (*Bunjinga* or *Nanga*) being transplanted from China to Japan at this time. A native of the province of Kii (present-day Wakayama prefecture), he was himself a painter of considerable refinement.

Nankai begins his essay by stating that *ki* 奇 (the odd, the eccentric) is the antithesis of *sei* 正 (the orthodox, correct, proper), and thus to prefer the odd is a kind of disease. He goes on to equate *sei* with *kō* 恒 (the unchanging, eternal), deeming *ki* to be far removed from both. But he also notes that the diligent practice of *sei* and *kō* never produces *shu* 趣, which we might translate here as aesthetic refinement, or simply art. Ordinary people hold to the orthodox and proper, whereas to delight in eccentricity makes one a renegade—but in the end it is only from the eccentric that art can be born. These ideas represent a genuine theory of *ki*.

Nankai's *ki* would later develop into the philosophy set out by Ban Kōkei in *Kinsei kijin den* (Biographies of Eccentrics of Recent Times, 1790). The individuals that Kōkei treats in his book are eccentrics of the type alluded to in the *Zhuangzi* as "standing aloof from other men, but . . . in accord with Heaven." Although they are regarded by society as home-wreckers, wastrels, and lunatics, their craziness and dissipation lead to artistic excellence. Among his examples Kōkei cites the Zen monk Baisaō (1675–1763) and the literati painter Ike no Taiga (1723–76).

Baisaō, a monk of the Ōbaku sect of Zen Buddhism, was at the center of an extensive network of literati and artists that had grown up around his practice of selling *sencha* tea (tea brewed from the leaves, as opposed to the powdered tea used in the tea ceremony). This Kyoto-based network included such representative artistic eccentrics as Ike no Taiga, the haiku poet Yosa Buson (1716–84), and Itō Jakuchū (1716–1800). *Ki* was in fact synonymous with the culture that flourished at the time.

In this chapter, I have taken up a series of important concepts underlying the sense of time in Japanese culture. In particular, I have turned the spotlight on how *hoka*—the Other, the external—has served as a wellspring feeding the currents of our imagination. And I have uncovered, too, how the concept of *ma* 間 conceals within it the mysteries of *ma* 真 and *kata* 片. My goal throughout has been to renarrate these concepts, as almost no one else has attempted to do, in terms of the story of the birth of imagery.

The perspective that I have raised in this discussion is, I believe, unprecedented and calls for further evaluation and study by others. Details aside, I think the main line of argument points to some very significant issues. But why is this perspective so important? I will make my appeal to you in the final two chapters.

CHAPTER 9   DREAMS

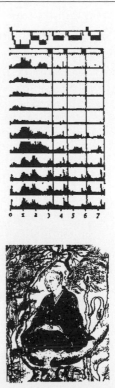

Between dreams and reality

"Asleep and dreaming what is it that we see? Is it first of all images and scenery? Does it have anything to do with what is visible and audible?" These are the opening lines of *Ways of Sleepers, Ways of Wakers* by the Belgian-born French poet and artist Henri Michaux (1899–1984), which recounts in roughly two hundred pages the dream life of its author. Michaux had previously compiled lyrical accounts of his experiences under the influence of mescaline—*Miserable Miracle* and *Paix dans les brisements* (Peace in the Breaking). *Ways of Sleepers, Ways of Wakers* extends these efforts into the realm of dreams. Michaux was an eccentric poet who was very fond of Yoshida Kenkō's *Essays in Idleness*.

For Michaux, dreams were reality. He believed that daytime waking consciousness and nighttime dreaming consciousness were directly linked, and that dream consciousness continued after waking.

This vision of the continuity of dreams and reality—*yume* and *utsutsu* in Japanese—is also found in indigenous cultures from the First Nations in Australia, Canada, and the United States to the San ("Bushmen") of southern Africa. In the modern West, the continuity between waking and dreaming began to be intentionally integrated into modern consciousness only from German Romanticism onward.

German Romanticism stressed the "night side" of human consciousness. In the late eighteenth century Johann Wolfgang von Goethe (1749–1832) wrote eloquently of the development of the individual spirit, and his ideas were taken up by figures such as Jean Paul (1763–1825), E.T.A. Hoffmann (1776–1822), Ludwig Tieck (1773–1853), and Novalis (1772–1801), who were increasingly drawn to the nocturnal. A contemporary of Goethe, the physicist Georg Christoph Lichtenberg (1742–99) influenced and supported the Romantics, declaring that the patterns of electrical discharge that he discovered represent the shapes of our dreams.

It was the German Romantics who first brought dreams into the broad daylight of intellectual discourse. It might be said that the first great leap of modern literature began with the attention focused on the language of dreams by pioneering writers such as Gérard de Nerval (1808–55).

Of course an emphasis on dreams was to be found, at least occasionally, in ancient Greek and medieval philosophy as well. Plato concluded the *Republic* (c. 380 BCE) with the Myth of Er, an account of the afterlife from a man who had a near-death experience. Cicero emulates this in the mystical Dream of Scipio, which closes his own meditation on the Roman republic, *De re publica* (On the Commonwealth), written between 54 and 51 BCE. Descartes (1596–1650) wondered what might happen if a man were carried to different places whenever he fell asleep and made to awaken there each time—a rather cruel experiment, like something out of a sci-fi movie. Yet all of this represents no more than a partial focus on dreams and is, moreover, confined to Europe.

The oldest extant dream book is from Assyria, from around 1800 BCE; astonishingly, the names of the scribes who recorded the dreams are given, and the dreams are listed in chronological order, like a card catalogue for a library of dreams. In ancient Egypt, dream books were written in both the Hieratic and Demotic scripts; the latter gave special attention to the dreams of women. In India in the fifth century BCE, a supplement to the *Atharva Veda* that later came to be known as the *Book of Dreams* provided a classification of dream imagery for prediction of future events.

Islamic culture also addresses the question of the reality of dreams. For example, Abd al-Ghani al-Nabulsi (1641–1731) wrote a six-hundred-page treatise on dream interpretation that did not question the objective validity of the information conveyed in dreams.

In short, historically, the world of dreams was initially accorded great significance but was then abandoned until the Romantics drew renewed attention to its significance.

For a year or so around the time I entered university, I made notes on my dreams every morning before getting out of bed. At first it was difficult to write about my dreams, but eventually I got to the point where I could recallthem pretty well. Strangely enough, when I did, I would get sleepy again. Not only that—I would lose track of whether I was asleep and dreaming, awake and remembering a dream, or awake in the midst of a dream. This phenomenon is known as hypnagogia or hypnagogic hallucination (though the terms are more usually associated with the state of entering sleep rather than waking up), and it is quite a strange sensation. However, I trained myself to keep writing (often nearly illegibly) and became able to make notes even in this hypnagogic state—until I fell asleep once more. This was usually a light sleep, and upon waking from it, I would begin writing again.

It was as if Morpheus, the god associated with sleep and dreams, had suddenly appeared to throw his black mantle over my vision. As my eyelids began to close I would say to myself, "Don't you dare fall asleep!" and managed to keep on writing. The result was that I would enter a state between dreams and waking. The self that was trying to stay awake struggled with the self that was falling asleep, and in the midst of it I was writing all kinds of things I would never have thought of in normal waking life.

The titan of Surrealism, André Breton (1896–1966), pioneered this type of writing under the name "automatism." And indeed, anyone can do it, and by so doing become a Surrealist. While I too use the method to amuse myself, I have little interest in works of literature and art produced this way. I am, nonetheless, fascinated by the strange linguistic realm opened up by this method, a blurred vision of a world neither quite of memory nor quite of dreams. My interest, in short, is to take a peek at the borderland between waking consciousness and sleep—and to ponder what this zone can offer.

The science of sleep

Contemporary science has yet to elucidate the true nature of sleep and dreams. Compared with scientific advances in other areas, it might be said that we still understand almost nothing in this regard. Nonetheless, a number of different hypotheses have been proposed.

First up is Sigmund Freud (1856–1939), who, despite the intense interest he displayed in the interpretation of dreams, did not provide us with much concerning the science (or neuroscience) of sleep. Freud believed that sleep is demanded by the subconscious, but his attention was almost exclusively focused on the inner realities of the ego and the workings of instincts and urges such as the id and libido. These were difficult to elicit in ordinary waking consciousness, but he believed that at night, as the body gives way to fatigue, the subconscious might take up the conductor's baton and summon them forth.

Ivan Pavlov (1849–1936), famous for his experiments with conditioned reflexes in dogs, claimed that in sleep the cerebral cortex is freed from its usual constraints. The cerebral cortex, particularly the frontal lobes, is responsible for planning and linguistic functions. In waking life it is tightly regulated, but when we fall asleep, these inhibitions are removed, giving the brain greater freedom. Pavlov believed that this results in dreams in which wishes and plans are fulfilled.

In 1928 Hans Berger (1873–1941), discoverer of brain waves and the electroencephalography (EEG) procedure for recording them, proposed that sleep provides rest for our parallax vision. Most animals, including fish and birds, have eyes located on the sides of their heads. But in the process of evolution, the eyes of humans migrated so that they both face forward from the front of the head, giving us depth perception and encouraging the development of our cognitive and planning capacities. During sleep, this parallax vision is put temporarily to rest—which also gives us the opportunity to dream.

The Swiss physiologist Walter Hess, who won the Nobel Prize in Medicine in 1949, was the first to discover the importance of the region of the brain known as the diencephalon (and particularly the hypothalamus). He proposed that sleep is a type of vegetative homeostatic state.

Hess thought that during sleep, the "animal" (sympathetic) functions of the body, which mainly have to do with arousal, are suppressed in favor of "vegetative" (parasympathetic) functions having to do with rest. As I mentioned at the beginning of chapter 2, "Paths," homeostasis is the self-regulating capacity of an organism to return to a particular physiological state: when we are hot, we sweat, and when we are cold, we get goosebumps as our body works to maintain its temperature equilibrium. In a way, it might be said that through sleep we return to a latent "plant-like" state in which dreams come to us as though reversing the flow of time from the remote past to our present.

As I suggest in chapter 6, "Flowers," plants and animals probably did not develop distinctly from one another, side by side; rather, one particular lineage within the plant world evolved over time into animals.

Plants have two modes of respiration: a diurnal cycle based on the assimilation of carbon dioxide through photosynthesis, and a nocturnal cycle that takes in oxygen and expels carbon dioxide. In terms of respiration, we humans follow the nocturnal cycle. Viewed in this way, the idea that in sleep we are returning to something like the memories of our vegetative past is quite intriguing—though this theory has no scientific substantiation.

The American sleep researcher Frederick Snyder, Institute of Mental Health, Washington, DC, argues that many organisms, and especially humans, sleep in order to conserve energy and maintain physiological balance. The English neurologist John Hughlings Jackson (1835–1911) thought that the function of sleep is to clear the mind of unneeded memories of the day's events and to consolidate ones more important to maintaining function. In other words, sleep is a kind of inventory control for memory. But Jackson's theory remains a bit unclear, since he never specified what standards went into determining the relative significance of memories, or lack thereof.

The Dutch scientist Serge Daan (1940–2018) suggested a similar idea—that sleep allows our system to reprogram. During sleep, and particularly while dreaming, the brain receives signals of some kind from the cerebral cortex that causes it to engage in processing the most recent unstored data for long-term retention. In other words, the cells of the cerebral cortex are temporarily holding a variety of new data that has not been sorted and catalogued, and sleep is our device for properly incorporating this data into the brain's operating system. Dreams give us glimpses of this underlying process.

So as we've seen, there are a number of different scientific hypotheses regarding sleep and dreams, though their validity has not yet been determined. However, a consensus seems to be evolving. We have discovered that there are two kinds of sleep: REM and non-REM (or NREM). REM stands for the Rapid Eye Movement that characterizes this phase of sleep; non-REM is the phase in which REM does not occur. REM sleep is also called dream sleep or D-sleep (for desynchronized); NREM is sometimes referred to as S-sleep (synchronized).

When we go to sleep, we first enter NREM sleep and then move into a REM phase. We then return to NREM sleep, once again followed by a REM phase. In other words, these phases recur cyclically during sleep. We also know that dreams seem to occur during the passage from one phase to the next.

Observation of NREM sleep shows that the entire body is engaged in subtle movement that appears to be synchronized to some type of stimulus. Exactly what that might be is still unknown, but as we enter sleep we appear to synchronize with something and the body engages in micromovements unlike those we exhibit in everyday activity.

Next we enter into REM sleep. This is the state in which we usually dream, and external observation shows that indeed our eyeballs are engaged in rapid movement. After a brief period of this REM sleep, we return once more to the NREM state, and then once more to REM. One cycle (from the beginning of one NREM phase to that of the next) normally takes about 90 minutes. Out of seven to eight hours of total sleep, five or six hours are spent in NREM sleep, and only one or two in REM sleep.

During sleep our body temperature lowers slightly, respiration and pulse slow (in NREM), and blood pressure falls. However, in REM sleep body movement becomes somewhat more active and respiration slightly irregular. Interestingly, men also commonly get erections during this phase of sleep.

It is unclear exactly when sustained dreaming takes place. It used to be thought that REM sleep was the locus of dreams, but now it has been determined that dreaming can occur in both REM and NREM sleep.

The materiality of dreams

A variety of chemical substances are secreted within the brain, including cerebral hormones and neurotransmitters. As I relate in chapter 2, "Paths," neurotransmitters are released by the neurons into the synapses, the small gaps in the neural network that serve as communication gateways. One class of neurotransmitters is monoamines, organic compounds containing a single amino group. Typical monoamines are noradrenaline, serotonin, and dopamine—all of which, together with another compound, acetylcholine, appear to have major effects on sleep and dreaming.

First to have its functions discovered was serotonin, which is active in regulating the duration of sleep. In addition, the groups of neurons containing serotonin appear to play some role in triggering the dream episodes that are part of REM sleep, while neuron groups containing noradrenaline and acetylcholine are thought to be involved in the manner in which dreams unfold.

The psychiatrist Allan Hobson, professor emeritus at Harvard Medical School, is one of the world's leading dream researchers. He is particularly interested in the function of acetylcholine. He developed the activation-synthesis hypothesis of reciprocal interaction between groups of neurons containing different neurotransmitters. Dreaming occurs when the one with acetylcholine predominates over the other. Hobson further hypothesized that the "victor" in this phase may be a network of neurons concentrated in the pons of the brainstem. Put as simply as possible, the theory posits that dreams arise out of a tug-of-war between groups of excitatory and inhibitory neurons.

Hobson's theory, first advanced in the 1970s, established a new bridgehead for dream research. By the late 1980s a number of researchers began to point out that substances in the brain other than hormones and neurotransmitters, such as enkephalin and the endorphins, seem to be involved in sleep and dreaming. Enkephalin and the endorphins are neuropeptides within the brain that might be described as endogenously generated opioids. In other words, our own brains produce substances similar to morphine that are utilized in various ways to regulate our systems.

News of this spread globally, touching off a race to discover new peptides. Japanese researchers such as Uchizono Kōji and Inoue Shōjirō joined in this quest, and during the 1980s a number of endogenous sleep-promoting substances were eventually isolated (such as the Delta-sleep inducing peptide, or DSIP)—all believed to be involved in supporting REM sleep. New substances of this kind continue to be discovered, and a number of scientists are still actively involved in research into the relationship between peptides and dreaming.

Another avenue of research looks at the regulation of dreams from the perspective of the internal clocks discussed in chapter 5, "Birds." An internal clock associated with dreams would naturally be geared to circadian rhythms and located in the brain. In fact, the most commonly accepted theory is that it is probably located in the suprachiasmatic nucleus of the diencephalon, because it has been demonstrated that when this brain structure is removed, circadian rhythms are lost.

I believe we have multiple internal clocks that synchronize to determine our sense of time. If more of these clocks are discovered, and more is understood concerning the mechanisms that produce neurotransmitters and amines, then the science of dreams should suddenly become a lot more interesting.

Analysis of dreams

Let's look at Zhuangzi's "Butterfly Dream" for a moment. Zhuangzi once dreamed he was a butterfly fluttering through the air. But when he awoke, he was assailed by doubt: Was he Zhuangzi who dreamed he was a butterfly, or a butterfly dreaming he was Zhuangzi? This is a richly suggestive question, one that has been considered a significant philosophical problem ever since.

Up to now, science has generally regarded dreams as nothing more than a by-product of waking life. But Zhuangzi's butterfly dream looks at the situation differently. One night I dream of being a butterfly. But perhaps I have actually always been a butterfly, and every night the butterfly has been trying to teach me that, though up to now I have not noticed it. Night after night the butterfly's message has been right there in my dreams, only I was unable to hear it because my sleeping was poor from eating too much, or being at odds with other people, or worrying. But then one night, as I sleep soundly, the message finally gets through: that perhaps I have not become a butterfly in my dream, but that the butterfly is dreaming it is me. This is the problem that Zhuangzi poses.

Zhuangzi's problem concerns not only dreams but also the vast realm of the subconscious or unconscious mind. John Lilly, author of *The Center of the Cyclone* (1972), inventor of the isolation tank, and dolphin researcher, is one man who plunged into what we might call the science of Zhuangzi's dream.

Zhuangzi's butterfly dream alerts us to the possibility that dreams and reality may not be such strictly separate realms. Even if they are separate, they may still possess common elements. Grasping the roots of this commonality appears to be one of the biggest issues for the future of the mind sciences.

Dream interpretation is not something that particularly interests me. Using symbols and metaphors from dream analysis to explore psychological states would be more intriguing if we could use them to get at some sort of larger pattern, but not if all we do is link them back to the dreamer's personal history. To me, attributing a person's dreams to his personality and temperament is akin to judging him based on unfair evidence, like a trial in absentia. I am much more interested in the nebulous "half-world" arising from the relationship between dreams and reality.

Bodhidharma's nine years of wall gazing was nine years in which the wall looked back at Bodhidharma. The wall was the dreaming butterfly; it had inserted itself into the space between dreams and reality. If this is so, then meditation bears some similarities to the combined state of *yume-utsutsu*, dreams *and* reality. The great medieval Tibetan sage and mystic Milarepa is said to have spent eight years in continual meditation in a cave in the mountains—but what did he see there? No doubt a cycle beyond that of birth and death.

Our lives are spent in a daily cycle in which the realm of night and of dreams holds a special place. In the daytime we talk to people, hate and love one another, read newspapers, watch television, and so on, and precisely because of this, we long for the night, fascinated by the dreams it brings.

For Bodhidharma staring at his wall for nine years, or Milarepa with his eight years in a mountain cave, the boundaries between one day and the next must have broken down, turning daily existence into one uniform unvarying stretch. When such a state is sustained over time, dreams and reality too exist in continuity.

It's possible that we have all been overthinking the idea of the realm of dreams as a unique and limited zone. Perhaps we haven't yet realized how intimately connected dreams are to ordinary consciousness.

It's true that the conditions of life in contemporary society demand a certain separation between day and night. Yet it is also possible to imagine that by pursuing a more meditative life—getting up every morning, doing some chores, eating a bit of porridge, communing with nature, and sitting—one could create a separate "dream community" here and now. What daily life would be like after seven or eight years of this strains my imagination, but even without any intense religious practice, there must be various ways of living such an existence. Children are able to imagine such a "dream community" through their daily absorption in creative play, perhaps even developing the ability to speak with creatures such as those depicted in Miyazaki Hayao's *My Neighbor Totoro*, 1988. Native Americans such as the Hopi, who traditionally live on three mesas in northern Arizona, incorporate such a community into their daily lives through kachina "dolls" inhabited by spirit beings.

The Hopi believe that each individual possesses something called the *hiqwsi* or "spirit breath," which might be loosely described as a "soul." Among other things, the *hiqswi* functions as a detective, judge, and mediator of the dreams of individual members of the community, which are understood as being recorded in a sort of collective dream archive—an archive curated by the *hiqswi*. In other words, the *hiqswi* serves as a sort of information-editing body transcending space and time.

So it would be interesting if we too, instead of analyzing our dreams, shared them with one another as a form of communication. It is certainly not impossible for us to speak with one another about the things that take place in our dreams. But this would require each of us to make the effort to remember, record, and share our dreams. And that is a lot of work.

Even so, many people have taken up this fascinating challenge. Among them are the Japanese monk Myōe (1173–1232), whom I will introduce a bit later, and the Marquis d'Hervey de Saint-Denys (1822–92).

Hervey de Saint-Denys should probably be in the *Guinness Book of World Records* as far as dream journals are concerned. In 1867 he published a book based on his dream journal, which ran to twenty-two notebooks. Even as a youth he is said to have kept a daily journal not of words but of sketched images. The conclusion that Saint-Denys drew from all this was that anyone can control dreaming. One strategy is to train ourselves to see the dreams that we want to see, rather than trying to remember the dreams that we had. Henri Michaux also took up this challenge.

Carl Jung also looked to dreams for evidence of a shared realm of consciousness, or what he called the "collective unconscious." In his view, dreams are simply individual expressions of this collective structure. Jung believed that dreams are expressions of "archetypes," motifs or patterns that enable human psychology to resonate within a shared realm that transcends the individual personality. He was interested in the way the collective unconscious shapes human societies through these universal archetypes, beginning with mythologies.

Freud, who was Jung's mentor, was influenced by the German naturalist Ernst Haeckel, who wrote, "ontogeny recapitulates phylogeny"—that is, individual development retraces the evolution of the species. Freud was not interested in Jung's concepts of universal archetypes or the collective unconscious, and instead focused on the analysis and definition of neuroses.

Jung's autobiography contains an account of a 1909 dialogue with Freud. One day the two were discussing the subject of paranormal phenomena, which Freud categorically rejected as occultism, arguing that everything has natural causes. Jung was so upset by Freud's comments that he felt his body burning, but just as he was about to retort, a large explosive sound came from the nearby bookcase. Jung immediately predicted to Freud that this inexplicable sound would be followed by another, and indeed it was. This was an example of what Jung would later call synchronicity—the idea that phenomena (here, Jung's burning sensation and the noise from the bookcase) can sometimes coincide despite having no apparent causal relationship, with no small significance for psychoanalysis.

Jung asked Freud what he made of the occurrence. Later, Freud responded in a letter with a mechanistic explanation, but Jung remained unpersuaded. Their divergence in this matter and others ended in the severing of their relationship a few years later.

From the standpoint of psychology as a discipline, it is difficult to assess the relative merits of Jung's approach to theory and therapy compared to Freud's. But one salient characteristic of Jung's methodology was the effort to link dreams into a web transcending individual consciousness. What drove Jung to embark on this interpretive adventure?

Dreams of gods, dreams of humans

Yumemi kozō (The Boy Who Had a Dream) is a well-known Japanese folk tale. In one version of this story, a boy has a dream—a dream so splendid and joyful that everyone wants to hear it. But the boy refuses to say anything, even to the village headman or the god Daikoku. Angered, the villagers drive the boy from the village. Lost in the woods, he encounters an old witch who asks him to tell her his dream in exchange for a magic fan that will let him fly through the air. But the boy deceives her: he grabs the fan and flies away, eventually reaching the ocean. There he meets a whale that possesses a needle with power over life and death; he tricks the whale into giving it to him and escapes. He reaches a castle town, where the entire population is mourning the death of the young princess. The boy uses the whale's needle to bring her back to life and is rewarded with gold and other treasures that he takes home to his village.

The key point to this story is that if you have a good dream and *do not* tell it to anyone, it will come true.

In a number of other stories, good dreams are bought and sold. In *Soga monogatari* (Tale of the Soga Brothers), Hōjō Masako marries Minamoto no Yoritomo, who later founded the Kamakura shogunate, thanks to buying an auspicious dream from her younger sister. This theme appears in many Japanese stories from ancient times to the present, though it is not unique to Japan but appears in folklore the world over.

Japanese mythology also includes a number of stories in which dreams play a crucial role. Emperor Sūjin, for example, is said to have sought guidance in his dreams for what he should do to alleviate a plague that was ravaging the land. As he slept, the deity Ōmononushi appeared to him, saying, "It is my will that things are thus. But if you find the one named Ōtataneko and cause him to worship me, then the troubles of the land will subside." The emperor sent out emissaries to find Ōtataneko, who (according to the *Kojiki*) was eventually located in the village of Minu in Kawachi. The emperor installed him as the chief priest of a shrine dedicated to Ōmononushi on Mount Miwa, and indeed, peace and prosperity were restored to the realm. The *Nihon shoki* account of the same episode states that the emperor resorted to oneiromancy after other forms of divination had failed to account for the disasters visited upon the country. In other words, by this time dreams were already being regarded as a more advanced form of divination than the use of oracle bones (turtle shells or deer scapula placed in a fire to produce cracks that could be read as auguries).

Emperor Sūjin seems to have had a particularly strong faith in the efficacy of dreams, resorting to them again when choosing a crown prince. Unable to decide between two sons, he ordered both of them to report their dreams to him. In those days, when one wanted to dream for the purpose of divination, there was a prescribed method that included cleansing one's body and hair and sleeping in a specially prepared bed. The two princes followed their father's instructions.

> The next dawn the elder brother, Toyoki no Mikoto, reported to the Emperor the story of his dream, saying: "I myself ascended Mount Mimoro, and turning to the East, eight times I flourished a spear, and eight times dealt blows with a sword."
>
> The younger brother, Ikume no Mikoto, reported the story of his dream, saying: "I myself ascended to the summit of Mount Mimoro, and stretched a cord to the four quarters with which to drive away the sparrows which fed upon the grain."
>
> The Emperor compared the dreams, and spake to his two sons, saying: "The elder of you turned to the East only, and it is therefore [fitting] that he should rule the Eastern Land. But the younger looked down generally over the four quarters, and he ought therefore to succeed to Our Dignity."[1]

Divination based on dreams (*yume-awase*) was so common at the time that a popular saying arose: "Even the crying stag follows the interpretation of a dream." The saying's origin is related in the *Nihon shoki* book that covers the reign of Emperor Nintoku.

Night after night in the seventh month, Emperor Nintoku heard the mournful cry of a male deer coming from the direction of Toga moor. But one night, it ceased. The next day a man presented a dead stag to the emperor. The emperor was saddened, realizing that this must have been the deer whose cries he had heard. The *Nihon shoki* then goes on to link this episode with the following story:

> There is a popular story that a long time ago there was a man who went to Toga, and spent the night on the moor. Now there were two deer which lay down beside him. When it was on the point of cock-crow, the male deer addressed the female: "This night I had a dream in which I saw a white mist come down copiously and cover my body. What may this portend?"
>
> The female deer answered: "If thou goest out, thou wilt certainly be shot by men and die, and so thy body will be smeared with white salt to correspond with the whiteness of the mist." Now the man who was spending the night there wondered at this in his heart. Before it was yet dawn, there came a hunter, who shot the male deer, and killed it. Hence the proverbial saying of the men of that day— "Even the belling male deer follows the interpretation of a dream."[2]

Dream divination makes frequent appearances in Heian sources as well. Even Sei Shōnagon, who generally comes across as a formidable personality in her *Pillow Book*, writes of her relief, after being frightened by an eerie dream, at being told by a dream interpreter that there was nothing to worry about. And in the "Wakamurasaki" chapter of *The Tale of Genji*, when it appears that Fujitsubo has become pregnant, Genji has a dream so unusual that he consults a dream interpreter.

Even today we can be startled by what we see in dreams, and it's reasonable to assume that in ancient times dreams must have felt even more vividly real. In those days, dream interpretation was the province of specialists called *onmyōji*, professional practitioners of yin-yang divination.

Other interesting aspects of dreams in the life of the ancient Japanese include the Yumedono 夢殿 or "Hall of Dreams" at the temple Hōryūji, where Prince Shōtoku (574–622) is said to have meditated, and the perspective on dreams displayed by the poets of the *Man'yōshū* anthology, in which the word "dream(s)"—*yume* in modern Japanese but pronounced *ime* when the *Man'yōshū* was written—appears nearly a hundred times.

Yumedono is written 夢堂 in a biography of Prince Shōtoku written in the late eighth century, *Jōgū kōtaishi bosatsu den*. The difference in kanji suggests that in Prince Shōtoku's day it might have been somewhat less grand than the octagonal structure we see today, which was built no earlier than the Tenpyō era (729–49). What did Prince Shōtoku do in this Hall of Dreams? *Konjaku monogatari* tells us that before entering the Yumedono, he performed a ritual cleansing. This alone doesn't indicate what he was up to after entering the building, but I suspect that he was actually using it not as a meditation hall but as a sacred bedchamber in which to await divinatory dreams.

As to the *Man'yōshū*, the reading *ime* used there for the character 夢 probably derived from 寝目 or 寝見 (literally, "sleep-eye" or "sleep-seeing"). The majority of dreams mentioned by the poets of the *Man'yōshū* were of a romantic nature. In particular, Ōtomo no Yakamochi wrote frequently of dreams of love.

ime no ai wa	Meeting in a dream
kurushikarikeri	is a cruel way to meet:
odorokite	for you wake,
kakisaguredo mo	suddenly groping, but nothing
te ni mo fureneba	is there for your hand to touch.[3]

hanekazura	In a dream I saw
ima suru imo o	the young maiden who now wears
ime ni mite	a feather chaplet,
kokoro no uchi ni	since when within my heart
koiwataru kamo	I drift on seas of longing.[4]

yoru hiru to	Whether night or day
iu waki shiranu	my love knows no difference—
a ga kouru	did my yearning
kokoro wa kedashi	heart perhaps appear to you
ime ni mieki ya	in a dream of desire?[5]

These three poems are quite straightforward. They all express a desire for dreams to be linked to reality, suggesting what strong faith the people of those times placed in dreams.

The following is another noteworthy poem, by Kasa no Iratsume:

wa ga omoi o	Have I let my love
hito ni shirure ya	slip out where the world may know?
tamakushige	I had a dream
hirakiaketsu to	where I saw my box of combs—
ime ni shi miyuru	and I was opening it![6]

A simple poem, but quite symbolic. The *kushige* in the third line (preceded by *tama*, meaning precious) was a lacquered box in which women kept their combs (*kushi*) and hair ornaments. As previously noted in chapter 3, "Deities," the pointed teeth of a comb, worn in the hair, were originally seen as a sort of antenna for channeling spiritual power, and this imbued the comb box itself with an aura of spirituality. The poet had a dream in which she opened this spiritual container—which was so easy to do that she feared the secrets of her heart might be equally open to others. That is the gist of the poem.

But I would like to note here that the box is a repository not only for combs but also for untold dreams and their unique space-time. In other words, it links the image of dreams to that of the magic box found in many folk tales.

Magic boxes (*tamatebako*) are boxes for the spirit. As we know from legends such as Urashima Tarō, and from the discussion in chapter 8, "Time," hollow objects like boxes function as models of negative space-time, of worlds beyond our ken. In other words, these boxes contain Mount Penglai or the Tokoyo, redolent with the fragrance of the sages and immortals. The poets of the *Man'yōshū* secretly carried this realm of the immortals in their hearts, where it was linked to secret loves, a fragile thing, something one could not risk opening.

It fascinates me that the dreams of the *Man'yōshū* poets and their contemporaries seem to overlap with an illusory realm we might call "the marketplace of love"—or, to put it differently, to them dreams were like a "market" or venue for exchanging feelings and thoughts, including those of a romantic nature.

There is an anecdote about an erotic dream of Empress Kōmyō's. One day, the empress visited a temple lecture hall, where she saw a beautiful image of the bodhisattva Jizō. She thought to herself that if there really were monks this lovely, then she would like to meet one. So she secretly had her ladies-in-waiting conduct a search, and after a while, news came that there was a monk named Jitchū who was even lovelier than the image of Jizō. The empress summoned him immediately and ordered him to bathe. As she secretly gazed upon him nude in the bath, she was smitten, and she fell into a dream in which she gave herself to him.

When she suddenly came to her senses, she saw that in the air above Jitchū, an eleven-headed avatar of the bodhisattva Kannon had revealed itself. Startled, she put her hands together in prayer, and was ashamed of her desires.

Jitchū is a historical figure who, according to some accounts, came to Japan from India. He is credited with founding the Shuni-e, a two-week repentance ceremony at Tōdaiji conducted to honor the Eleven-Headed Kannon. It is still famous today for the Omizutori ritual that comes near the conclusion of the ceremony.

It seems to me that in Japan erotic episodes such as this are too often hidden away. In European culture, to this day, the passions and seductions of the Roman and Greek gods are talked about openly and unabashedly. I think the time has finally come for us to acknowledge the natural eroticism inherent to Japanese myth and legend.

Haka and *ate*

Here I would like to address the core imagery of what I believe dreams express in the Japanese phenomenology of nature.

Let's begin with the opening lines of *Izumi Shikibu nikki* (The Diary of Izumi Shikibu, c. 1000): "She passed her nights and days distraught by the transience of this world, more fleeting than a dream." From the very beginning, Izumi Shikibu compares the reality of human life to dreams. Why? If we look at the literature of her time, appearing frequently is the phrase *yume yori mo hakanashi*, here rendered "more fleeting than a dream." This is the sensibility of the Heian court, which was different from that of the poets of the *Man'yōshū* and which prefigured the sense of *mujō*, or impermanence, that would prevail in medieval times.

"More fleeting than a dream" implies that dreams are evanescent, and that the real world is even more so. Here we should examine the *haka* in *hakanashi*, to which the critic Karaki Junzō was the first to call attention in his book *Mujō* (Impermanence, 1965).

In classical Japanese *haka* is a noun indicating progress or accomplishment in some task or endeavor, as we still see in modern expressions like *hakadoru* (to progress), *hakabakashii* (quick, rapid, satisfactory), or *haka ga yuku* (to progress, to move along smoothly). It is said to have originally been a unit of measure used in partitioning rice fields during planting and harvest; from it comes the verb *hakaru*, meaning to measure. *Haka* also carries the sense of an estimate, as in a rough perspective on or approximate clue to something.

Thus, etymologically *haka* carries an essentially positive image as a unit expressing degrees of progress, advancement, accomplishment. But when it is used in negative form, we arrive at *hakanashi*—which has a lonely, mournful quality, a sense of frustration and failure, or progress thwarted. Not only that: what begins as a simple feeling of lack of progress develops into a full-blown expression of *mujō*, the impermanence and insubstantiality of all phenomena. This is a rather dramatic transformation in meaning, even when taking the fundamental Japanese sensibility into account. *Hakanashi* evolved from the culture of the ancient imperial court through medieval times to inform our contemporary sense of *hakanai*.

We find an even earlier usage of *haka* than Izumi Shikibu's in the opening lines of *Kagerō nikki* (Kagerō Diary, c. 974): "There once was a woman who led a forlorn, uncertain life, the old days gone forever and her present status neither one thing nor the other."[7]

Kagerō nikki was written by an author we know only as "Mother of Michitsuna" when she was about thirty-three; it is a gem among the classics. The author is reputed to have been one of the rarest beauties of her day; when I first heard this I thought immediately of the actress Sakuma Yoshiko in the classic film *Gobanchō Yūgirirō* (House of the Evening Mists, 1963). In any case, what I want to note here is the word translated in the English as "forlorn" and "uncertain"—*monohakanaku*—which breaks down into *hakanashi* plus the prefix "mono-" evoking a sense of ineffability. The added element gives the word a broader resonance, demonstrating that *hakanashi* has moved from a simple negation of a unit of progress to an aesthetic sensibility in its own right.

Another point of interest is that both this quote from *Kagerō nikki* and the earlier one from *Izumi Shikibu nikki* contain the phrase *yo no naka* 世の中, which is described as being fleeting, transient, *hakanai*. In modern Japanese *yo no naka* usually means something like "the world," or "society," but in the literature of the imperial court, it had a strong connotation of relations between the sexes.

If this is the case, it would follow that the Heian aristocracy felt the transience of the world first of all in the fleeting nature of love between men and women, the vicissitudes of which consequently colored their perception of other worldly phenomena. Thus Karaki speaks of *hakanashi* as a supremely feminine sensibility, moreover describing *aware*, the pathos or deep emotion noted earlier as a key term in Japanese aesthetics, as a product of being moved by this sense of the transitory nature of life, and feeling profound empathy for it.

Yet if I may quibble with this analysis, I would say that the people of that era were using *haka* as a measure not only of the fragility of relations between the sexes, but also of the vanity of human life in general.

Such a viewpoint is more evident in the words of Murasaki Shikibu, who belonged to the generation following that of Mother of Michitsuna. Perhaps the best example I can give is Genji's famous pronouncement on the type of woman he favors, in the "Yūgao" chapter of *The Tale of Genji*: "It is frailty [*hakanabitaru*] that gives a woman her charm, though. I do not care for a woman who insists on valuing her own wits."[8] *Hakanabitaru* includes the root form of *hakanashi* plus the conjugated suffix *-bu* meaning to "become like" or "assume the characteristics of" something. In other words, here *hakanashi*, which began as a lament over an absence, has developed into a full-fledged state of being.

Of course, Murasaki Shikibu is using this "frailty" to describe a certain sort of femininity, so that it has not yet been extended to human existence as a whole. That comes soon enough, though, in the final ten "Uji chapters" of the novel.

The Uji chapters begin with the twenty-five-year-old Kaoru (who has been raised as Genji's son, though he was in truth fathered by another) fruitlessly courting the elder daughter of Hachi no Miya, an imperial prince who has secluded himself and his family in Uji. She dies without their relationship being consummated, and in the following chapter, "Sawarabi" (Bracken Shoots), Kaoru turns down a marriage proposal with these words: "Having seen with my own eyes the fragility of life and suffered so greatly from it, I feel that my own existence is blighted, and for that reason I could not under any circumstances consider taking such a step."[9] Here, his feelings at the death of the daughter of Hachi no Miya have clearly expanded to the world at large; "fragility" has become something attributable to this world of dreams.

In addition to this word *haka*, I would like to draw attention to the imagery associated with another, *ate*. This term appears in phrases such as *ate ga nai* or *atedo mo nai*, connoting aimlessness or purposelessness—like the ungraspable images of a dream. Saigyō's anthology *Sankashū* includes the following poem:

samidare wa	In fifth-month rains
yukubeki michi no	no trace of a path
ate mo nashi	where I can make my way,
ozasa ga hara mo	meadows of bamboo grass
uki ni nagarete	awash in muddy water.[10]

Saigyō's use of *ate mo nashi* here is identical to what we have been seeing with *hakanashi*: a reliable unit or standard of perception (*ate* or *haka*) has been lost or negated (*nashi*).

Etymologically, *ate* referred to a stand or board on which something was struck or cut. As far as I know the oldest example of such usage is in the chapter of the *Nihon shoki* chronicling the reign of Emperor Yūryaku, which mentions the use of a stone as an *ate*, with the kanji 質 for *ate*. Breast-plates and shoulder protectors are called *mune-ate* and *kata-ate*. In short, an *ate* indicated something offering reliance and support, and from this came expressions such as *ate ni suru* (to count on) and *ate ga hazureru* (to be disappointed in one's expectations).

Ate ga nai, atedo ga nai—to have no goal, no direction, no aim. This is sad, lonely, *hakanai*.

The last line of Saigyō's poem contains a pun on *uki*, which means both "floating" and "melancholy." Saigyō links the loss of direction (lack of *ate*) induced by the fifth-month rains with the floating, melancholy ephemerality of the flooding waters, in a dream-like echo of his own aimless wanderings. In other words, his poem captures how *ate* (and its absence or negation) gradually became a standard for taking the measure of a Japanese life.

For medieval poets, dreams were a world consigned to the transitory and ephemeral (which had no *haka*) and the aimless or purposeless (which had no *ate*). To me, their express choice of such a world, a world marked by absence, seems very Japanese.

yume no yo no	This world of dreams—
utsutsu nariseba	what if it were real?
ikagasemu	our only hope
sameyuku hodo o	is to await
mateba koso are	our waking.[11]

Myōe's long dream

In 1173, around the time that Saigyō was making his mark on the world, a boy was born into a powerful local family in the Aridagawa region of what is now Wakayama prefecture. At the age of eight he lost his mother; his father died in the autumn of the same year. Fated in this way to experience the transitory and impermanent nature of human life at a tender age, this young boy would grow up to become the famous Buddhist teacher Myōe— the author of the poem quoted just above.

As a boy, Myōe was called Yakushimaru because during her pregnancy his mother had made a pilgrimage to Jingoji in Kyoto and the deity enshrined there, the Medicine Buddha, Yakushi Nyorai.

Given the uncertainties of the age, one of strife and turmoil in which a sense of impermanence had become endemic throughout society, his mother no doubt made the trip clinging to the hope that her boy would be protected by the power of Yakushi. So it really was almost as though the young Yakushimaru was fated to take Buddhist vows after losing both his parents. Of course in those days, becoming a monk was not at all unusual. Myōe took the monastic precepts at Tōdaiji, the main temple of the Kegon sect. After mastering the Kegon teachings, he left the sect to study Zen. As noted earlier in the chapter "Buddhas," Zen in Japan was born from the Kegon sect, so Myōe might be said to have been riding that same trend.

Later, at the age of thirteen, Myōe would claim, "I am already old." This is a remarkable statement, but it was not a lament: Myōe saw it instead as a point of departure that would surely lead to something more. It would seem that from a very early age he had an extraordinarily clear perspective on the ways of the world, and its impermanence.

Beginning at the age of seventeen or eighteen and for the next forty years or so, Myōe would keep a dream journal, *Yume no ki*—no doubt the longest such work in medieval times. He appears to have been a dreamer from an early age, fascinated by the linkage between the worlds of dreams and reality, and positioning himself from the outset at the interface between the two.

As he reached maturity, Myōe became determined to go to India, believing that Japanese Buddhism would be doomed unless it connected itself more directly with the teachings of the original Buddha. But then, in his thirties, he experienced a series of dreams and oracles that became so famous it would later serve as the basis of the Noh play *Kasuga ryūjin* (The Dragon God of Kasuga).

The play begins with Myōe setting out from his retreat in the Toganoo district of northern Kyoto to pray at Kasuga Shrine in Nara for safe passage on the dangerous voyage to India. But at the shrine an old priest (actually a messenger of the Kasuga deity) tells him he should not go. Myōe protests that it surely cannot be undesirable for him to visit the land of Shakyamuni.

The old man asks whether he thinks anything might really be accomplished by going to India now, long after Shakyamuni has passed away. He tells Myōe that with the right perspective, Japan's Mount Hiei can become Mount Tientai, and Mount Yoshino can become Mount Wutai (mountains sacred to Buddhism in China). There is no need for him to travel to China and India because his proper place is here in Japan. Since there are people here who look up to him, he should think of them and stay in Japan to work for their salvation.

The old man then promises to show him something if he gives up the idea of going to India. Myōe consents, and Shakyamuni Buddha himself descends to Mount Kasuga, which is transformed into Vulture Peak. A spectacle similar to that of the opening passages of the *Lotus Sutra* ensues, and the life of Shakyamuni, from his birth to his entry into nirvana, is reenacted on the slopes of the mountain. When this pageant draws to a close, Myōe finally ceases all thought of going to India, realizing that everything in the world is right here.

Later, Myōe would become the abbot of Kōsanji in Toganoo and begin cultivating tea there. His tea spread rapidly throughout the country, together with the practices of tea drinking recently brought back from China by Eisai (1141–1215) as part of the Zen tradition. Myōe is thus regarded as one of the patriarchs of tea in Japan.

Before it developed into the formal ritual of the tea ceremony, one of the ways that tea was enjoyed in Japan was the "tea competition"—a party at which a number of different kinds of tea were served and participants vied to guess their provenance. In those days, Myōe's Toganoo tea was widely esteemed as the finest.

A portrait of Myōe at Kōsanji depicts him seated in meditation in the branches of a pine tree. It presents an image of him as a hermit, rarely seeing people, concentrated on his meditative practice. In the end, though, his form of Zen became only a minor strain in Japan.

As briefly mentioned in chapter 4, a Zen movement called the Nihon Daruma sect, led by Dainichi Nōnin, was gaining popularity at this time. In opposition to it, Eisai wrote a tract entitled *Kōzen gokoku ron* (Promotion of Zen for the Protection of the Country) in which he mounts an overtly political appeal for a different type of Zen. Meanwhile Dōgen had begun teaching his own type of Zen, which drew some of Nōnin's chief disciples. Myōe's solitary dedication to meditative practice resulted in him being left behind by these movements in Zen. But Myōe remained indifferent. He continued sitting, eventually erasing the boundaries of dream and reality, moving further and further into a realm where the two were indistinguishable—and so onward to the end of his life.

Painting of Myōe (1173–1232), thirteenth century. Kōsanji temple, Kyoto.

Myōe had wanted to die for a long time—since boyhood, in fact. But although he may have truly wished to take impermanence—*hakanasa*—to its ultimate conclusion, he ran up against the problem that if he did, that which was characterized by impermanence would disappear.

Caught in this dilemma, and wishing to look deep into the abyss of impermanence, he cut off one of his ears with a razor. In this he is often compared to Van Gogh—and it is a ghastly episode, no matter how many times we hear about it. Still, just as Van Gogh continued to paint, Myōe continued to record his dreams.

DREAMS

miru koto wa	All that we see
mina tsune naranu	in this world
ukiyo ka na	is impermanent
yume ka to miyuru	so impermanent
koto no hakanasa	it seems but a dream.

This poem was sent to Myōe by his uncle Jōkaku, who was a disciple of Mongaku. Myōe also studied with Mongaku, a warrior monk who appears in the *Tale of the Heike* as one of the advisors urging Minamoto no Yoritomo to commence hostilities against the Taira. We see him in chapter 6, "Flowers," as the formidable figure who once threatened to give Saigyō a beating. Jōkaku was a pretty impressive monk, too.

Myōe learned a lot from these two mentors. That he was able to master the complexities of the Kegon teachings probably speaks to the high quality of their instruction. In response to Jōkaku's poem, Myōe sent him this one:

nagaki yo no	You who know that this long dream
yume o yume zo to	of the world is truly a dream
shiru kimi ya	must help those
samete mayoeru	who are awake
hito o tasukemu	and have lost their way.

This poem implies that those inhabiting the world of dreams are the truly awakened ones, while those in the waking world are lost and confused. In his poem Jōkaku links dreams with impermanence, but Myōe suggests that those who are awake are lost because they are not dreaming hard enough. This sense of "not dreaming enough" is perhaps unique to Japanese thought; it appears quite clearly in this dialogue between Jōkaku and Myōe.

As one might expect, Myōe had a variety of strange dreams. I use the following one at the beginning of my book *Kūkai no yume* (Dreams of Kūkai).

One night, as he slept, Myōe encountered Kūkai walking along a mountain trail. The great teacher was chatting with a group of carpenters on the way to Jingoji, then under construction. Myōe drifted aimlessly along after them. The party entered the priest's quarters at Jingoji, where Myōe found Kūkai sleeping with his head nestled upon one of the tie beams of the pillars as a pillow. Two glittering orbs like crystal lay near his head. Looking more closely, Myōe discovered they were Kūkai's eyeballs. Thinking them as beautiful as plums, Myōe picked them up and was about to carry them off in his sleeve when he awakened from his dream.

The act of Myōe reaching out toward Kūkai in this dream is highly symbolic. The entire trajectory from Kegon to Shingon Buddhism is distilled into this single image. This is the sort of dream ordinary folks like us are never likely to have. There is a poem of Myōe's that beautifully expresses this genius of his. It is the sparest, most monotonous, and yet most deeply felt poem about the moon in the Japanese language:

aka aka ya	Bright, so bright!
aka aka aka ya	bright, bright, so bright!
aka aka ya	bright, so bright!
aka aka aka ya	bright, bright, so bright!
aka aka ya tsuki	bright, so bright!—the moon.

What a poem! All he does is exclaim the moon is bright—but what else could he do? This poem became so immensely famous that Myōe has ever since been known as the poet of the moon, as Saigyō is often called the poet of flowers.

Well, we've talked a lot about dreams, and to conclude this chapter I would like to introduce a selection of poems about dreams from the *Kokinshū* onward that I find interesting. The sixth poem, by Saigyō, encapsulates the theme of this chapter.

yadorishite	On a spring hillside
haru no yamabe ni	I took lodging for the night;
netaru yo wa	and as I slept
yume no uchi ni mo	the blossoms kept on falling—
hana zo chirikeru	even in the midst of my dreams.[12]

(Ki no Tsurayuki)

Suminoe no	To Suminoe shore
kishi ni yoru nami	waves advance across the sea:
yoru sae ya	must I see him
yume no kayoiji	even in the night look round
hitome yokuramu	and hesitate upon the path of dreams?[13]

(Fujiwara no Toshiyuki)

inochi ni mo
masarite oshiku
aru mono wa
mihatenu yume no
sameru narikeri

Harder to accept
than the loss of life itself—
this awakening
from an uncompleted dream
where I encountered my love.[14]

(Mibu no Tadamine)

kakikurasu
kokoro no yami ni
madoiniki
yume utsutsu to wa
yohito sadameyo

I wandered, too,
in heart-blinding darkness:
was it dream
or reality?
let others decide.[15]

(Ariwara no Narihira)

utsutsu ni wa
sa mo koso arame
yume ni sae
hitome o moru to
miru ga wabishisa

In the waking world
you must, I suppose, take care,
but how it pains me
that you should keep out of sight
even in the realm of dreams.[16]

(Ono no Komachi)

nakanaka ni
yume ni ureshiki
au koto wa
utsutsu ni mono o
omou narikeri

Though seeing each other
in dreams
is quite a joyous thing
it only increases my suffering
while waking.[17]

(Saigyō)

au to miru
koto o kagireru
yumeji ni te
samuru wakare no
nakaramashikaba

How I wish
I could dream
only of seeing you
and we did not have to suffer
the farewell of waking!

(Saigyō)

Yume to nomi
omoinasaruru
utsutsu koso
aimishi koto no
kai nakarikeri

Our encounters
real as they are,
seem like a dream
and our promises to each other
so futile.

(Saigyō)

In Myōe's and Saigyō's time, the folk songs known as *imayō* were popular.

Set to plaintive but beguiling melodies, these songs—which resemble the *iroha* song associated with Kūkai—were created in great numbers during this period. The retired emperor Go-Shirakawa was instrumental in popularizing them after years of study with a master of the form, a former courtesan named Otomae from Aohaka in Gifu. Among the *imayō* is a splendid song about dreams, one of the more famous collected in the twelfth-century anthology *Ryōjin hishō* (Songs to Make the Dust Dance).

Hotoke wa tsune ni imasedomo	The Buddha is always everywhere,
utsutsunaranu zo aware naru	but it's sad he remains hidden;
hito no oto senu akatsuki ni	at dawn when the human noise is still
honoka ni yume ni mietamau	in dreams I see his shadow.[18]

This song deftly expresses a number of the sentiments I have been discussing. The Buddha is forever omnipresent but cannot actually be seen. So where, then, does he become "real"? In dreams "at dawn when the human noise is still." Captured here is the idea of the complementary relationship between reality and dreams, interwoven with that of divine manifestation. The majority of the songs in *Ryōjin hishō* convey a blend of Buddhist and Shinto beliefs and are thus suited to expressing such ideas.

I will close this chapter with a selection of a few more poems from the *Shinkokinshū*. They are all masterpieces, and in all of them, the phenomena of nature flutter back and forth across the margins between dreams and reality.

haru no yo no	On this spring night
yume no ukihashi	my floating bridge of dreams
todaeshite	has broken away:
mine ni wakaruru	and lifting off a far peak—
yokogumo no sora	a cloudbank trailing in the sky.[19]

(Fujiwara no Teika)

sakurabana	Distant cherry blooms
yume ka utsutsu ka	were they a dream? reality?
shiragumo no	evanescent
taete tsurenaki	white clouds fade before my eyes
mine no harukaze	spring winds sweep across the peaks.[20]

(Fujiwara no Ietaka)

DREAMS

naku shika no
kowe ni mezamete
shinobu ka na
mihatenu yume no
aki no omohi wo

Awakened by mournful voices
of the belling deer
I go on yearning
sad autumn thoughts of a dream
begun yet left unfinished.[21]

(Jien)

mishi yume o
wasururu toki wa
nakeredo mo
aki no nezame wa
geni zo kanashiki

Though never for a moment
do I forget the dreams of the past
awakening in the autumn is
indeed
a painful thing.[22]

(Minamoto no Michichika)

haru no yo no
yume ni aritsu to
mietsureba
omohitaenishi
hito zo mataruru

In the fleeting dream
of a spring night he appeared
to me again so
now I find I await once
more someone I'd given up.[23]

(Ise)

yume ya yume
utsutsu ya yume to
wakanu ka na
ikanaru yo ni ka
mezamu to suramu

Are dreams dreams
or is reality a dream?
The answer I cannot tell;
in what world will I wake
from my delusion?[24]

(Akazome Emon)

CHAPTER 10   MOON

From mountains to birds

In the preceding nine chapters I have spoken of the phenomenology of nature in Japanese culture and provided a selective overview of the development of the imagery and the genealogy of the imagination residing within our collective memory. In this final chapter, I will conclude this exploration of the phenomenology of nature by raising the banner of the moon across the far reaches of time. But first I will summarize the main themes I have presented and include a few additional remarks on subjects not addressed earlier.

For the ancients, the mountains were another world—the beyond, the other shore. Mountains have been a preoccupation ever since what came to be called the *animus mundi* (world spirit) first emerged in human consciousness. From that point onward, there has been a continuous history of human effort, using the imagination, to scale the heights. Think of mountains as the body of Mother Earth. We were born of the sea, but it was by looking to the mountains that we attained our spiritual center (often referred to as a "womb"). Mount Sumeru, the world-mountain of Indian mythology, is a classic example of this concept of mountain as maternal form.

However, the history of human efforts to reach the mountains was paralleled by an equally strong resolve to *not* embark on that quest. Contrasting with the yearning for the other world—*there*—beyond the mountains was a powerful determination to create a maternal (or actually, paternal) form to take the place of the mountains right *here*, in this world. This was the seed from which the ancient state germinated. And throughout the history of human culture these two impulses—while not always diametrically opposed—have been at work, maintaining a strange and subtle tension.

In contrast to the paths and trails leading into the mountains are the roads connecting cultivated land. *Kuni*, the word for "domain," or "country," originally derives from *kune*, meaning a boundary or hedge and thus a symbol of the roads through the fields that provided the infrastructure upon which the ancient states were built.

Human paths are a legacy of the evolutionary event that took place when we first stood erect and began to walk upright. Of course animals had always created their own tracks, but humans quickly surpassed them. The Chinese character 道 (way, path, road, etc.) is a pictograph representing a band of walkers carrying the head of a sacrificial victim; it is a startling expression of the transition from animal tracks to paths made by men.

The roads built by humans became more numerous and soon began to cross. Crossroads spawned markets, markets gave birth to towns and cities. There is an expression in Japanese, *tsugō* 都合, made up of the characters for "town" and "coming together," suggesting more than one town linked by roadways. Today, the basic meaning of the word is "convenience," or "arrangements," something that transportation links between cities certainly support.

Roads created the circuits along which urban culture runs, but for a long time they were also where diseases and demons lurked in ambush. So people established boundaries and roadblocks, and chased out insects and other malign influences, all to invest the roads with new powers in order to welcome any beneficent deities that might also travel along them. These were the *sae no kami*, or *dōsojin*, which also served as prototypes for a variety of local deities. If one wished to access the power of the divinities, then an entire apparatus of worship and festivals was necessary to praise and venerate them.

The essence of the deities is expressed in the movement of invisible information. Such information manifests or appears to us after traveling from across the mountains or sea, and then returns from whence it came. Japanese deities—the *kami*—must be both welcomed and given a proper send-off. They're not much inclined to move unless called. So two basic methods were developed to accomplish this. The first was to prepare a *yorishiro*, a device that could subtly mark the visitation of a divinity. The archetype of the *yorishiro* was a carefully selected tree. But the fickle Japanese gods do not necessarily content themselves with such specified destinations, and might alight and inhabit a myriad of different objects. Japanese deities are present in such numbers that they were traditionally counted as *yaoyorozu no kami*, the "eight million gods."

Another method was to imagine deities assuming human form—as *marebito*, or strangers—to be greeted with courtesy, hospitality, and lively entertainment. The deities were greeted as "guests" coming from afar, honored here for a brief time, and then sent off once more to return to their distant homes. The various styles of welcoming and sending off the arriving and departing deities in different parts of the country are the origin of many of Japan's performing arts traditions.

Our cultural history emphasizes bearers of invisible information, like the wind and the birds, entities privy to the secrets of nature. They also embodied the breath that flows in and out of our bodies and were associated with the spirit of language within us which, riding on the breath, creates such a host of meanings. But the main reason that the wind and birds, these bearers of information from the unknown, were so venerated was that no one could see whence they came nor whither they would return.

Wind—風 (*fū* or *kaze*)—figures prominently in the Japanese language. Through the wind, we perceive the landscape (*fūkei* 風景) and scenery (*fūbutsu* 風物), foster a sense of taste and elegance (*fuzei* 風情, *fūshu* 風趣), and develop manners and customs (*fūzoku* 風俗, *fūshū* 風習). In part this is because a subtle sense of the seasons has been nurtured in Japan, but also because this sense of the passing seasons is closely identified with the shifting landscape of human ideas and feelings, seeing in them the fluctuations of what we might call "scenic energy" (*keiki* 景気).

A fresh wind blows away the stagnation of an established scene. Terminology such as *wafū* 和風 (Japanese style) and *karafū* 唐風 (Chinese style), or *kifū* 気風 (tone, spirit) and *shafū* 社風 (corporate culture), tells us that cultural patterns are also a type of "wind." Harbingers of change in such patterns elicited potent reactions in people and were labeled *ifū itei* 異風異体 (strange styles and forms), *fūryū* 風流 (aestheticism), or *fūkyō* 風狂 (eccentricity, madness).

Such "new waves" would eventually evolve into winds of change promoting eccentricity—*kabuki* 傾奇 and *basara* バサラ—which in the late Muromachi period would blow through even the realms of religion and politics. Figures such as Taira no Masakado (903–40), Ikkyū Sōjun (1394–1481), and Oda Nobunaga (1534–82) were either precursors or representatives of this powerful gale of eccentricity.

But extreme winds of this sort had already been blowing through the landscape of Japanese myth—as exemplified from earliest times by the "rough spirit" (*aratama*) of the storm god Susanoo. The roughness and wildness of this deity and others of his kind were born out of the untamed and unpredictable nature of the wind, an energy that would come to be known as *susabi*. *Susabi* could be written 遊び, connecting it with *asobi*, or "play," and giving support and encouragement to those elements in Japanese culture that took their pleasure to extremes. In other words, *susabi* was "play" taken over the top. And this led eventually to the spirit of *suki*, passionate devotion to the aesthetic realm.

This was no mere hedonism. The essence of such "deep play" was not individual pleasure but collaborative engagement in the game. This tendency gave impetus to a variety of aesthetic competitions, including poetry matches and linked verse, as well as the formation of theater troupes and other professional entertainers.

The "rough style" (*aragoto*) of Kabuki acting pioneered by figures such as Ichikawa Danjurō I (1660–1704), for example, has its roots here as well. The Ichikawa family took its cue from the fierce guardian deity Fudō Myōō enshrined at Naritasan Shinshōji temple in present-day Chiba prefecture.

Over time *susabi* would evolve into *sabi*, the ideal of lean or withered beauty often cited in connection with the haiku of Bashō and the tea ceremony, as I will discuss below.

From flowers to dreams

In earlier times, patterns and motifs, written language and spoken words— all possessed a spiritual power. Because of this, groups of people vied with one another over these cultural attributes. Indeed, even modes of speech, recreation, and play could become objects of conflict.

Victors would impose their patterns and styles on the vanquished; dominated groups would secretly attempt to preserve their own legacy for posterity. Thus certain linguistic styles or patterns of deportment acquired symbolic significance or were encrypted in various ways, becoming (in Japan) prayer formulas, pillow-words, poetic epithets, and forms of dance and song. The texts from ancient times—the *Kojiki* and *Nihon shoki*, the provincial gazetteers (*fudoki*), the *Man'yōshū*, and so on—are treasuries of such esoteric protocols and passwords. As Kūkai (774–835), founder of the Shingon sect of Buddhism, wrote, "Vibrating in each other's echoes are the five great elements. . . . All in the six sense-fields are letters."[1]

Yet gradually the power of ancient language was lost. One way to recover it, at least to a degree, and to find its lost protocols and secret passwords, was to uncover the common archetypal images embedded in folk tales by carefully teasing out and linking up the individual elements embedded in their narrative structures.

One such archetype we might call "negative space-time." Momotarō's peach, Issun Bōshi's bowl boat, Hanasaka Jijii's withered tree, Urashima Tarō's magic box—all of these are empty vessels enclosing negative space-time. And out of this negative space-time, the Japanese people have spun a phenomenology of the ceaselessly shifting cycles of nature and the vicissitudes of human fortune.

Some among the Japanese went even further: instead of doing the spinning, they sought to become one with what was being spun. These were the wanderers who, not content to simply devote themselves to aesthetic appreciation, renounced the world and took to the road. This type of spiritual wandering, which we might say began with the Buddhist priests Nōnin (d. 1196) and Saigyō (1118–90), not only took the form of actual physical travel, but also was pursued symbolically by Zeami (1363–1443) on the Noh stage, by Sesshū (1420–1506) on the silk and linen grounds of his paintings, by Murata Jukō (1423–1502) in a bowl of tea, and by Sen no Rikyū (1522–91) in a rustic hut in the midst of the city. The sensibility might be described by the single word *wabi* 侘び (simple and austere beauty). The culture of the Momoyama period was driven by the tension between it and its opposite, *ogori* (luxury or ostentation).

Another lineage, from Zen monk and *renga* poet Sōgi (1421–1502) to the haiku master Bashō (1644–94), rejected the dualism of *wabi* and *ogori*, and instead sought to embrace negative space-time and return to the vicissitudes of travel as a means of emptying the heart and mind. This represents the advance from *susabi* to *sabi*. *Sabi* may be written 寂び, suggesting the patina of age, or 然び, suggesting nature; in any case, it represented a sensibility seeking a return to the natural.

Observation in poetry of the changing phenomena of nature began with the invocation of the season (*kisetsu no yobiyose*), prominent by the *eighth century, as found in the Man'yōshū.*

First poetry, then gardens and objects used in the home—from textiles and ceramics to small furnishings—framed the perception of the seasons, creating models through which nature came to be viewed and appreciated. Poets such as Ōtomo no Yakamochi (718–85) and Yamabe no Akahito

(700–36) wrote of planting flowering grasses and trees in their gardens and sowing seeds. By this time the custom of consciously appreciating nature through the year—snow in winter, the moon in autumn, flowers in spring—was becoming established. Flowers could be picked and used to decorate one's hair; snowflakes or a reflection of the moon captured in a bowl. Although these were indirect forms of appreciation that were often smaller in scale, the critical idea was to capture the scenic energy (*keiki*) present in nature.

Japanese antiquity was also permeated to a surprising extent by Daoist notions of immortality and the Buddhist concept of impermanence, so that *keiki*, too, remained ever shifting, ever beyond one's grasp. In addition, the advent of millenarian *mappō* thought and the yearning for rebirth in the Pure Land that accompanied it brought a sense, even to the nobility of the imperial court, of the fragility and transience of the things of this world, inspiring the supremely feminine sensibility of *aware* (the pathos of things) and eventually giving rise to an aesthetics of overtones (*yosei*) and mysterious depth (*yūgen*).

Meanwhile in the male-dominated world of the warrior class, the sensibility of *aware* was turned inside out, transformed into the aggressively masculine stance of *appare*, as I described in the Introduction. This tension between *aware* and *appare*, however, did not endure; death was death, after all, and it made little difference whether one greeted it quietly, surrendering to the impermanence of all things, or willfully, on the battlefield.

And so the phenomenology of flowers, birds, wind, and moon faced the threat of sinking under the looming weight of this preoccupation with death and rebirth. But then, lifting it up, in serried ranks, marching into the cultural center of the capital from the mountains and countryside surrounding it, came the lively and rambunctious arts and sensibilities of *dengaku*, *sarugaku*, *furyū*, *imayō*, and *basara*.

This rustic backlash (*hinabi*) against the courtly elegance (*miyabi*) of the capital was evidence that the common people had remained uninfected by the influence of the concept of impermanence and the ethos that it inspired. In pursuing the poetics of nature in Japanese culture we tend to focus on the sensibility of the courtly elite. But what we really should take note of is the fact that whenever the rustic has supplanted the courtly, or emphasized the courtly elements in itself, it has been the harbinger of a fundamental stylistic shift in Japanese culture.

Of the ten keywords that we have been using to investigate the phenomenology of nature in Japanese culture, "flowers" is particularly prominent.
Flowers are of course the blooms of trees and plants, but they also represent human life and the passage of time and serve as temporary abodes
(*yorishiro*) for divinity or as offerings to the Buddha. The roots of ikebana
can be traced in part to offerings for a Buddhist altar.

However iconic the plum blossoms of the *Man'yōshū* and the cherry
blossoms of the *Kokinshū* may be to the Japanese imagination, the fundamental concept of "flower" in our culture is not limited to individual
types or species. In antiquity Mount Hiei, which looms over Kyoto, was
the representative mountain, and plum and cherry were the representative
flowers; but conversely, "flower" was a concept that expressed all the phenomena of nature and encapsulated the cycle of the seasons. It seems to
me that this is fully expressed by the following poem by Fujiwara no Teika
(1162–1241):

miwataseba	As I look about—
hana mo momiji mo	what need is there for cherry flowers
nakarikeri	or crimson leaves?
ura no tomaya no	The inlet with its grass-thatched huts
aki no yūgure	clustered in the growing autumn dusk.[2]

In this poem, there are neither cherry blossoms nor crimson maple leaves.
The season is late autumn, the time is dusk, the scene monochrome, reminiscent of an ink-wash painting. Yet the vibrant colors of spring blossoms
and autumn leaves are still glimpsed like a mirage. Teika's imagery simultaneously presents the desolate inlet at dusk that appears before his gaze
and the vivid hues that linger in his mind's eye. The cherry blossoms and
crimson leaves alluded to in his poem are one and the same with the archetypes that operate within the Japanese imagination.

It has long been a truism that the unique qualities of the Japanese religious
sensibility defy explanation—but a few phrases can bring them into focus.
Phrases like *shinbutsu shūgō* (amalgamation of the Japanese *kami* and buddhas), or *honji suijaku* (Japanese deities seen as avatars of Buddhist deities),
or *wakō dōjin* ("softening the radiance and becoming one with dust"; a
reference to the way in which the buddhas adapt their teachings to match
the capacities of their listeners). If the *kami* were expressions of a sense of

the activity of unseen presences in our world, then the buddhas were an attempt to express the possibility of salvation.

The cultural influence that the currents of Buddhism have exerted in Japan is impossible to sum up succinctly, in part because they met with such complex varieties of opposition, resistance, and accommodation. In addition, at some point buddhas were no longer part of our daily lives. My mother used to chant the mantra of Amida before going to sleep, but few people do such things anymore. The sense of buddhas as a living presence, coming and going in everyday life, found in classics such as *Konjaku monogatari* or *Ryōjin hishō,* is now long gone.

In such circumstances, rather than tracing the history of Japanese Buddhism, we should seek to revisit its roots, turning our attention to the thought and activities of the historical Buddha and his disciples. And indeed, this is precisely what Tominaga Nakamoto (1715–46) proposes in his critique of Buddhism in the mid-Edo period. Nakamoto argues that all religious and philosophical traditions are affected by a process of "layering" (*kajō*) or accretion, as generation after generation added new levels of interpretation (and misinterpretation) to the original teachings, and stresses the need for a return to the original sources. It seems to me that we would also be well advised to fully reacquire the Buddhist philosophies of interconnectedness, emptiness, and prajna (transcendental wisdom).

Today we are apt to forget how much of Japanese culture comes from Buddhist culture, or from the amalgamation of Buddhism and Shinto. In part this is due to the unfortunate impact of the anti-Buddhist campaign that followed the Meiji Restoration of 1868, but our history textbooks do not emphasize the seriousness of its impact.

I have just recapitulated the main themes of this book through to chapter 7, "Buddhas," and now I must say a few words about the scientific imagery I invoke in many places throughout the text. I have inserted various scientific commentaries not because I feel it necessary to provide scientific rationales for this exploration of the intuitive sensibility with which Japanese culture approaches nature. Rather, I did so because I want to demonstrate that concealed within science itself are insights and modes of thought that share common ground with that sensibility—what the mathematician Oka Kiyoshi (1901–78) once called the "science of the emotions" (*jōcho no kagaku*).

In ancient Greece, science was "the study of nature"—without nature, it was nothing. To study nature, one might engage in logical analysis and classification based on existing scientific knowledge or introduce new perspectives to address heretofore inexplicable problems. Either is in itself equally acceptable.

But it has become customary for contemporary science, rather than confronting the irrationality lying athwart unknown territories, to content itself with chipping away at small bits of the unknown from within the confines of areas whose rationality has been firmly established. Yet if we go on like this, science will soon reach a dead end. And indeed, although calls for paradigm shifts are being loudly voiced in a number of fields, we seem to have entered a period of stagnation.

One approach to breaking this deadlock is to introduce the perspective of information exchange and communication. Most scientific work—and progress—to date has focused on material phenomena, but this leaves a host of problems unexplained.

The migration of birds is not due to some material component inside them, nor can the opening of a flower be explained in purely material terms. In other words, once science began to engage with complex biological phenomena, it was forced to pay attention to how the communication of "information" operates to coordinate the disparate building blocks of an organism. If scientists were to analyze an organism by simply itemizing all of its constituent material elements, they would not, in fact, be able to put those elements back together again into a living thing. Reflecting on this, scientists gradually came to understand that life is built on the workings of information.

Our brains are the locus of perception and cognition, the seat of a complex information-processing system. Even if we accept that the flower we see exists outside of us, the fact that we can close our eyes and continue to see that flower demonstrates that we are managing that flower as information in our brains. This is the essence of images and the imagination.

In dreams we make extensive and creative use of such information, though dreams are not subject to our conscious will. Indeed, it would appear that these bits of information are freely arranging and editing themselves according to a logic of their own.

Supposing that one day we arrive at a science that accounts for such flows of information, it will probably turn out to be unexpectedly related to the ways in which we already encounter and experience the phenomena of nature in our culture.

One other point I would like to emphasize is that modest, seemingly inconsequential natural phenomena depicted in poetry and artwork—such as the flight of butterflies among spring flowers or the crying of insects amid autumn grasses—actually present quite significant challenges to the explanatory powers of science. Simply put, science will have reached its pinnacle when it can provide definitive answers to questions like the one posed in the Japanese song "Have the plums blossomed? O, when will the cherries flower?" But as yet, science cannot.

Let us turn at last to a discussion of the moon. I have already devoted an entire book to this subject—*Runatikkusu (Lunatics*, 1993). Here I will focus on some aspects of the phenomenology of nature in early modern and modern Japanese culture, with an emphasis on tracing the evolution of Japanese aesthetics from *wabi* to *sabi* during this period.

Mad about the moon

Years ago, I formed an association called the Japan Luna Society, and for a while its members—Chō Shinta, Kamata Tōji, Kusuta Eriko, Marino Louni, Minami Shinbō, Nakai Hideo, Shibuya Kyōko, Yamao Yūko, and other writers and people in the arts—met regularly on nights of the full moon to appreciate its beauty and discuss matters lunar. It wasn't much more than an occasion to gather for a potluck dinner and drink some sake, but once things got underway, we'd share poems and songs—and by the end of the evening hardly anyone had bothered to go up to the rooftop to look through the telescope that had been set up there.

The word "lunatic" means mad, demented, foolish, eccentric. In medieval Japan madness was associated with frenzied dancing, but in English, "lunatic" implies that a person has been driven insane by the influence of the moon.

The West has had its share of moon freaks—the French poet Jules Laforgue (1860–87), the German artist Friedrich Schröder Sonnenstern (1892–1982), and the Belgian painter Paul Delvaux (1897–1994) come to mind—while in China and Japan there were many more, including the Tang poet Li Bo (701–62) and the Edo-period poet and painter Yosa Buson (1716–84). What was it about the moon and night that appealed to these figures? What sentiments did they invest in the moon?

We all possess a yearning for the unknown—somewhere we might like to go, even if we don't know quite how to describe it—a place that, as I remark in chapter 9, "Dreams," is often conceived as "elsewhere," or "outside."

When we are walking down the street and someone asks where we are going, we usually have a clear destination and purpose. We are going shopping, or on our way to a coffee shop or a movie, or perhaps out on a daily walk and taking the long way back home. It's become rare to have no specific destination when we go out.

Indeed, if you are out wandering around these days with no apparent purpose, you might get stopped and questioned by the cops. Back in the day, the avant-garde theater legend Terayama Shūji (1935–83) used to enjoy wandering about his neighborhood in Shibuya, and at one point was stopped by the police for questioning. The incident was taken up by the newspapers, who mocked him as a Peeping Tom. Modern civil society is structured in such a way as to marginalize those without goals and purpose, as Walter Benjamin and Michel Foucault have argued in their writings. Perhaps this is because in recent times we have lost our appreciation for that "indescribable somewhere."

When the Apollo missions landed on the moon, many people expected that this would lead to its development, but I never thought anything of the sort. Instead, I sighed and said, "Well, now there's no place else to go." Such an ultimate "elsewhere" or "other world" as the moon is absolutely essential to humanity and to civilization, and it seemed to me a great mistake to trample on this final frontier.

It is absolutely crucial for us to have a sanctuary of some sort, to be able to respond to the question "Where have you been?" with something vague like, "Oh, nowhere in particular." This "nowhere" can be anywhere, a personal hideaway no one else knows about, or even just a movie house or a pachinko parlor—as long as it lies "elsewhere," beyond our mundane existence. Earth itself needs an elsewhere, a hideaway. And to me the moon has always seemed the best candidate for such a refuge.

There is nothing on the moon. And that's precisely what makes it so wonderful. That's my take on it. I don't think anything is likely to happen on the moon in the future. If it does, then we on Earth will be destroying something very precious. Even if someday we become able to travel freely in outer space, we should bypass the moon and leave it alone. I think an effort to colonize the moon and build bases there might actually herald the decline of the human spirit.

By the way, the moon is moving away from Earth. At this point, the rate is only about three or four centimeters annually, but who knows when it might suddenly speed up. Better take a good look while it is still here.

In Japanese culture, we see an attachment to the moon expressed to some degree as far back as the eighth-century *Man'yōshū* and tenth-century *Kokinshū* poetry anthologies; such feelings, however, do not reach an ardor approaching lunacy until about the time of the *Shinkokinshū*, at the beginning of the thirteenth century.

The *Kokinshū* contains 1,111 poems, only 31 of which feature the moon. The number of moon poems steadily increases in later anthologies—49 in *Gosen wakashū*, 60 in *Shūi wakashū*, 109 in *Go Shūi wakashū*, 154 in *Senzai wakashū*—reaching a peak of 300 in the *Shinkokinshū*.

This was the result of several factors. First, in the evolution of poetic sensibility from ancient to medieval times, there was a gradual shift in preference from poems set in spring to those set in autumn. Concurrently, a trend emerged toward the evocation of natural phenomena that inspired feelings of melancholy, cold, and solitude. The winter moon also appeared at this time as a poetic subject. As far as I am concerned, if your poetic sensibility stops with the autumn moon without advancing to the moon in winter, you are not a genuine moon fanatic.

Someone—albeit a fictional character—who expressed an early interest in the winter moon was none other than the Shining Prince, the protagonist of *The Tale of Genji*. In the "Asagao" (Bluebells) chapter, Genji says, "More than the glory of flowers and fall leaves that season by season capture everyone's heart, it is the night sky in winter, with snow aglitter beneath a brilliant moon, that in the absence of all color speaks to me strangely and carries my thoughts beyond this world; there is no higher wonder or delight."[3] Genji then has the bamboo blinds rolled up to reveal a winter snowscape illuminated by the moon. That the brilliance of the winter moon upon the snow speaks to him "strangely" and carries his thoughts "beyond this world" are signs that the prince indeed has a sense of what the moon is about.

This intense fascination with the winter moon was inherited by the poets Fujiwara no Shunzei and Myōe. We've already met Myōe in the preceding chapter. And Yoshida Kenkō also expressed an interest in the desolate moon of winter. Here are two poems, by Shunzei and Myōe:

tsuki sayuru   Out on the ice pack
kōri no ue ni   that glitters with cold moonlight,
arare furi   hail is falling
kokoro kudakuru   shattering my heart
Tamakawa no sato   at Tamakawa village.[4]

                                                    (Shunzei)

kumo o idete   Winter moon,
ware ni tomonau   coming out from the clouds
fuyu no tsuki   to accompany me—
kaze ya mi ni shimu   the wind is piercing, is it not?
yuki ya tsumetaki   and the snow so very cold.

                                                    (Myōe)

These poems are all the more interesting because they intimately link the winter moon to the body and mind of the poet. Although neither poem is much by way of technique, it is their committed engagement with the moon that makes them so appealing. Yet if I may be a bit harsh in my judgment, I think neither poem is at a level that fully sings of the moon. The level of expression I seek has not yet been attained by Shunzei and Myōe. Nor do Saigyō, Kamo no Chōmei, Yoshida Kenkō, or even the "chill melancholy" (*hiesabi*) of Shinkei really do justice to the moon.

So what form of expression suits my sense of the moon? Perhaps the following verses on the winter moon by Yosa Buson. With these we are at least beginning to get somewhere.

Kangetsu ya / mon naki tera no / ten takashi
Cold winter moon / over the gateless temple / the distant heavens.

Tsuki tenshin / mazushiki machi o / tōrikeri
The moon at zenith / as I pass through / these mean streets.

Kakekakete / tsuki mo nakunaru / yo samu kana
Waning, waning / the moon, too, almost gone / how cold the night!

Kangetsu ya / nokogiri iwa no / akarasama
Cold moon! / starkness / of the sawtoothed peaks.

Why were Shunzei and Saigyō unable to express themselves in this way? The fault did not lie with them; it was not their poetic sensibility that was deficient, but the times in which they lived. To reach a point where it could give voice to the moon as an "other world," the Japanese appreciation of natural phenomena first had to be honed by passage through a more tempestuous and dangerous historical period.

What follows is an overview of this evolution, which traces developments from Zeami to Buson and onward to the moon of modern poets such as Hagiwara Sakutarō (1886–1942) and Miyazawa Kenji, while at the same time summarizing developments in the Japanese sensibility through periods not yet touched on in this book.

The duality of *ogori* and *wabi*

The Noh master Zeami embodied the spirit of the Kitayama culture that reached its zenith under Shogun Ashikaga Yoshimitsu (1358–1408). His aesthetic was defined by a revival of the past and an embodiment of overtones (*yosei*) and mysterious depth (*yūgen*) that could also be regarded as the essence of Kitayama culture. In it was a longing for a kind of feminine luster recalling the elegant refinement (*miyabi*) of the ancient imperial court.

But the times would soon change. Shogun Yoshinori (the sixth shogun, Yoshimitsu's son) was hostile to Zeami and exiled him to the island of Sado. During his rule there were unprecedented famines, and a major peasant rebellion in 1428 signaled the beginning of an era of civil unrest and warfare. Yoshinori was succeeded as shogun by Yoshikatsu, still only a child, who died eight months later. His successor, Yoshimasa, was also only eight years old when he became the eighth Ashikaga shogun, and nothing in his experience prepared him to deal with the Ōnin War, which broke out in 1467 and, over the next decade, reduced the Kitayama culture to ashes.

The Higashiyama culture that replaced Kitayama culture was virtually its polar opposite. Nostalgia for the ancient elegance of the Japanese imperial court was supplanted by a fascination with the pomp and circumstance of a new wave of culture imported from China, while overtones and mystery were replaced by *wabi suki* (austere aestheticism). The Ōnin War had changed history, and the sensibility of artists with it—including the way they looked at the moon.

Is it really possible for the sensibility of an era to change so precipitously as a result of such an event? I certainly think so.

After the Ōnin War, most of Kyoto was smoking ruins. What would happen today if Tokyo were visited by disaster on a scale comparable to that wrought by the Great Kantō Earthquake of 1923 or the air raids of World War II? I think we would see the advent of a major and quite complex transformation that could not be reduced to a single phenomenon like the appearance of Taishō Democracy after the earthquake or the influx of American culture after the war.

Yet even if Tokyo were destroyed, it would not necessarily lead to a transformation in the urban culture throughout Japan. However, in the fifteenth century, urban culture was concentrated almost entirely in Kyoto. And so I would argue that a deep spiritual and stylistic gulf separates the Kitayama and Higashiyama cultures, no matter how connected they may seem on the surface. Ikkyū, whom I have already introduced as an eccentric in chapter 4, "Wind," was one of the spirits born of this new era. And even Shogun Yoshimasa (1436–90) wrote about the moon:

kuyashiku zo	Today I recall
sugishi uki yo wo	The sad world where I lived
kyō zo omou	With bitter regret—
kokoro kumanaki	My mind serene as I gaze
tsuki o nagamete	At a moon free of shadows.[5]

This poem does not express an especially highly developed sense of the moon, no matter how you look at it. But a sensibility that could look at the moon and feel bitter regret is something that simply didn't exist in or before Kitayama culture. Yoshimasa's moon, moreover, recalls for him a "sad," transitory world—*ukiyo*.

So what did the regretful Yoshimasa do? On the grounds of his villa in the Higashiyama district of eastern Kyoto, which later became the temple Jishōji, he built the Tōgudō buddha hall and the Silver Pavilion and immersed himself in the practice of *wabicha*, an austere form of the tea ceremony, under the tutelage of the master Murata Jukō. This did not simply stem from the difference in personalities between Yoshimitsu, who reveled in secular life, and Yoshimasa, who wanted to escape it. It was also the contrast between the Hana no Gosho ("flower palace"), Yoshimitsu's grand palace in the Muromachi district of Kyoto, and the sober and modest *shoin-zukuri* style of Yoshimasa's villa. It was the opposition between *ogori* (luxury, lavishness, excess) and *wabi* (poverty, austerity, restraint).

But it would also be wrong to let Yoshimasa's taste stand for everything in his era. During this same period, Zen monks began to practice monochromatic ink painting, members of the warrior class such as Kanō Masanobu (1434–1530) painted folding screens with themes of birds and flowers, and Buddhist monastics initiated ikebana. It was an era in which a variety of decorative arts reached an apex of ingenuity, as captured in the *Kundaikan sō chōki*, a reference manual and set of guidelines for the display of art compiled by Nōami (1397–1471), an artist and aesthetic consultant to the Ashikaga shoguns.

In other words, the sensibility that responds to the phenomena of nature was no longer confined to the poems and diaries of court nobility; an age had dawned in which that sensibility was also poured into ink painting and the arrangement of objects for display in the tokonoma, the decorative alcove that was one of the innovations of *shoin-zukuri* architecture. To put it even more boldly, adepts in the arrangement of objects began to sway the perception of nature.

It is in this context that *wabi* first emerges. This is because *wabi* is a sensibility that appears only after objects have become abundant, tastes for them have been finely honed, and the highly desirable ones whittled down to a precious few.

In the *Yamanoue no Sōji ki*, notes left by one of Sen no Rikyū's principal disciples, it is written that a *sukisha* (one of three types of tea master) is someone who "possesses nothing" while "holding determination in his heart." Similarly, the *Nanbōroku* (Southern Record), a collection of Rikyū's teachings on tea attributed (probably apocryphally) to his disciple Nanbō Sōkei, speaks of "the state of non-possession" (*mu ichimotsu no kyōkai*). The *Zencharoku* (The Book of Zen Tea), an Edo-period text attributed to Jakuan Sōtaku, describes *wabi* as "a sense of impoverishment, of things not going according to one's will, of faltering." *Wabi* clearly begins with an attachment to things, but it is a sensibility that is ultimately shaped by contemplating this attachment as an aesthetic mentality and taking the opposite stance of having too little.

This attitude was premised upon Murata Jukō's dictum that one should "blur the boundaries between Japan and China." What he meant was that while both Chinese and Japanese objects had their good points, overattachment to one or the other would only be confining; to break through the limits, it was better to pull back from making such distinctions altogether. The tea master Takeno Jōō (1502–55) declared that the origins of the tea ceremony lay in the act of offering tea and hospitality to a friend who had come to visit, where one "was retired and enjoying living apart from the things of this world (*butsugai*)." This *butsugai* was Jōō's "elsewhere," and it can also be seen as a rejection of the lavish sensibility (*ogori*) vis-à-vis material objects in Kitayama culture.

But the times would soon take another dynamic turn. Only twenty years after the Ōnin War had finally drawn to a close, the warlord Hōjō Sōun (1432–1519) occupied the province of Izu. It was the first of a succession of local conflicts that would plunge the country into more than a century of civil war known as the Sengoku ("warring states") period—bringing with it a general sense that the aesthetic extravagance of Kitayama culture was being eclipsed by the reality of extravagant displays of power.

The sensibility of *wabi* underwent a corresponding transformation. This was how Rikyū's sense of the tea ceremony and its "system interface" developed the taut intensity that was then overlaid on the austere *wabicha* of Jukō and Jōō. And it was here that the phenomenology of nature reached a bold and complete cultural expression, as epitomized by the famous story of Rikyū and the morning glories.

The warlord Toyotomi Hideyoshi, Rikyū's patron and the most powerful man in Japan at that time, had heard that the morning glories in Rikyū's garden would be at their peak on the day he was to go there for tea. He was looking forward to strolling among them in the garden. But when he arrived to take tea with Rikyū, there was not a morning glory to be seen. Puzzled, Hideyoshi entered the tea room—and found a single morning glory in a vase in the alcove. Rikyū had cut down all the others in the garden. This scene is vividly depicted in Teshigahara Hiroshi's film *Rikyū* (1989). Such boldness was completely unthinkable in the previous culture of flowers, tea, or hospitality. Something had radically shifted in the cultural response to nature.

It is often said that in the age of Oda Nobunaga and Toyotomi Hideyoshi, *wabi* and opulence coexisted. Nobunaga's castle at Azuchi and Hideyoshi's gilded teahouse were emblematic of this. But as in the contrast between the Kitayama and Higashiyama cultures, *wabi*/opulence was but one example of the many dualities that coexisted in the same era: great warlords and prosperous townsmen, castles and merchant shops, spears and guns, Buddhist sectarians and Christians, bird-and-flower paintings and genre paintings, the bodhisattva Miroku and the folk gods of good fortune.

In the Sengoku period, extravagance and poverty stood cheek by jowl. *Ogori* and *wabi*, previously locked in opposition to one another, for the first time found common ground. In the *Nanbōroku*, we find Rikyū himself saying that "it is not pleasing to take *wabi* to an extreme." It is here that the transition from *wabi* to *sabi* begins.

Later developments in the phenomenology of nature

What is *sabi*? In English it's often described as a quiet, aged beauty, but it's certainly a difficult word to define. Bashō, responsible for the supreme expression of this ideal, left no satisfying explanation of it—no doubt intentionally. One of Bashō's chief disciples, Mukai Kyorai, wrote in *Kyoraishō* (Kyorai's Notes, 1702–4) that "*Sabi* is the color of a verse. It does not refer [only] to poems that express tranquility or serenity." Bashō reportedly praised a haiku by Kyorai—"The custodians of the flowers / putting their white heads / together" (hanamori ya / shiroki kashira o / tsukiawase)—as "expressing the color of *sabi*." Bashō's travelogue *Nozarashi kikō* contains a haiku by a local poet named Gara—"Let me, too, become *sabi* / the wild camellia / beyond the plum blossoms" (ware mo sabi yo / ume yori oku no / yabutsubaki)—to which Bashō linked a verse of his own. But that is about it.

Yet even if Bashō left no detailed explanation of the nature of *sabi*, it is clear that the times could no longer be satisfied with *wabi* alone. They demanded the creation of a new sensibility to transcend the fusion of *wabi* with *ogori*. The literary scholar Matsuda Osamu offered a fresh perspective on *sabi* in his 1979 essay "Sabi iro no sekai," in which he notes that in *Shogenji kōsetsu yōshū*, an early seventeenth-century dictionary, the reading *sabi iro* is given to the compound 宿色 made up of the characters 宿 (here meaning "aged") and 色 (meaning "color").

Efforts at creating this new sensibility prior to Bashō include the stylistic innovations embodied in the boldly and playfully misshapen tea wares (*hyōgemono*) associated with the daimyo tea master Furuta Oribe (1544–1615), followed by the open, liberated designs of Kobori Enshū (1579–1647). The art of these two came to be known to later generations as *kirei sabi*, "beautiful *sabi*" or "refined rusticity"; along with the *hime* (elegant; literally, "princess") *sabi* of tea master Kanamori Sōwa, who was influenced by both Oribe and Enshū, it represented what we might call a transitional period in the aesthetics of *sabi*. The response to nature had finally entered a stage in which individual imagination and ingenuity became crucial.

But at the same time, *wabi* with an admixture of lavishness did not disappear as a style; nor can we say that the rather showy *kirei sabi* and *hime sabi* led directly to the *sabi* of Bashō. Rather, it seems to me that *kirei sabi* originated in the work of the artists Hon'ami Kōetsu (1558–1637) and Tawaraya Sōtatsu (d. 1643), received cultural validation as the aesthetic of the warrior-class tea masters Oribe and Enshū, and then mingled with a looser sensibility welling up among commoners, ronin, and artisans to produce what it finally became.

Indeed, we might say that the evolution of the *wabi* of the Momoyama period into the *sabi* of the Edo period began in the early seventeenth century with those who encountered Izumo no Okuni's *kabuki odori* and the genre paintings of Iwasa Matabei (which evolved into Kabuki and ukiyo-e, respectively).

In short, at this point in history it becomes impossible not to speak of developments in the phenomenology of nature as a single unified stream. The cultural response to nature in the Edo period was simply too diverse. Considerable individual creativity was displayed even within a single artistic school like the Kanō school, and artists in a number of other fields from ceramics to printmaking showed a dizzying and delightful ingenuity and variety. It was precisely these developments that would enable Buson's approach to the moon, discussed above.

The first noteworthy development in the evolution of the phenomenology of nature in the Edo period is Sōtatsu's rise from fan maker to master painter and artisan, backed by the power of the wealthy merchants of Kyoto. I am particularly fond of his folding screen *Narrow Path Amid Vines* (*Tsuta no hosomichi-zu*), but once I accompanied the photographer Jūmonji Bishin on a half-day shoot of Sōtatsu's famous screen painting of Bugaku dancers, and as I looked at this remarkable work I had a visceral sense that it was with Sōtatsu that Japanese design was first endowed with such power of detail. His almost tectonic approach to composition was unprecedented; at the same time his work embodies an undeniable sense of courtly elegance (*miyabi*). And as far as the moon is concerned, in *Poem Cards with Designs of Flowering Plants of the Four Seasons*, a collaboration between Sōtatsu and Kōetsu, the boldly rendered enormous half moon that serves as a recurring motif fundamentally demolishes all previous models for depicting the moon.

This is testament to the power of both Sōtatsu himself and the studio system that he devised, but another crucial factor is that the wealthy merchants and townsmen of the era had begun to erode at least a portion of the monopoly over aesthetic culture held until that point by the court nobility, the warrior houses, and the Buddhist and Shinto clergy. Otherwise Sōtatsu would have been unable to express *miyabi* in his work as he did, openly and without reserve, with the exuberant energy of the townsmen, thrusting the moon and flowers onto the center stage of his times.

The paintings of Ogata Kōrin (1658–1716), following Sōtatsu a generation or two later, have been criticized by some as being too one-dimensional, deficient in spiritual and imaginative depth—but I give him high marks for precisely this surface "flatness."

Kōrin largely drew on Sōtatsu in works such as *Rough Waves* and his series of screens *Waves of Matsushima*, which were painted as a direct challenge to Sōtatsu's masterful pair of screens on the same theme, leading to questions about his originality. But I think that for Kōrin, achieving a sense of sophistication was far more important than being original.

Kōrin transformed the imagery of flowers, birds, wind, and moon into a set of stylized modules and imparted to them a rhythm. This was something that Sōtatsu, intent on taking formal tension to its limits, was unable to accomplish. In short, the Rinpa tradition from Kōrin to Sakai Hōitsu (1761–1829) and Suzuki Kiitsu (1796–1858), and onward to Kayama Matazō (1927–2004) in modern times, was a lineage thoroughly acquainted with a sense of design.

This consciousness of design is also apparent, though I will not elaborate on it here, in the bold and immediate treatment of natural imagery by the ukiyo-e artists. Two well-known prints—*Famous Places in the Eastern Capital: Cherry Blossoms at Night in Yoshiwara Nakanochō* by Utagawa Hiroshige (1797–1858) and *Famous Places in the Eastern Capital: The New Yoshiwara* by Utagawa Kuniyoshi (1798–1861)—present us with an enormous midsummer moon, depicted as boldly as anyone could wish for, and completely devoid of subtle overtones (*yosei*) or mysterious depth (*yūgen*). These moons do not fiddle around with niceties of feeling: here, pure form captures the flag.

Late Edo culture is often said to have seen the rise of an aesthetic founded on *iki* 粋 and *tsū* 通, two terms that connote a modish elegance or chic, a mastery of contemporary style.

Iki began with the townspeople of the Osaka-Kyoto region, where it was pronounced *sui*. It seems to have originated in a pronunciation shift from *suki* (数寄 or 好き aesthetics, taste, liking). In Osaka, even today, those given to rather eccentric tastes or interests will be teased with the phrase, "Omae, suki ya nē!" (You're really *into* that, aren't you?). This was the sense that gave rise to *sui*.

In other words, with *sui*, the sense of *suki* as a passion for art or aesthetics that had been fostered in Kyoto radically changed character. Or, rather, it was not so much that the old notion of *suki* changed, as that it branched off into a fresh cultural sensibility, a new wave supplanting the old. From about the time of the popular writer Ihara Saikaku (1642–93) onward, a rather sunny and affirmative attitude with regard to erotic pleasure established itself in the Osaka-Kyoto culture, giving birth to an earthier, more human sense of *suki* than had existed before. This eventually made its way eastward to Edo, where the transition from *sui* to *iki* was effected. Or so it seems to me.

The Edo townspeople preferred *iki* over *sui* in part because *iki* 粋 was homophonous with *iki* 意気 (spirit, energy, will) and *ikiji* 意気地 (standing one's ground). The pursuit of this concept created a lineage that runs from the playwright Chikamatsu Monzaemon (1653–1725) through the novelist Izumi Kyōka (1873–1939) to the philosopher and cultural critic Kuki Shūzō (1888–1941), author of the 1930 study *Iki no kōzō* (The Structure of *Iki*).

In any case, at this point, *suki* (in its newly evolved guise as *iki*) became a matter of attitude, of verve. Taste could no longer be defined in terms of the language of the imperial court—*aware* and *okashi* and the like. This is the moon that rises out of the artistic panache of Hiroshige and Kuniyoshi, and that appears in the literary fantasies of Ueda Akinari (1734–1809) and Kyokutei Bakin (1767–1848).

Changes were also afoot in Kyoto. One was the new style of drinking *sencha* or leaf tea (as opposed to the *matcha* powdered tea favored in the formal tea ceremony) that was introduced by the Ōbaku sect of Zen and swiftly spread through the city, creating a new type of salon culture.

This *sencha* trend, strikingly similar to the popularity of coffeehouses that were the nexus of London culture during the same period in the eighteenth century, was initiated by a figure we met in chapter 8, "Time," the Ōbaku monk Baisaō, and rapidly adopted by the literati of Kyoto as a new aesthetic sensibility. The classic poetics of nature established by the court aristocracy and warrior elite would not do for these *sencha* salons, which would soon evolve a more sensual and romantic relationship to the world of nature.

This would find expression in the style of literati painting that is described by Gion Nankai and Ban Kōkei as "art in eccentricity" in chapter 8, which reached its fruition at exactly this time in figures such as Ike no Taiga, Yosa Buson, and Itō Jakuchū: the era in which Buson could finally— for the first time—write a haiku such as, "The moon at zenith / as I pass through / these mean streets."

Then, in the first few decades of the nineteenth century, there emerged a few personalities of remarkable intensity who frequented multiple salons and had everyone chattering about them, even the townsfolk. Representative of such figures was Nakajima Sōin (1779–1855), also known as Bunkichi, who was mentioned in a satirical verse: "For riches it's Tasuku; for Chinese poetry, San'yō; as a calligrapher, Nukina; for the Confucian classics, Ikai; and for style [*iki*], you have Bunkichi." Although a Confucian scholar by profession, Bunkichi built a residence for himself in the style of a restaurant, which he presided over as a man of taste and style, versed in Chinese and Japanese poetry, painting, and calligraphy, and a connoisseur of good food.

The modern moon

Among the poems left to us by Tominaga Tarō (1901–25), who departed the world at the age of twenty-four, is one entitled "Kage-e" (Silhouettes). This work I believe epitomizes the way modern Japanese see the moon.

> Beneath a half-waning Japanese moon
> hurry Tom Thumb and his wife.
> Both bent forward and brooding,
> the silhouettes of their noses garish.
> Treading the shadows of the trees
> patchily dyeing the bleached riverbank,
> scurrying along—what pursues
> their mismatched gait?

Holding hands the clownish shadows
pass—see now, there—already beneath the black finials
of the distant bridge.
The slapping of their shabby straw sandals
can no longer be heard.
The waning moon, tonight, has forgotten
the hour of its rendezvous with the willows.

The blend of arrogance and subservience in the Japanese national character has been shaped by the truly impoverished conditions of the everyday
life of ordinary people until the mid-twentieth century.

Up to this point, I have been considering the phenomenology of nature
in Japan essentially in terms of shifts in aesthetic and cultural sensibilities—but of course this is only one aspect of the broader life of Japanese
society. Those who with their bent backs and gnarled hands tended the
fields, wove cloth, drew water from rivers and wells to boil over brushwood
fires to gain a bit of warmth in the winter cold—they were the ones who
built Japan over many generations.

Tominaga's poem symbolizes this in the "half-waning moon" gleaming
in the sky high above the Tom Thumb couple. It is unclear whether this
moon is laughing or weeping at the sight of the poor Japanese husband
and wife, hard pressed by everyday life. Yet even so, the Japanese have
loved and sought a friend in the moon. The thought is one that inspires a
most indescribable, forlorn feeling.

Tominaga Tarō was a prodigy who died of tuberculosis at the age of
twenty-four. His influence was crucial to the poetry of Nakahara Chūya
(1907–37), who also died young but had an important impact on the novelist Ōoka Shōhei (1909–88) and the critic Kobayashi Hideo (1902–83).
Kobayashi encountered Rimbaud through Tominaga and Nakahara
and made a dashing debut on the Japanese literary scene, wielding a
French-influenced intellect like a knife. But eventually he developed an
interest in the philosophy of "sincerity" (*makoto*) that lay behind the Japanese Tom Thumb couple, and in his later years devoted himself to the
study of Motoori Norinaga, who had written extensively on the concept.

But it was not really Rimbaud's intellectualism that Tominaga and
Nakahara had imparted to Kobayashi, for it was the plight of the Japanese beneath their waning moon that the two tragic young poets had truly
wanted to address in the first place. Later, I will speak more of this in con-

nection with the moon, but here I will simply say that the "detour" that finally brought Kobayashi back around to Motoori Norinaga seems to me a classic example of the "errors of youth" experienced by many Japanese intellectuals.

Tominaga Tarō was born at the beginning of the twentieth century, in 1901. A host of other representative Japanese modernists were born just before or after him, including Anzai Fuyue, Hagiwara Kyōjirō, Inagaki Taruho, Kitagawa Fuyuhiko, Kitazono Katsue, Makino Shin'ichi, Miyazawa Kenji, Nakagawa Yoichi, Ryūtanji Yū, and Yoshida Issui—as well as Kobayashi and Nakahara. They all brought new forms of expression to the Japanese moon.

Their path to modernism was prepared by the staging of the modern moon by poets Kitahara Hakushū, born in 1885, and Hagiwara Sakutarō, born a year later. The following is from Kitahara's foreword to Hagiwara's first collection of poetry, *Tsuki ni hoeru* (Howling at the Moon, 1917).

> The electrical current of your feelings never ceases to congeal all liquids into solids. Its refinement—like that required for moisture to collect on a bamboo leaf, forming a single drop of dew, or for the fumes of rotten wine to shape into a transparent drop of ethanol on the cold crystal of the alembic—is no ephemeral thing. Your creed of sentimentalism lies in this power of concentration, which can condense into a single instant the infinitude of time it takes to turn coal into diamonds. The incredible secret of this mantra is known only to the poet.
>
> Howling at the moon—this is indeed your sad heart. Winter is here, and the white dog at my place, too, howls all the more. He howls at the cries of a single sparrow traversing the daytime sky. At night the sparkling frost will settle, and he will somehow sniff out the sound of its falling, and howl. All who look toward heaven but in fact inhabit this earth are a sad lot.
>
> There is a mournful howling. Something is howling hollowly. Simply hearing this lonely, disconsolate cry is chilling; and tonight I will hear that voice again from the other side of the bamboo grove. What pours down with it will crystallize like snow on the fresh leaves of the bamboo, and when I think of you, there will always be a pale blue moonlit sky overhead.

The language is certainly modern, but what is expressed is all part of the traditional poetics of nature. When Kitahara describes the image of moisture on a bamboo leaf forming into a single drop as a concentrated mantra that only a poet can understand, he calls to mind the *hiesabi* ("chill melancholy") sought by Zeami and Shinkei, as described in chapter 6, "Flowers."

In Kitahara's poem below, we see the moon appear in startling conjunction with the word *susabi*, which we have been tracing as a key concept in Japanese aesthetics throughout this book.

> The red three-day moon,
> the red three-day moon,
> today, too, in the bedchamber
> your child blew upon his silver toy whistle
> and it gives me peace,
> that playing (*susabi*).

In the poetry of Hagiwara Sakutarō, whom Kitahara championed, the moon appears dozens of times, in memorable lines such as "a moonlit night bright like a decorative gaslight." He seemed to want to use the moon as a symbol of all things. And anyone who has read the poems in *Tsuki ni hoeru* or *Aoneko* (Blue Cat, 1923) will no doubt agree that Hagiwara's poems are also filled with images of cherries, bamboo, chrysanthemums, pines, pine needles, wind, frost, flutes, seashells, jellyfish, crabs, fish, frogs, flies, horses, and so on. It is within the context of this Japanese imagery that he depicts the moon.

As one might imagine from the way he employed them, Hagiwara's appropriation of these images was a kind of manifesto for the modernization of the Japanese phenomenology of nature. He likely learned this stance from Kitahara and Yamamura Bochō (1884–1924), who added a sense of dynamic speed to the treatment of flowers, birds, wind, and moon in collections like *Kaze wa kusaki ni sasayaita* (The Wind Whispered to the Grass and Trees, 1918) and *Tsukiyo no botan* (Peonies in Moonlight, 1926).

I might also mention that in his later years, Hagiwara wrote a famous essay titled *Nihon e no kaiki* (Return to Japan, 1938) in which he makes the fairly obvious observation that the passion for Western culture of his generation actually stemmed from a sense of rivalry with the West.

Miki Rofū (1889–1984), of the same generation as Kitahara, also wrote a number of moon-themed poems, such as "Tsuki no naka" (In the Moon) and "Tsuki no fujin" (Ladies of the Moon). In the simply titled "Tsuki" (Moon), he writes,

> On a winter night without a single other thing,
> how sad,
> the heart of the moon
> comes calling.

If we recast this into the language of classical poetry, the sentiment expressed would be akin to something from Kamo no Chōmei or Yoshida Kenkō. I once heard the cabaret star Miwa Akihiro sing Miki's "Hakugetsu" (White Moon) and was literally unable to hold back the tears.

The racing moon

For a long time in Japanese aesthetics, the moon remained a static, painterly motif, but at some point in the transition from the late Edo to the Meiji period, it clearly picked up a sense of speed and movement. This is expressed with unprecedented deftness in a single line by the poet Anzai Fuyue (1898–1965): "The moon slid down like a ripe plum."

This new sense of the moon is expressed even more lucidly in the poetry of Miyazawa Kenji. As seen from lines of Miyazawa's such as "The moon is made of bumpy craters painted with mercury" from "Kaze no henki" (Eccentricities of the Wind), or "The shadow of a bird grazing the moon / The music box of the electric poles" from "Kūmei to shōi" (The Moon on the Water and the Wound), he invests the moon with fantastic imagery drawn from the new sciences of chemistry and electricity. Have a look at three of his *tanka*:

> Trees on the cemetery hill immersed in the weight of the moonlight containing molten lead.

> The sixteenth-day moon rising has emerged releasing the fragrance of a cold fruit.

> The mackerel sky sucking moonlight having formed dew the blue of the signal thumps down.[6]

The images in the last line—of the mechanical sound of a traffic light suddenly shifting at the moment mackerel clouds appear to drink in the moonlight—convey a sense of the moon that did not exist before Miyazawa. Likewise, the image of the moon as a cold fruit emitting an aroma reflects a sensibility that the literary history we know from the *Man'yōshū* onward could never have produced. And yet there is no doubt that in Miyazawa's moon we can see the same moon—that of the sixteenth night (*izayoi*), just past full and beginning to wane—that the Japanese have always loved.

Here, let me introduce a few more representative examples of how invested Miyazawa was in imagery of the moon. The first three deal with a red or blood moon.

> I alone unable to sleep unable to sleep hanging in the midnight window is a clay-singed moon.

> Without stars a red half-moon all alone falling down through the sky is nothing ordinary.

> A bloodshot bow-taut moon comes to my window midnight distorting its mouth.

> The thin mist the half moon has surreptitiously swept aside I walk past scattered and torn.

> The crescent moon exposing its dark eyelids hangs in the daybreak sky whitening.

> As the morning dawn's amber gleams whitening Andersen's moon has set.

> When the limp moon rises faint blue crows awake and call suspiciously.

> In the midst of a thinly crying moonlight gas a hinoki brushes snow from its branches.[7]

The "moonlight gas" of this last poem is definitely a modern expression, but its use in association with the snow shaken from the branches of the hinoki cypress works to present the traditional phenomenology of nature in updated form. This is also apparent in the following lines from the poem "Iwate Hospital":

> The moon distorted blood-hue
> tonight again climbs through cherry blossoms,
> and at the end of the patients' hall
> speaks omens of a catastrophe.[8]

Here, like Tominaga Tarō, Miyazawa is writing of a foreboding moment when the moon hangs at half mast in the Japanese sky, and although there was no particular need for him to insert the cherry blossoms, he deliberately chose the *sabi* of this image, reminiscent of Matsubayashi Keigetsu's painting *Shunshō kaei-zu* (Cherry Blossoms on a Spring Evening, 1939). So we see that even for Miyazawa, the traditional poetics of nature was indispensable.

Matsubayashi Keigetsu, *Shunshō kaei-zu* (Cherry Blossoms on a Spring Evening), 1939. Collection of the National Museum of Modern Art, Tokyo. Photo: MOMAT/DNPartcom.

The concern with the moon in Japan begins with Tsukuyomi, the moon deity. But for some reason, Japanese mythology rarely speaks of the moon. It is between the eras of the *Kokinshū* (905) and the *Shinkokinshū* (1205) poetry anthologies that the moon suddenly erupts from obscurity.

Yet all along, the moon has exerted a variety of influences on the lives of the Japanese people. One is the custom of drawing sacred water on the first night of spring (February 4 or 5 by the modern calendar) from a well lying in an auspicious direction; this water, called *wakamizu*, is tradition-ally associated with Tsukuyomi and with immortality. The Omizutori rit-ual at the Nigatsudō hall of Tōdaiji temple in Nara originated in such a water-drawing. Likewise, the Uesaku Festival, held every May on the night of the full moon at Kuramadera temple in Kyoto, originally involved par-taking of water purified by moonlight. The essay "Tsuki to fushi" (The Moon and Immortality) by the linguist and ethnologist Nikolai Nevsky (1892–1937) was one of the first to point to the connection between the moon, sacred water, and the idea of immortality.

As I have mentioned before in my book *Lunatics*, the tug-of-war that is the finale of almost every school athletic meet in Japan is a full-moon ritual in many parts of the country. Especially in southern Kyushu, people go into the surrounding hills on the night before the full moon to gather grasses to weave into the rope as well as (in some cases) headdresses for the participants. Better known, perhaps, from Kinoshita Junji's play *Nijūniya-machi* (The Twenty-Second Night Watch, 1946), are the *tsuki-machi* ("moon waiting") vigils that take place on certain nights in the lunar cycle, including the twenty-second. This is a custom heavily colored by Daoist influences, similar to the *Kōshin-machi* practice mentioned in chapter 2 of staying up all night on specific days to keep the "three corpses and nine insects" (*sanshi kyūchū*) in one's body from causing harm.

So as we can see, the moon is deeply rooted in many aspects of Japanese life. The poets and painters dealing with natural imagery in the traditional manner always tended to treat it abstractly, so that until the time of Buson representations of the moon seemed rather muted. Gradually, though, under the impact of the encounter with Western culture, the power of the previously static moon began to push its way to the fore.

We could see this as the manifestation of a new decadence, or of dandyism and anarchism. This is the type of moon, it seems to me, that appeared in all its glory in the lineage of Kitahara Hakushū and Hagiwara Sakutarō. By attaining modern time and space, the moon was finally able to come into its own. A telling example is the following poem by Nakahara Chūya, which suggests the moon's rays are so quick and forceful that they induce "fainting":

> In a tarnished silver window-frame, peacefully
> a spray of flowers, peach colored flowers.
> fainting from the moonlight,
> the garden earth a beauty spot.
> Ah, nothing matters, nothing matters;
> trees, play your parts discreetly.[9]

There is a famous line from Nakahara's poem "Moon": "The moon has eaten too many ginger buds." I'm especially taken with this line, which depicts a reddish-pink moon hanging over the red-latticed house in which sleep two sisters for whom he longs. Compared with the Western notion of the moon being made of green cheese, this seems to hit more solidly on the Japanese sense of the moon's color. Ginger versus green cheese: how different is the Japanese sense of color from that in the West.

Incomplete moons

We are nearing the end of this book. And in closing, I will give some hint of the unfathomable direction that all this talk of the moon is taking us by introducing a haiku poet and vagabond born just before Kitahara and Hagiwara who wrote of the Japanese moon with total freedom: Taneda Santōka (1882–1940).

Here are two of my favorite Santōka poems about the moon:

I'll leave a door open for the moon.

Brightness of the moon: back and front, crickets everywhere.[10]

Santōka was the son of a wealthy landlord in Yamaguchi prefecture. When he was young, his mother committed suicide. For a time he ran a sake brewery with his father, but it went bankrupt, and a few years afterward his wife divorced him.

This set him off on his life of wandering, or we might rather say drifting, but contrary to the common image of him, he was not a vagabond by nature. Before this point he had enrolled in the department of literature at Waseda University (withdrawing after less than a year, however) and joined Ogiwara Seisensui's avant-garde poetry magazine *Sōun* (though he soon quit). After the bankruptcy he first moved to Kumamoto with his wife and helped her run a picture-framing shop, then went back alone to Tokyo, where he found a job at the municipal library. In other words, he did try to make a go of things.

But after seeing Tokyo reduced to ashes by the fires that followed the Great Kantō Earthquake of 1923, he was overtaken by an urge to hit the road. First, he went to Kumamoto, where his ex-wife was living. There in 1924 he got into trouble with the law after stepping in front of an oncoming streetcar while dead drunk; he was consequently placed under the care of the abbot of the Sōtō Zen temple Hōonji, where he took monastic vows. He then set out on an alms-seeking pilgrimage that took him through Kyushu, western Honshu, and Shikoku. He was already forty-five years old. His feelings on commencing these wanderings are famously captured thus:

> The deeper I go the deeper I go green mountains.[11]

Santōka wrote a remarkable number of haiku about the moon. Out of the perhaps 1,500 haiku he wrote, it seems a third of them mention the moon, such as these:

> Evening moon—I guess I'd like to settle down about here.

> A full-bellied moon comes out.

> Three-day moon—I come back from buying tofu.

> The moon's too bright; drinking the illusions.

> Mr. Moon says to Mr. Jizō, "Sure is cold tonight!"

> The moon finds a traveler's sky in the depths of the water.

This last one is the essence of Santōka. I've also stared many times into ponds and puddles, seeing the moon and fantasizing traveling the sky with it. At times I've even imagined there must be something in the moon that hurries it across the sky, and us with it.

As humans we all carry around a sense of incompleteness, of missing some "other half" that keeps us from being whole. What exactly that other half is, we don't know. But we seem fated to always be journeying in search of it. Sometimes it can be found, in the same way that Cinderella was reunited with her missing slipper.

Then there are those who, while searching for what is missing from them, instead come to know the moon. Jules Laforgue and Taneda Santōka were poets of this type. We may resist the encounter, protesting that it will bring us nothing, but the moon, being the boundlessly charitable goddess that she is, puts herself before us nonetheless.

As I have said, the moon is the Other (*hoka*). This is the same as the *there* (*mukō*) that people in ancient times sensed in the mountains and the wind. So to me the moon must hold the potential to unite with us and make us whole, if only barely. Perhaps we are all travelers in search of a lunar companion.

At its very essence, what the appreciation of flowers, birds, wind, and moon—all the phenomena of nature that we have been examining in this book—offers us is a means to touch upon the boundaries of the world of the Other in search of that piece missing inside ourselves.

If you think about it, none of the natural phenomena we've been looking at are particularly out of the ordinary. It is rare for any human being to pass a day without coming into contact with flowers, birds, wind, moon, or other elements of the natural world. Meanwhile, take a look at us, the humans doing the appreciating: the things that are lacking in us and that we are searching for are all so messy and troublesome that we can't even say for sure what they are. The attempt to understand this lack has provided content to some three thousand years of philosophy, art, and performance. And yet the upshot is that we have not even managed to truly grasp what we are missing, even inside our individual selves.

But then, sometimes, our eyes alight on a flower, a bird, the moon. Or it doesn't even have to be anything so poetic—it could just as well be a utility pole, a cigarette, a hat. Nail scissors, a motorbike, cellophane. It doesn't matter what the objects themselves are, because even after our interaction with them, or even when they become broken or lost, the resonances of their power still remain, enabling us to establish contact with the various boundaries separating us from the "other" world—until all of a sudden we feel ourselves basking under the light of the moon.

In the end, the exploration of the phenomenology of nature in Japanese culture that I carry on in this book is all about the emergence of pairs and boundaries, about the history of the quest by various missing pieces to find their complements.

Right now it is clear that Japan as a country is seeking its missing parts. It is no longer sufficient for Japan alone to do well. Japan needs other pieces to make it whole, and more of them. And whatever happens with Japan, we will always need the phenomena of nature—flowers, birds, wind, and moon—as our companions.

NOTES

Translations of poetry and extracts not cited in the notes are by David Noble,
in consultation with Imoto Chikako.

CHAPTER
1

1. Marc Peter Keane, *The Japanese Tea Garden* (Berkeley: Stone Bridge Press, 2009), 38.

2. In Royall Tyler's translation of *The Tale of the Heike* (New York: Penguin Books, 2012), 356, this passage is rendered: "There is in Jambudvīpa a lake, with, in its midst, a crystal mountain that rises from the depths of the world, and on it dwell heavenly maidens."

3. *Ryōjin hishō* (Songs to Make the Dust Dance, 1169) is a collection of *imayō* popular songs compiled by the Emperor Go-Shirakawa; see Yung-Hee K. Kwon and Yung-Hee Kim, *Songs to Make the Dust Dance: The* Ryōjin Hishō *of Twelfth-Century Japan* (Berkeley: University of California Press, 1994).

4. This song recounts a passage in the Treasure Stupa chapter of the *Lotus Sutra*. *The Lotus Sutra*, translated by Burton Watson (New York: Columbia University Press, 1993).

5. This translation of poem 4511 appears in *The Man'yo-shu: A Complete English Translation in 5-7 Rhythm*, part II, vols. 8–14, translated by Suga Teruo (Tokyo: Kanda Institute of Foreign Languages, 1991), 417. It is described as one of three poems composed by Mikata no Ōkimi while looking at a garden.

6. This translation of poem 4512 appears in Edwin A. Cranston, *A Waka Anthology, Volume One: The Gem-Glistening Cup* (Stanford, CA: Stanford University Press, 1993), 481.

7. This translation of poem 452 appears in *The Manyōshū: The Nippon Gakujutsu Shinkōkai Translation of One Thousand Poems* (New York: Columbia University Press, 1965), 120.

8. See the chapter on Shitennōin in Edward Kamens and Howard I. Kamens, *Utamakura, Allusion, and Intertextuality in Traditional Japanese Poetry* (New Haven, CT: Yale University Press, 1997).

9. Cranston, *A Waka Anthology, Volume One*, 164.

10. Headnote from poem 478 by Mibu no Tadamine.

11. Translated by Sonja Amtzen. For the original text, see Mitani Ei'ichi et al. (eds.), *Ochikubo monogatari: Tsutsumi Chūnagon monogatari* (Tokyo: Shōgakukan, 2000), 195–6.

CHAPTER
2

1. See *Man'yōshū* 11:2506, translated by Gary L. Ebersole, *Ritual Poetry and the Politics of Death in Early Japan* (Princeton, NJ: Princeton University Press, 1989), 20.

CHAPTER
3

1. Poem 24 from *One Hundred Poets, One Poem Each: A Translation of the* Ogura Hyakunin Isshu, translated by Peter MacMillan, rev. ed. (New York: Penguin Classics, 2018), 30.

2. Haruo Shirane, *The Bridge of Dreams: A Poetics of* 'The Tale of Genji' (Stanford, CA: Stanford University Press, 1987), 156.

3. *The Tale of the Heike*, translated by Royall Tyler (New York: Penguin Books, 2012), book 3, 132.

4. Translation by Edwin A. Cranston, *A Waka Anthology, Volume One: The Gem-Glistening Cup* (Stanford, CA: Stanford University Press, 1993), 119–20.

5. Cranston, *A Waka Anthology, Volume One*, 406–7.

6. H.A.C. Dobbs, "The Time of Psychology and of Physics," *British Journal of the Philosophy of Science* 4, no. 14 (1953): 161–64.

CHAPTER
4

1. Romanization and translation by Haruo Shirane, *Traditional Japanese Literature, An Anthology: Beginnings to 1600* (New York: Columbia University Press, 2012), 88.

2. Paula Doe, *A Warbler's Song in the Dusk: The Life and Work of Ōtomo Yakamochi (718–785)* (Berkeley: University of California Press, 1982), 148.

3. Joshua S. Mostow, *Pictures of the Heart: The Hyakunin Isshu in Word and Image* (Honolulu: University of Hawai'i Press, 1996), 207.

4. *The Pillow Book* by Sei Shōnagon, translated by Meredith McKinney (London: Penguin Classics, 2006), section 187, 180.

5. Edwin A. Cranston, *A Waka Anthology, Volume One: The Gem-Glistening Cup* (Stanford, CA: Stanford University Press, 1993), 645.

6. Both *waka* translations are from Cranston, *A Waka Anthology, Volume One*, 18.

7. This poem by Ōtomo no Yakamochi appears in the *Man'yōshū*. See Cranston, *A Waka Anthology, Volume One*, 476.

8. Translation and romanization from Haruo Shirane, *Japan and the Culture of the Four Seasons: Nature, Literature, and the Arts* (New York: Columbia University Press, 2013), 40.

9. David Landis Barnhill, *Bashō's Journey: The Literary Prose of Matsuo Bashō* (Albany: SUNY Press, 2005), 13.

10. Translation from Helen Craig McCullough, *The Tale of the Heike* (Stanford, CA: Stanford University Press, 1988), 170–71.

11. Didier Davin, "Between the Mountain and the City: Ikkyū Sōjun and the Blurred Border of Awakening," *Studies in Japanese Literature and Culture* 2 (March 2019): 45–60.

12. Ryūichi Abé, *The Weaving of Mantra: Kūkai and the Construction of Esoteric Buddhist Discourse* (New York: Columbia University Press, 1999), 282.

13. Ibid., 278.

CHAPTER

5

1. Helen Craig McCullough, *Tales of Ise: Lyrical Episodes from Tenth-Century Japan* (Stanford, CA: Stanford University Press, 1968), 103.

2. Murasaki Shikibu, *The Tale of Genji,* translated by Royall Tyler (New York: Penguin Books, 2001), 445.

3. Helen Craig McCullough, trans., *Kokin Wakashū: The First Imperial Anthology of Japanese Poetry* (Stanford, CA: Stanford University Press, 1985), 232.

4. Translation by Donald Keene, from *Seeds in the Heart: Japanese Literature from the Earliest Times to the Late Sixteenth Century* (New York: Columbia University Press, 1999), 324.

5. Edwin A. Cranston, *A Waka Anthology, Volume One: The Gem-Glistening Cup* (Stanford, CA: Stanford University Press, 1993), 453.

6. This translation appears in *The Manyōshū: The Nippon Gakujutsu Shinkōkai Translation of One Thousand Poems* (New York: Columbia University Press, 1965), 161.

7. Gaston Bachelard, *The Poetics of Space*, translated by Maria Jolas (Boston: Beacon Press, 1994), 103.

CHAPTER
6

1. Edwin A. Cranston, *A Waka Anthology, Volume One: The Gem-Glistening Cup* (Stanford, CA: Stanford University Press, 1993), 312.

2. Helen Craig McCullough, *Tales of Ise: Lyrical Episodes from Tenth-Century Japan* (Stanford, CA: Stanford University Press, 1968), 153. She phoneticizes the third word as *yado* and not *niwa*, as Matsuoka does.

3. Haruo Shirane, ed., *Traditional Japanese Literature: An Anthology, Beginnings to 1600* (New York: Columbia University Press, 2008), 128.

4. These translations, romanization, and other information are taken from Steven D. Carter, *Traditional Japanese Poetry: An Anthology* (Stanford, CA: Stanford University Press, 1991), 374. Carter provides a complete translation of this 36-verse *kasen* sequence, with explanatory notes and commentary.

5. Shirane, *Traditional Japanese Literature*, 585.

6. Ryusaku Tsunoda, et al., *Sources of Japanese Tradition, Volume One* (New York: Columbia University Press, 1964), 283–85.

7. Burton Watson, *Saigyō: Poems of a Mountain Home* (New York: Columbia University Press, 1991), 36.

8. Ibid., 39.

9. Translation by Jack Stoneman, from Shirane, *Traditional Japanese Literature*, 578–79.

10. Shirane, *Traditional Japanese Literature*, 577–78.

11. Translated by Julia Winters Carpenter, Nakano Kōji, *Words to Live By: Japanese Classics for Our Time* (Tokyo: Japan Publishing Industry Foundation for Culture, 2018), 174–75.

12. Watson, *Saigyō*, 45.

13. Ibid., 46.

14. Shirane, *Traditional Japanese Literature*, 578.

15. Jin'ichi Konishi, *A History of Japanese Literature, Volume One: The Archaic and Ancient Ages*, translated by Aileen Gatten and Nicholas Teele (Princeton, NJ: Princeton University Press, 1984), 221.

16. Cranston, *A Waka Anthology, Volume One*, 648. Cranston does not attribute this to Fukumaro (grouping it instead in a section of anonymous poems).

17. The romanization and translation are taken from the *iroha* entry in *Japan: An Illustrated Encyclopedia* (Tokyo: Kōdansha, 1993), 624.

18. Anne Commons, *Hitomaro: Poet as God* (Leiden: Brill, 2009), 167. Commons says it is from the *Nirvana Sutra*.

19. Shirane, *Traditional Japanese Literature*, 633.

20. Hilda Kato, "The Mumyōshō of Kamo no Chōmei and Its Significance in Japanese Literature," unpublished M.A. thesis, Department of Asian Studies, University of British Columbia, 1964, 120.

21. Donald Keene, *Essays in Idleness: The* Tsurezuregusa *of Kenkō* (New York: Columbia University Press, 1998), 115.

22. Keene, *Essays in Idleness*, 119.

23. Ibid., 120.

24. Dennis Hirota, *The Wind in the Pines: Classic Writings on the Way of Tea as a Buddhist Path* (Fremont, CA: Jain Publishing Company, 1995), 170.

25. Hirota, *The Wind in the Pines*, 151.

CHAPTER
7

1. Michael Polanyi first introduced the concept of "tacit knowledge" in *Personal Knowledge: Towards a Post-Critical Philosophy* (Chicago: University of Chicago Press, 1958).

CHAPTER
8

1. Kawai Hayao, "The Hollow Center in the Mythology of Kojiki," translated by Hori Tadashi, *Review of Japanese Culture and Society* 1, no. 1 (1986): 72–77.

2. Edwin A. Cranston, *A Waka Anthology, Volume One: The Gem-Glistening Cup* (Stanford, CA: Stanford University Press, 1993), 473. This is one section of a longer poem.

3. Ibid., 584. This is one of three envoys to a longer poem.

4. This is an excerpt from a translation of poem 1753 that appears in *The Manyōshū: The Nippon Gakujutsu Shinkōkai Translation of One Thousand Poems* (New York: Columbia University Press, 1965), 220.

5. Cranston, *A Waka Anthology, Volume One*, 229. This is a fragment of a longer poem.

6. Murasaki Shikibu, *The Tale of Genji*, translated by Royall Tyler (New York: Penguin Books, 2001), 27.

7. Cranston, *A Waka Anthology, Volume One*, 179.

8. Ibid., 417.

9. This is poem 216 in volume 2 of the *Manyōshū*.

10. Cranston, *A Waka Anthology, Volume One*, 395. The romanization here follows Cranston.

11. This is poem 1194 in volume 7 of the *Manyōshū*.

12. Cranston, *A Waka Anthology, Volume One*, 358. This is one section of a longer poem.

13. This translation of poem 709 appears in *The Manyōshū*, 238.

14. Yoshida Kenkō and Kamo no Chōmei, *Essays in Idleness and Hōjōki*, translated by Meredith McKinney (Penguin, 2014), 127.

CHAPTER
9

1. W.G. Aston, trans., *Nihongi: Chronicles of Japan from the Earliest Times to A.D. 697* (Tokyo: Tuttle, 1972), 161. Note that *Nihongi* is another name for the *Nihon shoki*.

2. Ibid., 290.

3. Cranston, *A Waka Anthology, Volume One: The Gem-Glistening Cup* (Stanford, CA: Stanford University Press, 1993), 441.

4. Ibid., 581.

5. Ibid., 438.

6. Ibid., 568.

7. Helen McCullough, in *Classical Japanese Prose: An Anthology* (Stanford, CA: Stanford University Press, 1990), 102.

8. Murasaki Shikibu, *The Tale of Genji*, translated by Royall Tyler (New York: Penguin Books, 2001), 76.

9. Ibid., 925.

10. Burton Watson, *Saigyō: Poems of a Mountain Home* (New York: Columbia University Press, 1991), 60. Watson writes the fourth line as *ozasa no hara mo*, but we are using the standard romanization of that line (*ozasa ga hara mo*).

11. This is poem no. 626 in the *Shin chokusen wakashū*.

12. Steven D. Carter, *Traditional Japanese Poetry: An Anthology* (Stanford, CA: Stanford University Press, 1991), 104.

13. Edwin A. Cranston, *A Waka Anthology, Volume Two: Grasses of Remembrance* (Stanford, CA: Stanford University Press, 2006), 44.

14. Helen Craig McCullough, *Kokin Wakashū: The First Imperial Anthology of Japanese Poetry* (Stanford, CA: Stanford University Press, 1985), 137.

15. Haruo Shirane, ed., *Traditional Japanese Literature: An Anthology, Beginnings to 1600* (New York: Columbia University Press, 2008), 164.

16. McCullough, *Kokin Wakashū*, 146.

17. These three poems by Saigyō are nos. 581–583 in the *Sankashū*.

18. Yung-Hee K. Kwon and Yung-Hee Kim, *Songs to Make the Dust Dance: The Ryojin hisho of Twelfth-Century Japan* (Berkeley, University of California Press, 1994), 62.

19. Carter, *Traditional Japanese Poetry*, 196.

20. Laurel Rasplica Rodd, *Shinkokinshū: New Collection of Poems Ancient and Modern* (Leiden: Brill, 2015), 92–93.

21. Ibid., 190.

22. This poem is no. 791 in the *Shinkokinshū*. It forms a pair with no. 790, which refers to the death of Michichika's father earlier that spring.

23. Rodd, *Shinkokinshū*, 190.

24. This poem is no. 1972 in the *Shinkokinshū*.

CHAPTER
10

1. Ryūichi Abé, *The Weaving of Mantra: Kūkai and the Construction of Esoteric Discourse* (New York: Columbia University Press, 1999), 281.

2. *Shinkokinshū* IV: 363. Translated by Earl Miner, *An Introduction to Japanese Court Poetry* (Stanford, CA: Stanford University Press, 1968), 13.

3. Murasaki Shikibu, *The Tale of Genji*, translated by Royall Tyler (New York: Penguin Books, 2001), 445.

4. Steven D. Carter, *Traditional Japanese Poetry: An Anthology* (Stanford, CA: Stanford University Press, 1993), 150.

5. Donald Keene, *Yoshimasa and the Silver Pavilion: The Creation of the Soul of Japan* (New York: Columbia University Press, 2006), 95.

6. Translation by Hiroaki Sato (unpublished), 2019.

7. Ibid.

8. Ibid.

9. Paul St. John Mackintosh and Maki Sugiyama, *The Poems of Nakahara Chūya* (Leominster, UK: Gracewing, 1993), 6.

10. Translation by Hiroaki Sato (unpublished), 2019.

11. *For All My Walking: Free-Verse Haiku of Takeda Santōka with Excerpts from His Diary*, translated by Burton Watson (New York: Columbia University Press, 2003).

ABOUT THE AUTHOR

Matsuoka Seigow (b. 1944) is executive director of the Editorial Engineering Laboratory (EEL), known for research and development in information culture and technology. He is also president of ISIS (Interactive System of Inter Scores) Editorial School, in Tokyo. In his twenties, he founded the popular arts magazine *Yū*, which published until 1982. He developed a unique methodological worldview, which he calls "editorial engineering." His ideas are published in innovative forms spanning the written word, film and video, multimedia, and the internet. Major published works include *Kokka to "watakushi" no yukue* (My Future and the Future of the Nation, Shunjūsha, 2015); *Nihon to Nippon: Yomitobashi Nihon bunkafu* (Nihon and Nippon: A Quick Guide to Japanese Culture, Kōsakusha, 2014); *Nihon ryū* (The Japanese Way, Chikuma Shobō, 2009); *Nihon suki* (Japanese Taste, Chikuma Shobō, 2007); *Nihon to iu hōhō: Omokage, usturoi no bunka* (Japan as Method: A Culture of Fleeting Images, NHK Shuppan, 2006); *Furajairu: Yowasa kara no shuppatsu* (Fragile: Starting from Weakness, Chikuma Shobō, 2005); *Kūkai no yume* (Dreams of Kūkai, rev. ed., Shunjūsha, 2005); *Runatikkusu: Tsuki o yūgaku suru* (Lunatics: Voyages of Discovery about the Moon, Chūōkōron Shinsha, 2005); and *Chi no henshūkōgaku* (Editorial Engineering for Intelligence, Asahi Shimbunsha, 2001). *Sen'ya sensatsu* (A Thousand Books for a Thousand Nights; https://1000ya.isis.ne.jp) is a popular book navigation website launched by Matsuoka in 2000. He has been a visiting professor at the University of Tokyo (1994–97) and a professor at Tezukayama Gakuin University (1998–2004), in Osaka.

ABOUT THE TRANSLATOR

David Noble is an award-winning translator living on the Olympic Peninsula in Washington State. He grew up in Nashville, Tennessee, where he completed an undergraduate degree at Vanderbilt University, followed by graduate studies in Japanese language, history, and literature at the University of Chicago and Princeton University. He served as executive editor of *Japan: An Illustrated Encyclopedia* (Kōdansha, 1993) and worked for five years at Weatherhill, Inc. in New York City before establishing an independent practice as a Japanese-English translator, editor, and book designer. He has translated more than a dozen books in the fields of history, political science, and the humanities.

（英文版）花鳥風月の科学

Flowers, Birds, Wind, and Moon: The Phenomenology of Nature in Japanese Culture

2020年3月27日　第1刷発行

著　者　　松岡正剛
訳　者　　デヴィッド・ノーブル
発行所　　一般財団法人出版文化産業振興財団
　　　　　〒101-0051 東京都千代田区神田神保町2-2-30
　　　　　電話　03-5211-7283

ホームページ　https://www.jpic.or.jp/

印刷・製本所　　大日本印刷株式会社

Heterick Memorial Library
Ohio Northern University

DUE	RETURNED	DUE	RETURNED
1.		13.	
2.		14.	
3.		15.	
4.		16.	
5.		17.	
6.		18.	
7.		19.	
8.		20.	
9.		21.	
10.		22.	
11.		23.	
12.		24.